# MMPI & MMPI-2
## Interpretation Manual
## for
## Counselors and Clinicians

### 4th Edition

**Jane C. Duckworth, Ph.D.**

Professor Emerita of Psychology —
Counseling
Department of Counseling Psychology
and Guidance Services
Ball State University

**Wayne P. Anderson, Ph.D.**

Professor of Psychology—Counseling Psychologist
Counseling Services
University of Missouri-Columbia

**ACCELERATED DEVELOPMENT**

A member of the Taylor & Francis Group

## MMPI & MMPI-2: Interpretation Manual
## for Counselors and Clinicians,  Fourth Edition

1 2 3 4 5 6 7 8 9 0 BRBR 9 8 7 6 5 4

First Edition Copyright 1975
Second Edition Copyright 1979
Third Edition Copyright 1986


Technical Development:     Virginia Cooper     Marguerite Mader
                          Delores Kellogg     Janet Merchant
                          Cynthia Long        Sheila Sheward


A CIP catalog record for this book is available from the British Library.

⊗ The paper in this publication meets the requirements of the ANSI Standard Z39.48-1984 (Permanence of Paper)

### Library of Congress Cataloging-in-Publication Data
Duckworth, Jane C.
     MMPI & MMPI-2: interpretation manual for counselors and clinicians/Jane C. Duckworth, Wayne P. Anderson.—4th ed.
        p.      cm.
     Includes bibliographical references and index.


     1. Minnesota Multiphasic Personality Inventory.  I. Anderson, Wayne P.  II. Title  III. Title: MMPI and MMPI-two
     BF698.8.M5D8   1994                                94-19528
     155.2'83—dc20                                      CIP

ISBN 1-56032-377-9

For additional information and ordering, please write or call:

**ACCELERATED DEVELOPMENT**
**A Member of the Taylor & Francis Group**
1900 Frost Road, Suite 101
Bristol, Pennsylvania 19007-1598
1-800-821-8312

that if a client answers those items the usual MMPI profile can be scored. However, we would recommend not stopping at 370 items since items beyond number 370 are needed for some of the scales that may be of interest to clinicians (e.g., the new content scales and additional validity scales).

Another disappointment for some test users is the fact that the MMPI-2 reading level is higher than the reading level of the MMPI. The MMPI-2 has an eighth-grade level whereas the original MMPI has a sixth-grade reading level. We have found, however, that test takers who might be expected to have a lower reading level than the eighth grade are able to understand and answer the MMPI-2 items as long as they can read and the testing situation is arranged so that the test taker feels comfortable asking questions about the test if he or she should run into difficulties with any of the items. When these two things are present in the testing situation, we have found that individuals who would have been able to take the MMPI with its sixth-grade reading level also can take the MMPI-2 in spite of the higher reading level reported for the MMPI-2. For those individuals who have difficulty reading the test items, an audio-taped version of the test is available.

The MMPI-2 is designed to be given to individuals 18 years of age and older. The MMPI-A, the new version of the MMPI for adolescents, is to be used for individuals younger than 18. This adolescent version of the test has items written specifically for adolescents, and its norms are based upon a wide variety of adolescent populations. The original version of the MMPI was given to both adolescents and adults, but different norms were used for the two populations. With the MMPI-2, a different test will need to be used for the adolescent population. While we have some references to adolescents in the interpretation section of this book, we will be concentrating upon the adult population that is tested with the MMPI and MMPI-2. We have listed two books (Archer, 1992; Butcher & Williams, 1992) in a list of suggested readings (see p. 10) that we recommend for those who are testing adolescents.

first on the MMPI profile so that the test-taking attitude of the person can be taken into account in interpreting the clinical scales that appear in the second section of the profile.

In addition to these two sets of scales, over 550 experimental scales were developed for the original MMPI to measure such diverse areas as alcoholism, ego strength, dominance, anxiety, and status needs. Some of these additional scales that we have found especially useful are included in the supplementary scale section of this book. Scoring keys for these scales are available from Psychological Assessment Resources, Inc., P.O. Box 98, Odessa, FL 33556. Profile sheets for plotting these scales also are available from PAR.

## THE MMPI-2

A recent development for the MMPI has been the publication of a new version of the test, the MMPI-2 (Butcher, Dahlstrom, & Graham et al., 1989). The MMPI has been changed and updated in four ways to become the MMPI-2: new items have been added, new norms have been derived, new T-score distributions have been made, and new scales have been added to the test while other scales (some of the MMPI additional scales and the Wiggins Content scales) have been dropped. The implications of these changes for counselors and clinicians are many and will be discussed throughout this book.

Before discussing the four changes that have been made to create the MMPI-2, some information regarding the new test is in order. The MMPI-2 has 567 items instead of 566 items which the original MMPI has. This number of test items is a disappointment to individuals who had hoped that the MMPI-2 would be shorter than the MMPI, thus making it easier to give to people who have difficulty concentrating for long periods of time. However, the new test items have been arranged such that all of the items in the basic validity and clinical scales are contained within the first 370 items, so scales, **5** and **0,** have since been added to the clinical scales. Originally the MMPI clinical scales were intended to place persons into various diagnostic categories. Designers of the test expected that people taking the test would have an elevation on one scale, which would then indicate the diagnosis for that person such as schizophrenic, hypochondriac, and so forth. It soon was discovered that this was a very limited approach, and consequently, three major developments occurred.

First, MMPI interpreters began describing the behavior associated with the various elevations instead of just placing people into diagnostic categories. This development provided information useful to the counselor and clinician in the treatment of the person.

The second development was to use the varying scale elevations to differentiate intensity of behavior and thinking. For example, scale **2,** which was originally only interpreted as depression, is now used to differentiate between people who are feeling "blue" (lower elevations) from those who are severely depressed (higher elevations).

The third major interpretative development of the MMPI was the use of the whole profile for analysis, rather than only one, two, or three high points. This approach has added subtlety and richness to the interpretations.

An initial improvement on the original MMPI, occurring soon after it was developed, was the addition of four validity scales to the clinical scales to measure the test-taking attitude of the person. This addition is one of the major strengths of the MMPI. These validity scales note the number of items omitted (**?** scale), the amount of obvious social virtues claimed by the person (**L** scale), the amount of "different" or bad experiences the client is reporting (**F** scale), and the amount of good feelings the person is reporting (**K** scale). No other psychological instrument, to our knowledge, is so thorough in attempting to determine the client's mental set at the time of test administration. These validity scales are typically shown

# CHAPTER I

# INTRODUCTION

This MMPI book has been written primarily for counselors and clinicians who work with three types of populations: university counseling center clients, private practice clients, and mental health clinic clients. These populations are not usually psychotic or neurotic but are likely to be people who are functioning adequately in their world but having problems in one or two areas. These problems may be longstanding ones, but more usually they are the result of situational pressures and stresses. These pressures may range from mild (such as selecting an academic major) to severe (such as divorce or death in the family).

The MMPI was developed in the 1930s and 1940s as a complex psychological instrument designed to diagnose mental patients into different categories of neuroses and psychoses. Since that time its use has extended to all kinds of settings, including employment agencies, university counseling centers, mental health clinics, schools, and industry. Its use also has been expanded to include research and personnel screening. Most importantly, its diagnostic origins have been expanded to include a person's behavior, attitudes, thought patterns, and strengths—data that are extremely useful to the practicing counselor and therapist.

The MMPI as originally constructed had eight clinical scales (scales **1** through **4** and **6** through **9**). Two additional

# LIST OF TABLES

# LIST OF FIGURES

# TABLE OF CONTENTS

Because many of you are still using the MMPI, I also have included information regarding this test, especially pertinent research findings that have been published since the last edition of this book in 1986. I believe much of the information that is given for the MMPI is also useful for the MMPI-2 with the modifications that I have suggested in Chapter II, Interpreting the MMPI, and at the beginning of each of the validity and clinical scales. All of the research reported that is prior to 1989 has been developed using the MMPI. Since 1989, research regarding the MMPI-2 has started to appear while articles using the MMPI also have continued to be published. In order to distinguish which test has been used in the research that I am reporting, you can use the following guidelines. When the research that is being reported has used the MMPI-2, I have indicated that in my report of that research. When there is no indication that the MMPI-2 was used, then you can assume that the data being reported were generated from the MMPI.

I hope you find this book to be useful for the individuals who you treat as you make the transition from the MMPI to the MMPI-2. I am looking forward to receiving feedback from you regarding your use of the book and your suggestions for making it better for future editions.

Jane Duckworth

July 1994

# PREFACE

This is a transition book, a book that reflects the transition from the MMPI to the MMPI-2. Because the MMPI-2 is so new, five years old, there is still much that is unknown about it and its application to the population with which this book is mainly concerned (e.g. normal people under stress whether in mental health clinics, private practice, or college counseling centers). This lack of knowledge about the specific applications of the MMPI-2 to the individuals who most of us deal with has meant that adaptations are necessary in order to use this new test. Primarily these adaptations have meant taking research material that was developed from the original MMPI and trying to fit it to the MMPI-2. I have tried to do this in each of the sections dealing with the validity, clinical and supplementary scales of the test. I have tried out these suggested adaptations with clients who I have treated in the past five years, since the publication of the MMPI-2, and have been satisfied that these are the best ways to use this new test. Whether I still will agree with all of these adaptations after further years of working with the test is unknown as of now, but hopefully, most of them will stand the test of time.

How successful these adaptations are to the clients who you treat is also unknown at the present time. This is where you can be of immense help in developing future editions of this book. In the back of the book is a feedback page for you to suggest articles that you have found useful and for you to give suggestions about interpreting the MMPI-2 that you have found helpful with your clients. I do read every one of the feedback pages that is sent to me, and many of the suggestions that you have given me in the past have been incorporated into this latest edition of the book.

Another change on the MMPI-2 is that clinical problems are indicated on the MMPI-2 profile when a validity or clinical scale score reaches 65 T-score points or above, whereas for the original MMPI, problems were not indicated for an individual until a validity or clinical scale reached 70 T-score points or above. Why the change was made from 70 to 65 T-score points is not completely clear. One of the few statements found in the literature that relates to this change is given by Butcher (1990) who stated, "Clinical research with the MMPI-2 shows that interpretations of the clinical scales are significant at elevations of T > 65" (p. 26).

One additional minor change has been made on the MMPI-2 profile sheet and that is that the **?** validity scale is now shown as a raw score only and is not plotted on the clinical profile as it was on the MMPI. The rest of the MMPI-2 profile looks exactly like the one for the MMPI. These are three validity scales (the **?** scale having been moved), **L, F,** and **K,** and ten clinical scales: **1** (Hypochondriasis), **2** (Depression), **3** (Hysteria), **4** (Psychopathic Deviate), **5** (Masculine-Feminine Interests), **6** (Paranoia), **7** (Psychasthenia), **8** (Schizophrenia), **9** (Hypomania), and **0** (Social Introversion-Extroversion).

As was mentioned before, the MMPI-2 has been changed and updated in four ways. The first of these changes is in the items themselves. Many of the original MMPI items were obscure, and others were offensive to some individuals, such as items related to religious beliefs and bowel and urinary functioning. Thirteen of these items were dropped from the MMPI-2. Other items were edited to eliminate ambiguity and/or sexist wording. In spite of these changes, it should be emphasized that the items that make up the validity and clinical scales of the MMPI are essentially unchanged except for the elimination of the 13 items based on their content. It is for the rest of the items on the test, those items that are scored in scales other than the validity and clinical scales, that major changes have occurred for the MMPI-2. The significance of changes for these scales will be commented upon later in this chapter and also in the interpretation section of this book.

A second change for the MMPI-2 is the new normative group that has been derived for the test. The original MMPI norm group was based upon people tested in the 1930s. This group was comprised primarily of white, middle-class individuals from Minnesota. The new MMPI-2 norms are derived from a sample that is much more representative of the present population of the United States. Great care was taken by those individuals responsible for revising the test to include various ethnic and racial groups in the new normative sample. Also different geographic areas besides Minnesota were used so that the new sample more closely match that of the total United States. The 1980 census was used to derive target parameters for the new normative group, and the MMPI revisers succeeded in matching many of them. The MMPI-2 norm group does match the US population in ethnic diversity, geographic distribution, and age distribution more closely than did the old norm group. However, the new norm group does differ significantly from the 1980 census in years of education and occupational status. The new group is significantly higher than individuals in the 1980 census on both of these dimensions.

A third change that has been made on the MMPI-2 is the derivation of new T-score distributions for the eight clinical scales (**1**-Hypochondriasis, **2**-Depression, **3**-Hysteria, **4**-Psychopathic Deviate, **6**-Paranoia, **7**-Psychasthenia, **8**-Schizophrenia, and **9**-Hypomania) that traditionally have been considered true clinical scales. It has long been apparent to users of the original MMPI that the distributions of these eight clinical scales were not all the same. For example, it is not unusual to see a **2** scale (Depression) elevation of 100 T-score points in a clinical population, yet it is very unusual for the **6** scale (Paranoia) to be above 80 T-score points. These differences in clinical scale distributions had to be learned in an assessment class or picked up through using the MMPI with a number of individuals.

The new MMPI-2 has uniform clinical scale distributions; that is, the eight clinical scales now have the same range and distribution. This has made a major impact on the way the clinical scales look on the MMPI-2 profile sheet. It is now possible for some scales to be higher on the MMPI-2 profile (scale **6**, for example) than they were on the original MMPI profile, and it is also possible for some scales to be lower on the MMPI-2 profile (scales **4** and **8**, for example) than they were on the original MMPI profile. These differential changes mean that the types of two-point codes and the numbers of them that are found in various populations may be changed. For example, in a recent study (Cole, 1991), the predominant two-point codes found in a prison population using the MMPI-2 were found to be different than those found by Megargee and Bohn in their study of a prison population (Megargee & Bohn, 1979). These differences in two-point code frequencies and other problems with the new uniform T-scores will be discussed in the introductory remarks for each of the clinical scales.

The fourth major change for the MMPI-2 has been the addition of new scales. There are now four sets of scales available for the MMPI-2 in addition to the traditional validity and clinical scales. Some of these scales are updated versions of scales that were available for the original MMPI, e.g., the Harris and Lingoes subscales (Harris & Lingoes, 1955) and the Weiner-Harmon Subtle-Obvious subscales (Weiner, 1948), but others are new to the MMPI-2, e.g., some of the supplementary scales and new content scales. Each set of scales has it own scoring keys and accompanying profile sheet.

The Harris and Lingoes subscales (Harris & Lingoes, 1955) are used to refine the interpretation of six clinical scales (**2**-Depression, **3**-Hysteria, **4**-Psychopathic Deviate, **6**-Paranoia, **8**-Schizophrenia, and **9**-Hypomania). Interpretations for these subscales are given at the end of each of the appropriate clinical scale sections.

Another set of scales carried over from the MMPI is the Weiner-Harmon Subtle-Obvious subscales (Weiner, 1948). Five MMPI clinical scales (**2**-Depression, **3**-Hysteria, **4**-Psychopathic Deviate, **6**-Paranoia, and **9**-Hypomania) have been divided into subtle and obvious items and are made into obvious and subtle scales for each of these clinical scales. Greene (1991) used these scales to help determine the validity of an MMPI or MMPI-2 and found them useful in detecting under-

and overreporting of pathology when this might not be apparent using the **L, F,** and **K** validity scales alone. His method of using these subtle-obvious scales is very helpful when working with MMPIs given by individuals going through custody evaluations where there may be underreporting of pathology. These scales also are useful for evaluating individuals who are undergoing disability evaluations where there may be overreporting of pathology. Greene's (1991) book should be referred to for further information regarding these scales.

A third set of scales that is available for the MMPI-2 is called the Supplementary Scales. These 18 scales have been chosen by the MMPI revisers as additions to the basic validity and clinical scales. Four of these scales were scored on the original MMPI (**A**-Anxiety, **R**-Repression, **Es**-Ego Strength, and **MAC-R**-MacAndrew Alcoholism Scale) and were discussed in previous editions of this book as well as in the supplementary scale chapter of this current book. These scales are basically unchanged on the MMPI-2, although two of the scales, scales **R** and **Es,** have been shortened. The **R** scale has been reduced from 40 items to 37, and **Es** has been changed from 68 items to 52. The **MAC-R** scale, while not different in number of items for the two versions of the test, has had four of its items changed.

There are four additional scales that were scored on some computer scoring programs for the original MMPI. These scales are **O-H**-Overcontrolled Hostility, **Do**-Dominance, **Re**-Social Responsibility, and **Mt**-College Maladjustment. These scales are discussed in a number of books (Caldwell, 1988; Duckworth & Anderson, 1986; Graham, 1987; Greene, 1980; Levitt, 1989), and updated information regarding the **Do** and **Re** scales is included in the supplementary scale section of this book.

The next seven supplementary scales are two gender-role scales (**GM**-Gender Role-Masculine and **GF**-Gender Role-Feminine), two post-traumatic stress scales (**PK** and **PS**), and three new subscales for the **O** scale, Social introversion (**Si1, Si2,** and **Si3**). The final three scales of this supplementary scale section are new validity scales designed to evaluate random responding (**F**B), inconsistency (**VRIN**-Variable Response

Inconsistency), and the tendency to answer yes or no regardless of item content (**TRIN**-True Response Inconsistency). These last three scales are discussed in the validity scale section of this book, whereas the gender role, post-traumatic stress, and **O** scale subscales are covered in the supplementary scale chapter.

The fourth and final set of additional scales that are available for the MMPI-2 are new content scales (Butcher, Graham, Williams, & Ben-Porath, 1990). Many users of the original MMPI are familiar with the Wiggins Content Scales (Wiggins, 1966), a set of 13, non-overlapping scales that measure the major content areas of the MMPI. The new MMPI-2 content scales are similar to the Wiggins scales in many respects, but there are some differences. These content scales are also discussed in the supplementary scale chapter of this book.

Besides these four sets of additional scales, the MMPI-2 has two sets of critical items (Koss & Butcher, 1973; Lachar & Wroebel, 1979). The item numbers for these two sets of critical items are available in the MMPI-2 Manual (Butcher et al., 1989). When test takers endorse critical items, they are saying that they have problems or behaviors that may be of interest to a clinician. Critical items are subject to a test taker's tendency to over- or underreport pathology and therefore need to be used with caution as indicating accurate representations of the problems that a person has. They do however seem to be useful as an indication of what the test taker is willing to say is the matter with him or her.

In contrast to the original MMPI where there are two versions of the test for adults, the booklet form and Form R, the MMPI-2 has only one version. However, the test can be purchased in three different formats—hardcover, softcover, and audiocassette for clients who cannot read. There are five sets of scoring keys and a corresponding profile sheet for each of the sets of keys. The five sets of keys are the validity and clinical scales, Harris and Lingoes subscales, supplementary scales, subtle-obvious scales, and content scales. The MMPI-2 is available from many test distributors, but the main source of test material and scoring keys is National Computer Systems (NCS) (1-800-NCS-7271).

The MMPI-2 can be computer scored by some test companies, including NCS. NCS has a number of options for computer scoring, including a mail-in service or a Microtest system, which uses your own personal computer and printer for scoring the test. In contrast to the few companies that do MMPI-2 scoring, there are many companies that do computer interpretations of the test. Some of the most popular of these services are those provided by NCS (interpretations by Dr. James Butcher), the Caldwell Report (interpretations by Dr. Alex Caldwell), Psychological Assessment Resources (interpretations by Dr. Roger Greene), and Western Psychological Services (interpretations by Drs. Philip Marks and Richard Lewak).

The new MMPI-2 is a challenging test for those of us who do personality assessment. It has many positive features that were not available on the original MMPI, but it also presents many challenges. It will take much time and research before we know how to use this test to its fullest potential, but it is hoped that this book will help in that process.

## RECOMMENDED BOOKS

The following are some books that we have found useful in our work with the MMPI/MMPI-2.

Archer, R.P. (1992). *MMPI-2: Assessing adolescent psychopathology*. Hillsdale, NJ: Lawrence Erlbaum.

Butcher, J.N., & Williams, C.L. (1992). *Essentials of MMPI-2 and MMPI-A interpretation*. Minneapolis: University of Minnesota Press.

Greene, R.L. (1991). *The MMPI-2/MMPI: An interpretive manual*. Boston: Allyn and Bacon.

Lewak, R.W., Marks, P.A., & Nelson, G.E. (1990). *Therapist guide to the MMPI & MMPI-2: Providing feedback and treatment*. Muncie, IN: Accelerated Development, Publishers.

# CHAPTER II

# INTERPRETING THE MMPI

Like any other high level skill, learning to interpret the MMPI takes time. This is a test where much of what one can say is dependent on the interaction of many factors. To the reader, learning all of these factors may seem to be a massive task. This interaction, however, is what makes the test such a rich source of information about clients. Its complexity adds to rather than detracts from its value as an appraisal instrument.

In this section, we first will discuss some general interpretation strategies: (1) how to use sub-groupings of scale items, especially for scales that are less elevated; (2) how one clinical scale modifies the interpretation of another; and (3) how the supplementary scales can be used to add to the predictive power of the test. Then we will discuss how to interpret what some people consider very difficult tests, those that are only moderately elevated. A richness of material is available that we believe has been relatively untouched except in the previous editions of this book and a few research articles (e.g., Kunce & Anderson, 1976).

After this discussion about interpretation in general, we will conclude this chapter with specific comments about interpretation of the new MMPI-2.

# ITEM SUBSCALES

Many of the clinical scales on the MMPI and MMPI-2 are made up of subscales consisting of items that are similar in content. When working with a client, knowing which of these subscales are being endorsed is useful in obtaining a more accurate picture of what the person is feeling and thinking.

Many people have suggested subscales for the MMPI clinical scales. The most known are those that have been developed by Harris and Lingoes (1955). They subjectively divided scales **2, 3, 4, 6, 8,** and **9** into groups of items that had similar content. For example, scale **4** (anger) was divided into four subscales—familial discord, authority conflict, social imperturbability, and alienation. The clinical scales that were not made into subscales were found to have uniform content and therefore could not be divided. We believe that knowing which subscale a client/patient is endorsing is helpful in order to get the most accurate picture of how that client or patient is feeling, thinking, and behaving.

We find subscales to be especially useful when the client or patient has a clinical scale at the lower end of the clinically elevated range. At this level the person may be choosing items from only one or two of the subscales rather than all of them. For example, a person with a **4** scale of 75 could have that elevation because of endorsing items reflecting family problems (family discord), whereas another test taker could have an elevation on the **4** scale because he or she is denying social anxiety and dependency needs (social imperturbability). When a scale score is above 80 T-score points, however, the person most likely is answering at least some items from all the subscales in order to get that scale elevation, and therefore, the subscales are not as useful.

# CLINICAL SCALE INTERACTIONS

Clinical scale interactions become important to answer two questions: (1) how is the highest point scale interpretation *modified* by other scale elevations? and (2) how does a scale *modify* other scales when it is a lower point in a two- or three-point code?

The interpretation of any one scale will be modified by the other scales that are elevated along with it. In each scale chapter in this book, we discuss high-point codes. These are usually two-point codes, but some three-point codes are included when the third scale seems to be an important modifier of the two higher scales. The second and third highest scales may modify the highest scale in ways that change what is said about an individual. Sometimes the scale that has the lower elevation accentuates or makes more pathological the behavior or emotions indicated by the high-point scale. At other times a lower elevation may repress or diffuse the behavior or emotion, and at still other times it may significantly change the interpretation of a scale. With scale **4** as an example, let us examine these three possibilities. An individual who has a high **4** with no other significant elevations is usually seen as impulsive, rebellious, egocentric, and having poor relationships with parents and authority figures in general. This individual also has low frustration tolerance. This combined with poor self-control often results in aggressive outbursts.

An elevation on scale **9** (psychic energy) will accentuate the characteristics we expect of a **4** scale elevation, making the pathological characteristics not only more likely to appear but energizing them. Therefore, an individual with a **4-9** pattern would tend to be even more impulsive and irresponsible than one with just a high **4** scale. The **9** scale adds a dimension of restlessness and a need for stimulation, which "pushes" these individuals into trouble. On the other hand, an elevation on scale **3** (denial) will moderate the effects of the **4** scale, and the usual behavior connected with a scale **4** elevation will be seen only on relatively rare occasions, usually as sudden anger or rage, to a degree that is inappropriate to the situation. Most people will see this acting out as out of character for the individual since under ordinary conditions the person will be quiet and somewhat withdrawn.

The addition of a high **8** scale along with the high **4** scale also changes the interpretation of the **4** scale elevation, since the **8** scale elevation adds a more pathological dimension of confusion and bad judgement. Individuals with **4-8** elevations tend to have long histories of problems as a result of their not understanding social norms and chronically misinterpreting the expectations of others. While an individual with a high **4** scale is frequently likeable on initial contact, individuals who have the **4-8** combination usually are not.

We have been discussing how a particular high point is modified by the addition of another scale elevation. We also can look at what a particular scale does to other scales when it is the second highest scale and modifies the highest one. From the above discussion, we should suspect that a high scale **9** tends to energize other scales and that a high scale **3** tends to modify or lessen the pathology of other scale elevations.

An elevated scale **8** also modifies other scale interpretations. A high scale **8** by itself usually reflects an individual who has difficulty relating to others, is confused, and may be actually delusional or hallucinating. When scale **8** is the second highest score in a two-point code, different aspects of the scale will be apparent, and the interpretation of the high point will need to be modified accordingly. For example, when scale **1** is the highest point, it indicates considerable bodily concern and symptoms that are not logically connected to any standard illness. When scale **8** is added as a secondary elevation, these bodily concerns take on a bizarre quality, one where the somatic concerns may be of a delusional nature. As was already mentioned, when the **8** scale elevation is secondary to a high scale **4**, the delusional quality of the **8** scale is not as apparent; instead the bad judgment and chronic inability to relate to others becomes more noticeable. Finally, when the **8** scale is secondary to scale **7** (anxiety) we are not as likely to see either delusions or bad judgment; instead we see a pattern of chronic worry and tension, an awareness and a concern on the part of the patient that his/her thoughts are inappropriate. Thus, it is important to look at the interaction of the two or three highest scales to interpret a profile accurately.

Of additional interest is whether a secondary clinical scale elevation activates or modulates the behavior, thoughts, and feelings indicated by the highest scale. The following is a listing of the clinical scales and our assessment of their activator/modulator potential when they are elevated secondary to another clinical scale:

Scale **1 Hs** - Hypochondriasis (physical complaints) modulator;

Scale **2 D** - Depression (depression) modulator;

Scale **3 Hy** - Hysteria (denial) modulator;

Scale **4 Pd** - Psychopathic Deviate (anger) activator;

Scale **5 Mf** - Masculinity-Femininity (masculine-feminine interests) for men—modulator, for women—activator;

Scale **6 Pa** - Paranoia (suspiciousness) activator;

Scale **7 Pt** - Psychasthenia (anxiety) activator;

Scale **8 Sc** - Schizophrenia (confusion) activator;

Scale **9 Ma** - Hypomania (energy) activator; and

Scale **0 Si** - Social Introversion (extroversion-introversion) modulator.

## SUPPLEMENTARY SCALES

We have found the supplementary scales in Chapter V of this book to be of real value in interpreting profiles. We regularly use some of them to (1) modify the interpretation of the clinical scales, (2) help with our predictions about therapy outcomes, and (3) add new information not available from the clinical scales.

One of the most useful scales for modifying the interpretation of the clinical scales is the **Es** scale (Ego Strength). We find that the ego strength scale indicates whether or not to use attenuated pathology interpretations, suggested by Graham and McCord (1982), for scales that are moderately elevated or to go with interpretations that suggest more positive characteristics (Kunce & Anderson, 1976, 1984). (See the next section, moderate scale elevations, for a more complete discussion of other cues for using the pathological or positive interpretations.) When a clinical scale is above 65 and the **Es** is below 50, we use the more negative interpretation for the clinical scale. For example, with a scale **4** elevation of 70 and an **Es** of 40, we would give a more pathological interpretation. We would speak of an impulsive, rather unreliable individual who has frequent minor problems with authority figures. On the other hand, if the scale **4** was 70 and the **Es** score was 60, we would speak of an individual who is enterprising, social, and probably dedicated to making some changes in the social system but from a non-hostile stance.

Second, even in those individuals where their profiles are such that one would tend to use the more pathological interpretations (i.e., they are elevated markedly), the **Es** can be used to modify the interpretation. Anderson and Kunce (1984) have found that clients in a university counseling center who have an elevated **8** scale show different degrees of pathology, not so much on the basis of the height of the **8** scale score but on the difference between the **8** scale and the **Es** scale scores. That is, a moderately elevated **8** scale with a very low **Es** was more predictive of bizarre ideation than a high elevation on the **8** scale with an elevated **Es**.

How responsive an individual will be to treatment is often predicted from the clinical scales. The usual expectation is that an individual with a **1-3** pattern will be rather unresponsive to psychological interventions, while an individual with a **2-7** profile will be actively involved in and responsive to psychotherapy. Some supplementary scales add another dimension to therapy predictions since they can predict additional ways in which the individual will help with his/her own therapy or ways in which resistance will be shown. The relationship between the **A** scale and the **R** scale is an example. The **A** and **R** scales both were derived from a factor analysis of the original MMPI. The **A** scale relates to the client's feelings of being psychologically disturbed and taps a general maladjustment dimension. It intercorrelates highly with most measures of pathology on the MMPI. The **R** scale on the other hand does not correlate highly with many other scales and seems to tap a dimension of control of feelings that can be of a repressive nature. In any case, when the **A** scale is elevated above 55 T-score points and **R** is below 50 T-score points, therapy tends to proceed quite well. The person is both feeling disturbed (**A** scale) and not repressing the awareness of these feelings (**R** scale). On the other hand, when both the **A** and the **R** scales are above 55 T-score points, elevation of the **R** scale seems to prevent the client from discussing pertinent material even though the person recognizes being psychologically disturbed (**A** scale).

Finally, the supplementary scales may add information about a client/patient that is not given by the clinical or validity scales. The **Dy** and **Do** scales (Dependency and Dominance) on the original MMPI can be most useful in indicating how a person will react interpersonally. If the **Do** scale is about 50 T-score points and the **Dy** scale is below 50, the individual likes taking charge of his/her life and is not psychologically over-dependent on others. If, however, both the **Do** and **Dy** scales are above 50 and the **Dy** scale is higher than the **Do** scale, the person is likely to be passive-aggressive. This type of individual tends to be a game player and while saying one thing, "help me run my life (**Dy**)," really has a stake in making sure the individual who is trying to help does not succeed, "see, you can't do it well either (**Do**)." Passive-aggressiveness is not indicated by any of the validity or clinical scales. The only place it can be seen clearly on the MMPI is on the relative elevations of the **Dy** and **Do** scales.

Other supplementary scales can add information not indicated by validity or clinical scales. Each supplementary scale's contribution to an MMPI interpretation is discussed in the appropriate scale section of that chapter. Being aware of these scales' contributions can enhance the accuracy and applicability of your MMPI interpretations.

# MODERATE SCALE ELEVATIONS

While the MMPI originally was developed for diagnosing psychiatric patients, the use of the test has been broadened to include individuals with a variety of nonpsychiatric problems. In most populations if all of an individual's T-scores on the MMPI profile fall between 45 and 60, we usually can not make a very individualized report on that person's personality characteristics. However, when profiles have moderate elevations (60-65 T-score points, MMPI-2; 60-70 T-score points, MMPI), we have found that some things can be said about the personalities of these individuals.

In a nonpsychiatric setting, however, when one has a profile with moderate elevations, a problem exists in deciding what kind of interpretive approach should be used. A very frequent approach is to interpret the moderately elevated scale scores as if they indicated lesser degrees of the pathology that is connected with higher elevations. Graham and McCord (1982) represented this position when they stated

> Probably the most commonly used approach is to generate for our normal subjects what Dahlstrom and Welsh (1960) have called "psychologically attenuated" descriptions of more clear cut psychiatric patients. We determine what a more elevated score on a particular scale would mean for a clinical subject, and we modify the inferences subjectively for our more moderately elevated score for our normal subject. For example, if we would characterize a psychiatric patient with a T-score of 90 on scale **2** as depressed, a normal person with a T-score of 65 or 70 probably would be described as unhappy or dissatisfied. (p. 4)

Struck with the discrepancies between the potentially pathological implications of moderately elevated scores and the good personality adjustment of individuals in some populations who have these elevations, Kunce and Anderson (1976, 1984) have asked the question, "Why would well-functioning, academically able individuals score in a pathological direction on some of the scales?" Their investigation of the literature led them to believe that in some populations moderate scale elevations on the MMPI are related to positive personality traits. Their position on this point, therefore, is in opposition to that held by Graham and McCord (1982).

Kunce and Anderson argued (1984) that while a certain scale configuration often may be associated with certain kinds of pathology in a psychiatric setting, a similar profile may or may not be connected with the same pathology in a nonpsychiatric setting. Thus, it does not follow that a nonhospitalized person who has a moderately elevated peak score on the scale **8** will show schizophrenic symptomatology, even though this might be true for persons hospitalized for schizophrenia.

Kunce and Anderson postulated an underlying personality dimension for each scale that could have either negative or positive characteristics when it is moderately elevated. In a psychiatric population, the characteristics the client/patient will show are almost always the negative aspects of the dimension, but these same moderate elevations may be related to positive traits in other populations. For example, Kunce and Anderson believe the dimension underlying scale **7** is organization. Under conditions that we will be discussing in this section, individuals with moderate elevations on this scale tend to show a good ability to organize. They are punctual, decisive and methodical, and could function well in managerial positions. A problem arises when individuals with these moderate elevations are put under stress. When this happens, the scale **7** scores of the individuals with positive traits will probably become more elevated, and their behavior will become maladaptive. They may develop an overreliance on obsession with minutia and engage in ritualistic behaviors or constant checking (e.g., to see if they have locked the door). What had been a personality asset paradoxically degenerates into ineffectual adjustment. However, maladaptive personality characteristics are most likely to be transitory reactions rather than enduring traits.

In the appropriate chapters on the clinical scales, we will discuss the possible positive interpretations for each scale. But to help the clinician follow our reasoning on this point, we will point out the underlying dimensions for each scale and a sample positive term that would apply for moderate elevations for each of the clinical scales: scale **1**, conservation (conscientious); scale **2**, evaluation (deliberate); scale **3**, expressive (optimistic); scale **4**, assertion (venturesome); scale **5**, role-flexibility (dilettante); scale **6**, inquiring (investigative); scale **7**, organization (methodical); scale **8**, imagination (creative); scale **9**, zest (eager); scale **0**, autonomy (independent).

This raises the question of when does a clinician use an attenuated pathology approach and when does he/she use a more positive interpretation for moderate scale elevations. Three groups of factors exist and in various combinations help build the case for using either the attenuated pathology approach or the positive strengths approach to interpreting profiles that have scale elevations in the moderate range. These factors are (1) the reason the test was administered, (2) the personal characteristics of the test taker, and (3) other test scale variables, such as the supplementary scale elevations.

## REASONS FOR TAKING THE TEST

Under the following conditions, the clinician should ask in each instance if a more positive approach might be called for in interpretation of the MMPI. When the test is being used for the following conditions, a more positive interpretation may be appropriate:

1. for personnel screening where the psychological adjustment of the applicant is not critical,

2. to help agencies and courts in making judgments in cases such as child custody,

3. for students in graduate classes where taking the test is part of the learning situation,

4. with a normal population as part of a research study, and

5. for clients in college counseling centers and in private practice.

The use of the MMPI with three of these groups merits further explanation.

### Students in Classes

Our experience has been that well functioning graduate students often have moderately elevated clinical scales. When they take the test for a graduate course in testing and find that they have moderate elevations, especially on scales **4** and **9,** these students may become overly concerned about their adjustment. Instructors need to recognize that for most of these students, the more positive description of the underlying dimension gives an interpretation that is closer to the actual behavior (and strengths) of these students.

### Research Studies

Two examples of the MMPI used for research will be discussed: one where we feel the authors made a mistake by using an attenuated pathology explanation, and a second where the author recognized that a more positive set of descriptors was needed. The first is a study by Rosen and Rosen (1957), where a group of successful business agents were selected for study. They found that these agents had mean T-scores greater than 60 on scales **1, 3, 4, 6,** and **9.** These authors interpreted these scores as reflecting the high stress that these men felt from their jobs. Given that these subjects had been selected as outstanding performers and that their **Es** scores averaged greater than 60, the authors explanation might have been reformulated and the subjects described as optimistic, energetic go-getters.

A second example, one where the author did not conclude that moderate elevations meant attenuated pathology, is found in MacKinnon's (1962) work with creative architects. MacKinnon emphasized that when the creative architects' MMPI scales scores were moderately elevated, these scores did not have the same meaning for their personality functioning that it would for other persons. These creative architects were getting along well in their personal lives and professional careers. He felt that the manner in which these creative subjects described themselves in the MMPI as well as in their life history interviews was less suggestive of psychopathology than it was of good intellect, complexity and richness of personality, lack of defensiveness, and candor in self-description, in other words, an openness to experience and especially an openness to the experience of one's inner life.

## Clients Seen in Private Practice

When the MMPI is used with some client populations, the therapist may be misled if only the negative descriptors for moderate scale elevations are used. As the public becomes more psychologically sophisticated and people are increasingly willing to seek help with their personal problems, more persons who are basically well adjusted and who have a minimum of personality problems will consult psychologists for help. The clinician must be careful not to over-read scale elevations with this group. These clients bring many positive personality characteristics to therapy in spite of their moderately elevated scale scores on the MMPI.

Along these same lines, Daniels and Hunter (1949) found that occupational groups differed on their mean MMPI profiles. For some groups, moderate elevations appeared to be normal and not an indication of attenuated pathology. For those readers who would like further evidence on this issue, we would suggest an article by Kunce and Callis (1969), "Vocational Interest and Personality."

While we are stressing that the clinician should be alert to the possibility of using positive interpretation in non-psychiatric populations, even among hospitalized psychiatric patients moderate elevations may have positive characteristics connected to them. After considerable experience with different client populations, Hovey and Lewis (1967) prepared a library of statements for each scale of the MMPI but with a difference. They included positive traits that they found to be associated with elevated scores as well as negative traits. They felt that one apparent advantage of their library of terms over some other systems was that it contained a substantial portion of non-negative and positive statements. They believed this was one way to avoid descriptions of patients only in terms of liability statements.

Hovey and Lewis went on to state that their experience indicated that T-scores around 60, rather than 50, are optimal for most of the clinical scales. They also observed that when some T-scores are under 50, they are likely to reflect negative characteristics, just as they do when they approach a 75 T-score. However, Hovey and Lewis recommended that when the clinician in a psychiatric setting is selecting positive statements for a profile, he/she be aware that a T-score of 75 is the upper limit for using positive traits. Also, they suggested, based upon their evidence, that positive statements should be used with caution if the score for scale **F** is above 70, if scale **8** is above 80, or if any two scales are above 80. In our discussion of individual scales, we will include the positive statements suggested in the work of Hovey and Lewis (1967) as well as those given by Kunce and Anderson (1976, 1984).

## SUBJECT'S PERSONAL CHARACTERISTICS

Some personal characteristics of the individual who has taken the MMPI also would lead us to consider a more positive interpretation of moderately elevated scores. Some of these characteristics are

1.  present functioning,
2.  past social history,
3.  intelligence and educational level, and
4.  openness to admitting personal inadequacies.

### Present Functioning and Past Social History

If the individual is "making it," that is, is successful in some occupation and reports that in general his/her life is going well, positive interpretive statements probably apply. This also is true if the test taker reports that his/her past life has been well-adjusted.

## Intelligence and Educational Level

Both of these factors seem to be connected with higher scores on some scales of the MMPI. Researchers usually find that more intelligent college students routinely have moderately elevated scores on some scales with no more symptoms of pathology than shown by college students in general. A representative study is the one done by Kennedy (1962) on the MMPI profiles of a group of mathematically gifted adolescents who had an average IQ of 135. The mean scores for males on scales **2, 3, 5, 7,** and **8** were 58, 66, 64, 58, and 59 respectively. The moderately elevated scores for females were scale **3**-60 and scale **K**-57. The reader should keep in mind that this means that many of the gifted students had scores higher than these means. The average age of this group was 17, and they did not show any clinically evident signs of psychopathology.

A number of other studies also support the position that college students tend to have higher than average scale scores on the MMPI and also frequently have more positive personality characteristics (Goodstein, 1954; Norman & Redlo, 1952; Rosen, 1956).

## Openness to Personal Inadequacies

Gilliland and Colgin (1951), working with MMPIs of 14 groups of students from three campuses, found that normal college students typically were moderately elevated on a number of scales. At one university, 39% of the students had one score over 70, 14% had two scores over 70, and 7% had three scores over 70. Rather than accept the conclusion that a high level of abnormality existed in these groups, the authors concluded that college students were less inhibited and freer to give answers that indicate deviations from normal since they had less at stake than hospitalized patients. Whatever the cause, they felt that extreme caution and tentativeness should be attached to any pathological diagnosis given to this population based upon personality test score alone.

# SUPPLEMENTARY SCALE VARIABLES

A third consideration in the interpretation of moderately elevated scores is the presence or absence of other elevations, particularly on some of the supplementary scales. The research evidence on the ego-strength scale is an example. With populations such as college students and creative individuals, ego-strength scale scores tend to be elevated above 60 T-score points. As has been mentioned before, our interpretation policy has been that one should take a positive interpretative stance when confronted with moderately elevated scores on the psychiatric scales if they are accompanied by elevated ego-strength scores (Barron, 1969; Kleinmuntz, 1960; Kunce and Anderson, 1976).

We also feel that a normal **F** (50 T-score points or below) and an elevated **K** (above 55 T-score points) in a nonpsychiatric population warrant considering a positive interpretation of moderately elevated scale scores. As the reader will see in our section on validity scales, we believe the evidence supports the conclusion that in a nonpsychiatric population, high **K** represents something very close to good ego strength and self-respect.

In summary, we suggest two ways of approaching the interpretation of a nonpsychiatric population MMPI profile that has scales with moderate elevations: (1) attenuated pathology, or (2) positive strengths. The reasons for taking the test, the personal characteristics of the individual, and other scale levels, especially the supplementary scales, should all be considered in making the decision as to which interpretation to use. As a final suggested guideline, if false negatives (labeling people pathological when they are not) are more undesirable in interpretations for your population, then use the positive strength interpretations. If false positives (labeling people psychologically healthy when they are not) are undesirable in interpretations for your population, then use the attenuated pathology interpretations.

# MMPI-2 INTERPRETATION

A new version of the MMPI, the MMPI-2, has been published. This has led to some new challenges regarding test interpretation. Following are some general comments concerning the interpretation of this new test. More detailed information is presented in each of the validity and clinical scale sections.

Since the MMPI-2 was published in 1989, there have been many articles (Dahlstrom, 1992; Graham, 1991; Strassberg, 1991; Vincent, 1990) regarding the comparability of the two versions of the test and the best way to interpret the revised version. Most researchers agree that the test items that make up the validity and clinical scales of the two tests are very similar and the raw scores for these scales are comparable even though some items have been removed from five of the clinical scales.

The difference between the two tests comes when the raw scores are converted to the new uniform T-scores and plotted on the MMPI-2 profile forms. When this happens, the profiles for the two versions of the test may look quite different, because each of the scales on the profile has been affected differently by the conversion to uniform scores. For example, the same raw scores for scales **2, 4,** and **8** are 5 to 10 score points lower on the MMPI-2 than they are on the original MMPI. On the other hand, similar raw score points on the **L** scale will generate a 10 T-score point higher score on the MMPI-2 than on the MMPI. Strassberg (1991) has developed tables (Tables 3.1 and 3.2, pp. 42-43.) that illustrate the T-score differences between the two tests for various scale elevations. Numbers in the tables that have a minus sign in front of them show T-scores that are *lower* on the MMPI-2. Numbers in the tables that are positive show T-scores that are *higher* on the MMPI-2.

Dahlstrom (1992) has done another comparison of the MMPI and MMPI-2, this time of the two-point codes. His tables showing the two-point codes for the same test scored on the two different sets of norms (Tables 4.1 and 4.2, pp. 86-87) indicate how codetypes are changed when these two T-score distributions are used.

These differences in T-score distributions need to be considered when an MMPI-2 is to be interpreted since most of the research regarding the meanings of two-point codes as well as individual scale elevations comes from work done with the original MMPI. Caldwell (1992) has suggested that until research regarding the meaning of MMPI-2 codetypes is established, MMPI-2 raw scores be plotted on both the original MMPI profile and the new MMPI-2 profile. He recommended that the profile interpretation be done using the codetype elevations shown on the original MMPI profile so that the research information that has been derived from the original MMPI can be used. The MMPI-2 profile will help clinicians become familiar with how the test would look using the new T-scores.

Graham (1990) has suggested another approach to the dilemma of two different T-score distributions for the MMPI and MMPI-2. He advocated using MMPI research data for an MMPI-2 profile when that profile is a clearly delineated one- or two-point code. He defined clearly delineated as the most elevated scale or scales are at least 5 T-score points above the next highest scale. If Graham's advice is followed, plotting MMPI-2 raw scores onto both the MMPI-2 and MMPI profiles could be eliminated for those MMPI-2 profiles with clearly delineated codetypes. This would save time, since about a third of the profiles derived from a clinical population are well-defined profiles. However, for the two-thirds of the MMPI-2 profiles that are not clearly defined, we recommend plotting the MMPI-2 raw scores on both the MMPI and MMPI-2 profiles.

After the information regarding the client from the basic validity and clinical scales is considered, the supplementary scales can be consulted for further information and interpretation refinements. As was already mentioned in Chapter I, these supplementary scales are a mixture of some scales that were developed for the MMPI, such as **A, R, Es, MAC, O-H, Do,** and **Re,** and some new scales that have been developed for the MMPI-2.

Some of the supplementary scales that we have discussed in previous editions of this book are not included in the MMPI-2 supplementary scales, namely **Lb, Dy, Pr, St,** and **Cn**. Most of the items that make up these scales are still available in the MMPI-2; therefore, it is possible to score and interpret them. The MMPI-2 items that make up these scales are listed in Table 5.3, p. 298, and the tables to convert the raw scores for these scales into T-scores are in Tables 5.5 and 5.6, pp. 300-303.

The research that has been published so far regarding the new MMPI-2 supplementary scales indicates that some of them seem to be useful for enhancing MMPI-2 interpretation, while others have received mixed reviews. These research studies are discussed in the supplementary scales chapter of this book (Chapter V).

In the supplementary scale chapter we also include a discussion of the new MMPI-2 content scales. These content scales are sometimes similar to those developed by Wiggins (1966), but sometimes they are quite different.

We use content scales as indications of the test takers' diagnoses of their problems. The content scale items are obvious in nature and, therefore, when individuals endorse them, they are saying that these are problems that they believe they have, or these are problems that they want us to believe they have. Frequently the elevations on the content scales are different from those on the client scales of the test, and these differences cause interesting interpretation dilemmas. How to resolve these dilemmas is discussed in the content scale section of the supplementary scale chapter.

## SUMMATION OF INTERPRETIVE STRATEGIES

The following is a summation of the interpretive strategies that we suggest you use with the MMPI-2.

1.  After administering and scoring the MMPI-2, plot the validity and clinical scale raw scores on the MMPI-2 profile sheet.

a. If the MMPI-2 profile has one or two scale elevations that are 5 to 10 T-score points above the next highest scale, use the scale interpretations that are given in the appropriate high-point sections of this book. (It is highly likely that the profile on the MMPI-2 and the original MMPI are quite similar and, therefore, the research based upon the original MMPI can be used.)

b. If the MMPI-2 profile does not have a clearly defined profile or is within normal limits, transfer the MMPI-2 raw scores onto an MMPI profile sheet, and then use the MMPI profile to interpret the test. (The majority of the research literature for the test has been gathered from data derived from the original MMPI profile, and therefore, where the MMPI-2 and MMPI profiles differ for an individual, the original profile is the most appropriate one to use.)

2. Use the supplementary scales to modify and enhance the interpretations generated from the validity and clinical scales; however, be judicious in your use of the new supplementary scales because of the limited research that has been done with some of them.

3. Use the content scales as indicators of what test takers want you to know about their problems. Elevations on these scales are useful to indicate areas to talk about at the beginning of therapy. Clients recognize these area as problems and usually see them as appropriate topics for therapy sessions. (Whether the problems indicated on the content scales are also what the therapist sees as problems for the individual will take some time to assess. The clinical scales are usually the most accurate assessment of the individual's problem areas, but these problems may not be seen by the client initially. It will take time to build rapport before the therapist is able to work directly on the issues and behaviors indicated by the clinical scales if the client does not see them initially.)

# FORMAT AND USE OF THIS MANUAL

The following format is used in this book for the chapters on the validity, clinical, and supplementary scales (Chapters III-V. An introduction and general information about each scale is presented, then high score interpretations are given, usually divided into moderate elevations (60-65, MMPI-2; 60-70, MMPI) and marked elevations (>65, MMPI-2; >70, MMPI). These interpretations are followed by low score interpretations and then codetype interpretations. All clinical scales in the codetypes are in the marked elevation range, unless otherwise noted, and are listed in order from the highest to the lowest peaks. If a scale in a codetype is lower than a T of 50, the symbol "-" above the scale number is used, for example **5** in **4-5̄**.

Information should be gathered from the chapters concerning the validity, clinical, and supplementary scales according to the high and low points present in the profile to be interpreted. The T-score range between 45 and 60 is not usually interpreted for the validity and clinical scales. A profile may be interpreted using only the high and low score sections, or it may be interpreted using codetypes (with or without the information in the high and low score sections) if the profile scales are high enough to be in a codetype (>65, MMPI-2; >70, MMPI).

For the reader who is new to interpreting the MMPI/MMPI-2, the best way to become acquainted with the various scales is to read the introductory remarks for each of the scales. As you continue to work with the MMPI, the more detailed information listed under the high and low points of the scales becomes useful. Finally, as you become yet more skilled in the usage of the test, the codetypes with their more intricate interpretations become useful. A word of caution is necessary about the clinical scale combinations. Only the highest two or three scales are considered as a codetype. The other elevated clinical scales should be interpreted by referring to the respective high-point sections of the scales involved.

We recommend that the whole book be read through first in order to get the total picture of the MMPI we are presenting. After the overview, separate sections can be used as needed.

# CHAPTER III

# VALIDITY SCALES

Of primary consideration in the interpretation of any inventory is the attitude of the person taking the test. Most inventories either have no way to check this attitude or have a simplistic approach to the problem. The MMPI is unique in this area. Four scales were developed for the original MMPI to measure the test-taking attitude of the subject—the **?**, **L, F,** and **K** scales. Of these scales, two (**L** and **K**) were designed to measure the person's trying to look better on the test than he/she really is, and one (the **F** scale) was designed to measure the person's trying to look worse on the test than he/she really is. The **?** scale measures how many questions the client has left unanswered on the test and, thus, can show the person's resistance to the test, confusion, or the fact that he/she did not have time to finish. These validity scales can be interpreted either individually or in combinations.

For the original MMPI, the **?** scale did not usually have to be interpreted because it rarely had enough raw score points to be scored on the profile sheet. Similarly, the **L** scale was only rarely above a T-score of 60; therefore, the interpretation of this scale usually used only the low end of the scale (the person is not trying to look good on the test). Only the **F** and **K** scales varied considerably; therefore, the various interpretations of them were considered carefully.

These same general guidelines also apply to the new MMPI-2. Instead of the **?** scale appearing on the test profile, however, the number of items left unanswered on the test is indicated as a raw score number. The number of items left unanswered is still low on the MMPI-2, and therefore this scale is not usually a factor in validity considerations.

A second change for the MMPI-2 in the general guidelines given above is the fact that the **L** scale T-score distribution has been elevated so that what was once 60 T-score points on the MMPI is now 70 T-score points on the MMPI-2. (See the **L** scale section for further information.) It still holds true, however, that the **L** scale for normal individuals in various types of stressful situations is rarely clinically elevated on the MMPI-2, so this scale typically does not have to be interpreted. The **F** and **K** scales are still the usual validity scales that are interpreted out of the four validity scales from the original MMPI.

The new MMPI-2 has added three new validity scales to the four that are on the MMPI. These new scales—**F**ʙ, **VRIN,** and **TRIN**—will be discussed after the **?, L, F,** and **K** scales in this chapter. Since these new validity scales have only been available for such a short time, research regarding them is just now being published, and the best use of them for various populations still remains to be discovered. Our coverage of them in this book will necessarily be brief until more research information is available. We encourage you to explore using these new scales before coming to definite conclusions as to what they show for the people you treat.

Greene (1991) has a very important chapter in his new book, *The MMPI-2/MMPI: An Interpretive Manual,* that discusses these new validity scales and MMPI/MMPI-2 validity issues at length. We highly recommend this chapter to you since it is the best review of the relevant issues concerning MMPI validity issues available.

# ? SCALE

## (Cannot Say Scale)

This scale is no longer scored as a separate scale on the MMPI-2; instead the number of items that are left unanswered are indicated as a raw score number. Since the number of items left unanswered is typically small, it makes sense to just note this number rather than plotting it on a profile. All of the interpretation hints given below still apply to the MMPI-2.

The **?** scale raw score is simply the number of items the client has left unanswered. Omission of items is largely dependent upon the subject's response set, which in turn is usually influenced by the instructions given. If the instructions call for all items to be answered, they usually are. MMPIs are usually given with these instructions, and most people leave few, if any, questions unanswered.

The usual number of items omitted is from zero through six, with a mode of zero and a median of one. When more than six items are not answered, the interpreter should look at the items omitted to see if a pattern exists. If a pattern occurs, it may indicate an area that the client does not want to consider, or about which confusion exists. This knowledge can be useful in counseling the person.

The omission of more than 12 items is unusual. When a large number of items are omitted, the most likely reason is because the person did not have enough time to finish the test. A glance at the answer sheet should confirm whether or not this is true.

## GENERAL INFORMATION

1. The **?** scale raw score is the number of test questions a person does not answer.

2. Normal people decline few items on the MMPI. Thus, this scale tends to be highly skewed, with zero to six being the usual number of unanswered items. The mode for this scale is zero, and the median is one question unanswered.

3. The number of items omitted is largely dependent upon the subject's response set, which is usually influenced by the testing instructions given. If the instructions are for all items to be answered, they usually are answered.

4. When items are left unanswered, it might be useful to see if a pattern exists for the unanswered items; that is, they may all be related to a certain topic such as sex or family. This topic may be an area of concern for the client.

5. The reason people leave items unanswered may range from lack of knowledge about the item to defensiveness. See the high score section of this scale for the various reasons for omissions.

6. The effect of a high **?** score, if the omissions are scattered throughout the test, can be a general lowering of the entire profile without much distortion of the pattern, except for the women's scale **5**. For this one scale, the more items that are omitted, the higher the T-score becomes.

   The presence of a high **?** score, however, does not always mean that the profile is too low to interpret because the motivations leading the subject to omit items also may lead him/her to choose an unusual number of deviant responses.

7. If the high **?** score is the result of the person not finishing the test and leaving items unanswered at the end, the validity and clinical scales are relatively unaffected if the first 400 items (370 items, MMPI-2) have been answered. However, the supplementary scales are affected by the item omissions and should not be interpreted.

8. There is considerable consistency over time for this scale. That is, a person will have approximately the same score on it if the test should be given a second time.

# HIGH SCORES

(>20 unanswered items, MMPI-2)

(T = 70 or above, MMPI)

1. High scores may indicate the following:

    a. Indecision about the question and not wanting to be incorrect in answering either way.

    b. Indecision or obsession with the "right" answer.

    c. Defensiveness (wanting to look good). These people do not know what answer would be the most favorable one for them to choose. Therefore, they do not answer the question.

    d. Not wanting to answer the question, but also not wanting to say "no" to the tester. Therefore, the client takes the test but leaves many questions unanswered.

    e. Distrust of the tester's motives.

    f. Lack of ability to read or comprehend all items.

    g. Not enough time to finish the test. This would be shown when only items toward the end of the test are omitted.

    h. A seriously depressed patient who finds the items beyond his/her capacity for decision.

    i. Aggression toward the test or tester.

    j. Mental confusion whereby the person does not realize he/she has omitted questions.

2. In some research studies, MMPI tests with a large number of omitted items are considered invalid. The cut-off number varies with the research project, but a number recommended by Butcher & Williams (1992) is 30.

# LOW SCORES

(0-6 unanswered items, MMPI-2)

(T = 50 or below, MMPI)

1. Low scores are more likely to be obtained when the testing instructions call for answering all the items.

2. Even when only six items are omitted, a review of the omissions may reveal a pattern.

3. People may not answer questions about certain areas for the following reasons:

    a. because they are not sure what they feel or believe about an area,

    b. because they cannot face their feelings about an area,

    c. because they do not trust the counselor to keep the test answers confidential, and/or

    d. because the items pertain to one or more areas of life that these people have not experienced.

## SUMMARY OF ? SCALE INTERPRETATIONS

| Number of Items Omitted | Interpretations |
| --- | --- |
| 0 thru 6 | This is the typical number of items omitted. |
| 7 thru 20 | The subject would prefer not answering questions about one or more areas. |
| 20 or above | Scores in this range may indicate lack of time to complete the test, indecision, defensiveness, not wanting to answer the questions, distrust, lack of reading ability, aggression, depression, or confusion. |

# L SCALE

## (Lie Scale)

This validity scale has been greatly affected by the change from the MMPI to the MMPI-2. It has been recognized for years that the **L** scale on the original MMPI was given T-scores that were at least 10 T-score points too low when in the elevated range. We had noted this in previous editions of the book and had considered the scale to be clinically elevated when it reached 55. The new distribution of this scale for the MMPI-2 has corrected this problem so that now the T-scores are much higher than they were on the original MMPI profile. For example, a raw score of 10 on the **L** scale for the original MMPI that would have been at 70 T-score points is now around 80 T-score points (Strassberg, 1991, see Tables 3.1 and 3.2). Since most people that we test do not endorse many **L** scale items, this redistribution of T-scores will not affect the MMPI-2 profiles that we see. However, if you work with a population that does have **L** scale raw scores of six or more, you will see a difference on the MMPI-2 profile and will need to adjust for it.

In addition to this change in the distribution of T-scores, the revisers of the MMPI have made another change for the **L** scale. In the original MMPI, the T-score distributions were the same for men and women; in the new MMPI-2, they are different. This difference is not great but it is there. In general, at the higher elevations, women will have a higher T-score than men for the same raw score.

This scale is usually measuring the degree to which a person is trying to look good in an obvious way. The higher the scale, the more the individual is claiming socially correct behavior. The lower the scale, the more the person is willing to own up to general human weaknesses.

Our experience indicates that the **L** scale is nearly always below a T of 50 and is rarely above a T of 60 (70 on the MMPI-2). People scoring at a T of 55 or above (65 or above on the MMPI-2) may be presenting themselves as morally righteous, although this in fact may not be true. A naive job applicant, for example, may have an elevated **L** because he/she wishes to impress the person doing the hiring.

In mental health centers, an elevation on this scale frequently indicates a naive person who has not thought deeply about human behavior, particularly his/her own. In a college setting, an elevated **L,** particularly with a slightly elevated **3** scale, indicates people who like to look on the bright side of life and do not like to think bad thoughts about themselves or others. Thus, the exact inference to be construed from an elevated **L** depends upon the person's background, setting, and purpose for taking the inventory.

Scores at the low end of this scale indicate a person who is not socially naive, at least not to the extent of claiming social virtues he/she does not have.

## GENERAL INFORMATION

1. The 15 items of the **L** scale attempt to identify people who will not admit to human foibles, such as telling white lies or getting angry. Such persons may wish to be seen as perfectionistic, or they may be naive.

2. The **L** scale items are seen as positive attributes in our culture. However, most people, excepting the most conscientious or naive, do not see such attributes as being true of themselves.

3. The **L** scale may indicate the following:

   a. The way the person actually sees himself/herself, that is as morally straight.

   b. The degree to which a person may be attempting to "look good" by choosing the response that is more socially acceptable.

   c. The person's tendency to cover up and deny undesirable personal faults.

4.  Caldwell (1994) believes this scale may measure a person's fears of shame and moral judgment. If a person has these fears, he/she will deny moral fault and therefore score high on this scale.

5.  The mean raw score for this scale is close to zero, and the modal raw score is 4.

6.  The **L** scale tends to be higher for older people, a finding that suggests greater conservatism among older age groups (Colligan, Osborne, and Swenson et al., 1984).

7.  Mexican-Americans score higher on the **L** scale than whites. Hibbs, Kobas, and Gonzales et al. (1979) feel this may be due to cultural factors.

8.  The **L** scale is negatively correlated with education. That is, the more education the subject has, the more likely the **L** scale is to be low (Colligan et al., 1984).

9.  Text-retest reliabilities for this scale for the MMPI-2 are .77 for males and .81 for females (Butcher et al., 1989).

10. Although most people do not score high on this scale, in one study (Gravitz, 1970), using the MMPI with normal subjects, four items of this scale (items 15, 135, 165, 255) were endorsed in the scorable direction by more than half of the subjects, while just under half answered four other items in the scorable direction. Thus, eight of the 15 items in this scale were answered in the scorable direction by almost half of the subjects.

11. Under instructions to present oneself in the most favorable light, the **L** scale tends to elevate.

## TABLE 3.1
### T-score (K-corrected) Differences
### between MMPI-2 and MMPI (Males)

| MMPI-2 T score | L | F | K | Hs | D | Hy | Pd | Mf | Pa | Pt | Sc | Ma | Si |
|---|---|---|---|---|---|---|---|---|---|---|---|---|---|
| 40 | -1 | -9 | -7 | -5 | -8 | -9 | -8 | -13 | -8 | -7 | -8 | -7 | -2 |
| 42 | -1 | -8 | -6 | -5 | -9 | -9 | -8 | -13 | -8 | -7 | -8 | -7 | -2 |
| 44 | 0 | -8 | -6 | -4 | -8 | -10 | -9 | -13 | -7 | -8 | -7 | -8 | -2 |
| 46 | 1 | -8 | -6 | -4 | -9 | -9 | -9 | -13 | -7 | -7 | -8 | -8 | -1 |
| 48 | 2 | -7 | -6 | -4 | -9 | -9 | -9 | -13 | -7 | -7 | -8 | -9 | -1 |
| 50 | 2 | -7 | -6 | -3 | -8 | -8 | -10 | -14 | -7 | -7 | -8 | -9 | -1 |
| 52 | 2 | -6 | -6 | -3 | -8 | -8 | -10 | -15 | -6 | -7 | -8 | -10 | -1 |
| 54 | 3 | -5 | -5 | -3 | -9 | -8 | -10 | -15 | -6 | -7 | -8 | -10 | 0 |
| 56 | 3 | -5 | -5 | -3 | -9 | -7 | -10 | -15 | -5 | -7 | -9 | -9 | 0 |
| 58 | 4 | -4 | -4 | -3 | -9 | -6 | -10 | -15 | -5 | -7 | -9 | -9 | -2 |
| 60 | 5 | -3 | -4 | -3 | -9 | -6 | -10 | -14 | -4 | -7 | -9 | -9 | -1 |
| 62 | 5 | -3 | -4 | -3 | -10 | -6 | -9 | -14 | -4 | -7 | -9 | -8 | -1 |
| 64 | 5 | -2 | -4 | -3 | -11 | -5 | -10 | -14 | -3 | -7 | -9 | -8 | -1 |
| 66 | 5 | -1 | -4 | -4 | -11 | -5 | -9 | -14 | -2 | -7 | -9 | -8 | -1 |
| 68 | 6 | -1 | -4 | -4 | -12 | -4 | -10 | -14 | -2 | -7 | -9 | -7 | 0 |
| 70 | 7 | 0 | -4 | -5 | -12 | -4 | -10 | -14 | -1 | -7 | -10 | -6 | 0 |
| 72 | 8 | 0 | -3 | -5 | -12 | -3 | -9 | -14 | -1 | -7 | -10 | -6 | 0 |
| 74 | 8 | 0 | -2 | -5 | -13 | -2 | -9 | -14 | -1 | -7 | -10 | -6 | 1 |
| 76 | 8 | 0 | -2 | -5 | -13 | -2 | -9 | -14 | -1 | -6 | -11 | -6 | 1 |
| 78 | 8 | 1 | -2 | -6 | -14 | -1 | -9 | -14 | 0 | -6 | -11 | -5 | 1 |
| 80 | 9 | 1 | -2 | -7 | -14 | -1 | -9 | -15 | 0 | -6 | -11 | -5 | 1 |
| 82 | 10 | 2 |  | -7 | -15 | -1 | -8 | -15 | 1 | -6 | -12 | -4 | 2 |
| 84 | 10 | 3 |  | -6 | -16 | 0 | -9 | -15 | 1 | -6 | -12 | -3 | 2 |
| 86 | 11 | 3 |  | -7 | -17 | 0 | -8 | -15 | 1 | -6 | -11 | -3 | 2 |
| 88 | 11 | 4 |  | -7 | -17 | 1 | -8 | -15 | 2 | -6 | -12 | -3 | 3 |
| 90 | 11 | 5 |  | -8 | -17 | 2 | -7 | -15 | 2 | -6 | -12 | -2 | 3 |
| 92 | 12 | 6 |  | -8 | -18 | 2 | -8 | -15 | 3 | -6 | -12 | -2 | 3 |
| 94 | 12 | 7 |  | -9 | -18 | 3 | -7 | -15 | 3 | -5 | -13 | -2 | 3 |
| 96 | 13 | 7 |  | -9 | -19 | 3 | -7 | -15 | 3 | -5 | -13 | -1 | 4 |
| 98 | 14 | 8 |  | -9 | -20 | 4 | -7 | -15 | 3 | -5 | -13 | 0 | 4 |
| 100 | 14 | 9 |  | -10 | -20 | 5 | -7 | -15 | 4 | -5 | -14 | 0 | 4 |

**Note:** Tables 3.1 and 3.2 are from "Interpretive dilemmas created by the MMPI-2" by D.S. Strassberg, 1991 and 1992, *Journal of Psychopathology and Behavioral Assessment*, 1991, Volume 13, pp. 53-59, and 1992, Volume 14, pp. 93-94. Published by Plenum and reprinted by permission.

## TABLE 3.2
### T-score (K-corrected) Differences
### between MMPI-2 and MMPI (Females)

| MMPI-2 T score | L | F | K | Hs | D | Hy | Pd | Mf | Pa | Pt | Sc | Ma | Si |
|---|---|---|---|---|---|---|---|---|---|---|---|---|---|
| 40 | -2 | -7 | -7 | -4 | -5 | -8 | -7 | 3 | -8 | -6 | -6 | -4 | -4 |
| 42 | -1 | -7 | -6 | -3 | -4 | -7 | -7 | 4 | -8 | -6 | -7 | -5 | -4 |
| 44 | 0 | -6 | -6 | -3 | -3 | -7 | -8 | 4 | -8 | -6 | -7 | -5 | -3 |
| 46 | 1 | -5 | -5 | -2 | -2 | -7 | -8 | 4 | -8 | -5 | -6 | -6 | -3 |
| 48 | 1 | -5 | -5 | -1 | -3 | -7 | -8 | 4 | -7 | -4 | -6 | -6 | -3 |
| 50 | 2 | -4 | -5 | -1 | -4 | -6 | -9 | 5 | -7 | -4 | -5 | -7 | -3 |
| 52 | 2 | -4 | -5 | -1 | -4 | -6 | -9 | 4 | -7 | -3 | -5 | -7 | -3 |
| 54 | 3 | -3 | -5 | 0 | -4 | -5 | -9 | 4 | -6 | -3 | -5 | -7 | -4 |
| 56 | 4 | -3 | -5 | 1 | -4 | -5 | -9 | 4 | -6 | -3 | -4 | -7 | -4 |
| 58 | 4 | -2 | -4 | 1 | -4 | -5 | -9 | 4 | -6 | -2 | -4 | -6 | -4 |
| 60 | 5 | -1 | -3 | 1 | -4 | -4 | -9 | 5 | -5 | -2 | -4 | -6 | -4 |
| 62 | 6 | -1 | -3 | 1 | -3 | -3 | -8 | 5 | -4 | -3 | -4 | -6 | -4 |
| 64 | 6 | 0 | -3 | 1 | -3 | -3 | -8 | 6 | -4 | -2 | -4 | -5 | -4 |
| 66 | 6 | 1 | -3 | 1 | -3 | -3 | -8 | 6 | -3 | -2 | -5 | -5 | -4 |
| 68 | 7 | 2 | -3 | 1 | -3 | -2 | -8 | 6 | -3 | -1 | -5 | -5 | -3 |
| 70 | 8 | 3 | -2 | 1 | -3 | -2 | -8 | 6 | -3 | -1 | -5 | -4 | -3 |
| 72 | 8 | 4 | -2 | 1 | -3 | -1 | -8 | 6 | -2 | -1 | -5 | -4 | -3 |
| 74 | 9 | 5 | -1 | 2 | -1 | 0 | -8 | 6 | -2 | -1 | -5 | -4 | -3 |
| 76 | 10 | 5 | -1 | 2 | -1 | 0 | -7 | 7 | -1 | -1 | -5 | -5 | -3 |
| 78 | 10 | 6 | -1 | 2 | -1 | 0 | -7 | 7 | -1 | 0 | -5 | -4 | -3 |
| 80 | 11 | 6 | 0 | 2 | -1 | 1 | -7 | 7 | -1 | 0 | -5 | -4 | -2 |
| 82 | 11 | 6 | 0 | 2 | -1 | 2 | -7 | 8 | -1 | 0 | -5 | -4 | -2 |
| 84 | 12 | 7 | | 2 | -1 | 2 | -6 | 8 | 0 | 0 | -5 | -3 | -2 |
| 86 | 13 | 8 | | 1 | 0 | 3 | -6 | 9 | 0 | 0 | -5 | -3 | -2 |
| 88 | 14 | 9 | | 1 | 0 | 3 | -6 | 9 | 1 | 0 | -6 | -3 | -2 |
| 90 | 14 | 9 | | 1 | 0 | 4 | -6 | 9 | 1 | 1 | -5 | -2 | -2 |
| 92 | 14 | 10 | | 1 | 0 | 5 | -5 | 10 | 1 | 1 | -5 | -2 | -1 |
| 94 | 15 | 11 | | 2 | 0 | 5 | -6 | 10 | 2 | 1 | -6 | -2 | -1 |
| 96 | 15 | 12 | | 2 | 0 | 5 | -5 | 10 | 2 | 1 | -5 | -1 | -1 |
| 98 | 16 | 13 | | 2 | 1 | 6 | -5 | 11 | 3 | 1 | -5 | -1 | |
| 100 | 17 | 14 | | 2 | 1 | 7 | -4 | 11 | 3 | 2 | -6 | -1 | |

Negative numbers in Tables 3.1 and 3.2 represent instances in which the MMPI-2 T-score is less than that of the MMPI for the same raw score, while positive numbers represent a *higher* T-score for the MMPI-2. In some instances, these different scores represent extrapolations from the MMPI and MMPI-2 tables from which they were derived.

Under these instructions, the tendency is for the **L** and **K** scales to elevate and for the **F** scale to be in the average range. These three scales thus form a "V." See Figure 3.6.

# HIGH SCORES

(T = 65 or above, MMPI-2)

(T = 55 or above, MMPI)

### Moderate and Marked Elevations

1.  Persons who score high on this scale may actually see themselves as virtuous, scrupulous, conforming, and self-controlled.

2.  Caldwell (1985) has hypothesized that an **L** scale in this range measures the fear of being judged unworthy or bad.

3.  High scores on this scale in individuals with adequate intelligence may reflect the use of repression, especially rigid denial (Trimboli & Kilgore, 1983).

4.  High **L** scores also may indicate

    a.  Naive people.

    b.  People who repress or deny unfavorable traits in themselves.

    c.  People applying for jobs who want to look good on the test.

    d.  People with below average intelligence.

    e.  People with elementary school education.

f.  People with rural backgrounds.

g.  Ministers or people with strict moral principles.

h.  People with socioeconomic or cultural deprivation—ghetto or ethnic minority backgrounds (Dahlstrom, Welsh, & Dahlstrom, 1972).

5.  A high **L** score may indicate that the clinical scales are depressed. This fact should be taken into account in reading the profile.

   If the clinical scales are elevated while the **L** scale is in this range, this means that the person's defenses are not working well enough to keep problems under control.

6.  An extremely high **L** scale > 80 may indicate an all false response set. See Figures 3.1 and 3.2.

## LOW SCORES

(T = 45 or below, MMPI-2 and MMPI)

1.  Low scores indicate an ability to acknowledge general human weaknesses.

2.  The person who scores low may see himself/herself as nonrighteous and relaxed.

3.  Low scores are typical of the college population. However, a socially sophisticated and/or educated person may score low on **L** and still be trying to "look good." In this instance, the **K** score may be elevated.

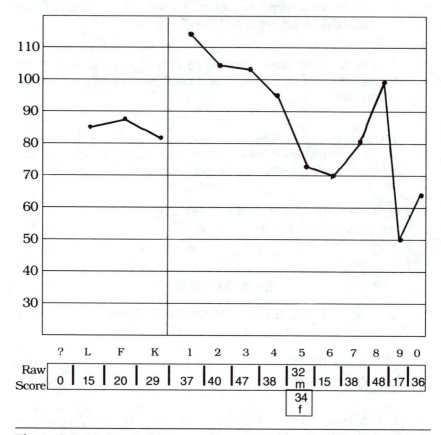

**Figure 3.1.** MMPI all false response set.

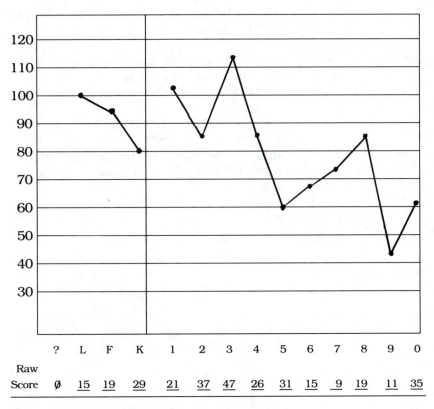

| | ? | L | F | K | 1 | 2 | 3 | 4 | 5 | 6 | 7 | 8 | 9 | 0 |
|---|---|---|---|---|---|---|---|---|---|---|---|---|---|---|
| Raw Score | Ø | 15 | 19 | 29 | 21 | 37 | 47 | 26 | 31 | 15 | 9 | 19 | 11 | 35 |

**Figure 3.2.** MMPI-2 all false response set.

# SUMMARY OF L SCALE INTERPRETATIONS

| T-score | | Interpretations |
| MMPI-2 | MMPI | |
|---|---|---|
| < 50 | < 50 | These people are willing to admit to general human faults. |
| 50-60 | 50-55 | These people are presenting themselves as, or may actually be, virtuous, conforming, and self-controlled. |
| > 60 | > 55 | Scores in this range may indicate naive people, people who repress or deny unfavorable traits, or people applying for jobs who want to make a favorable impression. |

# F SCALE

## (Infrequency or Feeling Bad Scale)

This scale is one of the scales that has been changed the most in the conversion from the old MMPI to the new MMPI-2. Four items were deleted and twelve were rewritten. In addition, the T-score distribution for the scale has been changed so that it is higher on the MMPI-2 than the MMPI for similar numbers of item endorsement (Strassberg, 1991). (See Tables 3.1 and 3.2, pp. 42-43.) For example, endorsing 12 MMPI **F** scale items, which is 70 T-score points on the original MMPI, now becomes 79 T-score points on women's MMPI-2 profiles and 73 T-score points on men's MMPI-2 profiles. Given that many people consider that the **F** scale at certain elevations indicates an invalid test, these new distributions may mean that the rules regarding validity will need to be reevaluated.

A second point to be made about the new **F** scale is that there are now separate T-score distributions for men and women, as can be seen in the example given in the previous paragraph. This was not true on the original MMPI. Because of these new distributions, women will show up more elevated on the **F** scale than men for comparable raw score points. How this will affect the interpretation of women's MMPI-2 profiles vis a vis men's remains to be seen.

Given these two changes in the T-score distribution of the **F** scale on the new MMPI-2, it is highly recommended that the MMPI-2 raw scores for this scale be plotted on both the MMPI-2 and the original MMPI profile sheets so the changes can be seen and accounted for. In addition, it is recommended that the **F** scale elevation on the original MMPI be used when doing a test interpretation. While this may underestimate the **F** scale a little, given that four items have been dropped from the new **F** scale, we feel that this is the most accurate way to use the MMPI-2 **F** scale until more research based upon the MMPI-2 is available.

Experience with mental health clinic and college counseling populations suggests that the **F** scale is nearly always measuring the degree to which a person's thoughts are different from those of the general population. Only rarely is an elevated **F** indicative of purposeful faking-bad in these populations. As the elevation increases, subjects report an increasing number of unusual thoughts and experiences. With a college population or with creative people, different thoughts, to a mild degree, are not uncommon, and an **F** of 60 to 65 may be quite typical. When people become involved in unusual religious, political, or social groups, they frequently have elevations on the scale as high as 75. However, when elevations go beyond 75, usually the person is using the **F** scale to request help by reporting many unusual thoughts and happenings.

In a mental health setting, elevations do not have to be as high as 75 for the request-for-help interpretation to be made. For example, a T of 65 in this population may indicate that the person is having difficulty in some area of life. As the elevation increases, the person tends to report an increasing number of problem areas and a greater severity of problems.

Elevations above 100 in either population limit the profile as an instrument for diagnosis. With an elevation above 100 (MMPI) or 90 (MMPI-2) on **F,** usually an elevation occurs on all of the clinical scales. Such a profile generally indicates that the person is unable to pinpoint any one area of concern and is reacting to everything.

Low **F** scores usually indicate a person who feels he/she is relatively free from stresses and problems.

## GENERAL INFORMATION

1. The **F** scale consists of 64 questions (60 MMPI-2) not answered in the scored direction by 90 percent of the normal population.

2. As the **F** scale becomes elevated, the person is saying more unusual things about himself/herself. This may be

for many different reasons. See the high score section for the various interpretations.

3. Special comparisons are usually made with the **K** scale for diagnostic clarification. See the **F-K** Index, pp. 81-82.

4. Schenkenberg, Gottfredson, and Christensen (1984) have found that younger people in a psychiatric population score higher on the **F** scale than older patients.

5. The **F** scale score tends to decrease with age for low and high IQ subjects but remains relatively constant for average IQ subjects (Gynther & Shimkunas, 1965).

6. Test-retest reliabilities on the MMPI-2 are .78 for men and .69 for women. The scale is particularly sensitive to fluctuations in a person's psychological state or to treatment.

7. Blacks tend to score high on this scale (Gynther, 1961; Gynther, 1972).

   In a prison population, Blacks tended to score higher than whites on this scale (as well as higher on scales **8** and **9**) (Holland, 1979).

8. Mexican-Americans tend to score higher than whites on this scale (as well as higher on the **L** scale). Hibbs et al. (1979) felt that this may be due to cultural factors.

## HIGH SCORES

### Moderate Elevations

(T = 60 through 70, MMPI-2 and MMPI)

1. Scores in this range may indicate one special area of concern, for example, family problems, religious problems, or health problems (Dahlstrom et al., 1972).

2. Elevations on **F** at this level, with clinical scales above 70, may indicate that the person has become used to having the problems indicated by the clinical scale elevations and is not too worried about them.

3. People who think differently from the general population score in this range (creative people, some college students).

4. Very compulsive people who are trying hard to be frank may score in this range (Good & Brantner, 1974).

5. Social protest or emotional commitment to a different-thinking religious and/or political movement may lead to elevations at this level. If the elevation on the **F** scale is for this reason, the clinical scales tend not to be elevated.

6. In a study comparing 26 personal injury malingerers to 21 nonmalingers, Lees-Haley (1991) has found that using an MMPI-2 **F** scale T-score of 65 or greater would correctly classify 81% of the malingerers and 100% of the nonmalingers.

## Marked Elevations

(T = 70 or above, MMPI-2 and MMPI)

### T = 70 through 80

See also the **F-K** Index, pp. 81-82.

1. These elevations may be indicative of unusual or markedly unconventional thinking as a way of life, especially for some college students.

2. Occasionally people who are intensely anxious and want to be helped score in this range. They also may score above 80 T-score points.

3. There may be some symptom exaggeration (Butcher & Williams, 1992).

4. Another cause for elevation of this scale is difficulty in reading or interpreting test statements because of poor reading ability or emotional interference. Because some of the more difficult items to read on the MMPI are on the **F** scale, it is possible for a poor reader to get an elevation on this scale.

5. Young people struggling with problems of identity frequently score in this range.

### T = 80 through 90

See also the **F-K** Index, pp. 81-82.

1. Before the profile can be considered valid, it must be determined whether or not the person (1) was out of contact with reality, (2) had a low reading level, or (3) was purposely malingering.

   a. Once the interpreter is satisfied that these causes are not in operation, profiles with this high an **F** score can be read and interpreted.

   b. In situations where elevated **F** scale scores can be interpreted, the person's problems are such that he/she truly may have very atypical experiences which are reported in the **F** scale items. (Dahlstrom et al., 1972). Occasionally people with these atypical experiences will score as high as T = 100 or above and still have a valid profile.

2. Scores this high may occur because of a "cry for help."

3. People who are severely disturbed and uncooperative subjects with behavior problems may score in this range.

4. The person may want to appear unconventional. This desire is not unusual for adolescents (Carson, 1972).

5. Hyer, Fallon, Harrison et al. (1987) have found that if people are classified as exaggerating pathology when the **F** scale is >87 (20 items endorsed), one-half of the individuals in three groups of Vietnam veteran inpatients suffering from PTSD would be classified as symptom exaggerators.

### T = 90 through 100

See the **F-K** Index, pp. 81-82.

1. Scores in this range may indicate a random marking of the test. This random marking may be purposeful or the result of the fact that the person is illiterate and does not want to admit it. The person also may be confused, have a psychological disorder, or have brain damage. See the random response profile, Figures 3.3 and 3.4.

2. Scores in this range also may indicate a person whose problems are such that he/she truly has very atypical experiences which are reported in the **F** scale items.

3. Shondrick, Ben-Porath, and Stafford (1992) have found that a large percentage of individuals (32% of the men and 21% of the women) in their sample of a forensic population undergoing court-ordered evaluations showed invalid profiles on the basis of elevations on the **?, F, F**ᴮ**,** or **VRIN** scales on the MMPI-2. Those with the more severe offenses showed a greater proportion of invalid profiles. These authors felt that some of those MMPI-2s that were declared invalid by these scales may have been valid pictures of severe pathology. These authors further suggested that there is a need to investigate the

appropriateness of the currently proposed cutoffs for the **F** and **F**ʙ scales with this population.

4. Wetter, Baer, Berry et al. (1993) found that individuals who were given information regarding post-traumatic stress disorder (PTSD) and paranoid schizophrenia and asked to fake one of these disorders on the MMPI-2 were detected by the **F, Fʙ, F-K,** and Dissimulation (**Ds,** Gough, 1954) scales. **F** $\geq$ 96 T-score points identified 78% of the faked PTSD profiles; **F** $\geq$ 104 T-score points identified 95% of the faked schizophrenic profiles.

### T = 100 or above

See the **F-K** Index, pp 81-82.

1. Scores of 100 or above may show confusion on the client's part in marking the items.

2. The person may be deliberately trying to look bad. See Figures 3.5 and 3.6, and the Random and All True Response Set profiles (Figures 3.3, 3.4, 3.7, and 3.8).

3. These scores may reflect the severity of psychopathology the person is experiencing or highly specialized and atypical experiences in the individual's life.

4. When **L** and **K** are low (T = 45 or below), an **F** elevation of T = 100 or above may indicate an All True Response Set. See Figures 3.7 and 3.8. On the MMPI-2, the **VRIN** validity scale (see p. 76) should be elevated if the true response set is operating.

5. These scores may reflect scoring errors.

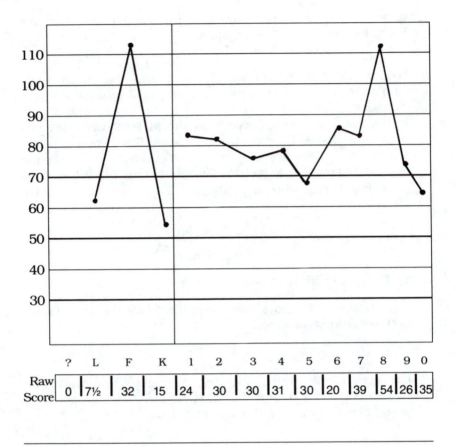

| Raw Score | ? | L | F | K | 1 | 2 | 3 | 4 | 5 | 6 | 7 | 8 | 9 | 0 |
|-----------|---|-----|----|----|----|----|----|----|----|----|----|----|----|----|
|           | 0 | 7½ | 32 | 15 | 24 | 30 | 30 | 31 | 30 | 20 | 39 | 54 | 26 | 35 |

**Figure 3.3** MMPI random response set.

6.  Gynther, Altman, and Warbin (1973 a) and Gynther, Altman, and Sletten (1973) have found that white psychiatric patients with T > 100 on the **F** scale have higher scores on withdrawal, poor judgment, thought disorders, and reduced speech than other patients. The phrase that best describes these patients is "confused psychotic." These terms do not apply to patients generating obviously faked MMPIs. For Blacks, those scoring above 100 were seen as no different from Blacks with scores below an **F** of 100.

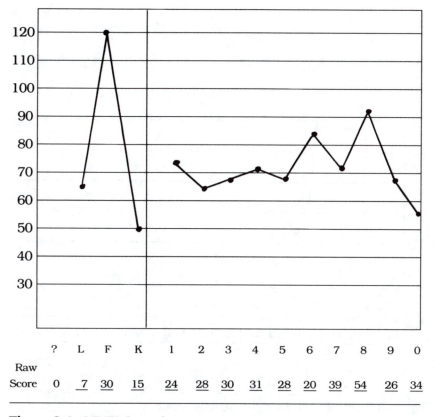

| | ? | L | F | K | 1 | 2 | 3 | 4 | 5 | 6 | 7 | 8 | 9 | 0 |
|---|---|---|---|---|---|---|---|---|---|---|---|---|---|---|
| Raw Score | 0 | 7 | 30 | 15 | 24 | 28 | 30 | 31 | 28 | 20 | 39 | 54 | 26 | 34 |

**Figure 3.4.** MMPI-2 random response set.

7.  Evans and Dinning (1983; Evans, 1984) have found that for male psychiatric inpatients, consistent responders (shown by a low **VRIN** and **TRIN** on the MMPI-2) with high **F** appeared to exaggerate pathology, while inconsistent responses were indicative of random responding, perhaps due to psychotic thought disorders that made them too confused to take the MMPI conscientiously.

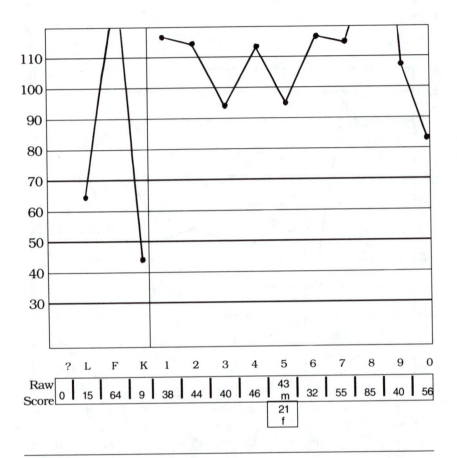

| Raw Score | ? | L | F | K | 1 | 2 | 3 | 4 | 5 | 6 | 7 | 8 | 9 | 0 |
|---|---|---|---|---|---|---|---|---|---|---|---|---|---|---|
| | 0 | 15 | 64 | 9 | 38 | 44 | 40 | 46 | 43 m | 32 | 55 | 85 | 40 | 56 |
| | | | | | | | | | 21 f | | | | | |

**Figure 3.5.** MMPI "All Deviant" response set.

## LOW SCORES

(T = 40 or below, MMPI-2)

(T = 45 or below, MMPI)

1. These scores may indicate normal persons who are relatively free from stress.

2. Adjectives that have been suggested to describe low scorers are sincere, calm, dependable, honest, simple, and conventional.

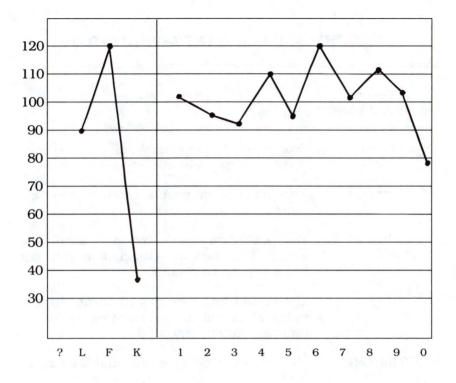

**Figure 3.6.** MMPI-2 "All Deviant" response set.

3. Low scores tend to indicate honestly reported records in college samples.

4. People in this range may have a high degree of social conformity (Caldwell, 1985).

5. The **F** scale score tends to reach this range after therapy.

# SUMMARY OF F SCALE INTERPRETATIONS

| T-score (MMPI and MMPI-2) | Interpretations |
| --- | --- |
| 50 or below | Scores in this range may indicate a normal person relatively free from stress. |
| 50 thru 60 | The majority of people score within this range. |
| 60 thru 70 | The person may have concerns about one area of life, such as religion or health, but is not too worried about it. |
| | The person may be involved in an atypical political or social organization or in an unusual religious group. |
| 70 thru 80 | This person may be upset and asking for help. |
| | A person with a score in this range may have had difficulty in reading or interpreting the test. |
| | The person may think somewhat differently than the general population. This is especially true if the **8** scale is above 70. |
| | College students with identity problems may score in this range. |
| 80 thru 90 | At this level, before interpreting the MMPI, check that the person was not out of contact with reality, did not have a low reading level, or did not have reason to malinger. |
| | If the elevation is not because of any of these reasons, then the person's problems |

are such as to give him or her a long list of bizarre, peculiar, and atypical experiences.

This may be a person who is anxious (check the **7** scale) and asking for help.

90 thru 100     This may be a random marking of the test. It may or may not be deliberate.

If this is not a random marking of the test, then the person's problems may have produced a long list of bizarre, peculiar, and atypical experiences.

100 or above     A score in this range may indicate confusion in marking items.

The confusion usually is not deliberate at this level.

This score may indicate that the person is deliberately trying to look bad.

It may reflect the severity of psychopathology of the person.

With low **L** and **K** (T = 45 and below), an **F** score in this range may indicate an All True Response Set. See Figures 3.7 and 3.8.

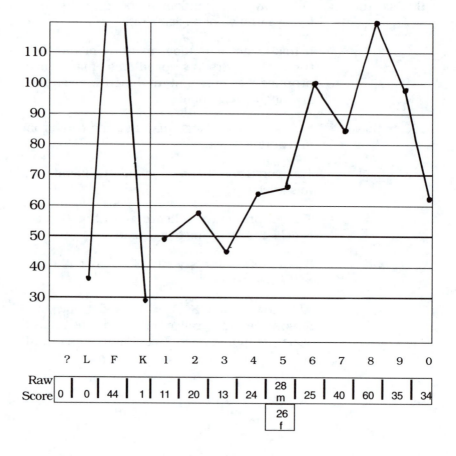

| Raw Score | ? | L | F | K | 1 | 2 | 3 | 4 | 5 | 6 | 7 | 8 | 9 | 0 |
|-----------|---|---|----|---|----|----|----|----|--------|----|----|----|----|----|
| | 0 | 0 | 44 | 1 | 11 | 20 | 13 | 24 | 28 m / 26 f | 25 | 40 | 60 | 35 | 34 |

**Figure 3.7.** MMPI all true response set.

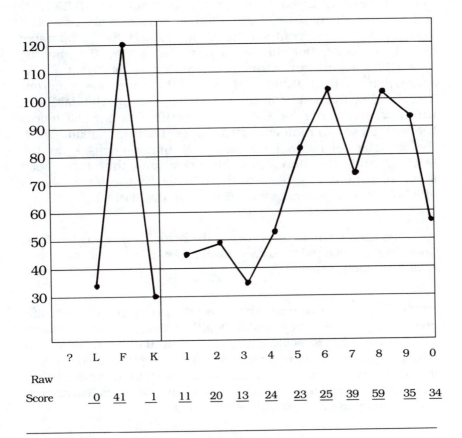

| | ? | L | F | K | 1 | 2 | 3 | 4 | 5 | 6 | 7 | 8 | 9 | 0 |
|---|---|---|---|---|---|---|---|---|---|---|---|---|---|---|
| Raw Score | | 0 | 41 | 1 | 11 | 20 | 13 | 24 | 23 | 25 | 39 | 59 | 35 | 34 |

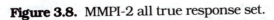

**Figure 3.8.** MMPI-2 all true response set.

# K SCALE

## (Correction Scale)

In contrast to the **L** and **F** validity scales, the **K** scale has not been changed to a great extent on the MMPI-2. It is true that the T-score distribution for the **K** scale has been lowered 5 T-score points (Strassburg, 1991) for comparable raw score points, but this is compensated for by the lowering of MMPI-2 significant clinical elevations to begin at 65 T-score points. (See Tables 3.1 and 3.2.) There are different T-score distributions for men and women on the MMPI-2, which was not true for the original MMPI, but the differences between these distributions seem to be relatively small. Thus, the **K** scale seems to have had only minor changes on the MMPI-2 and, therefore, the interpretations that have been given for various elevations of the **K** scale for the MMPI should also hold true, in general, for the **K** scale on the MMPI-2.

This scale measures defensiveness and guardedness. Therefore, it evaluates some of the same behavior as the **L** scale but much more subtly.

In order to evaluate the **K** scale properly, the specific population, college or mental health center, must be noted. In addition, the **K** scale interpretation must be modified for special groups of people within these populations. In this introduction are discussed the usual interpretations for the two major populations with whom this book is concerned and, when appropriate, modifications are noted.

In a college population, a T-score on this scale between 55 and 70 (50 and 65, MMPI-2) is typical. People scoring in this range are indicating that their lives are satisfactory, that they are basically competent, and that they can manage their lives. Such scores are usual for people coming for counseling about an academic major or for students taking the MMPI as part of some experiment. When T = 70 or above for the **K** scale, (65 or above, MMPI-2), these people are indicating not only that they are competent people and can manage their own lives, but also that they are a bit cautious about revealing themselves. Such scores are usually attained when a person is defensive, and/or when the test administrator does not fully explain the reason for the test, the use to which it will be put, or the confidentiality of the results.

When **K** is below 45 (40, MMPI-2) and the **F** scale is elevated above 60 T-score points, the college student may be experiencing some stress. The **K** scale score usually elevates to the 55 through 65 (to through 65, MMPI-2) range when the stress is alleviated.

When **K** is below 45 (40, MMPI-2) and the **F** scale is elevated above 60 T-score points, the college student may be feeling that life has been rough, that he/she has had fewer advantages than most people.

In a mental health setting, if the client is having difficulties, he/she usually scores below 45 (40, MMPI-2) on the **K** scale. The severity of the problem usually is indicated by how low the **K** score is (the lower the score, the more severe the problem). Below a T-score of 35, the prognosis for successful therapy is poor. A score in this range does not indicate that the person will or should be hospitalized for his/her problem, but more that the person is unable to improve at this time. Scores between 35 and 45 (35 and 40 MMPI-2) typically reflect situational difficulties, such as marriage, family, or job problems.

Elevations over 60 are unusual in the mental health population and for people who do not have some college education and/or are unsuccessful in business. Typically such scores are attained by persons who see others as having problems, e.g., the other mate in marriage counseling. A person in this range also may be bringing someone else in to be counseled, such as a parent who brings a child in with school difficulties. As the **K** goes above 60, defensiveness is usually present. When the person has a T-score over 70 (65, MMPI), the prognosis for the person recognizing problems he/she may have is poor. Marks, Seeman, and Haller's (1974) "**K+**" profile should be studied for further information concerning this pattern. See point 7 under the marked elevations.

College counseling and mental health centers personnel frequently evaluate persons for other agencies. In these instances, the above rules for interpretation of the **K** scale do not always hold since the person may have an ulterior motive for taking the test, rather than just taking it to tell how he/she is at the moment. Persons applying for jobs and students being screened for specific programs (doctoral admissions, for example) may have a T-score of approximately 70 (65, MMPI-2). Conversely, persons applying for such things as disability pensions (where the person wishes to look bad) tend to have unusually low **K** scores and elevated **F** scores.

Persons under scrutiny by the courts may have either high or low **K** scores, depending upon their situations. If the person is seeking parole or wishes to win custody of his/her child, a high **K** score may be obtained. If the person is seeking to avoid a sentence by appearing to be mentally ill, a low **K** score may result. Therefore, in these special instances, the examiner must know the purpose of the examination and what the person expects to gain from it.

When the **L** scale, the **3** scale, and/or the **R** scale are elevated with the **K** scale, the diagnosis of defensiveness is reinforced. The person not only does not want to look bad to others (**L** and **K** elevations), he/she does not want to think badly of others (**3** scale elevation), and he/she also does not want to look or talk about certain areas of life (**R** scale elevation).

## GENERAL INFORMATION

1.  The **K** scale of 30 items was chosen as a correction factor to sharpen the discriminatory power of certain clinical scales, specifically scales **1, 4, 7, 8,** and **9.**

2. The **K** scale was developed after the other validity scales when it was noted that there was no correction for defensiveness on the test.

3. The **K** scale was developed to measure how much the examinee wished to "look good" on the test. The higher the **K** score the more the indication was that the person desired to look good, and thus, a portion of the **K** score was added to five clinical scales (**1, 4, 7, 8,** and **9**) to correct for this attitude. These five clinical scales were the only ones seemingly affected by this "looking good" attitude; therefore, the correction is applied only to them.

4. In spite of **K** correction additions to clinical scales, high scores on **K** usually are associated with lower profile elevations, whereas low scores on **K** are usually accompanied by higher profile elevations (Dahlstrom et al., 1972).

5. High scores on the MMPI-2 **K** scale (>65) also are accompanied by average to low scores on the MMPI-2 content scales.

6. This is a subtle scale. The items are not as obvious as those on the **L** scale. The **K** scale is thus intended to detect defensiveness in psychologically sophisticated people.

7. This scale may measure the intactness of the individual's psychological defenses.

8. Caldwell (1977) has hypothesized that the **K** scale may measure a fear of emotional intensity and an avoidance of intimacy when it goes over 65 T-score points for non-college populations and above 70 T points for college populations.

   He also has hypothesized (1985) that elevations on this scale are associated with a marked constriction of affective responsiveness.

9. Some authors (Adams, 1971; Dahlstrom et al., 1972) have suggested that **K** scores in the 60 through 70 (60 through

65, MMPI-2) range do not always mean covering up more subtle atypical psychological characteristics, but may at least in part reflect a true assertion of psychological health, especially for females, college students, and people from higher socioeconomic levels. When the **K** scores go above a T of 70, however, the authors feel the scores do seem to reflect defensiveness for these groups.

10. Generally speaking, therapy prognosis tends to be poor with high scale scores (>70, MMPI; >65, MMPI-2).

11. Test-retest reliabilities for this scale on the MMPI-2 are .84 for men and .81 for women (Butcher et al., 1989).

12. Hibbs et al., (1979) have found that older women score higher on this scale.

13. In one study of a normal population, the women's mean score was 55 on this scale (Colligan et al., 1984).

14 A fairly high negative correlation occurs between the **K** and **F** scales and between the **O** and **K** scales.

15. Under ideal self-instructions ("take this test trying to look as good as possible"), the **K** scale tends to become elevated to the moderately elevated range.

16. Post therapy profiles tend to show an increase in **K**.

## AVERAGE SCORES

(T = 40 through 60, MMPI-2)

(T = 45 through 60, MMPI)

1. An average score on the **K** scale is an indication of a balance between self-disclosure and self-protection.

2. Adults with elementary school education and lower middle-class socioeconomic status generally will score in this range (Dahlstrom et al., 1972).

3.   Occasionally, people with higher socioeconomic status (including college students) will score in the range between 45 and 50. In such cases, these people may be undergoing some stress and thus do not feel as good about their lives as others of their socioeconomic level usually do.

# HIGH SCORES

### Moderate Elevations

(T = 60 through 65, MMPI-2)

(T = 60 through 70, MMPI)

1.   Scores of moderate elevation are typical for people in the upper-middle class and lower-upper class, and for college students.

2.   These people tend to have good mental health. They are independent and are easily capable of dealing with their day-to-day problems. The generally favorable view they show of themselves on the **K** scale is correct and therefore appropriate.

3.   If someone from the lower socioeconomic class has this elevation, it is more likely to reflect some defensiveness or a set toward looking socially desirable.

4.   Job applicants may appear at this elevation because they wish to make a good impression.

### Marked Elevations

(T = 65 or above, MMPI

(T = 70 or above, MMPI-2)

See also Figures 3.1 and 3.2, the All False Response Set profiles, and Figures 3.9 and 3.10, the All Nondeviant Response Set profiles.

1.   The usual reason for this elevation is that the person is impelled to present a psychologically healthy appearance to others.

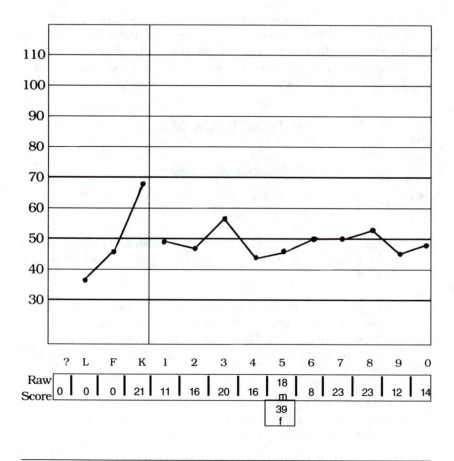

| | ? | L | F | K | 1 | 2 | 3 | 4 | 5 | 6 | 7 | 8 | 9 | 0 |
|---|---|---|---|---|---|---|---|---|---|---|---|---|---|---|
| Raw Score | 0 | 0 | 0 | 21 | 11 | 16 | 20 | 16 | 18 m | 8 | 23 | 23 | 12 | 14 |
| | | | | | | | | | 39 f | | | | | |

**Figure 3.9.** MMPI "All Nondeviant" response set.

Limits may exist to this defensiveness, however, so that it may not include the obvious items of the **L** scale. Thus, extremely high elevations on the **K** scale may not be accompanied by high scores on the **L** scale.

2. The person tends to restrict his/her emotions and appears calm and even-tempered.

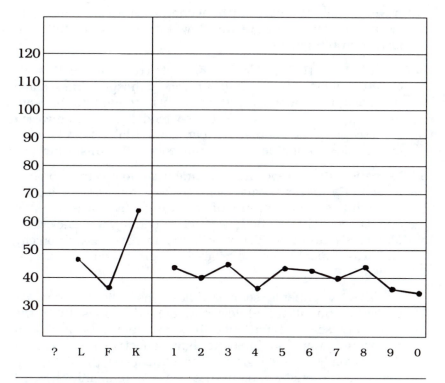

**Figure 3.10.** MMPI-2 "All Nondeviant" response set.

3. Elevations on this scale may reflect the use of repression and rationalization as defense mechanisms (Trimboli & Kilgore, 1983).

4. Because women tend to judge themselves more harshly than do men on a test such as the MMPI, a high **K** score by a woman is likely to reflect psychological effectiveness rather than defensiveness (Dahlstrom et al., 1972).

5. A high **K** score is associated with the low probability of delinquency, especially with females (Carson, 1969).

6. A very high **K** score with accompanying clinical scale elevations may indicate an unwillingness or inability to look at problem areas.

7. Marks et al. (1974) found a **K+** pattern (only the **K** scale elevated above 70) in their university hospital and clinic population. People with this pattern tended to be shy, inhibited, and defensive. They also tended to be uninvolved in activities. The Marks, Seeman, and Haller book should be consulted for further information concerning this pattern.

8. **K+** patients in a psychiatric inpatient setting were compared to non **K+** patients also with unelevated MMPIs and a randomly selected group of inpatients by Barley, Sabo, and Greene (1986). Both sets of patients with unelevated MMPIs (**K+** and non **K+**) were found to have less chronicity and less time in the hospital than the randomly selected patients.

   The **K+** patients somatized less than did the non **K+** patients and also had fewer suicidal histories than the randomly selected patients; however, both **K+** and non **K+** groups were as likely to have affective disorders as the randomly selected group. The patients in the **K+** group were more overactive than those in the randomly selected group and were more likely to have psychotic diagnoses. There were striking similarities and differences between the **K+** group in this population and the **K+** group described by Marks et al. (1974).

## LOW SCORES

### Low Range

(T = 30 through 40, MMPI-2)

(T = 35 through 45, MMPI)

1. People may have scores in this range for one of two reasons.

   a. They may have problems that they are quite willing to admit. This interpretation is likely to be true if the **F** scale is elevated into the moderately elevated range. If they do have problems, they are often sarcastic and caustic concerning themselves and the world (Carson, 1972).

(1) These people may not feel good about themselves and may also feel that they lack the skills to deal with their problems. If this is so, the **Es** scale is usually low.

b. They believe life has been rough for them and that they have not had some of the advantages that others have had. This interpretation is likely to be true if the **F** scale is not elevated.

(1) This belief may be an accurate perception because people scoring in this range frequently have had a deprived family background and/or limited income.

### Markedly Low Range

(T = 35 or below)

1. A person with a score in this range is too willing to say uncomplimentary things about self and tends to exaggerate his/her faults (Carson, 1972).

2. The person may have answered items on the test so as to create the impression that he/she is undergoing a serious emotional problem.

3. Scores below a T of 35 may arise from any of the following (Dahlstrom et al., 1972):

a. Special pleading for help or attention.

b. A general state of panic in which the person believes that his/her world or the control over his/her destiny is rapidly disintegrating.

c. Deliberate malingering.

4. When the **K** score is in this range, the **F** scale and the clinical scales usually are high.

# SUMMARY OF K SCALE INTERPRETATIONS

| T-score MMPI-2 | MMPI | Interpretations |
|---|---|---|
| <35 | <35 | The client may have deep emotional difficulties and feel quite badly about them. He or she also may be deliberately malingering or pleading for help. |
| 35-40 | 35-45 | People with this range of scores feel they are not as well off as most people. This appraisal may be accurate. |
| | | People in this range may be having some situational difficulties. If they are, the **F** scale will be above 60. |
| 40-60 | 45-60 | The majority of people score in this range. |
| 60-65 | 60-70 | A person in therapy with this score tends to blame others for his/her problems or feels that it is the other person who needs counseling. |
| >65 | >70 | The client may be defensive (as the T-score increases, the client is more defensive) and does not wish to look at difficulties. The likelihood of the client recognizing the need for him/her to change or for his/her life to change is poor. |

### Relation to Research Scales

**Es** scale—If the **K** scale is below 45 T-score points (40, MMPI-2) and the **Es** scale is low, the person may be feeling badly about self as well as his/her life situation.

# MMPI-2 VALIDITY SCALES
## F𝐁, VRIN, TRIN, and S

As has already been mentioned in the chapter on the development of the MMPI-2, three new validity scales were added to the test when it was originally published in 1989. These validity scales are **F𝐁**, **VRIN**, and **TRIN**. The scales are designed to be used in conjunction with the original MMPI validity scales as additional checks on test-taking attitude. Greene's *MMPI/MMPI-2 Interpretive Manual* (1991) has an excellent chapter on these scales and how they fit into the overall picture of determining the validity of an individual's MMPI-2.

The **F𝐁** scale is made up of 40 items that were infrequently endorsed by people in the MMPI-2 normative sample. These items, however, appear in the latter half of the test, whereas the **F** scale items appear in the first half of the test. Thus, the **F𝐁** provides the same information regarding random or unusual responding in the latter half of the test that the **F** scale does for the first half of the test. While the **F** scale indicates this type of responding for the part of the test that includes the clinical scales, the content and supplementary scales of the MMPI-2 have items that are in the latter half of the test and thus are not covered by the **F** scale but are covered by the **F𝐁** scale.

When a clinician intends to use only the clinical scales for an interpretation, the **F** scale elevation will be the only scale that needs to be interpreted; however, if a clinician intends to use the content and/or the supplementary scales as well as the clinical scales, the **F𝐁** also must be looked at to be sure that it is in the appropriate range, preferably below 65 T-score points. The higher the **F𝐁** scale, the more likely the test taker is indicating random or unusual responding. The **F** scale summary chart on page 62 can also be used for the **F𝐁** scale, since elevations on the **F𝐁** have the same interpretations as comparable elevations on the **F** scale.

When both the **F** and **F**<sub>B</sub> scales are within acceptable ranges, then the clinical, content, and supplementary scales can be used without worrying about random responding or a test bias towards reporting bad things in the person's life. If the **F** scale is elevated but the **F**<sub>B</sub> isn't, then the clinical scales have been affected by this test-taking bias, but the latter half of the test has not. If the **F** scale is within reasonable limits but the **F**<sub>B</sub> scale is not, the clinical scales can be used but the content and supplementary scales should not be since the test taker started to respond differently in the latter half of the test and endorsed many unusual items. If both the **F** and **F**<sub>B</sub> scales are too elevated, the test is invalid and needs to be discarded or retaken.

The second new validity scale on the MMPI-2 is the **VRIN** or Variable Response Inconsistency scale. This scale is similar to Greene's Carelessness Scale (Greene, 1978), that is used with the original MMPI. The **VRIN** consists of 67 pairs of items that are either very similar or very opposite in content. If individuals are inconsistent in their endorsement of the two items that make up a pair, they will get a point on the **VRIN** scale. Elevations on this scale, therefore, indicate random responding or, at the least, carelessness in how questions are answered. If both **VRIN** and **F** are elevated on a test, this is a pretty clear indication that the test taker was answering in a random manner since both scales measure this tendency. If, however, the **F** scale is elevated but the **VRIN** is not, then it is likely that the **F** scale is indicating an unusually high endorsement of bad feelings by the client but not randomness since the **VRIN** scale is not elevated. Thus, the **VRIN** can help with **F** scale interpretations in clarifying whether the **F** scale is elevated because of random responding or because of deliberate endorsement of unusual items that make up the **F** scale.

The third new validity scale of the MMPI-2 is the **TRIN** or True Response Inconsistency scale. This scale was designed to measure "yea-saying" or "nay-saying." It consists of 23 pairs of items with opposite content. If individuals answer both of the items in a pair True they will get a point on the **TRIN** scale, if they answer both of the items in a pair

False, they will have a point taken away from the **TRIN** scale. Thus, if there is a consistent bias to answer True on the **TRIN** items, the test taker will have a high raw score on this scale. If there is a consistent bias to answer False on this test, this will be shown as a low raw score on the **TRIN** scale.

A constant of 9 is added to the scale in order to avoid a negative score. For example, if a client endorsed two, true-item pairs and seven, false-item pairs, his/her score would be 2 - 7 + 9 or 4(F). The **TRIN** raw scores are plotted such that abnormally high raw scores ("yea-saying") and abnormally low raw scores ("nay-saying") are indicated as elevations on the profile, and a T or F is added to indicate which tendency is being endorsed.

These three new validity scales are additional helps in determining whether a profile has been answered in a random manner (**F**<sub>B</sub> and **VRIN**), or with a consistent response set (**TRIN**). Recently an additional validity scale has been introduced, the **S** scale (Butcher, 1993; Butcher & Han, 1993), which is designed to measure defensive underreporting of symptoms. This new 50 item scale is designed to measure a bias towards reporting unusually positive adjustment and lack of moral or personal flaws. It was developed by contrasting the answers given by a group of individuals applying for highly desirable jobs with those answers given by the individuals in the MMPI-2 normative group. The scale has five subscales of items: belief in human goodness, serenity, contentment with life, patience/denial of irritability and anger, and denial of moral flaws. The scale is available in a new computer scoring service available from NCS. Because this scale is so new, it remains to be seen how useful it will be in discriminating test takers who are unduly stressing how good they are from those individuals who actually are highly competent and free from the majority of life's stresses.

# L-F-K SCALE

In addition to looking at validity scales separately, the patterns produced by three of them (**L, F,** and **K**) also should be reviewed. Six validity patterns are presented in this section. The last two are less common than the others but are still seen occasionally, usually in the mental health center setting.

1.  The solid line pattern (Figure 3.11) is the one usually obtained with clients who admit emotional difficulties and request help. The **L** and **K** are typically below a T of 50, and the **F** is above a T of 60. The higher the **F** scale (dashed line), the more the person is saying he/she feels bad. When the **F** scale gets above 80 in this profile, possibly the client is exaggerating his/her symptoms, perhaps to be helped sooner. It is important in this profile that **L** and **K** are below 50 and that **F** is above 60.

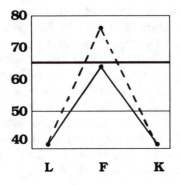

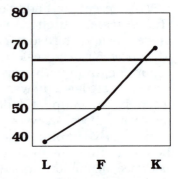

**Figure 3.11.** **L-F-K** profile (elevated **F** scale).

**Figure 3.12.** **L-F-K** profile (elevated **K** scale).

2.  Figure 3.12 is a typical validity scale profile for a job applicant, for those in counseling for vocational and/or educational help, and for those coming to counseling to help someone else.

The validity scale profile in Figure 3.12 is usually accompanied by unelevated clinical scales except perhaps for scales **5** and **9**. For a profile with this validity scale pattern, see Figures 3.9 and 3.10, the All Nondeviant Response Set profiles.

3. People with the pattern shown in Figure 3.13 are presenting themselves in the best possible light. They feel very good about themselves and tend to deny common human foibles. They also tend to be simplistic and to see their world in extremes of good and bad. This profile is frequent for naive job applicants, public office holders, and strict, moralistic individuals.

4. People with the profile shown in Figure 3.14 (solid line) tend to have long-standing problems to which they have become adjusted to the extent that they feel O.K. about themselves (**K** scale) while still admitting to some bad feelings, usually about their situations (**F** scale). As the **F** scale becomes elevated (dashed line), these people still feel rather secure about themselves, but they are more worried about their problems.

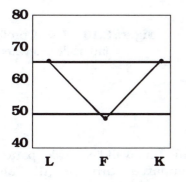

**Figure 3.13.** **L-F-K** profile (elevated **L** and **K** scales).

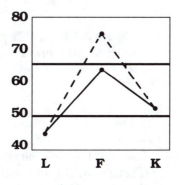

**Figure 3.14.** **L-F-K** profile (elevated **F** and **K** scales).

5. Figure 3.15 is an unusual profile but still found frequently enough to be included in this section. The solid line is usually associated with a naive, unsophisticated person who is feeling bad. The person with this pattern is saying many of the same things as someone with the Figure 3.11 profile, but he/she has in addition a lack of sophistication. Even when the **F** scale is greatly elevated (dashed line), the person still shows the same behavior as long as the **L** scale is near 65 and the **K** scale is below 50.

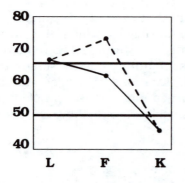

**Figure 3.15.** **L-F-K** profile (elevated **L** and **F** scales).

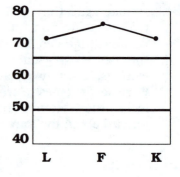

**Figure 3.16.** **L-F-K** profile (all scales elevated).

6. The total profile accompanying this validity scale pattern (Figure 3.16) should be compared with the All False Response Set profiles. The possibility is that the person with this validity pattern has answered the test from a response set of marking false to questions rather than from his/her own feelings. The All False Response Set profile is illustrated in Figures 3.1 and 3.2.

# F MINUS K INDEX

## (Also called the Dissimulation Index)

The **F** minus **K** index was developed to detect faking bad and faking good profiles. The index number is obtained by subtracting the *raw score* of **K** from the *raw score* of **F**. If the resultant number is positive and above 11, the profile is called a "fake bad" profile. The person is trying to look worse than he/she really is. If the resultant number if negative, the profile is called a "fake good" profile. The person is trying to look better than he/she really is.

We do not use this index very much in our work with university and mental health clients. The "fake good" part of the index is usually grossly inaccurate for these populations, and the "fake bad" part can have another very dissimilar interpretation. In addition to the person scoring positively on this index because he/she is faking bad, a second interpretation can be made that the person really is feeling bad and the scales are accurately reflecting this fact.

We tend to suspect that the faking bad interpretation is the correct one when the client is seeking some disability compensation, is wanting to be judged insane by a court and thus escape some punishment, or stands to gain by seeming to be extremely mentally ill.

## GENERAL INFORMATION

1. This index is found by subtracting the raw score on the **K** scale from the raw score on the **F** scale. Positive scores are in the symptom-exaggeration direction ("fake bad"), and minus scores are in the defensive direction ("fake good"). However, the index is much more successful in detecting the former test-taking attitude than the latter.

2. The problem with detecting "fake good" profiles is that college students and people with good mental health tend

to get elevated **K** scores and low **F** scores which, while accurately reflecting their psychological health, are incorrectly read as "faking good" by this index.

3.  Because of these problems for the "fake good" direction of the index, the recommendation is that this index be used only for detecting "fake bad" profiles, and then only when the person is suspected of having something to gain by looking bad. If the person is not trying to look bad, then an **F-K** raw score difference of 9 or more usually is an indication of actually feeling bad.

4.  In one study of a normal population, the fake bad index worked best if **F-K** > 7 or **F**>15. The fake good index worked best if **F-K** $\geq$ -11, but this index was not as accurate as the fake bad index (Grow, McVaugh, & Eno, 1980).

5.  In the same study, for clinical populations, faking bad was best discovered with an **F-K** index > 7 or **F** > 15. The fake good index worked best when **F-K** <-11.

6.  Hyer, Woods, Harrison et al. (1989) have found that when the **F-K** index was used, a high percentage of Vietnam veterans had an overreporting pattern. There was a pattern of increased overreporting with higher Post-traumatic Stress Disorder scale scores (Keane, Malby, & Fairbank, 1984).

7.  In a study comparing 26 personal injury malingerers to 21 nonmalingers, Lees-Haley (1991) has found that using an **F-K** score of -4 or greater would correctly classify 85% of the malingerers and 100% of the nonmalingers. An **F-K** index of -8 or greater would correctly classify 85% of the malingerers and 90% of the nonmalingers.

# CHAPTER IV

# CLINICAL SCALES

A history of the MMPI clinical scales development and construction is available in Greene's *MMPI-2/MMPI: An Interpretive Manual* (1991). The clinical scale section of the MMPI profile is composed of ten scales, each with a number, abbreviation, and formal name. These scales are as follows:

**1** Hs   Hypochondriasis
**2** D     Depression
**3** Hy   Conversion Hysteria
**4** Pd   Psychopathic Deviate
**5** Mf   Masculinity-Femininity
**6** Pa   Paranoia
**7** Pt   Psychasthenia
**8** Sc   Schizophrenia
**9** Ma   Hypomania
**0** Si    Social Introversion

In actual practice, the formal names and abbreviations are not usually used. The names are long and in many instances do not convey a clear picture of what is being measured by the scale. We prefer to use the numbers for the scales because they are neutral and are the way the scales usually are reported in the research literature.

Most practitioners tend to view the clinical scales as giving some indication of problem areas for a client. We feel such a viewpoint is incomplete because these scales also can, in some instances, indicate strengths and/or coping behaviors for the person.

For example, an elevation on scale **5** is fairly typical for college educated males in the arts (music, drama, literature, and art). An elevation on this scale shows aesthetic interests, and as such would be quite advantageous to an arts major. However, engineers with such an elevation on scale **5** may have a problem because their great interest in aesthetics may conflict with the demands from the engineering profession for "scientific rigor." Therefore, elevations on the clinical scales must be evaluated in terms of the person's situation.

In all of these clinical scales, the behavior or emotion mentioned as being the meaning of that scale is most clearly seen when that scale is the highest one in the clinical section of the profile; otherwise the behavior or emotion may be partially masked or modified by the higher scale(s).

The term "elevation" as used with the clinical scales usually indicates that a scale score is above 65 T-score points (70, MMPI). We have noted trends in behavior at lower T-score levels. Consequently, we have devised two categories of elevations: Moderate Elevation refers to T-scores of 60-65 (MMPI-2) or 60-70 (MMPI), and Marked Elevation refers to T-scores of 65 and above (MMPI-2) or 70 and above (MMPI). This division of elevations into categories is a convenience and should not be taken as absolute. This is particularly true when a score is on the borderline between the Moderate and Marked Elevations categories, i.e., at 65 T-score points for the MMPI-2 or 70 T-score points for the MMPI. Then the judgment of the tester must be used to determine if the Moderate or Marked Elevation interpretation is most appropriate.

We also have included information on clinical scale low points. The information about the low end of the scales is scanty because little is written or researched about persons receiving such scores. Nevertheless, we do see some trends in these areas that can be useful.

A final section in this chapter deals with the first three clinical scales, **1, 2,** and **3,** and their various combinations. We have found these combinations to be useful in interpreting profiles for individuals with various physical problems and/ or chronic pain and, therefore, have included a section about them in this book.

# SCALE 1

## (Hs, Hypochondriasis Scale)

This scale has been affected by the redistribution of the clinical scales in their transformation from linear T-scores on the MMPI to uniform T-scores on the MMPI-2. The distribution of the **1** scale for women has not been changed significantly, but the distribution of this scale for men has (Strassberg, 1991). (See Tables 3.1 and 3.2, pp. 42-43.) The scale has been lowered for men, such that in the 60 and 69 range it is 5 T-score points lower on the MMPI-2 than it was on the original MMPI. This lowering effect increases as the T-scores get higher; however, Dahlstrom (1992) has found that this is one of five clinical scales that appeared as first or second high points more frequently when MMPIs were rescored using MMPI-2 norms. This seemed to be due to the fact that some other MMPI-2 clinical scales were lowered even more drastically in the transition from the MMPI to the MMPI-2. He also found that the single largest increase in codetype when these MMPIs were rescored occurred for the 13/31 code, from 28 profiles (2.5%) using the MMPI norms to 61 profiles (5.4%) using the MMPI-2 norms. (See Tables 4.1 and 4.2.)

Given these findings, we suggest that you use caution in interpreting MMPI-2 profiles for which the **1** scale is either the highest or second highest clinical scale elevation. We suggest you score MMPI-2 raw data onto the original MMPI profiles before using the information related to codetypes in this scale section.

Scale **1** is a straightforward scale that measures the number of bodily complaints claimed by a person. This scale does not distinguish actual from imagined physical difficulties.

When this scale is below 45 T-score points (MMPI) or 40 T-score points (MMPI-2), the person generally is seen as an alert, capable who tends to deny bodily complaints. This T-score is the normal level of the scale for persons in the medical profession and related areas (nurses, physical therapists,

**TABLE 4.1**

Frequencies (and Percentages) of High-Point Pairs for 1,138 Males
on K-Corrected Norms for the MMPI (Below the Diagonal)
and MMPI-2 (Above the Diagonal)

| MMPI | MMPI-2 1 | 2 | 3 | 4 | 5 | 6 | 7 | 8 | 9 | 0 | Scale[a] Totals |
|---|---|---|---|---|---|---|---|---|---|---|---|
| 1 | — | 35 | 61 | 21 | 14 | 18 | 15 | 26 | 31 | 24 | 245 |
|  |  | (3.1) | (5.4) | (1.8) | (1.2) | (1.6) | (1.3) | (2.3) | (2.7) | (2.1) | (10.8) |
| 2 | 26 | — | 48 | 13 | 22 | 21 | 11 | 3 | 6 | 67 | 226 |
|  | (2.3) |  | (4.2) | (1.1) | (1.9) | (1.8) | (1.0) | (0.3) | (0.5) | (5.9) | (9.9) |
| 3 | 28 | 26 | — | 23 | 65 | 54 | 3 | 4 | 29 | 15 | 302 |
|  | (2.5) | (2.3) |  | (2.0) | (5.7) | (4.7) | (0.3) | (0.4) | (2.5) | (1.3) | (13.3) |
| 4 | 16 | 30 | 29 | — | 20 | 29 | 14 | 17 | 37 | 19 | 203 |
|  | (1.4) | (2.6) | (2.5) |  | (2.6) | (2.5) | (1.2) | (1.5) | (3.3) | (1.7) | (8.9) |
| 5 | 19 | 90 | 92 | 78 | — | 47 | 15 | 12 | 42 | 38 | 285 |
|  | (1.7) | (7.9) | (8.1) | (6.9) |  | (4.1) | (1.3) | (1.1) | (3.7) | (3.3) | (12.5) |
| 6 | 2 | 12 | 16 | 12 | 49 | — | 9 | 8 | 31 | 23 | 240 |
|  | (0.2) | (1.1) | (1.4) | (1.1) | (4.3) |  | (0.8) | (0.7) | (2.7) | (2.0) | (10.5) |
| 7 | 2 | 21 | 4 | 11 | 27 | 5 | — | 26 | 23 | 37 | 153 |
|  | (0.2) | (1.8) | (0.4) | (1.0) | (2.4) | (0.5) |  | (2.3) | (2.0) | (3.3) | (6.7) |
| 8 | 11 | 20 | 8 | 29 | 33 | 9 | 25 | — | 29 | 9 | 134 |
|  | (1.0) | (1.8) | (0.7) | (2.5) | (2.9) | (0.8) | (2.2) |  | (2.5) | (0.8) | (5.9) |
| 9 | 8 | 11 | 27 | 58 | 122 | 20 | 18 | 33 | — | 14 | 242 |
|  | (0.7) | (1.0) | (2.4) | (5.1) | (10.7) | (1.8) | (1.6) | (2.9) |  | (1.2) | (10.6) |
| 0 | 4 | 34 | 3 | 3 | 43 | 4 | 8 | 4 | 8 | — | 246 |
|  | (0.4) | (3.0) | (0.3) | (0.3) | (3.8) | (0.4) | (0.7) | (0.4) | (0.7) |  | (10.8) |
| Scale[b] | 116 | 270 | 233 | 266 | 553 | 129 | 121 | 172 | 305 | 111 | |
| Totals | (5.1) | (11.9) | (10.2) | (11.7) | (24.3) | (5.7) | (5.3) | (7.6) | (13.4) | (4.9) | |

[a]Frequency with which each scale is highest or second highest in the profile for MMPI-2 norms.
[b]Frequency with which each scale is highest or second highest in the profile for MMPI norms.

**Note:** From "Comparability of two-point high-point code patterns from original MMPI norms to MMPI-2 norms for the restandardization sample" by W. G. Dahlstrom (1992), *Journal of Personality Assessment*, 59, pp. 153-164. Reprinted with permission.

TABLE 4.2

Frequencies (and Percentages) of High-Point Pairs for 1,462 Females on K-Corrected Norms for the MMPI (Below the Diagonal) and MMPI-2 (Above the Diagonal)

| MMPI | MMPI-2 | | | | | | | | | | Scale[a] |
| | 1 | 2 | 3 | 4 | 5 | 6 | 7 | 8 | 9 | 0 | Totals |
|---|---|---|---|---|---|---|---|---|---|---|---|
| 1 | — | 25 | 94 | 6 | 30 | 11 | 16 | 10 | 22 | 50 | 264 |
|   |   | (1.7) | (6.4) | (0.4) | (2.1) | (0.8) | (1.1) | (0.7) | (1.5) | (3.4) | (9.0) |
| 2 | 17 | — | 48 | 26 | 40 | 31 | 22 | 4 | 9 | 76 | 281 |
|   | (1.2) |   | (3.3) | (1.8) | (2.7) | (2.1) | (1.5) | (0.3) | (0.6) | (5.2) | (9.6) |
| 3 | 55 | 40 | — | 44 | 82 | 72 | 5 | 4 | 38 | 12 | 399 |
|   | (3.8) | (2.7) |   | (3.0) | (5.6) | (4.9) | (0.3) | (0.3) | (2.6) | (0.8) | (13.6) |
| 4 | 6 | 46 | 112 | — | 41 | 44 | 11 | 24 | 47 | 13 | 256 |
|   | (0.4) | (3.1) | (7.7) |   | (2.8) | (3.0) | (0.8) | (1.6) | (3.2) | (0.9) | (8.8) |
| 5 | 3 | 6 | 18 | 19 | — | 50 | 12 | 16 | 85 | 76 | 432 |
|   | (0.2) | (0.4) | (1.2) | (1.3) |   | (3.4) | (0.8) | (1.1) | (5.8) | (5.2) | (14.8) |
| 6 | 5 | 32 | 57 | 92 | 11 | — | 16 | 12 | 44 | 46 | 326 |
|   | (0.3) | (2.2) | (3.9) | (6.3) | (0.8) |   | (1.1) | (0.8) | (3.0) | (3.1) | (11.1) |
| 7 | 5 | 27 | 7 | 16 | 2 | 13 | — | 21 | 21 | 36 | 160 |
|   | (0.3) | (1.8) | (0.5) | (1.1) | (0.1) | (0.9) |   | (1.4) | (1.4) | (2.5) | (5.4) |
| 8 | 5 | 8 | 24 | 65 | 8 | 23 | 17 | — | 37 | 14 | 142 |
|   | (0.3) | (0.5) | (1.6) | (4.4) | (0.5) | (1.6) | (1.2) |   | (2.5) | (1.0) | (4.9) |
| 9 | 24 | 15 | 47 | 129 | 31 | 92 | 14 | 54 | — | 19 | 322 |
|   | (1.6) | (1.0) | (3.2) | (8.8) | (2.1) | (6.3) | (1.0) | (3.7) |   | (1.3) | (11.0) |
| 0 | 13 | 106 | 20 | 28 | 19 | 62 | 20 | 16 | 33 | — | 342 |
|   | (0.9) | (7.2) | (1.4) | (1.9) | (1.3) | (4.2) | (1.4) | (1.1) | (2.3) |   | (11.7) |

Scale[b] 133 297 380 513 117 387 121 220 439 317
Totals (4.5) (10.2) (13.0) (17.5) (4.0) (13.2) (4.1) (7.5) (15.0) (10.8)

[a] Frequency with which each scale is highest or second highest in the profile for MMPI-2 norms.

[b] Frequency with which each scale is highest or second highest in the profile for MMPI norms.

**Note:** From "Comparability of two-point high-point code patterns from original MMPI norms to MMPI-2 norms for the restandardization sample" by W. G. Dahlstrom (1992), *Journal of Personality Assessment*, 59, pp. 153-164. Reprinted with permission.

etc.). Others who also may receive a scale score at this level are the children of those in the medical profession, the children of hypochondriacs, and student nurses. These people have been around illness a lot and have seen others use it as a manipulative device. They do not wish to be classified with these manipulators and, therefore, they deny they have illnesses and tend not to seek medical help in the early stages of real somatic complaints.

In recent years we have been seeing people with low scale 1 scores who do not fit the above categories. For these people, what seems to be the common reason for the low scores is that they have negative feelings toward illness and see it as a sign of some weakness. Frequently, joggers and health food enthusiasts score in this range.

Most people score in the 45 through 60 range on this scale for the original MMPI and in the 40 through 60 range for the MMPI-2. This range indicates that these people have the usual number of physical complaints. T-scores of 60 through 70 on the MMPI, 60 through 65 on the MMPI-2, are common for persons who are physically handicapped. Persons with scores in this range who do not have such a physical disability may be suffering from a cold or some other illness and thus may be feeling slightly "under the weather."

As the elevation on this scale increases, and it is the highest scale elevated, people tend to use bodily complaints (either real or imagined) to avoid dealing with psychological difficulties and to manipulate those around them. When the manipulation does not work, particularly with physicians and counselors, clients may shop around until a physician or counselor is found who can be manipulated. Thus, the higher the elevation, the less likely the person is to stay in productive counseling.

When this scale is elevated above 70 (MMPI) or 65 (MMPI-2), and is not the highest scale, it may indicate that the person is having physical problems related to the emotion or behavior shown by the highest scale. For example, if the 7 scale is the highest scale and the 1 scale also is elevated but lower than the **7** scale, the person would be having physical problems that he/she most likely would see as the result of the high anxiety that is present.

Kunce and Anderson (1976, 1984) have hypothesized that the underlying dimension of this scale is conservation. When the characteristics measured by a scale **1** are working in the positive direction as shown by a moderate elevation in a psychologically normal person, the individual will be conscientious, careful, considerate, and sincere. These individuals seem to be unusually responsive to their environment and tune not only into changes in their bodies but also into the immediate environment around them, e.g., heat and light. A person with a moderate elevation, thus, may be interested in both personal health and ecological problems. Even in a person who is otherwise well adjusted, stress may turn these positive characteristics into transitory irritability, dependence, and bodily preoccupations.

Elevations above 70 on scale **1** are rare in college populations but are found frequently in mental health clinic populations. We have found about 10% of the people in our mental health clinic populations scoring above 70 (MMPI) or 65 (MMPI-2) on this scale. This elevation is more likely to be on a man's profile than a woman's; however, when either one has an elevation on this scale and it is the highest scale, it usually indicates behavior of long standing.

## GENERAL INFORMATION

1. The 33 items of this scale (32 items, MMPI-2) are fairly obvious questions having to do with bodily problems.

2. We believe this scale to be "characterological"; that is, elevations on the scale tend to reflect long-term behavior.

3. Caldwell (1985) has hypothesized that people with this scale as their highest elevation are concerned about their bodily functions because of conditioning experiences of having their physical health seriously threatened.

4. When the person is actually physically ill and this scale is markedly elevated, the person is likely to be using the physical illness in a manipulative way to control others.

5. When no physical illness exists and this scale is elevated, the person tends to be using vague somatic complaints in a manipulative way to control others around him/her.

6. Gass (1992) has found 21 MMPI-2 items that reflect neurologic symptoms; twelve of them are on the **1** scale. These items are 10(F), 45(F), 47(F), 53(T), 141(F), 152(F), 164(F), 173(F), 175(F), 224(F), 247(F), and 249(F). In a group of 110 patients with cerebrovascular disease (CVD), he found that, on the average, five of these items were endorsed, thereby raising this scale 13 T-score points. Scales **2, 3,** and **8** also are affected by the inclusion of these items.

   Gass recommended scoring a CVD patient's MMPI-2 profile twice, once in the standard manner and again after eliminating the pathologically endorsed CVD items. He felt that the adjusted MMPI-2 profile would give a more accurate estimate of the psychological functioning of this type of patient.

7. Bowler, Rauch, Becker, and Hawes (1989) and Bowler, Mergler, Rauch, and Bowler (1992) have found that the **1** scale can be significantly elevated by organic solvent toxicity. Scales **2, 3, 7,** and **8** may be similarly affected.

8. Borden, Clum, and Broyles (1989) studied 91 patients with anxiety disorders and found that those with panic attacks had higher scores on the **1** scale. These authors suggested that somatic preoccupation might play a role in the etiology of panic attacks.

9. The **1** scale tends to be higher for older people from a normal population, perhaps reflecting greater somatic concern (Colligan, Osborne, Swenson, & Offord, 1989). Schenkenberg et al. (1984) also have found that older

people from a psychiatric population score higher on the **1** scale.

10. Hibbs et al. (1979) have found that men score significantly higher than women on this scale (as well as scale **9**). They suggested that this may be due to a sex-role sanctioning of somatizing behavior.

11. Test-retest reliability is high—85 (Butcher et al., 1989). Scale **1** is one of the most stable scales for clinic populations.

# HIGH SCORES

## Moderate Elevations

(T = 60 through 65, MMPI-2),

(T = 60 through 70, MMPI)

1. Physically ill persons may score in this range.

2. Kunce and Anderson (1976) have hypothesized that when this scale is in the moderate range (and there are no other elevated clinical scales except perhaps the **5** scale for men), it may measure a constructive concern for one's own and others' physical well-being.

## Marked Elevations

(T= 65 and above MMPI-2),

(T = 70 and above MMPI)

Behaviors mentioned for this elevation are most clearly seen when this scale is the highest of the clinical scales.

1. People with scores in this range tend to see themselves as having some physical problems. If this is the highest clinical scale, they may be using the problems to manipulate others. They tend to complain a great deal and are whiny.

2. In addition, they may be very cynical and defeatist, especially toward those who are helping them. The following adjectives frequently are used to describe these people: unambitious, stubborn, and egocentric.

3. Elevations on this scale tend to reflect the use of displacement to cope with anxiety (Trimboli & Kilgore, 1983).

4. The higher the score on this scale,

   a. The more manipulative the client is with his/her physical complaints.

   b. The more unable he/she is to cope with life.

   c. The more he/she has the attitude "you must take care of me."

   d. The more the person uses his/her somatic complaints to get out of responsibility and to gratify dependency needs.

5. This scale may measure dependency needs that are channeled into claims of physical illness. These people force others to take care of them; thus, their dependency needs are met.

6. People with scale **1** scores in this range tend to "shop" for physicians and may see one after another, or several at one time.

7. In therapy, persons with high **1** scores tend to frustrate the therapist in any efforts toward psychological change since they see their illness as physical not psychological. This elevation is associated with poor progress in psychotherapy.

8. In one study of medical patients, people who had high scale **1** scores did not have successful lower back surgery (Long, 1981).

# LOW SCORES

(T = 40 or below, MMPI-2)

(T = 45 or below, MMPI)

1. These scores may indicate people who have been closely associated with others who have used illness in a manipulative way. Because they do not want to appear hypochondriacal themselves, they reject even admitting a normal amount of aches and pains.

2. These people may also take pride in their good health and do not like to see themselves as ill even to the point of ignoring illness until it becomes quite severe.

3. People with these scores are described as alert, capable, and responsible. They seem to be free from hampering inhibitions and undue concern about the adverse reactions of others.

4. Keiller and Graham (1993) have found that low scores on the MMPI-2 **1** scale indicate someone who is not likely to worry about health or to complain about bodily aches and pains.

# CODETYPES

All scales in the codetypes are at a T-score of 65 or above (MMPI-2) or 70 or above (MMPI) and are listed in order from the highest to the lowest peaks. The scales in the codetype must be the highest clinical scales on the profile.

### Spike 1

1. Test takers with the **1** scale as their only elevation usually have a long history of vague physical complaints (Greene, 1991).

2. Despite having these complaints, these individuals do not seem to be unduly depressed or upset about them except

when significant others do not pay sufficient attention to their complaints.

**1-2** See also point 1a in the **1-2-3** Triad profile, p. 158.

1.  People with the **1-2** codetype tend to see themselves as ill and typically are depressed about this illness.

2.  They usually have pain, fatigability, and overevaluation of their physical complaints.

3.  Greene (1991) has found that people with this combination complain about pain and somatic discomfort, especially in the digestive tract. They tend to react to stress with physical symptoms and resist psychological explanations for their discomfort.

4.  Caldwell (1974) has hypothesized that this combination possibly indicates a phobic fear of death.

5.  State hospital and mental health clinic inpatients with this pattern, **1-2/2-1,** were found to have multiple somatic complaints, insomnia, and physical problems. However, they seemed to be less disturbed than other state hospital patients. Older males tended to have histories of alcoholism. These findings may not apply to females (Gynther, Altman, Warbin, & Sletten, 1973).

6.  Adolescents in treatment with this **1-2/2-1** pattern (Marks et al., 1974) were referred to treatment because of being shy and overly sensitive. They were also excessively fearful. The Marks, Seeman, and Haller book should be consulted for further information about this profile.

7.  Archer (1992) reports a low frequency of adolescents with this profile type on the *MMPI-A.*

8.  For internal medicine patients with this codetype, males had two different sets of symptoms. One group of men complained of marked epigastric distress, usually of the upper gastrointestinal tract. The other group complained

of tension and depression. Both groups of men were competitive and industrious, but immature and dependent. Though they dreaded increased responsibilities, they maintained their normal level of efficiency in spite of their worries (Guthrie, 1952).

9. Male college counselees with these scores tend to have tension, insomnia, insecurity in heterosexual relationships and other social situations, worry, and introversion.

10. Female college counselees with these scores (especially with a low **5** scale) tend to have headaches, depression, worry, anxiety, shyness, social insecurity, and indecisiveness (Drake & Oetting, 1959).

**1-2-3** See also the **1-2-3-$\overline{5}$** pattern, p. 96, and point 1b in the **1-2-3** Triad pattern, p. 159.

1. People with this pattern are depressed, and have loss of interest, apathy, and tension (Lachar, 1974).

2. A person with this pattern (called the **1-2-3** slope) usually is male, tends to be in declining health, and feels "over the hill." He usually had poor health in childhood. Also, he does not tend to take risks or to change jobs frequently. He may feel a profound sense of loss of body functioning (Caldwell, 1972).

3. Some persons with valid physical disabilities that result in declining health also have this pattern. However, in this instance not all three scales are above 70.

4. Gilberstadt and Duker (1965) found this **1-2-3** pattern in a VA hospital male population. Men with this pattern usually reacted to stress with physiological symptoms. They tended to lack aggressiveness and sexual drive.

5. In contrast to patients with high **1, 1-3,** and **1-3-4** profiles, patients with **1-2-3** codetypes in one study tended to have successful lower back surgery (Long, 1981).

## 1-2-3-4

1. Gilberstadt and Duker (1965) found this **1-2-3-4** pattern in a VA hospital male population. Men with this pattern tended to be demanding and dependent. They developed somatic symptoms, especially ulcers and gastrointestinal disturbances. They tended toward alcoholism, which appeared to be associated with physiological hyperactivity of the gastrointestinal tract.

2. Fowler and Athey (1971) also have found the same behavior as Gilberstadt and Duker for this codetype: general psychological discomfort, depression, hostility, and heavy drinking.

3. In a more recent study (Alfano, Nerviano, & Thurstin, 1987), alcoholics with this profile pattern were described as preoccupied with physical illness and unlikely to seek psychotherapy for their problems.

4. This person may have a history of gastrointestinal difficulty. He or she may be prone to ulcers (Caldwell, 1974).

## 1-2-3-$\overline{5}$ (5 scale T = 45 or below)

See also point 1b in the **1-2-3** Triad profile, Figure 4.1, p. 159.

1. Women with this combination tend to have masochistic behavior with self-depreciation, long-suffering sacrifice, and unnecessary assumption of burdens and responsibilities (Dahlstrom et al., 1972).

## 1-2-3-7

1. Individuals with this codetype have anxiety, tension, fearfulness, and an inability to be assertive (Friedman, Webb, & Lewak, 1989). They also have physiological complaints and, therefore, are likely to be seen in medical centers or for disability evaluations.

2.  To properly evaluate disability clients who have this pattern, an important procedure is to take a thorough medical history and to look at scores on the dependency scale (**Dy**) and the social responsibility scale (**Re**). If no long history of previous illnesses is present and the individual has a normal **Dy** scale (below 50) and a high **Re** scale (above 50), most likely the person has a disability with multiple symptoms that has developed recently with concomitant reactive depression and anxiety.

3.  Gilberstadt and Duker (1965) found this **1-2-3-7** pattern in a VA hospital male population. Men with this pattern tended to have physical complaints that may or may not have been real. They usually were weak, fearful, and unable to take ordinary stresses and responsibilities.

4.  In an internal medicine population, very few of the men with this pattern had demonstrable physical problems. Women with this codetype had a varied set of physical complaints, including epigastric distress. They complained of tension, depression, lack of energy, occasional attacks of dizziness, and fear. These women were willing to accept a chronic level of maladjustment; therefore, they showed poor response to treatment (Guthrie, 1952).

**1-3**  See also the **1-3-K** codetype, p. 100; the **3-1** codetype, p. 148; and the **1-3** Triad profile, Figure 4.2, pp. 159-160.

1.  A person with this codetype tends to convert his/her psychological difficulties into physical problems. Pain is a frequent complaint and gastrointestinal problems are common.

2.  The lower the **2** scale, especially if it is 10 points or more below the **1** scale, the more likely the person is to have become adapted to his/her physical problems.

3.  Keller and Butcher (1991) have suggested, however, that the relative elevations of scales **1, 2,** and **3** on the MMPI-2 not be interpreted too rigidly since the **2** scale will be

lower relative to the other scales compared to profile results obtained from the original MMPI.

4. The closer scale **3** is to scale **1,** the more tempered the pessimistic complaining attitudes shown by the high **1** scale.

5. Clients with a **1-3** codetype are more likely to show more somatization features than the histrionic features characteristic of clients with a **3-1** codetype (Greene, 1991).

6. This codetype is more frequent with women and older persons. Physical symptoms tend to increase in times of stress. People with this codetype are very difficult to deal with in psychotherapy because they see their problems as physical in origin.

7. Elevations on these two scales cannot be used reliably to distinguish functional disorders from actual physical disorders (Schwartz & Krupp, 1971).

8. Marks et al. (1974) found this **1-3/3-1** pattern in a university hospital and outpatient clinic. It tended to be a female profile. A woman with this pattern usually had a somatic complaint. Her behavior could best be described as agitated, depressed, and confused, with periods of weakness, forgetfulness, and dizziness. The Marks, Seeman, and Haller book should be consulted for further information concerning this pattern.

9. In one sample of psychiatric inpatients, people with a **1-3** codetype showed significantly more somatic concern than other patients (Lewandowski & Graham, 1972).

10. Gynther, Altman, and Sletten (1973) also have found that psychiatric inpatients with this pattern, **1-3/3-1,** have an unusual amount of bodily concern.

11. Adolescents in treatment with this **1-3/3-1** pattern (Marks et al., 1974) were referred for treatment because of attention seeking behavior and somatic concern. They saw themselves

as physically ill. The Marks, Seeman, and Haller book should be consulted for further information concerning this pattern.

12. Archer (1992) has found that adolescents with this codetype on the MMPI-A were frequently referred to treatment because of academic problems or concerns.

13. Patients with this "Conversion V" profile on the MMPI who reported chest pain were found to be free of significant artery disease (Barefoot, Beckham, Peterson, & Haney, 1992). These authors found an inverse relationship between elevation on the conversion V scales and severity of coronary artery disease.

14. The **1-3** pattern was one of the codetypes found for females with closed head injuries (Alfano, Neilson, Paniak, & Finlayson, 1992). The elevations on the **1** scale for closed head patients may be influenced by 14 scale items that are descriptive of some of the physical and cognitive symptoms that occur with head injuries (Gass, 1991).

15. Thirty-nine percent of patients with an MMPI **1-3/3-1** pattern in one study had organic diagnoses; thirty-four percent had psychological diagnoses. However, 66% of the psychological diagnoses were found in the group members who were under 40. In other words, the older people with **1-3/3-1** patterns in the study tended to have organic problems, whereas the younger people with this pattern had psychological problems (Schwartz, Osborne, & Krupp, 1972).

16. In one study (Long, 1981), patients with this codetype did not have successful lower back surgery.

17. Wiltse and Rocchio (1975) have found that for patients treated by chemonucleolysis and laminectomy for low back syndrome, the relative elevations of the **1** and **3** scales on MMPIs administered before the treatment were predictive of successful recovery.

When both scales were 84 or above   10% had good recovery
When both scales were 75 to 84   16% had good recovery
When both scales were 65 to 74   39% had good recovery
When both scales were 55 to 64   72% had good recovery
When both scales were 54 or below   90% had good recovery

When patients were high (above 70) on only one of the scales, the patient had a 39% chance of good recovery.

### 1-3-K

1. With the **1-3-K** combination if the person has had surgery, the individual may have intractable post-operative pain (Caldwell, 1974).

### 1-3-2

1. Gilberstadt and Duker (1965) found this **1-3-2** pattern in a VA hospital male population. Men with this pattern tended to be extroverted, sociable, and highly conforming. Under stress, they tended to develop psychosomatic illnesses.

### 1-3-4

1. In one study (Long, 1981), patients with this combination did not have successful lower back surgery.

2. Caldwell (1985) has found that when patients have this profile, they are more likely to sue their doctors for malpractice.

### 1-3-7

1. Gilberstadt and Duker (1965) found this **1-3-7** pattern in a VA hospital male population. Men with this pattern tended to have severe anxiety attacks and were clinging people. Under stress they developed psychosomatic illnesses.

### 1-3-8

1. A person with this profile tends to have physical problems that seem strange, odd, or do not make sense.

2. A family background of psychosis and/or childhood deprivation may exist (Caldwell, 1972).

3. This type of person seems to need structure. He/she tends to do well in school when the school is structured. However, when this structure or a significant relationship is gone, bizarre symptoms may be seen (Caldwell, 1972).

4. Gilberstadt and Duker (1965) found this **1-3-8-(2)** pattern in a VA hospital male population. The **2** scale is elevated above 70, but it is not necessarily the next highest scale after the **8.** Men with this pattern tended to have confused thinking, suspiciousness, and jealousy. These researchers hypothesized that these men may have somatic illnesses to defend against their schizophrenic tendencies.

## 1-3-9

1. Gilberstadt and Duker (1965) found this **1-3-9** pattern in a VA hospital male population. Men with this pattern tended to have chronic organic illnesses, frequently with organic brain dysfunction. Temper outbursts were seen at times, and occasionally these people became combative and disruptive.

## 1-4

1. This combination is not found frequently but, when present, is more likely a man's profile than a woman's. There may be severe hypochondriacal symptoms, especially headaches. People with this combination may be rebellious but not express this directly. They tend to be pessimistic, grouchy, bitchy, and dissatisfied.

2. Gynther, Altman, and Sletten (1973) have found that psychiatric inpatients with this pattern, **1-4/4-1,** may have a drinking problem. These researchers found almost no females with this pattern.

3. Adolescents in treatment with the **1-4/4-1** pattern (Marks et al., 1974) were referred, typically by the courts, because

they were defiant, disobedient, and impulsive. They were seen as aggressive, outspoken, resentful, and self-centered. The Marks, Seeman, and Haller book should be consulted for further information about this profile.

## 1-5

1. Tanner (1990a) found six people with this codetype in a psychiatric center. They were passive, indecisive and dependent. They constantly complained and seemed to use their physical symptoms to provide an acceptable way to avoid family and work responsibilities. These individuals typically were diagnosed as having hypochondriasis or conversion reactions. Their response to treatment was poor.

2. For men, this combination may suggest multiple surgeries. For women, the **1-5̄** also would suggest the same (Trimboli & Kilgore, 1983).

3. Adolescents in treatment with this **1-5/5-1** pattern (Marks et al., 1974) were referred because of their hyperactivity. They tended to be impulsive and effeminate. They presented themselves as physically ill and had had significant amounts of illness as children. The Marks, Seeman, and Haller book should be consulted for further information concerning this pattern.

## 1-6

1. This is a rare codetype. Greene (1991) reports people with it as having some form of somatization disorder plus hostility, which they frequently do not recognize.

2. Adolescents in treatment with this **1-6/6-1** pattern (Marks et al., 1974) were referred for emotional overcontrol. Family

disruption was frequent for these adolescents. They were defensive and evasive, egocentric, self-centered, and self-indulgent. They did not report physical complaints however. The Marks, Seeman, and Haller book should be consulted for further information concerning this pattern.

## 1-7

1. Individuals with this codetype have physical complaints that reflect the anxiety that they also have (Greene, 1991).

## 1-8

1. These people have physical complaints that may be quite bizarre or odd.

2. They may be socially inept and inadequate and feel alienated and different from other people (Greene, 1991).

3. This codetype was found among drug abusers who had attempted suicide, but it was not found for drug abusers who had not attempted suicide (Craig & Olson, 1990).

4. Adolescents in treatment with the **1-8/8-1** pattern (Marks et al., 1974) presented themselves as physically ill. As children they had been seriously ill, and currently only one-half of them were in good health. They were seen as insecure, unambitious, and constantly demanding attention. The Marks, Seeman, and Haller book should be consulted for further information concerning this pattern.

5. Archer and Klinefelter (1992) reported that adolescents with this codetype may have elevated MacAndrew Alcoholism scales. Attempted suicides are also frequent.

$\boxed{\textbf{1-9}}$ See also the **9-1** combination, p. 276.

1. This person may have somatic complaints but also a lot of energy.

2. He/she is usually quite tense and may be distressed by an inability to attain high goals (Lachar, 1974).

3. This person tends to be one who has coronary attacks (Caldwell, 1972).

$\boxed{\textbf{1-0}}$

1. These people are typically shy and insecure and may report only a limited number of physical symptoms (Greene, 1991).

$\boxed{\textbf{2-1-3}}$ See the **2-3-1** codetype, point 3, p. 119.

$\boxed{\textbf{2-3-1}}$ See p. 119.

$\boxed{\textbf{2-3-1-7}}$ See p. 119.

$\boxed{\textbf{2-7-3-1}}$ See p. 127.

$\boxed{\textbf{2-8-1-3}}$ See p. 133.

$\boxed{\textbf{3-2-1}}$ See p. 150.

$\boxed{\textbf{8-1-2-3}}$ See p. 254.

# SUMMARY OF SCALE 1 INTERPRETATIONS

| T-score MMPI-2 | MMPI | Interpretations |
|---|---|---|
| <40 | <45 | With a score in this range, a person is denying bodily complaints. This is typical of people in the helping professions, children of these people, and people with hypochondriacal parents. Runners and health conscious individuals also may score in this range. |
| 40-59 | 45-59 | The majority of people score in this range. |
| 60-65 * | 60-70 * | This level is usual for persons with valid bodily complaints. |
| >65 | >70 | If this is the highest clinical scale, the person tends to use bodily complaints to avoid emotional situations and also uses these complaints as a way of manipulating others. The person may be whiny, complaining, and making others miserable. As the scale is elevated, these people tend to be defeatist, to solicit help from others, and then to sabotage this help. They may "shop" for physicians and/or counselors. |
| | | If this scale is not one of the highest scales, then the person usually has physical complaints as a result of the problem indicated by the highest clinical scale(s) and may not be using the physical complaints in a manipulative way. |

See notes on the next page.

Notes for "Summary" on prior page.

* This interpretation applies only when there are no marked elevations on the clinical scales.

# SCALE 2
## (D, Depression Scale)

Scale **2** is one of the clinical scales most affected by the change from the MMPI to MMPI-2. Three items have been deleted from the scale and two have been rewritten. In addition, the redistribution of the T-scores in the transformation to uniform T-scores has *lowered* elevations of this scale significantly for men but not for women (Strassberg, 1991). (See Tables 3.1 and 3.2, pp. 42-43.) Dahlstrom (1992) has found that this is one of five clinical scales that appeared as first or second high points less frequently when MMPIs were rescored using MMPI-2 norms. (Scales **4, 5, 8,** and **9** were the other scales similarly affected.) (See Tables 4.1 and 4.2, pp. 86-87.) Munley and Zarantonello (1989) also have found that scale **2** is one of the scales most prominently affected by the transformation from linear T-scores to uniform T-scores for the MMPI-2.

We recommend plotting MMPI-2 raw scores on both the MMPI-2 and MMPI profile sheets so that this redistribution can be easily seen and taken into consideration. Since scale **2** has been one of the most frequently elevated clinical scales, especially for people coming in voluntarily for counseling, it is important to interpret this scale accurately. Since most of the research regarding this scale is based upon MMPI T-scores, it is most appropriate, we feel, to use these T-scores for interpretation until more research is available based upon the MMPI-2.

Two observations should be noted in evaluating scale **2.** First of all, this is a mood scale. It measures the degree of pessimism and sadness the person feels at the time the MMPI was administered. Thus, a change in mood will lower or raise this scale. Second, scale **2** is rarely elevated by itself; usually at least one or two other scales also are elevated. These other scales can be helpful in determining how the depression is shown.

When the T-score is between 60 and 65 (MMPI-2) or 60 and 70 (MMPI), a mild dissatisfaction with life may exist, but either the dissatisfaction is not enough for the person to be really concerned or the dissatisfaction is of long standing and the person has learned to live with it. When scale **2** is at 60 and scale **9** is low, the person may have taken the inventory at the bottom of a mood swing (for example during a post-exam let-down) or at the end of a long work day.

As the elevation increases, the person's attitude changes from sadness to gloom (T = 80) to all pervasive pessimism about self and the world (T = 90 or above).

Low scale **2** scores (45 or below, MMPI; 40 or below, MMPI-2) indicate that the person is cheerful, optimistic, and easygoing. However, these attitudes should be checked in terms of their appropriateness for the person's situation, particularly if a tragedy has occurred recently.

Kunce and Anderson (1976, 1984) have hypothesized that evaluation is the underlying dimension on this scale; that is, the person has an inclination for sorting out good from bad, right from wrong. A moderate elevation on scale **2** in an individual who has good mental health would indicate a person who is realistic and objective. In addition, he/she is likely to be deliberate and contemplative. When placed under stress, this same individual could show transitory worry and anxiety with feelings of guilt connected with an overly critical attitude toward his/her own behavior.

Scientists such as mathematicians, physicists, engineers, and chemists tend to have moderately high scores on this scale (Kunce & Callis, 1969; Norman & Redlo, 1952), which is consistent with the realistic and objective dimensions of this scale. Hovey and Lewis (1967) found that when scale **2** is elevated along with scale **3,** these individuals are ambitious, conscientious, industrious, and take responsibilities seriously.

Scale **2** is one of the most frequent high points on a profile for clients in college counseling centers and mental health clinics. It usually indicates a reaction to problems that are pressing on the person.

# GENERAL INFORMATION

1.  This 60-item scale (57 items, MMPI-2) concerns poor self-concept, sadness, pessimism, and a lack of hope.

2.  Harris and Lingoes (1955) have subjectively divided scale **2** into 5 subscales: subjective depression, psychomotor retardation, physical malfunctioning, mental dullness, and brooding. The interpretation for these subscales are shown on p. 138.

3.  Scale **2** is the most frequent high point in psychiatric profiles.

4.  This scale measures people's present attitudes about themselves and their relationship with others. It is the best scale for measuring a person's present feelings of contentment and security.

5.  Riley and McCranie (1990) found the Self-critical scale of the *Depressive Experiences Questionnaire* significantly and positively related to severity of depression, especially for males.

6.  Caldwell (1985) has hypothesized that people who have this scale as one of their highest have a fear of irretrievable loss or a fear of hope.

7.  Trimboli and Kilgore (1983) have found that the relative elevation of scale **2** is the best single index of the extent to which an individual's typical defenses are being breached.

8.  This scale quickly reflects changes in a person's day-to-day feelings. Therefore, it tends to be a fairly changeable scale. The retest reliabilities for this scale on the MMPI-2 are .75 for men and .77 for women (Butcher et al., 1989).

9.  An accurate interpretation of scale **2** relies on the rest of the profile. Therefore, high-point combinations should be considered carefully.

10. This scale tends to decrease in elevation on a retest, even without intervening therapy.

11. Women who have an elevated scale **2** tend to report depression significantly more often (2 to 1) than men who have an elevated scale **2.**

12. Scale **2** tends to be higher for older people, perhaps reflecting greater dysphoric emotional tone (Colligan et al., 1984). This scale is negatively correlated with education.

13. Maffeo, Ford, and Lavin (1990) also found a relationship between high scale **2** scores and age in men. These authors also found a significant negative relationship between education and depression.

14. Priest (1993) has found a group of 12 age-related items on the MMPI-2 that older (over 64), nondepressed people endorsed in the depressed direction, thus raising their depression T-scores. These items are 10(F), 29(F), 37(F), 43(F), 68(F), 134(F), 147(T), 178(F), 188(F), 189(F), 226(F), and 260(F). If an older individual is being tested, and has an elevated score on the **2** scale, it would be prudent to see how many of the items from this normal aging scale have been endorsed before diagnosing an individual as depressed.

15. Bolla-Wilson and Bleecker (1989) also have found that the increased prevalence of depression in older adults on self-report depression scales (such as the **2** scale) is due to the report of more somatic items or physical symptoms rather than true depressive symptomatology.

16. The obvious items in this scale (Weiner, 1948) are highly correlated with other measures of depression, whereas the subtle items are not (Nelson, 1987; Nelson & Cicchetti, 1991). The validity of the **2** scale may be enhanced when the subtle items are excluded from the total item set.

17. A series of studies report research on the **2** scale for individuals with various types of physical problems.

a.  Gass (1992) found 21 MMPI-2 items that reflected neurologic symptoms; seven of them are on the **2** scale. These items are 10(F), 31(T), 45(F), 141(F), 147(T), 148(F), and 175(T). In a group of 110 patients with cerebrovascular disease (CVD), he found that, on the average, three of these items were endorsed, thereby raising this scale eight T-score points. Scales **1, 3,** and **8** also are affected by the inclusion of these items.

b.  Gass recommended scoring a cerebrovascular patient's MMPI-2 profile twice, once in the standard manner and again after eliminating the pathologically endorsed CVD items. He felt that the adjusted MMPI-2 profile would give a more accurate estimate of the psychological functioning for this type of patient.

c.  In a study (Light, Herbst, Bragdon, & Hinderliter, 1991) of depressed patients with myocardial ischemia, patients tended to report angina pain more frequently during exercise testing than nondepressed patients. They also rated the pain as more severe.

d.  The **2** scale was the mean high point for a group of females with closed head injuries (Alfano et al., 1992). The mean group two-point code was **2-3.** The authors pointed out that these scale elevations were at least partly the result of the endorsement of items reflecting physical and cognitive symptoms caused by the closed head injury.

e.  Chronic pain patients' scores on the MMPI scale **2** were found to be positively correlated with self-blame and negatively correlated with perceptions of social support (Kleinke, 1991).

f.  Keller and Butcher (1991) have found that chronic pain patients look somewhat less depressed on the MMPI-2 (have lower **2** scale scores) and less characterological (lower **4** scale scores) than they do on the original MMPI.

g.  A 20 year follow-up study of 1,522 men who participated in a health study found a relationship between elevation on the **2** scale and incidence of cancer and mortality (Persky, Kempthorne-Rawson, & Shekelle, 1987). These authors suggested that psychological depression may promote the development and spread of malignant neoplasms.

h.  Women with PMS had higher scores on the **2** scale during the luteal phase of their menstrual cycles than women without PMS (Trunnell, Turner, & Keye, 1988); however, the two groups of women did not differ on the **2** scale during the follicular phase of their menstrual cycles.

## HIGH SCORES

### Moderate Elevations

(T = 60 through 65, MMPI-2)

(T = 60 through 70, MMPI)

1.  A person with a score in this range may have a feeling that something is not right, but he/she does not always recognize this feeling as depression.

2.  Kunce and Anderson (1976) have hypothesized that when this scale is in the moderate range (and there are no other elevated clinical scales except perhaps the **5** scale for men), it may measure a penchant for sorting out what is right and wrong, what is good and bad. An existential questioning may occur about life and its meaning.

3.  College freshmen with this elevation tend to report more homesickness than freshmen without elevations on this scale (Rose, 1947).

4.  With a scale **2** score in this range and a **9** scale score on or near a T of 45, the MMPI may have been taken

when the person had had a long hard work day, had a cold, or was at the bottom of a mood swing.

## Marked Elevations

(T = 65 and above, MMPI-2)

(T = 70 and above, MMPI)

The behaviors mentioned for this elevation are seen most clearly when the scale is the highest of the clinical scales.

1. A person with a **2** scale score at the lower end of this range may be withdrawn but may not show the typically tearful depression associated with higher elevations.

2. A person with a **2** scale elevation above a T of 80 tends to be self-deprecating, withdrawn, and may be feeling guilty. If the person is feeling guilty, the **Es** scale also will be below 45 T-score points. The higher the **2** scale becomes, the more these symptoms are seen, together with an overriding feeling of hopelessness.

3. Marked elevations on this scale may reflect a lack of psychic energy (confirmed by scale **9** below 50 or the lowest point on the clinical scales) and social withdrawal (confirmed by an elevated scale **0**). This combination of lethargy and interpersonal isolation may make traditional psychotherapy inappropriate prior to chemotherapy.

4. Other high scales should be checked to determine how the depression is being felt and/or shown; for example, a high scale **7** with the high scale **2** usually means the person is in an agitated, depressed state.

5. Suicide risk tends to be greater when scale **2** is elevated with scale **4** and/or scale **8** or scale **9** (Trimboli & Kilgore, 1983). MMPI-2 items 150, 506, 520, and 524 which reflect suicidal ideation should be routinely checked when the **2** scale is elevated.

6. Streit, Greene, Cogan, and Davis (1993) conducted a study comparing patients who had MMPI scale **2** scores 12 or more T-score points above their Wiggins (1966) **DEP** (Depression) content scale T-scores (2 > **DEP**) with patients who had MMPI scale **2** scores 12 or more T-score points below their **DEP** scores (**DEP** > 2). They found that the 2 > **DEP** patients appeared to be more classically depressed without the psychotic features that were characteristic of the **DEP** > 2 patients. The 2 > **DEP** patients more likely had codetypes that included the **2** scale and rarely had a codetype that included the 8 scale. The **DEP** > 2 patients had a greater number of codetypes that included the **8** scale and displayed classical clinical features of psychoses.

7. Anderson, Kunce, and Rich (1979) have found a **2-4** profile (**2**=70, **4**=67) as one of three sex offender profiles (the others were **F-6-8** and **4-9**). These people had a greater incidence of serious crimes than the other sex offenders. They also tended to be older and less educated. Two-thirds of these men had a history of alcohol abuse, and one-half of them had served time for previous crimes.

8. When trying to differentiate between patients with schizophrenia and those with major depression, Ben-Porath, Butcher, and Graham (1991) found that both groups had similar scores on the **8** scale (Schizophrenia), but male depressives were higher on the **2** scale and lower on the **9** and **F** scales than schizophrenic patients. Female depressives also were higher on the **2** scale and lower on the **F** scale, and in addition, were higher on the **7** scale (Psychasthenia).

9. In a study, Coons, Bowman, and Milstein (1988) found the majority of 50 patients with a diagnosis of multiple personality disorder to be women with elevated **2** scales. These women had histories of suicide attempts, repeated amnesic episodes, and childhood trauma, particularly sexual abuse.

10. One study has found that university students with high **2** scale scores had more inwardly directed hostility and a diminished sense of control over their anger (Biaggio & Godwin, 1987).

11. Female college students who score high on the **2** scale are self-blaming and have a feminine rather than an androgynous orientation (Anderson & Leitner, 1991). They also are more introverted and show more global symptomatology.

# LOW SCORES

(T = 40 or below, MMPI-2)

(T = 45 or below, MMPI)

1. People with this level of scale **2** tend to be optimistic, gregarious, and alert.

2. These people seem to have a naturalness, buoyancy, and freedom of thought and action.

3. Low scale scores on the MMPI-2 indicate people who are cheerful and self-confident. They also are less likely to worry about their health, or to worry and fret over little things, than people in general (Keiller & Graham, 1993).

4. The lack of inhibition seen in a person with a low scale **2** score may sometimes lead to negative reactions from others.

5. These scores tend to be seen more often with younger people, because scale **2** tends to become elevated with age.

6. Seventeen men who scored low on the **2** and **0** scales when they took the MMPI as part of employment screening were compared to 142 men randomly selected from the same population (Venn, 1988). They showed some

indications of low frustration tolerance, poor impulse control, and a desire to "show off" in their employment history and screening interview.

# CODETYPES

All scales in the codetypes are at a T-score of 65 or above (MMPI-2) or 70 or above (MMPI) and are listed in order from the highest to the lowest peaks, unless otherwise noted. The scales in the codetypes must be the highest clinical scales on the profiles.

For all the combinations involving scales **1, 2,** and/or **3,** also see the Triad profiles, pp. 158-162.

| **1-2-3** | See p. 95.

| **1-2-3-4** | See p. 96.

| **1-2-3-5** | See p. 96.

| **1-2-3-7** | See p. 96.

| **1-3-2** | See p. 100.

| **1-3-8-2** | See the **1-3-8** combination, point 4, p. 101.

| **Spike 2** |

1. When the **2** scale is elevated by itself, it usually indicates a clearcut, uncomplicated reactive depression (Lachar, 1974).

2. Kelley and King (1979a) have found that college counseling center clients with a spike **2** profile were reactive depressives. They were tense, nervous, and indecisive. They also had a great deal of rage.

3. When the **2** scale is the only one above 70 and scale **9** is the low point of the profile, the depression is usually mild, but the person may complain of fatigue and loss of energy. These complaints tend to yield readily to supportive therapy (Guthrie, 1949).

**2-1** See the **1-2** combination, p. 94; also point 1b in the **2-1-3/2-3-1** Triad profile, p. 160.

1. The **2-1** profile was one of six MMPI profile types found in a VA inpatient population of alcoholic males (Alfano et al., 1987). This group of 20 men also had the **3** and **7** scales elevated, although to a lesser extent than the **2** and **1** scales. Alfano et al. labeled this group Chronic-organic. This group of men showed restless depression with tension and anxiety. The members of the group were older than the average patient in the unit, and there was a higher percentage of retirees. The group also showed greater organic impairment.

2. This was the mean codetype for 96 patients who had had strokes two and one-half years before being tested on the MMPI (Gass & Lawhorn, 1991). When answers reflecting bona fide stroke symptoms were removed from the scoring, the elevations on scale **1** were significantly reduced.

**2-1-3** See the **2-3-1** combination, point 3, p. 119; also point 1a in the **2-1-3/2-3-1** Triad profile, Figure 4.3, pp. 160-161.

1. This pattern was found in a group of male alcoholics. Also found were the **2-4-7, 4-9,** and **8-7-6** patterns (Conley, 1981).

**2-3** See also point 1c in the **2-1-3/2-3-1** Triad profile, Figure 4.3, pp. 160-161.

1. People with the **2-3** combination typically are seen as overcontrolled. They may be unable to start things or to complete them once they are started. They lack interest and involvement in life (Graham, 1977).

2. They are insecure persons who keep things inside themselves and are unable to express their feelings (Dahlstrom et al., 1972).

    a. They lack interest or involvement in things and feel constantly fatigued, exhausted, nervous, and inadequate.

    b. They are frequently described as inadequate and immature.

    c. Their troubles are typically of long standing.

    d. Their response to treatment is poor.

3. These two points elevated together indicate ineffective use of repressive and hysteroid defenses (Greene, 1991).

4. This codetype is much more common for women than for men. It indicates a lowered standard of efficiency for prolonged periods of time (Graham, 1977).

5. Gynther, Altman, and Sletten (1973) found that a group of psychiatric inpatients with the **2-3/3-2** pattern showed depressed mood and decreased activity. A person with the **2-3** pattern also had feelings of helplessness and multiple somatic complaints.

    a. Men may complain of lack of recognition on their jobs or of not being promoted when they should be, but they are adequate on their jobs. (Dahlstrom et al., 1972).

    b. Women frequently have family or marital mal-adjustments, but divorce is rare (Dahlstrom et al., 1972).

6. Adolescents in treatment with the **2-3/3-2** pattern (Marks et al., 1974) were referred because of poor relationships with their peers. They were lonely people with long histories

of personal isolation. They tended to overcontrol their impulses. They did not tend to have histories of drug abuse. The Marks, Seeman, and Haller book should be consulted for further information concerning this pattern.

7. Lewandowski and Graham (1972) have found that patients with the **2-3** pattern have significantly less conceptual disorganization, unusual mannerisms and postures, suspiciousness, hallucinatory behavior, and unusual thought content than patients with other patterns.

8. Internal medicine patients have the same symptoms as **1-2/2-1** patients (Guthrie, 1952).

---

| **2-3-1** | See point 1a in the **2-1-3/2-3-1** Triad profile, Figure 4.3, pp. 160-161.

1. People with this pattern tend to be smiling depressives. They smile while they cry, and they do not know why. They deny aggression and hostility, and usually are inhibited. This profile is frequent for people with deteriorating neurological diseases (Caldwell, 1972). Fifty percent of the people with this pattern in one population had lost their parents when they were young (Caldwell, 1985).

2. People usually have at least moderate distress and multiple somatic complaints. They have learned to tolerate the unhappiness and, therefore, may have poor motivation for treatment (Lachar, 1974).

3. Marks et al. (1974) found this **2-3-1/2-1-3** pattern in a university hospital and outpatient clinic. People with this pattern showed a combination of depression and somatic complaints. They saw themselves as physically sick. The Marks, Seeman, and Haller book should be consulted for further information concerning this profile.

---

| **2-3-1-(7)** |

1. In this pattern, the **7** scale is also elevated above 70 but is not necessarily the next highest scale. People with

this pattern tend to be older than patients in general. They feel they cannot get things done and are pessimistic. Their somatic complaints are secondary to their depression (Caldwell, 1972).

**2-4** See also the **4-2** combination, p. 177.

1. People with this pattern tend to vacillate between anger and depression. The higher the **2** scale the more prominent the depression. They feel frustrated by their own lack of accomplishment and are resentful of demands placed on them by others.

2. They tend to have behavioral difficulties that have developed over time. They may be remorseful after acting out but do not seem sincere about this remorse. They tend to run from people's expectations for them and from their own problems.

3. The person cannot take pressure in therapy, and if it is applied, he/she will leave. Prognosis for change is poor.

   a. He/she will change jobs or leave town but will not confront the therapist directly.

   b. If the person cannot run from therapy, he/she will tend to have a "spontaneous" recovery.

   c. He/she will be superficially deferent to the therapist.

4. If these scales are both highly elevated, suicidal ideation and attempts may occur. The attempts are usually to get other people to feel guilty (Graham, 1977). MMPI-2 items 140, 506, 520 and 524, which reflect suicidal ideation, should be checked.

5. Gynther, Altman, and Warbin (1972) and Gynther, Altman, and Sletten (1973) have found psychiatric patients with this pattern, **2-4/4-2,** are apt to show less psychotic pathology and fewer defects in judgment and orientation than the typical state hospital inpatient. Both males and

females are more likely to be diagnosed as alcoholic than patients with other MMPI patterns. Females are more likely to show depressive symptoms and males are more likely to have had a job loss than the average patient. There may be a recent history of suicidal behavior.

6. Adolescents in treatment with the **2-4/4-2** pattern (Marks et al., 1974) were referred for treatment because of difficulty concentrating. They tended to resent authority figures, were argumentative, and were afraid of involvement with others. They had a history of drug usage and tended to escape their problems by running away, using drugs, or attempting suicide. The Marks, Seeman, and Haller book and Archer's (1992) book should be consulted for further information concerning this profile.

7. Megargee and Bohn (1979) found a group of incarcerated criminals (Group George) with the **2-4/4-2** codetype predominating (53% of the group). They did not have extensive criminal records, were bright, and were well educated. Many of the men were drug pushers but did not use drugs themselves. They seemed to be career criminals and, in spite of making a good prison adjustment, had a high recidivism rate.

8. Walsh, Penk, Bitman, Keane, Wickis, and LoCastro (1990) found these elevations to be the mean MMPI codetype for a group of 64 VA male substance abusers. Those patients also had elevated **7, 8,** and **9** scales. The MMPI-2 mean profile for these patients showed only the **4** scale as significantly elevated.

9. In one study, this codetype was consistently found in profiles of DWI offenders and alcoholics (Sutker, Brantley, & Allain, 1980).

10. In another study, the **2-4/4-2** profile occurred most frequently in four alcoholism treatment centers. It accounted for 12 to 21% of the profiles in any one facility (Schroeder & Piercy, 1979).

11. Kelley and King (1979a) found the **2-4/4-2** codetype in a college counseling center. Clients with this profile were

depressed, impulsive, and had a history of physical problems. Females were usually seen to have a personality disorder and to be in situational distress. Males had many characterological symptoms such as impulsivity, drug abuse, and criminal records, yet they were guilt ridden, depressed, and unable to sleep.

12. Clients in another college counseling center with this code were difficult clients with whom to work because they dropped out of therapy when pressure was put upon them to improve. Their main symptoms included depression, disturbed home life, few friends, and sexual problems. Therapists who used a supportive, non-demanding approach made more progress than therapists who used confrontive or uncovering therapies (Anderson & Bauer, 1985).

## 2-4-6

1. Fifty male and fifty female cocaine abusers produced elevations on these three scales (Denier, Thevos, Latham, & Randall, 1991).

## 2-4-7 See the 2-7-4 codetype, point 3, p. 127.

1. Caldwell (1985) found that people with this pattern tend to get into trouble with alcohol even when the **MAC** scale (p. 374) is not elevated. They drink to relieve their depression and may have episodic bouts of drinking.

2. This pattern was found in a group of male alcoholics. Also found were the **2-1-3, 4-9,** and **8-7-6** patterns (Conley, 1981).

## 2-4-8

1. Persons with this pattern have a high incidence of sexual difficulties (Caldwell, 1972).

2. This pattern is found frequently in people with suicidal ideation and multiple suicide attempts (Caldwell, 1985).

3. MMPI-2 items 150, 506, 520, and 524, which reflect suicidal ideation, should be routinely checked.

## 2-5

1. Tanner (1990a) found 19 cases of this codetype in a group of psychiatric patients. All of these patients were male. The **2-5** profile was more common for inpatients, and the **5-2** profile was more common for outpatients.

   a. As a group, they had difficulty with heterosexual relationships with most of them being divorced or separated. They had a high incidence of job dissatisfaction, job-related injuries, and medical leaves.

   b. These individuals came in with a variety of physical complaints. Physically, most were slender and well groomed. Many of them had histories of multiple drug abuse.

   c. They had good social skills and, despite their depression, handled their interviews well. They were most frequently diagnosed with depressive disorders, but a minority were seen as manic or bipolar. The latter were likely to have prison records and to have engaged in illegal activities.

2. Adolescents in treatment with the **2-5/5-2** pattern (Marks et al., 1974) were referred because of poor relationships with their siblings. They tended to be indecisive, shy, hypersensitive, suspicious, and negative. They were seen as unmasculine and rarely dated. They also had anti-social activities such as breaking and entering and stealing. The Marks, Seeman, and Haller book should be consulted for further information concerning this profile.

3. College students with this profile codetype are usually anxious and have a history of physical complaints and difficulties. They also have a history of dating infrequently (King & Kelley, 1977b).

1. These people are touchy, take offense easily, and become tired and depressed quickly.

2. A great deal of other directed anger exists along with fatigue and depression.

3. They tend to induce rejection by others.

4. This profile indicates an agitated, depressed person who gets others involved in his/her problems (Caldwell, 1974).

5. Little change is likely in therapy over time and prognosis is poor.

6. Kelley and King (1979a) found the **2-6/6-2** profile code in a college counseling center. These clients were all women who came to counseling following a recent breakup with a boyfriend. They had numerous physical complaints; were dependent, moody, and tearful; and had recently lost weight. They had suicidal thoughts and indeed had made suicide attempts in the past. They used alcohol to excess and had a high frequency of alcoholic relatives. They were diagnosed as latent schizophrenics in spite of their depressive features.

### 2-6-7

1. In one study (Schotte, Maes, Cluydts, & de-Doncker, 1991), patients with a DSM-III avoidant personality disorder diagnosis had a **2-6-7** mean profile.

**2-7** See also the **7-2** combination, p. 236.

1. These people tend to be very anxious and depressed and have feelings of worthlessness. They also tend to be agitated and obsessed about their problems.

2. They tend to have distress, neurasthenia (weakness), and lack of self-esteem and self-confidence (Lachar, 1974).

3. They usually anticipate problems before they occur and over react to minor stress. Somatic problems are typically seen (Graham, 1977).

4. A person with this elevation usually has been an achiever in the past and, with lower **2-7** elevations, may be an achiever still. Generally, the person has been successful in his/her field. Then something goes wrong and the person reverts to child-like behavior and cannot do anything. This is especially true when scale **3** also is elevated (Caldwell, 1972).

5. This codetype reflects acute distress. More severe deterioration is shown by an accompanying rise on scale **8** (Trimboli & Kilgore, 1983).

6. Suicidal preoccupation may be present with these people (check MMPI item 339 or MMPI-2 items 150, 506, 520, and 524). The possibility of suicide is greater when the person does not act depressed than when he/she appears deeply depressed (Good & Brantner, 1961).

7. This person is usually a good candidate for psychotherapy, because he/she is hurting so much. However, with extreme elevations, the agitation and worry may be so excessive that the person cannot sit still for therapy (Carson, 1969). Consequently, these people may need medication to quiet them so that they can participate in therapy.

8. Greene (1991) has found that it may be possible to look at the third highest clinical scale to refine the interpretation given for the **2-7** codetype. He has found three codetypes that are useful—the **2-7-3/7-2-3,** the **2-7-4/7-2-4,** and the **2-7-8/7-2-8.**

9. Marks et al. (1974) found the **2-7** pattern in a university hospital and outpatient clinic. These people tended to be seen as depressed and anxious. They also tended to be perfectionistic and compulsively meticulous. Because they felt they must live up to their own high expectations, they tended to be self-punishing and felt hopeless. The

Marks, Seeman, and Haller book should be consulted for further information concerning this profile.

10. Gilberstadt and Duker (1965) found the **2-7-(3)** pattern in a VA hospital, male population. The **3** scale elevation is above 70, but it is not necessarily the next highest scale in the profile. A man with this pattern was usually a chronically anxious, ambitious person. When he was unable to tolerate stress, he tended to become depressed, self-deprecating, inadequate, and clinging.

11. Gynther, Altman, and Warbin (1973c) and Gynther, Altman, and Sletten (1973) have found psychiatric inpatients with the **2-7/7-2** pattern to have more suicidal thoughts and feelings of worthlessness than patients in general. When patients had the **2-7** pattern, they had a "loss of interest" as well. They were less evasive, unrealistic, angry, hostile, deluded, and antisocial than patients in general. These researchers found this code pattern to be quite similar to the **2-7-8** pattern and questioned the need for a separate three-point codetype.

12. Adolescents in treatment with the **2-7/7-2** pattern (Marks et al., 1974) were tearful, restless, nervous, and anxious. They also were depressed, passive, and nonassertive. The Marks, Seeman, and Haller book should be consulted for further information concerning this profile.

13. Kelley and King (1980) found the **2-7/7-2** profile code in a college client population; however, too few females were found to analyze. Males had many neurotic features typical of an obsessive-compulsive individual, such as perfectionism, rumination, and meticulousness.

14. These people tend to have test anxiety in college with obsessive thinking and rigidity. They also are introverted, dependent, self-conscious, or insecure. They have conflicts at home usually with their mothers or siblings. They also tend to be nonverbal (Drake & Oetting, 1959).

`2-7-3/7-2-3` See also the **2-7** pattern, point 4, p. 125.

1. Greene (1991) reported that individuals with this codetype are likely to be docile, passive individuals who are most comfortable in very dependent interpersonal relationships. Additional information regarding this codetype is available in Greene's book.

`2-7-3-1`

1. These people may be socially dependent, but they are not typically a member of any group (Caldwell, 1972).

2. They tend to have much self-pity and self-blame (Caldwell, 1972).

`2-7-4`

1. Greene (1991) has found that individuals with the **2-7-4/7-2-4** codetype are likely to be chronically depressed with feelings of inadequacy and guilt. Additional information regarding this codetype is available in Greene's book.

2. Gilberstadt and Duker (1965) found the **2-7-4-(3)** pattern in a VA hospital male population. The **3** scale is elevated above 70, but it is not necessarily the next highest scale after the **4** scale. A patient with this profile tended to be a hostile, passive-aggressive, anxious, immature person who also had feelings of inferiority. Chronic alcoholism also was found with this pattern. The alcoholism tended to be associated with the anxiety and tension.

3. Marks et al. (1974) found this **2-7-4/2-4-7/4-7-2** pattern in a university hospital and outpatient clinic. People with this pattern tended to be depressed and have many worries. They were usually described as passive aggressive, generally tearful, full of fear, nervous, and irritable. The Marks, Seeman, and Haller book should be consulted for further details concerning this profile.

4. If a person with this codetype is an alcoholic and stops drinking and then his/her life situations gets better, the person may become depressed and revert back to alcohol (Caldwell, 1972).

5. A man with this profile may have been a mama's boy, and his mother always came to his rescue. He often marries a woman similar to his mother, and if the wife also tries to rescue her husband and is unsuccessful, she may become sick (Caldwell, 1972).

6. Women with this profile tend to be daddy's girls. They may have long affairs with married men. They may have problems because of poor relationships with others and want to be rescued (Caldwell, 1972).

7. This was the MMPI codetype of a group of 20 agoraphobics who had current panic attacks (Brown, Munjack, & McDowell, 1989). Twenty agoraphobics who did not have current panic attacks had much lower MMPI profiles with only the **2** scale in the elevated range.

8. A group of females who reported general difficulties with eating had elevations on these scales (Anderson & Meshot, 1992). They also complained about anxiety and depression.

9. Females with this combination and a low **5** scale tend to show the same behavior as men with the **2-7-5-(4)** pattern.

## 2-7-5-(4)

1. In this pattern the **4** scale is elevated above 70, but it is not necessarily the next highest scale after **5**. Males with this combination usually try to look weak and submissive (Carson, 1969).

   a. They are self-effacing and try not to show any strength.

b. They seem to ask others to act superior to them and are usually most comfortable when others act this way toward them.

2. Males with this combination tend to be ambivalent and have a sense of failure (Caldwell, 1972).

$\boxed{\textbf{2-7-8}}$ See also the **2-7** pattern, point 8, p. 125.

1. This is one of the most frequent profile patterns found in a psychiatric population. Long-standing distress and obsessional features are likely to exist (Lachar, 1974).

2. Greene (1991) has found that individuals with the **2-7-8/7-2-8** codetype are likely to have multiple symptoms such as depression, nervousness, and obsessions. They typically complain of difficulty in thinking and concentrating. They also may have suicidal ruminations. Items 150, 506, 520, and 524 on the MMPI-2 need to be checked to see if they have been endorsed by the individual. Further information regarding this profile type can be found in Greene's book (1991).

3. Gilberstadt and Duker (1965) found this **2-7-8-(4-0-1-3-5-6)** pattern in a VA hospital male population. Scales **4, 0, 1, 3, 5,** and **6** are elevated above a T of 70, but they are not necessarily the next highest scales in the profile after **2, 7,** and **8.** A man with this pattern tended to be depressed, shy, quiet, withdrawn, and anxious. He usually felt inadequate in all areas of his life. He may have had bizarre thinking and flat affect.

4. Marks et al. (1974) found this **2-7-8/8-7-2** pattern in a university hospital and outpatient clinic. A person with this pattern was typically described as tense, anxious, and depressed with confused thinking and much self-doubt. The Marks, Seeman, and Haller book should be consulted for further information concerning this pattern.

5. This codetype was one of six MMPI codetypes found in a VA inpatient population of alcoholic males (Alfano et al., 1987). The **4, 0,** and **6** scales also were elevated but to a lesser extent than the **2, 7,** and **8** scales. Alfano et al. (1987) labeled these individuals the "bright unrealistic" patients. These men averaged much higher on their verbal and abstract IQs than the alcoholic group in general. They also tended to be much younger than the other patients. Individuals with this profile tended to have a high degree of chronic subjective distress—low energy, depression with a great deal of obsessiveness, fear, tension, and anxiety. There tended to be a high degree of psychosocial incapacity. This was a group of younger, less deteriorated alcoholics.

6. Kelley and King (1979b) found the **2-7-8/7-2-8** profile in a college mental health clinic. Only males reported difficulty concentrating. They also tended to complain of affective or eating problems. Females with this profile type had many neurotic symptoms. They were tense, nervous, and had respiratory somatic complaints. They also had crying spells, appetite and weight loss, sleep disturbance, fatigue, and feelings of inferiority.

7. In a study of 106 college students who had elevations on these three scales (Balogh, Merritt, Lennington, Fine, & Wood, 1993), those students with the **2** scale as the highest of the three scales seemed to have schizotypal features including distorted thinking, paranoid ideation, and social impairment. These authors believe that the **2-7-8** profile when the **2** or **8** scales are the highest is promising as an index of schizotypy. When the **7** scale was the highest in the profile, schizotypal features were not found.

## 2-7-8-(0)

1. In this codetype, the **0** scale is elevated, but it is not necessarily the next highest scale after **8.** For people with

this pattern, there usually are chronic depression, introversion, and shyness (Caldwell, 1972).

2. Over a period of time, the psychomotor responses in these clients may slow up. These clients appear to have mood swings, but in reality they have been steadily slowing down with occasional bursts of energy (Caldwell, 1972).

3. He/she usually is negative concerning his/her achievements. A person with this profile is a problem in therapy because he/she tends to intellectualize endlessly (Caldwell, 1972).

4. A person with this profile may report incidents of teasing in early childhood. This person may feel that he/she is the inferior member in the family (Caldwell, 1972).

## 2-8

1. Greene (1991) has indicated that there may be different interpretations for this codetype, depending upon whether the **2** scale is the highest or the **8** scale is the highest. When the **2** scale is the highest, individuals are experiencing depression with anxiety. They should be evaluated to see if a thought disorder is also present. When the **8** scale is the highest, individuals are much more likely to have a thought disorder and also depression. Bizarre somatic symptoms may be seen.

2. A person with this profile tends to be withdrawn because of feelings of worthlessness. He/she tends to have severe depression with anxiety and agitation and a fear of loss of control (Lachar, 1974). The individual is usually confused and may have difficulty concentrating.

3. He/she tends to be agitated, tense, and inefficient. Such persons are likely to say they are physically ill and have symptoms such as dizziness, blackouts, nausea, and vomiting (Graham, 1977).

4.  Usually a history of repeated hurts in childhood exists. The person now fears being hurt more and therefore runs from closeness (Caldwell, 1972).

5.  Caldwell (1985) has found that if the **4** scale is not significantly elevated, psychotropic medicines work well with these people. If the **4** scale is also elevated, people do not respond well.

6.  If both scales are highly elevated, this codetype may indicate serious pathology.

7.  Marks et al. (1974) found the **2-8/8-2** pattern in a university hospital and outpatient clinic. People with this pattern were usually anxious, depressed, and tearful. They tended to keep people at a distance and were afraid of emotional involvement. They tended to fear loss of control and reported periods of dizziness and forgetfulness. The Marks, Seeman, and Haller book should be consulted for further information concerning this profile.

8.  Gynther, Altman, and Sletten (1973) and Gynther, Altman, Warbin, and Sletten (1972) found that psychiatric inpatients with this **2-8/8-2** pattern showed symptoms of depression such as suicidal thoughts or attempts. The suicidal ideation may be in the form of a specific plan. For this codetype, different diagnostic implications are associated with the **2-8** and the **8-2** codes.

    a.  With a **2-8** profile, somatic delusions may be present.

    b.  For the **8-2** profile, one or more symptoms of schizophrenia, i.e., hallucinations or delusions of persecution, may be present.

9.  Adolescents in treatment with the **2-8/8-2** pattern (Marks et al., 1974) were referred to therapy because of being emotionally inappropriate. They were nervous, anxious, and timid. They appeared fearful of emotional involvement and had inner conflicts about sexuality and emotional dependency. Almost one-half of these adolescents had

made suicide attempts. They were frequent truants. The Marks, Seeman, and Haller book should be consulted for further information concerning this profile.

10. Kelley and King (1980) found the **2-8/8-2** profile in a college client population. These people had disruptive thoughts and social withdrawal. They tended to be diagnosed as schizophrenic. Females had more affective features and were diagnosed schizoaffective. They also abused many types of drugs. Males were more flat and apathetic and had more somatic symptoms and motor peculiarities such as tics.

11. Palmer, Lambert, and Richards (1991), in their study of 214 women with PMS, found three profile types, two of which were elevated on these two scales. The first type also had elevations of the **3, 4, 6, 7,** and **0** scales when they were experiencing PMS but within normal limits profiles when they were not experiencing PMS.

   The second profile type was less elevated on these two scales and had no other clinical scales significantly elevated.

## 2-8-1-3

1. People with this profile tend to have somatic complaints, chronic tension, and dramatic tremors. They may have intellectual confusion (Caldwell, 1972).

2. They may attempt to promote rescue by their therapists but will back off when the therapists try to help them. This type of person often sets the therapist up with the result that the therapist gets angry at him/her (Caldwell, 1972).

3. If these people are older than 40, they may complain of having thinking and recall problems. They may show organic deficits in testing, but they are not really as bad as the tests indicate. Their slowness causes the low scores on these tests (Caldwell, 1972).

1. Kelley and King (1980) found the **2-8-7/8-2-7** profile group in a college client population had suicidal ideation. In addition, males had disruptive and tangential thought processes, inappropriate affect, and were disoriented, all suggestive of psychosis. However, they did not display overt psychotic symptoms. They were depressed, had difficulty in concentration, and loss of interest. Females were seen as neurotic. They had difficulty concentrating and had made suicide attempts. They had no thought disorder but had derealization, la belle indifference, perfectionism, and alcohol abuse. Thus, men and women with this profile were quite different.

| 2-9 | See also the **9-2** codetype, p. 276.

1. A person with this codetype may show agitated depression with the depression sometimes masked by activity.

   The person with the **2-9** codetype is different from the person with the **2-7** codetype in that less obsessive thinking and rigidity is seen, and more motor activity is evident.

2. A feeling of pressure for the client without euphoria and grandiosity may be observed in people with high **2** and **9** scale scores. This pressure usually alternates with fatigue. The prognosis is good for these people (Caldwell, 1972).

3. Graham (1977) has hypothesized that this code may be found primarily for people who have feelings of inadequacy and worthlessness but are trying to deny them.

4. This person, when a child, may have had to be emotional to get attention (Caldwell, 1974).

5. Heavy drinking may be present for men with this pattern.

6. This codetype was found in drug abusers who attempted suicide but was not found for drug abusers who did not attempt suicide (Craig & Olson, 1990).

7. This profile when seen in older people may indicate a brain lesion or deterioration (Lachar, 1974).

8. Aggressive and antagonistic behavior is found in college counselees with this pattern. They also tend to rationalize a great deal (Drake & Oetting, 1959).

2-0 | See also the **0-2** codetype, p. 288.

1. This codetype may indicate a socially withdrawn and introverted person with a mild but chronic and characterological depression. This depression may be related to poor human relations and inadequate social skills. He/she tends to be inhibited, shy, and timid (Webb, McNamara, & Rogers, 1981).

2. Tanner (1990b) found 19 cases of this codetype in a psychiatric clinic. Three-quarters of these patients were female and single. They typically were depressed and dissatisfied with themselves as well as uncomfortable in social situations.

   a. These patients were insecure and had obsessive ruminations, complaints of memory deficits, and poor concentration. Despite these problems, these patients typically had good employment histories.

   b. The most frequent diagnoses were depression and inadequate or schizoid personality disorder. These patients showed little improvement over time.

3. VA males with this codetypes were found to be socially insecure and withdrawn. They were unhappy, tense, lacked effective social skills, and tended to have insomnia (Hovey & Lewis, 1967).

4. Adolescents in treatment with the **2-0/0-2** pattern (Marks et al., 1974) were nervous and anxious, listless, apathetic, shy, and overly sensitive. They had few friends, and they did not enjoy social gatherings. They felt inferior and were viewed by their therapists as schizoid. The Marks, Seeman, and Haller book should be consulted for further information concerning this profile.

5. This codetype occurs more frequently on the MMPI-A than it did on the original MMPI (Archer, 1992).

6. College students with this profile codetype frequently seek counseling (especially men). They are unhappy, introverted, and lack social skills.

7. Clients in a university counseling center who had these profile elevations were more likely to remain in therapy 13 sessions or more than clients with lower scores on these two scales (Elliott, Anderson, & Adams, 1987).

8. Kelley and King (1979a) have found college clients with the **2-0/0-2** profile tended to have academic problems and an inability to choose a career. They were described as indecisive by counselors.

**3-2-1** See p. 150.

**4-6-2** See p. 183.

**4-7-2** See p. 185.

**4-8-2** See p. 188.

**4-8-9-2** See the **4-8-9** codetype, point 4, p. 189.

**6-4-2** See p. 221.

**8-1-2-3** See p. 254.

**8-2-4** See p. 255.

**8-4-2** See the **8-2-4** pattern, point **1**, p. 255.

# SUMMARY OF 2 SCALE INTERPRETATIONS

| T-score MMPI-2 | MMPI | Interpretations |
|---|---|---|
| <40 | <45 | These people are cheerful, optimistic, and outgoing. |
| 40-60 | 45-60 | The majority of people score in this range. |
| 60-65* | 60-70* | With this range of scores, a mild dissatisfaction with life may be present, or a long-term situation exists with which the person has learned to live. The person with a **2** scale in this range may not be aware of the dissatisfaction until questioned about it. |
| 65-75** | 70-80** | At this level, usually a general sadness either about life or the world exists. This sadness tends to be situationally specific or temporary in nature. If the person is feeling guilty or self-deprecating, the **Es** scale will be below 45 T-score points. |
| 75-85** | 80-90** | At this level, gloom is usually the theme. Not much exists about which to feel good. If the person is feeling guilty or self-deprecating, the **Es** scale will be below 45 T-score points. |
| >85** | >90** | An all-evasive pessimism is present. Nothing is positive in the person's world. All is dark. If the person is feeling guilty or self-deprecating, the **Es** scale will be below 45 T-score points. |

*This interpretation applies only when there are no marked elevations on the clinical scales.

**This interpretation applies mainly when this is the highest scale or part of a two-point code.

# HARRIS AND LINGOES SUBSCALES FOR SCALE 2

| Subscales | Interpretation |
|---|---|
| D1 Subjective Depression (32 items) | This person is pessimistic and complains about lack of motivation and energy to cope with problems. |
| D2 Psychomotor Retardation (14 items) | He/she is lethargic and lacks energy. |
| D3 Physical Malfunctioning (11 items) | This individual complains about physical problems that typically accompany depression. |
| D4 Mental Dullness (15 items) | This person feels incapable of processing information as he/she used to do. |
| D5 Brooding (10 items) | He/she ruminates about his/her problems. |

# SCALE 3

## (Hy, Hysteria Scale)

Scale **3** has not been affected as much as some others by the conversion of the MMPI to the MMPI-2; however MMPI-2 T-scores will be higher for comparable raw scores at the higher ranges of the scale (T = > 80 for women and > 90 for men) (Strassberg, 1991). (See Tables 3.1 and 3.2, pp. 42-43.) Dahlstrom (1992) has found that this is one of five clinical scales that appear as first or second high points more frequently when MMPIs were rescored using MMPI-2 norms. (Scales **1, 6, 7,** and **0** were the other scales similarly affected.) He also found that the single largest increase in codetype when these MMPIs were rescored occurred for the **1-3/3-1** code, from 28 profiles (2.5%) using the MMPI norms to 61 profiles (5.4%) using the MMPI-2 norms. (See Tables 4.1 and 4.2, pp. 86-87.)

Given these findings, we suggest that you use caution in interpreting MMPI-2 profiles in which the **3** scale is either the highest clinical scale elevation or the second highest elevation. The information derived from studies done with **3** scale elevations on the original MMPI may not always be appropriate for similar elevations on the MMPI-2. Since this scale is one that is frequently elevated for chronic pain patients or other individuals who are being seen for medically related problems, only those studies that have specifically used the MMPI-2 to derive their data should be relied upon. An alternate approach is to rescore the test using the MMPI-2 raw scores on the original MMPI profile. This profile then could be used with the research that has been generated using the original MMPI.

One way many people avoid facing difficulty and conflict is to deny such situations exist. Scale **3** measures the amount and type of such denial. This characteristic tends to be a way of life and may be so ingrained that the person is not even aware that such a defense mechanism is being utilized. These people are extremely difficult in therapy, because they may adamantly refuse to recognize obvious realities.

Interpretation of scale **3** is a bit complicated and involves at lease three steps. First, evaluate the elevation of scale **3** itself to determine what information it gives about the client. A low scale **3** score (<45 MMPI, <40 MMPI-2) indicates a person who tends to face reality head-on in a tough, realistic manner. He/she may be caustic and questioning and believes that people in general see others in a too trusting and optimistic way. Scores in the moderate range—45 to 60, MMPI; 40 to 60, MMPI-2—are not interpreted. As the scale elevates above the moderate range, the person tends to "think positively" and to prefer not to think about unpleasant things. Above a T of 65 (MMPI-2) or 70 (MMPI), the person is probably not able to see unpleasantness and "bad things" (except as qualified in the next paragraph). In addition, people with elevated scale **3** scores are usually very social but quite shallow in their relationships. Women tend to have a sensuous, flirtatious quality about them.

Second, the actual areas of denial can be determined by comparing the elevation of scale **3** with the elevations on the other clinical scales. Generally, symptoms indicated by scales with scores above scale **3** are seen and acknowledged by the client, while those indicated by scales with elevations below scale **3** are denied or not seen. For example, if scale **3** is at T of 80, scales **2** and **8** at a T of 90, and scales **4** and **7** at a T of 70, the person usually is aware of being depressed (scale **2**) and confused (scale **8**) but probably will deny or not see the fighting (scale **4**) and agitation or anxiety (scale **7**) shown by the two scales lower than scale **3.**

Third, if the elevation on this scale is > 70 on the MMPI or > 65 on the MMPI-2, it should be compared with scales **1** and **2** (see the Triad Profiles). These other two scales influence the interpretation of scale **3** and therefore also have to be considered. Figures 4.1 through 4.5 are illustrations of the Triad Profiles, pp. 158-162.

Kunce and Anderson (1976, 1984) have hypothesized that expression is the underlying dimension on this scale. Individuals with moderate elevations where a positive interpretation is called for are emotional, sensitive, generous, affectionate, optimistic, and friendly. People who work with this person are likely to find him/her enthusiastic, enterprising, and clever. This individual likes to have things pleasant and cheerful. Stress may turn these virtues into psychomatic reactions or denial.

When the **3** scale is moderately elevated with the **2** scale, individuals are ambitious, conscientious and take their responsibilities seriously. With a moderately elevated **4** scale, they may have some assertiveness/anger, but their ability to inhibit and control are good. Finally, a moderately elevated **9** scale gives the individual a flare for the dramatic and an openness with others.

Scale **3** is more typically elevated on women's profiles than it is on men's. The behavior measured by scale **3** is much more likely to be considered "good" behavior for women than it is for men, because the person tends to be passive and agreeable even though not quite accurately seeing other people's behavior or her own.

In college populations, a clinically elevated scale **3** is rare, but moderate elevations (60 to 70, MMPI, or 60 to 65, MMPI-2) for women are seen more frequently.

## GENERAL INFORMATION

1. This scale consists of 60 questions that are divided into two different categories, one centering around bodily problems and one rejecting the possibility that the person is in any way maladjusted or has problems.

2. For most people who take the inventory, these categories tend to be mutually exclusive. However, for some people who have elevated scale **3** scores, the categories do fit together so that these people acknowledge many physical problems but deny that they are worried about them.

3. Harris and Lingoes (1955) have subjectively divided the **3** scale into 5 subscales: denial of social anxiety, need for affection and reinforcement from others, lassitude-malaise, somatic complaints, and inhibition of aggression. The interpretations for these subscales are shown on p. 157.

4. Keller and Butcher (1991) have suggested that the relative elevations of scales **1, 2,** and **3** on the MMPI-2 not be interpreted too rigidly since the **2** scale will be lower relative to the other scales compared to profile results obtained from the original MMPI.

5. When scale **3** is moderately elevated, a denial of problems (a "Pollyanna" attitude) may be all that is seen. When scale **3** becomes markedly elevated, however, physical complaints and denial become more prominent.

6. People with even moderate elevations on this scale, if this is one of the highest on the profile, tend to inhibit direct expression of anger (Trimboli & Kilgore, 1983).

7. McGrath and O'Malley (1986) have found that the best indicator of denial of psychological factors associated with a physiological disorder is an elevation on this scale with simultaneous elevations on scales **K** and **1.** They found it unwarranted to suggest the presence of hysteroid features in a person on the basis of an elevated **3** scale alone.

8. Caldwell (1974, 1985) has hypothesized that a profound fear of emotional pain may exist with these people. To be rejected by or to lose a loved one is painful, and these people have a high incidence of such loss of love in childhood. The only way to deal with the pain is to shift attention away from it and deny that it exists.

9. Women with an elevated scale **3** (70 or above) tend to have an underlying sensuality and sexuality that become more obvious and denied as the scale is elevated and the scale **5** scores become lower (45 or below).

10. This is considered a character scale (Trimboli & Kilgore, 1983).

11. A large sex difference exists in respect to the frequency of scale **3** peaks. For women, scale **3** elevations are common; however, for men such peaks are unusual (Dahlstrom et al., 1972).

   Yet in a recent study of a normal population, the men's mean score was 57 on this scale (Colligan et al., 1984).

12. Test-retest reliabilities for this scale on the MMPI-2 are .72 for men and .76 for women (Butcher et al., 1989).

13. In a study (Wilson, 1980) comparing the subtle and obvious items of this scale (Weiner, 1948), the obvious items were more predictive than the subtle ones.

14. Hibbs et al. (1979) have found the **3** scale to be higher for both younger and older subjects, perhaps reflecting heightened sensitivity to physiological processes for the adolescent and preoccupation with physical vulnerability for the older subjects.

15. Schenkenberg et al. (1984) also have found that older people from a psychiatric population score higher on scale **3**.

## HIGH SCORES

### Moderate Elevations

(T = 60 through 65, MMPI-2)
(T = 60 through 70, MMPI)

1. People with moderate elevations on scale **3** tend to be optimists and to think positively about people.

2. Kunce and Anderson (1976) have hypothesized that when this scale is in the moderate range (and there are no

other elevated clinical scales except perhaps the **5** scale for men), it may measure being in touch with one's positive emotions and an ability to show these emotions readily.

## Marked Elevations

(T = 65 or above, MMPI-2)
(T = 70 above, MMPI)

The behaviors mentioned for this elevation are most clearly seen when the scale is the highest of the clinical scales for the profile.

1. People with elevations this high tend to have denial, suggestibility, and functional physical complaints. They also tend to be naive and self-centered. They are likely to be exhibitionistic, extroverted in their relations with others, and superficial. In addition, they tend to have a great lack of insight into their own and other's motivations and actions.

2. Elevations on the **3** scale may reflect the use of the defense mechanism of repression (Trimboli & Kilgore, 1983).

3. When a person has a high scale **3,** the individual is not likely to be diagnosed as psychotic, even when other clinical scales are high.

4. Elevations of **3** and **K,** when scales **F** and **8** are low, may indicate a constricted, over-conventional person (Lachar, 1974).

5. People with this elevation initially express enthusiasm about psychological treatment, because they have a strong need to be liked and accepted.

    a. However, they cannot stand questioning of their way of looking at the world.

    b. They can make inordinate demands of the counselor or therapist.

c.  They tend to want concrete solutions from the therapist while they resist developing insight into their problems.

d.  College males with this elevation tend to come in for only one interview. They want immediate solutions to their problems, and where these are not available, they leave.

6.  Gass (1992) has found 21 MMPI-2 items that reflect neurologic symptoms; 13 of them are on the **3** scale. These items are 10(F), 31(T), 45(F), 47(F), 141(F), 148(F), 152(F), 164(F), 172(T), 173(F), 175(T), 224(F), and 249(F). In a group of 110 patients with cerebrovascular disease (CVD), he found that, on an average, five of these items were endorsed, thereby raising this scale 9 T-score points. Scales **1, 2,** and **8** also are affected by the inclusion of these items.

Gass recommended scoring a CVD patient's MMPI-2 profile twice, once in the standard manner, and again after eliminating the pathologically endorsed CVD items. He felt that the adjusted MMPI-2 profile would give a more accurate estimate of the psychological functioning for this type of patient.

7.  Bowler et al. in two studies (1989, 1992) have found that the **3** scale can be significantly elevated by organic solvent toxicity. In addition, scales **1, 3, 7,** and **8** can be similarly affected.

8.  High scores on this scale were correlated with high ratings of pain by 72 chronic back pain patients (Kleinke & Spangler, 1988).

9.  College counselees with a scale **3** this high tend to present problems rooted in an unhappy home situation.

a.  The prominent pattern seen involves a father described as rejecting, to which women react with somatic complaints and men with rebellion or covert hostility.

b. Their specific worries are concerned with scholastic failure, difficulties with authority figures, and lack of acceptance by their social group.

10. The behavior seen in point 9b with college students also is seen in clinic populations with work failure substituting for scholastic failure.

11. With scale **0** low, male college counselees tend to show aggressiveness and generally extroverted behavior.

12. College women with this scale elevation are described by their peers in rather uncomplimentary terms such as irritable and having many physical complaints. However, they see themselves as trustful, alert, friendly, and loyal.

## LOW SCORES

(T = 40 or below, MMPI-2)
(T = 45 or below, MMPI)

1. People with these scores may be caustic, sarcastic, and socially isolated (Carson, 1972).

2. They tend to feel that life is hard and tough (Carson, 1972).

3. They may have narrow interests.

4. Men with low MMPI-2 scores on the **3** scale were likely to be seen as shy by their partners (Keiller & Graham, 1993).

## CODETYPES

All scales in the codetypes are at T-scores of 65 or above (MMPI-2) or 70 or above (MMPI) and are listed in order from the highest to the lowest peaks. Scales in the codetypes must be the highest ones on the profile. For all codetypes using scales **1, 2,** and **3,** see the Triad Profiles, p. 158.

**1-2-3** See p. 95.

**1-2-3-4** See p. 96.

**1-2-3-5** See p. 96.

**1-2-3-7** See p. 96.

**1-3-K** See p. 100.

**1-3-2** See p. 100.

**1-3-4** See p. 100.

**1-3-7** See p. 100.

**1-3-8** See p. 100.

**1-3-9** See p. 101.

**2-1-3** See the **2-3-1** codetype, point 3, p. 119.

**2-3-1** See p. 119.

**2-3-1-7** See p. 119.

**2-7-3** See p. 127.

**2-7-3-1** See p. 127.

**2-7-4-3** See the **2-7-4** codetype, point 2, p. 127.

**2-8-1-3** See p. 133.

1. People with this scale as their only high point are conventional people who emphasize their harmony with other people and are incredibly optimistic (Greene, 1991).

| 3-1 | See also the **1-3** codetype, p. 97; and the **3-1** Triad profile, p. 161.

1. In contrast to the **1-3** combination, people with a **3-1** pattern tend to have symptoms that are relatively specific and of a somewhat more episodic nature. They tend to have a long history of insecurity and immaturity. They also tend to develop physical symptoms when under stress.

2. Because people with a high scale **3** tend to deny that things are going badly, the whining and complaining about physical problems typically seen in persons with high scale **1** scores is modified when the **3** scale is higher than the **1** scale.

   People with this scale combination tend to try to charm people into taking care of them with their illnesses rather than coercing people as those with a **1-3** combination tend to do.

3. The lower the **2** scale, the more adapted the person has become to his/her problems and the more chronic it may be.

4. Marks et al. (1974) found this **3-1/1-3** pattern in a university hospital and outpatient clinic. This profile tended to be of a female. A woman with this profile usually had a somatic complaint. Her behavior could best be described as agitated, depressed, and confused, with periods of weakness, forgetfulness, and dizziness. The Marks, Seeman, and Haller book should be consulted for further information concerning this profile.

**3-1-K** See the **1-3-K** codetype, p. 100.

**3-2** See also the **2-3** codetype, p. 117; and the **3-2-1** Triad pattern, point 1a, p. 162.

1. Women with the **3-2** codetype tend to have a history of marital difficulties, but no divorces (Guthrie, 1949).

    a. They frequently are sexually frigid and not interested in sexual activity with their husbands.

    b. They tend to complain about the infidelity and drinking of their husbands.

    c. They tend to be conscientious and easily hurt by criticism.

2. Men with this pattern tend to be ambitious and conscientious (Dahlstrom et al., 1972; Guthrie, 1949).

    a. They may have much anxiety and show the physical effects of prolonged tension and worry. One of the main areas of concern for these men is their work.

    b. They may have stomach problems that could result in ulcers.

3. Internal medicine patients with this codetype tended to see the physician for only one visit. For those who did continue treatment, their physical symptoms did not change. Even though the **2** scale is elevated, little depression was evident. They seemed to be insightless, non-introspective people who were very resistant to psychotherapy (Guthrie, 1952).

**3-2-1** See also **3-2-1** Triad profile, point 1b, p. 162.

1. Patients with this pattern may have periodic hysterical attacks with palpitations, sweating, fear, and exhaustion (Lachar, 1974).

2. For a woman, this pattern tends to be a hysterectomy or gynecological complaint profile. Typically, she has had a lifelong history of ill health. Women with this pattern rarely date and usually are sexually inhibited. If they do marry, they may be sexually frigid (Caldwell, 1972).

3. Women with this profile may be quite involved with their parents in a symbiotic fashion. Frequently, these women report that their mother has physical problems about which the mother does not complain (Caldwell, 1972).

4. Marks et al. (1974) found this **3-2-1** pattern in a university hospital and outpatient clinic. The pattern usually was for a woman who was described as anxious, tense, depressed, and tearful with somatic complaints. These researchers also found a high probability of hysterectomy and gynecological complaints. The Marks, Seeman, and Haller book should be consulted for further information concerning this profile.

**3-4** See also the **4-3** codetype, p. 178.

1. Scale **4** shows the amount of aggressive or hostile feelings the person has, while scale **3** indicates the controls the person has available. In this **3-4** pattern, since scale **3** is higher than scale **4,** the aggressions and hostilities shown by the **4** scale would tend to be masked and only shown indirectly, most likely passive-aggressively, because of the denial and controls shown by the higher **3** scale.

2. These people tend to be very immature. They may satisfy their own aggressions and hostilities in an indirect manner by having friends who are acting out.

3. In a VA hospital, men with this combination tended to have many socially unacceptable impulses with a fairly effective inhibitory or suppressive control. They tended to be passive aggressive.

4. Adolescents in treatment (Marks et al., 1974) with the **3-4/4-3** pattern were referred for sleep difficulties and sometimes suicidal thoughts. They tended to resent their sisters. The majority were heavy drug users, and one-third had made suicide attempts. The Marks, Seeman, and Haller book should be consulted for further information concerning this pattern.

5. Archer (1992) reported adolescents with this codetype have somatic complaints and do not see themselves as emotionally distressed, yet they have problems with impulse control and histories of suicide attempts.

6. Internal medicine patients with this profile code and the **3-6** code tend to show some of the same behavior. They typically are women who have a superficial outlook on life and an inability to recognize the shortcomings of either themselves or their friends. In spite of this, the interpersonal relations of these women are tenuous, and many experience well-rationalized hostility toward their immediate family (Guthrie, 1952).

7. Kelley and King (1979a) found only female clients in a college counseling center with a **3-4/4-3** profile. They were coming to therapy for marital problems, particularly sexual difficulties. They were excitable and complained of hostile feelings and aggressive outbursts. They also had many physical complaints. These women tended to overcontrol their anger and express it in irrational outbursts of rage.

## 3-4-5

1. These men are typically immature and sexually inadequate. Exhibitionism, voyeurism, and a need for more than usual sexual stimulation are possible (Lachar, 1974).

1. Tanner (1990a) found 10 cases with **3-5/5-3** codetypes. Eight of the 10 were males. These clients tended to be very positive about their therapists until they were pushed to work in their sessions. They were described as manipulative, immature, and demanding by their therapists.

   The men had many physical complaints such as ulcers, low back pain, headaches, or impotency. They were typically unhappy with their jobs and had job connected disability claims.

   The most likely diagnoses given to clients with this profile configuration were personality disorder, conversion reaction, or hypochondriasis.

2. College-educated males with histrionic features might have this codetype (Greene, 1991).

3. Adolescents with this codetype are rare (N = 11), but when they were found (Marks et al., 1974), they were withdrawn and inhibited, overcontrolling their impulses. Forty-three percent were found to have weight problems. The Marks, Seeman, and Haller book should be consulted for further information.

4. Nelson and Marks (1985) found 23 individuals who participated in a career evaluation program with this MMPI codetype. These two scales were not necessarily above 70 T-score points but were above 60. These individuals described themselves as pleasant but hard-hearted. They considered themselves as straightforward but definitely not approachable by others.

**3-6** See the **6-3** codetype, p. 221.

1. This individual tends to deny his/her own hostilities, aggressions, and suspicions.

2.  He/she may be hard to get along with because the underlying hostility and egocentricity of this person are likely to be apparent the closer you get.

3.  When these two scales are elevated, the person's anger is usually easily seen by others, but the individual typically is unaware of it.

4.  A person with this pattern may tend to have deep and often unrecognized feelings of hostility toward family members. These feelings, when awareness of them exists, are unusually rationalized away.

5.  He/she may report moderate tension and anxiety, but these do not seem to be acute or incapacitating. The person may be mildly suspicious and resentful of others as well as self-centered (Graham, 1977).

6.  Adolescents in treatment with the **3-6/6-3** pattern (Marks et al., 1974) were referred for a variety of reasons. One-third had attempted suicide. They were suspicious, obsessional, and resentful. The Marks, Seeman, and Haller book should be consulted for further information concerning this pattern.

## 3-7

1.  Some chronic physical symptoms resulting from chronic anxiety are likely with these people.

2.  Women with this combination together with a low scale **0,** usually lack academic drive, are anxious, and have insomnia.

## 3-8

1.  These people complain of problems in thinking clearly.

2. Possibly they may have delusional thinking. They may have bizarre physical problems.

3. They may have much psychological turmoil and have difficulty making even minor decisions (Graham, 1977).

4. People with this combination may have brief, highly sexualized psychotic episodes, for which they are amnestic (Trimboli & Kilgore, 1983).

5. Marks et al. (1974) found this **8-3/3-8** pattern in a university hospital and outpatient clinic. This profile tended to be of a woman who was having difficulties thinking and concentrating. She usually was seen by others as apathetic, immature, and dependent. The Marks, Seeman, and Haller book should be consulted for further information concerning this profile.

6. College students with this pattern tend to be indecisive, confused, worrying, and report a lack of knowledge or information.

## 3-9

1. These people may be dramatic, superficially open, and highly visible in social situations.

2. They may have episodic attacks of acute distress (Dahlstrom et al., 1972).

3. The physical problems of this group may involve acute attacks (Greene, 1991). They may develop medically atypical or medically impossible symptoms that yield to superficial treatment.

4. Kelley and King (1979a) found the **3-9/9-3** profile code in a college counseling center. Female clients typically had come in because of difficulty with an instructor (to

whom some of them were sexually attracted). They were seen by their counselors as defensive and were diagnosed frequently as hysterical in spite of having depression and disturbed thought processes. These women seemed to be in acute distress precipitated by the interpersonal conflict with their instructors.

### 3-0

1. Greene (1991) reports that people with this rare codetype describe themselves as conventional and law abiding. They are very shy and socially reserved.

### 4-3-$\bar{5}$    See pp. 180.

### 8-1-2-3    See p. 254.

# SUMMARY OF 3 SCALE INTERPRETATIONS

| T-score | | Interpretations |
| MMPI-2 | MMPI | |
|---|---|---|
| <40 | <45 | These people tend to be caustic and tough. They may believe that others are too optimistic about life. Men with scores in this range on the MMPI-2 may be shy. |
| 40-59 | 45-59 | The majority of people score in this range. |
| 60-65* | 60-69* | These people tend to look on the "bright side" and are usually positive about people. They like others to feel good and are usually pleasant to be with. |
| >65** | >70** | Persons at this level tend to be naive, lack insight, and deny psychological difficulties. They also tend to be uninhibited and visible in social situations (particularly when there is a low **2** scale). There may be some irritability and somatic complaints (especially when scale **1** is also elevated). When people with this scale as one of their highest scales have their way of thinking questioned, the questioning usually meets with denial and hostility. If they are in counseling, although they may claim they are interested in working and say they need therapy, they are in fact usually looking for simplistic, didactic answers that do not require them to evaluate their emotions or actions realistically. If they are required to do this, they tend to terminate counseling prematurely. Women with this elevation tend to be sensual and flirtatious and prefer male therapists. |

\* This interpretation applies only when there are no marked elevations on the clinical scales.

\*\* This interpretation applies mainly when this is the highest scale or part of a two-point code.

## HARRIS AND LINGOES SUBSCALES
## FOR SCALE 3

| Subscales | Interpretation |
| --- | --- |
| Hy 1 Denial of social anxiety (6 items) | This individual is strongly denying problems with shyness or difficulty in social situations. |
| Hy 2 Need for affection (12 items) | He/she denies any critical attitudes towards others. He/she has strong needs for attention and/or affection. |
| Hy 3 Lassitude-Malaise (15 items) | This person reports symptoms of poor health such as tiredness, weakness and fatigue. |
| Hy 4 Somatic Complaints (17 items) | He/she has somatic complaints that seem to be due to repression and conversion of affect. |
| Hy 5 Inhibition of Aggression (7 items) | This individual denies hostile or aggressive feelings. |

# THE TRIAD PROFILES

Traditionally, scales **1, 2,** and **3** are called the "neurotic triad." However, we feel this choice of terms is unfortunate for many reasons, not the least of which is that these scales do not differentiate neurotics from other groups of people. Consequently, we prefer to call these scales "The Triad," which eliminates the negatively loaded and ambiguous adjective, "neurotic." Interpretations of some selected Triad patterns follow.

## 1-2-3

1. In this pattern, scale **1** must be higher than scale **2,** and scale **2** must be higher than scale **3.** This pattern is usually associated with males, and generally indicates a concern about physical problems. This concern is used frequently as a means of not facing emotional problems.

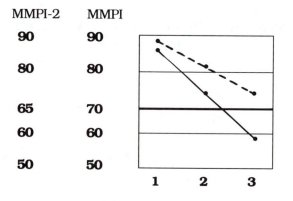

| MMPI-2 | MMPI |
|--------|------|
| **90** | **90** |
| **80** | **80** |
| **65** | **70** |
| **60** | **60** |
| **50** | **50** |
| **1** | **2** | **3** |

**Figure 4.1.** **1-2-3** triad profile.

a. At lower elevations (solid line) (scales **1** and **2** above 70 and scale **3** lower than 70), mental health clients tend to be irritable, to overevaluate minor dysfunctions, and to use physical complaints seemingly to avoid thinking about psychological problems. College counselees with such a profile are usually anxious, insecure in social situations, and have insomnia or headaches. (See also the **1-2** codetype, p. 94.)

b. A markedly elevated **1-2-3** profile (dashed lines) is called a "declining health" profile. A person with this pattern is usually over age 35 and feels "over the hill." (See also the **1-2-3** codetype, p. 95.) This pattern is common in VA populations, male welfare and social security disability claimants, and long-term alcoholics. Females rarely have this elevated pattern; however, those who do and who also have a low **5** scale tend to be masochistic.

## 1-3

1. This is one of two patterns known as the "conversion V" (see the **3-1** pattern for the other). For this pattern, scale **1** must be at least 5 T-score points greater than scale **3,** and the **2** scale must be at least 10 T-score points lower than the 1 and 3 scales. The general meaning of the **1-3** pattern is that persons with it convert psychological stress and difficulties into physical complaints. The wider the T-score spread between scale **2** and scales **1** and **3,** the more severe, long-standing, and resistant to change are the physical complaints as shown by the fact that the person is no longer depressed about them.

Caution must be used with the MMPI-2, however, since the **2** scale has been lowered significantly. See the general information section, scale **3,** p. 141.

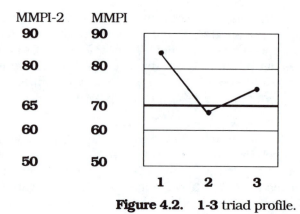

**Figure 4.2.** **1-3** triad profile.

a.  People with this profile tend to be somewhat pessimistic and complaining. They also may have gastrointestinal complaints. With this pattern, there may or may not be valid physical complaints. The interpretation is that the real or imagined complaints are used to avoid facing up to emotional difficulty. (See also the **1-3** codetype, p. 97.)

---

| **2-1-3/2-3-1** |

1.  These two patterns generally are considered to be interchangeable at the higher elevations. However, at the lower levels, each should be dealt with separately.

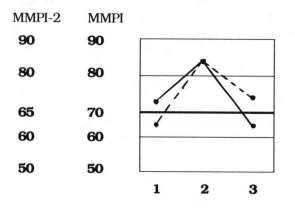

**Figure 4.3.** **2-1-3/2-3-1** triad profile.

a. Persons with marked elevations on all three scales tend to be anxious and depressed with long-standing physical problems and gastrointestinal difficulties. (See the **2-3-1** codetype, p. 119.)

b. When scales **1** and **2** are elevated but scale **3** is not (solid line), refer to the **1-2** profile, p. 94.

c. When scales **2** and **3** are elevated but scale **1** is not (dotted line), people usually are overcontrolled with bottled-up emotions. They frequently are fatigued, nervous, and filled with self-doubt, which prevents them from doing anything. Their difficulties are generally of long standing, and they frequently are described as inadequate and immature. (See also the **2-3** codetype, p. 117.)

---

| 3-1 |
|---|

1. This is one of the two patterns known as the "conversion V" (the other is the **1-3** pattern). Interpretation of this pattern is similar to the **1-3** pattern with some modifications. When the **3** scale is higher than the 1 scale, the person tends to be optimistic about his/her physical symptoms, instead of pessimistic about them as people with the **1-3** pattern are. These people play down their physical complaints, and they also deny that the physical complaints may have a psychological basis. Thus, they tend to be difficult in therapy. The physical complaints of this group in general are more specific and less global, in contrast to the **1-3** pattern. (See also the **3-1** codetype, p. 148.)

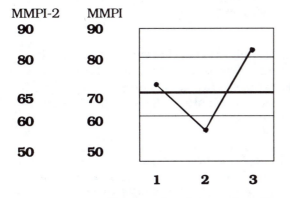

**Figure 4.4.** **3-1** triad profile.

1. The **3-2-1** slope in general is associated with females and is commonly called the "hysterectomy profile." As its name implies, females with such a pattern usually present gynecological complaints.

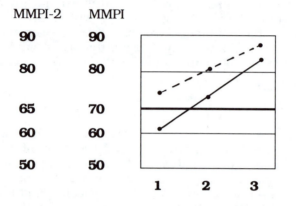

**Figure 4.5.** **3-2-1** triad profile.

a. At the lower levels (solid line), women may report marital difficulties such as frigidity, lack of sexual desire, and husbands with infidelity and drinking problems. (See the **3-2** codetype, p. 149.)

b. At the higher elevations (dashed line), a history of female operations is quite common. These women may be aversive to sex, have a life-long history of ill health, and may have symbiotic relationships. (See also the **3-2-1** codetype, p. 150.)

2. Males rarely have this profile. However, when they do, the scores are usually at the lower levels. Such men usually have physical problems as the result of prolonged stress and worry.

# SCALE 4

## (Pd, Psychopathic Deviate Scale)

Scale **4** is one of the clinical scales that has been lowered significantly on the MMPI-2. This is due to the transformation from linear T-scores to uniform T-scores and the use of the new normative group. The difference between the T-scores is as much as 10 T-score points for men and 8 T-score points for women at the 65 T-score level (Strassberg, 1991). (See Tables 3.1 and 3.2, pp. 42-43.) The lowering of T-scores for this scale means two-point codes involving the **4** scale are less likely for the MMPI-2 (Dahlstrom, 1992). See Tables 4.1 and 4.2, pp. 86-87, for a summary of the differences found for the codetypes of the MMPI-2 restandardization sample when their tests were scored using MMPI and MMPI-2 norms.

This lowering of scale **4** on the MMPI-2 means that those populations that typically generate high **4** profile codetypes are likely to have different profiles with the MMPI-2. Indeed Megargee (1993) has found this to be true for the classification system he developed for criminals using the MMPI. He has found that his original rules for classifying criminals according to their MMPIs are not applicable to the MMPI-2. He is now working on a new set of rules using the MMPI-2, which he believes will be superior to the old rules based upon the MMPI. A book with the results of his research in this area will be available in the near future.

Because of these differences on scale **4** for the MMPI-2 compared to the MMPI, we feel it is very important not to use research based upon MMPI studies for MMPI-2 profiles until it is proven to be applicable for the MMPI-2. Again we urge clinicians to transfer the MMPI-2 raw scores onto the original MMPI profile sheet and use the elevations from the MMPI profile to determine the codetype for the profile. This is especially important for those profiles where the **4** scale is in the 70 to 75 T-score range on the original MMPI. On the MMPI-2, this same raw score would be below the 65 T-score line and, therefore, would not be considered an elevation or interpreted when it would have been on the original

MMPI. If you are working with a population where diagnosing deviancy is an issue, you could be missing significant elevations if you relied solely upon MMPI-2 profiles combined with MMPI research data.

The key phrase for an elevation on this scale is "fighting something." The exact nature of the conflict and its appropriateness depends upon the target (parents, friends, spouse, society, or school), the amount of confusion connected with the fighting out (particularly as indicated by scale **8**), and the context in which it occurs. Thus, value judgments (for example, high **4** behavior is bad) are inappropriate to apply to elevations of this scale without some awareness of the person's situation. At the lower elevations of this scale, the fighting out may not be overt but rather a covert feeling that something or someone other than the client needs to be changed—"I'm right and you're wrong." Others with this elevation may be having situational stress such as marital problems, and a gradual decline in this scale is observable as the problem is resolved.

Kunce and Anderson (1976, 1984) have hypothesized an underlying dimension, assertiveness, for this scale. In individuals with good ego strength, a moderate elevation on scale **4** (60-70, MMPI; 60-65, MMPI-2) can reflect positive personality traits: enterprising, assertive, frank, and adventurous. These individuals adjust rapidly to new situations and show initiative and drive. A fair number of occupations have members who show moderate elevations on scale **4**; for example, authors, editors, commercial artists, athletic coaches, and physicians (Daniels & Hunter, 1949). When frustrated, these positives can turn to aggression and maladaptive social behavior.

Hovey and Lewis (1967) saw the positive traits of people with an elevated scale **4** as adventurousness, sociability, and energy. When coupled with a moderately high **3,** the individual has some socially unacceptable impulses but also fairly effective controls.

T-scores in the moderately elevated range are quite common in both mental health clinics and college counseling center populations. This range is more typically seen in men than in women, but both may have elevations in this range. This range of scores frequently is seen for college students concerned with peaceful societal change and persons in helping professions such as social work or psychology.

The permanence of a fighting-out pattern appears to be correlated with age. An elevated **4** is common with adolescents, particularly those in difficulty with family, school, or the law. In most cases, the **4** scale elevation disappears as the person becomes older. However, if the **4** scale is still in the marked elevation range by the age of 40, it usually is indicative of long-standing self-centered behavior. Fighting out at this age may be shown by marital problems, alcoholism, or difficult interpersonal relationships.

An interesting relationship exists between the **4** and **5** scales. When the **4** scale is clinically elevated and the **5** scale is within 15 T-score points for males or below 40 for females, then the fighting out shown by the **4** scale is tempered in such a way that the fighting tends to be more covert than overt.

Persons with a low scale **4** can be described as conventional and concerned with correct social appearances. They are basically non-fighters and prefer a quiet, uneventful life. This non-fighting may have come about because of one of three reasons:

1. The person may have been born with a very easygoing nature.

2. He/she at one time might have been a fighter but because this behavior was so painful or nonproductive, the person switched to being a non-fighter.

3. The person grew up in a family where fighting was the norm and he/she vowed not to have that kind of life.

As Carson (1972) has noted, these people may have a great capacity for tolerating a dull, boring life. One peculiarity noted by Meehl (1951) that we also have found in the mental health clinic and college counseling center populations is that persons with scale **4** scores in this range may be uninterested in sexual activity.

The **4** scale is frequently a high point for college student profiles and for people coming into mental health clinics who are in trouble with the law.

## GENERAL INFORMATION

1. The scale **4** consists of 50 items that concern social imperturbability and a lack of general social adjustment, such as family or authority problems and social alienation.

2. Harris and Lingoes (1955) have subjectively divided the **4** scale into four subscales, one of which is divided into two. The five subscales are familial discord, authority conflicts, social imperturbability, social alienation, and self-alienation. The interpretations of these subscales are shown on p. 195.

3. This scale may measure a continuum ranging from inhibited overconformity on the low end to rebellious, antisocial acting out of impulses on the high end (Lachar, 1974).

4. The major features of a person with a high **4** scale may be as follows:

    a. A tendency to see others as needing to change due to a belief that "I'm right and you're not."

    b. An emotional shallowness toward others that makes it difficult, if not impossible, to empathize with someone else's pain.

    c. An inability to profit from experiences, both good and bad (Dahlstrom et al., 1972).

d. A revolt against family and/or society (such as school, religion, or politics). If this is true, the **Re** scale will be below 50 T-score points. For the **Re** scale, see p. 346.

5. This scale tends to be stable over time and, therefore, most likely reflects a characteristic way of dealing with others. It may reflect a way of dealing with significant others that is maladaptive and, therefore, causes problems in relationships.

6. Caldwell (1985) has hypothesized that people with this scale as one of their highest have a fear of caring. They have come from a home where they felt no caring, and they have shut down their own caring as a defense against hurting.

7. Often the person with the **4** scale as the highest clinical scale above 70 goes undetected until he/she is in a situation demanding responsibility, loyalty, or an appreciation of social mores (Dahlstrom et al., 1972).

8. The older a person is with a high **4**, the less likely the scale will decline in elevation with time.

   a. At approximately age 40, this elevation on scale **4** most likely reflects long-standing self-centered behavior.

   b. At age 65 or above, this elevated score more likely reflects social alienation, apathy, absence of pleasure, and lack of involvement, rather than antisocial behavior (Good & Brantner, 1974).

9. The **4** scale is a frequent peak point for males and often appears in a variety of high point combinations on the MMPI. Other scales suppress (scale **5**) or activate (scale **9**) the behavior seen in scale **4.**

   a. When scales **1, 7,** or particularly **2** are high with scale **4,** the delinquency rate is reduced below the level expected for boys in general (Dahlstrom et al., 1972).

b. When scales **8** and **9** are high with scale **4,** the delinquency rate is greatly increased (Dahlstrom et al., 1972).

10. Gynther, Burkhart, and Hovanitz (1979) have found that the obvious items on this scale (Weiner, 1948) are better predictors than the subtle and neutral items. However, the subtle items make a small but unique contribution.

11. Snyder and Graham (1984) also have found that the obvious items are the most useful.

12. Scale **4** scores tend to be lower for older people in a nonpsychiatric population, perhaps reflecting fewer feelings of impulsivity and rebelliousness (Colligan et al., 1984).

13. Hibbs et al. (1979) have found the **4** scale to be higher for younger people.

14. Schenkenberg et al. (1984) also have found that younger people in a psychiatric population score higher on this scale than older people from this population.

15. High **4** scores tend to characterize Blacks more than Whites (Hokanson & Calden, 1960; Mitler, Wertz, & Counts, 1961).

16. Test-retest reliability is .81 for males and .79 for females (Butcher et al., 1989). Scale **4** tends to be subject to maturational changes as well as shifts because of psychological treatment.

17. Anderson and Holcomb (1983) found one of their 5 groups of murderers had an MMPI pattern with the highest scale **4** at 67. These murderers had the highest IQ and were the oldest of the five groups. They were more likely to kill a friend or relative. Sixty percent of the crimes they committed had a sexual element. Their profiles resembled Megargee and Bohn's (1979) Item group.

18. A study of 600 small-town police officers over a 13-year period by Bartol (1991) to find out which ones were likely

to be terminated for poor performance, produced an "immaturity index" made up of a combination of scales **4, 9,** and **L** raw scores. A cutoff score of 49 was a good predictor of termination. High **3** and **K** scores added to the accuracy of this measure.

19. The **4** scale is more prominent in profiles of husbands and wives in marriage counseling than in profiles of husbands and wives from the general population (Arnold, 1970; Ollendick, Otto, & Heider, 1983).

20. Two studies show that the **4** scale may be elevated when there is marital distress.

    a. Elevations on this scale and the Family Problems (**FAM**) content scale of the MMPI-2 were highly correlated with reported marital problems (Hjemboe & Butcher, 1991), but neither of these two scales identified a majority of the marital counselees studied. The authors felt that these two scales are most useful in identifying and describing particular types of marriage counselees rather than as general prediction indices.

    b. Snyder and Regts (1990) also have found the **4** scales to be highly correlated with marital distress. However, it also identified many happily married individuals and missed many highly distressed people.

    It is very important, therefore, to get corroborating data before assuming this scale diagnoses marital difficulty.

21. Closed head injured adults were grouped into recovery levels and it was found that nonrecovered subjects scored significantly higher on the **4** scale (Walker, Blankenship, Ditty, & Lynch, 1987).

22. In a study involving 101 college undergraduates, Lilienfeld (1991) found the **4** scale to be correlated with measures of negative emotionality and emotional maladjustment, which are hypothesized dimensions of psychopathy, but

the **4** scale was not highly correlated with measures of fearlessness, another hypothesized dimension of psychopathy. These results might indicate that the **4** scale is not an adequate measure of psychopathy. The **ASP** (Antisocial Practices) content subscale on the MMPI-2 may be a better measure of psychopathy since Lilienfeld found in his study that it correlated with both negative emotionality and fearlessness.

# HIGH SCORES

## Moderate Elevations

(T = 60 through 65, MMPI-2)

(T = +60 through 70, MMPI)

1. Kunce and Anderson (1976) have hypothesized that when this scale is in the moderate range and no other clinical scales are clinically elevated except perhaps the **5** scale for men, the **4** scale may measure a readiness to assert oneself and to express one's physical energy and drive. People scoring in this range may adjust rapidly to new situations and show initiative and drive.

2. For college students with the **4** scale in this range and good ego strength (**Es** above 50), the individual may be energetic, enterprising, venturesome, and social (Munley & Gilbert, 1965).

3. Marks et al. (1974) found that the mean score for this scale for their adolescent populations in counseling was a T of 68.

## Marked Elevations

(T = 65 or above, MMPI-2)

(T = 70 or above, MMPI)

The behaviors mentioned for this elevation are most clearly seen when the scale is the highest of the clinical scales.

1.  Elevations on this scale tend to reflect hostility toward social sanctions, authority figures, and a variety of parental surrogates. The focus of the anger is diffuse and well-rationalized (Dahlstrom et al., 1972).

2.  People with high scores on this scale are described by their mates as moody, irritable, unpleasant, resentful, and craving attention (Hjemboe & Butcher, 1991). Women with high scores are also described as easily upset, hostile, jealous, and difficult to get along with.

3.  This elevation often indicates a resentment for rules and regulations.

    Depending upon other high peaks, the resentment and asocial feelings may be shown many different ways. See the codetype section for further information.

4.  People with **4** scale elevations as the highest elevated clinical scale score tend to make good first impressions, but after longer acquaintance their unreliability and self-centeredness becomes apparent.

5.  Many people at this elevation seem unable to plan ahead. They tend to disregard the consequences of their actions and not profit by them.

6.  Elevations of this scale reflect heavy reliance on the defense mechanisms of externalization, acting-out, and rationalization or intellectualization (Trimboli & Kilgore, 1983).

7.  Some people in this range may be reacting to situational pressures that require them to act out against their own or others' morals; for example, getting a divorce. They may return to the nonclinical range for the scale when the situational pressure is gone.

8.  Therapy seems to be less effective in changing a person with a marked elevated **4** scale than is age. However, the higher the intelligence, the more likely a person with

a high **4** scale can be channeled by therapy into constructive pursuits by appealing to the person's self-interest. "You can get what you want by changing your behavior." The underlying self-interest is not changed however.

9.  A series of studies of sex offenders by Hall, Maiuro, Vitaliano, and Proctor (1986); Hall (1989); Hall, Graham, and Shepherd (1991); and Hall, Sheperd, and Mudrak (1992) has shown that the **4** scale is frequently elevated for these offenders.

    a.  In a study by Hall et al. (1986), men who had committed sex offenses against children typically had a generally disturbed MMPI profile with the **4** and **8** scales as the most frequent elevations. There were no significant relationships between codetype and incest/nonincest, rape/nonrape, or male/female victim.

    b.  In a later study involving 81 offenders who had sexually assaulted children, Hall (1989) found that 54% of the offenders had the **4** scale as one of their two highest scales. The author felt that the MMPI has little usefulness in differentiating types of sexual offenders but thought it was useful in describing their pathology and as an aid in treatment planning.

    c.  In yet another study, Hall et al. (1991) found two MMPI profile clusters for a group of sex offenders, one of which had the **4** scale as a prominent feature of the two-point code. These individuals were impulsive and antisocial with low frustration tolerance. In addition, they were poor therapy risks. These authors found that the age of the victim was not related to the personality characteristics of the offender as shown by the MMPI.

    d.  Hall et al. (1992), in a study contrasting child sexual and nonsexual offenders, found three profile clusters that did not differentiate on the basis of the crimes committed. Cluster 1 was a **4-9** profile, Cluster 2 was a **4-8/8-4** profile, and Cluster 3 had an elevated **8** scale.

10. Roman and Gerbing (1989), in a study of 340 male forensic state hospital patients, found seven MMPI cluster profiles. The **4** scale was the highest or second highest elevation in 32% of the profiles.

11. Walfish et al. have found in a series of studies (1990, 1991, 1992) involving cocaine addiction that the **4** scale is a typical elevation.

    a. Walfish, Massey, and Krone (1990) found significant elevations on the **4** and **9** scales in a group of 268 cocaine addicts who went into residential treatment for their addictions. They also had elevations on the **2, 6,** and **7** scales.

    b. Forty-two nurses under treatment for alcoholism or opiate addiction in a residential treatment unit had significant elevations on the **4** scale (Walfish, Stenmark, Shealy, & Krone, 1991).

    c. Walfish, Stenmark, Shealy, and Krone (1992) found, however, that for a group of 73 women in residential treatment for codependency, there was no prominent codetype. The one that was found most often, although only in 19% of the cases, was **4-8/8-4.** The next most likely codetype in 12% of the cases was **2-4/4-2.** These results suggest that there are many different types of codependents.

12. In a study of heroin addicts (Craig, 1984a), 44% of the cases had the **4** scale as one of the highest points. Twenty-one percent of the cases were **4-9/9-4,** 14% were **4/2-2/4,** and 9% were **4-8/8-4.**

13. In counseling centers, high **4** counselees may not show the classic amoral, asocial behavior, but the scale elevation may be an index of rebelliousness rather than an indication of acting out impulses (Mello & Guthrie, 1958). Typically these people also will have a low **Re** scale (see p. 346).

14. Huesmann, Lefkowitz, and Eron (1978) have proposed an MMPI measure of aggressive acting out that consists of adding the T-scores of the **F, 4,** and **9** scales. This composite was found to be useful in a college population for identifying individuals with higher self-ratings on a hostility inventory (Schill, Wang, & Thomsen, 1986). The composite did a better job of identifying these individuals than considering elevations on the **4** and **9** scales separately or the two scales together.

15. Female medical patients with this elevation may have recurrent marital difficulties and illegitimate pregnancies. Their medical symptoms tend to be mild in nature and overshadowed by their behavioral problems (Mello & Guthrie, 1958).

## LOW SCORES

(T = 40 or below, MMPI-2)

(T = 45 or below, MMPI)

1. People with these scores tend to be very conventional and may be concerned with social status. They may have a great capacity for a boring, routine life.

2. People with low scores on this scale on the MMPI-2 are likely to be pleasant and are unlikely to be resentful, angry, or having difficulties with others because of antisocial behavior (Keiller & Graham, 1993).

3. Low scores, especially with **3** scale elevations, may indicate repressed aggressive and assertive tendencies (Graham, 1977).

4. The low scores also may indicate people who have low sexual interest. The indication is particularly true when scale **4** is the low point of the profile (Meehl, 1951).

5. These scores tend to characterize older people (Canter, Day, Imboden, & Cluff, 1962; Swenson, 1961).

# CODETYPES

All scales in the codetypes are at a T-score or 65 or above (MMPI-2) or 70 or above (MMPI) and are listed in order from the highest to the lowest peaks. The scales in the codetype must be the highest clinical scales on the profile.

| 1-2-3-4 | See p. 96.

| 1-3-4 | See p. 100.

| 2-4-7 | See p. 122 and the **4-7-2** pattern, p. 185.

| 2-4-8 | See p. 122.

| 2-7-4 | See p. 127.

| 2-7-4-3 | See the **2-7-4** pattern, point 2, p. 127.

| 2-7-5-4 | See p. 128.

| 3-4-5 | See p. 151.

| Spike 4 |

1. Gilberstadt and Duker (1965) found a spike **4** pattern (only **4** scale elevated) in a male VA hospital population. A person with this pattern tended to be irresponsible, impulsive, egocentric, and emotionally unstable. He also tended to have a low frustration tolerance.

2. The spike **4** profile is one that frequently is found in criminal populations.

   a. Megargee and Bohn (1979) found a group of incarcerated criminals with a spike **4** pattern, which Megargee and Bohn labeled the Delta codetype. These criminals were hedonistic, amoral people with little ability to postpone gratification, but without the hostility and alienation found when the **8** scale also was elevated with the **4.** These individuals were typically charming, intelligent, and manipulative, with little anxiety and guilt regarding their asocial behavior. This group was one of the brightest of the ten groups that they found.

   b.   Anderson et al. (1979) found a spike **4** profile as one of three profiles in a group of sex offenders. (The other two profiles were **F-6-8** and **2-4**.) These men had the best preincarceration adjustment. They also had less severe adjustment problems on their units compared to the other sex offenders.

   c.   One of four MMPI cluster profiles found in a sample of incarcerated homicide offenders had an elevation on this scale (spike **4**) and a relatively low **0** scale (Kalichman, 1988). (The other profile clusters were a within-normal-limits profile, a **4-2** profile, and a **4-9** profile.) The spike **4** group typically knew their victims who were typically females. The author speculated that these offenders may be individuals who are most likely to be domestic homicide offenders. The profile is similar to the Delta codetype (Megargee & Bohn, 1979).

   d.   Hutton, Miner, and Langfeldt (1993) found a group of criminals in their forensic psychiatric population that closely resembled group Delta in their MMPI profiles. These individuals showed the greatest criminal versatility in their committing of offenses that ranged from rape and/or theft to drug violations. They also tended to have juvenile records. Their most frequent diagnosis was Antisocial Personality Disorder or Cluster B diagnosis.

3.   College students with a spike **4** profile were in academic and/or legal difficulties. They had a significantly higher rate of past crime than other students (King & Kelley, 1977a).

4-1 See the 1-4 codetype, p. 101.

4-2 See also the 2-4 codetype, p. 120.

1. People with the **4-2** codetype may seem to be depressed and feeling guilty, but they are not always very convincing or sincere in these feelings. The elevations on the **2** scale also may be because they are depressed about being "caught."

2. People with the **4-2** pattern say one thing, but their behavior is the opposite. For example, they may be self-condemning but act out continuously (Caldwell, 1972).

3. They tend to put their problems on other people so that other people will feel guilty (Caldwell, 1972).

4. When a person with an elevated **4** scale gives responses that indicate difficulty with parents and family, the usual interpretation is that the client, in fact, is the difficult one, and the family often has put up with considerable disruption from him/her. However, when the **2** scale is also elevated, the family may truly have been difficult in some way, such as one parent being alcoholic or emotionally explosive. The client's report may reflect a real situation rather than a psychopathic interpretation of reality.

5. One of four MMPI cluster profiles found in a sample of incarcerated homicide offenders had elevations on these two scales as well as a slight elevation on the **8** scale (Kalichman, 1988). (The other profiles were a within-normal-limits profile, a spike **4** profile, and a **4-9** profile.) These individuals tended to have violent behavior and substance abuse.

6. Several studies have found the mean profile of child molesters to be **4-2** (Erickson, Luxenberg, Walbek, & Seely, 1987; Panton, 1979). Erickson et al. (1987) found that

the child molesters in their sample of convicted sex offenders were almost exclusively extrafamilial offenders. They also had a **4-8** profile. Intrafamilial offenders most typically had **4-3/3-4** or **4-7/7-4** profiles. Erickson et al. cautioned, however, that their findings do not support any one MMPI profile as typical of a particular type of sex offender and, therefore, they felt that MMPI profiles should not be used to diagnose whether or not a person is a sex offender, but rather that they would be most useful for presentence evaluation and monitoring long-term treatment progress.

7. The **2-4/4-2** codetype occurred most frequently in four alcoholism treatment centers. It accounted for 12 to 21% of the profiles in any facility (Schroeder & Piercy, 1979).

8. In a recent study of heroin addicts (Craig, 1984a), 14% had the **4-2/2-4** profile. The only code with a higher percentage of cases was the **4-9/9-4** code.

9. Anderson and Bauer (1985) have found that college students with high **4-2** (and also elevated **7** and **8** scales) had

   a. poor relationships with the opposite sex,
   b. significantly more depression than other clients,
   c. low self-esteem,
   d. many problems with their families,
   e. rigid rules,
   f. dependency, and
   g. no improvement in therapy.

---

**4-3** See also the **3-4** codetype, p. 150, and the **4-3-5̄** combination, p. 180.

1. The elevation of scale **4** indicates the amount of aggressive or hostile feelings present, while the elevation of scale **3** indicates the repressive or suppressive controls available. Consequently, because scale **4** is higher than scale **3** in this codetype, the controls seen in scale **3** are not always adequate limits. Therefore, the person tends periodically to break out into violent behavior.

2. The relationship between scales **3** and **4** serves as an index of whether persons will control and inhibit their socially unacceptable impulses, particularly aggression and hostility (Greene, 1991). People with the **3** scale higher will show their hostile feelings indirectly, maybe even passive-aggressively, whereas people with the **4** scale higher will have poorly controlled anger and hostility that is expressed in a cyclic fashion.

   a. A life-long pattern may exist of overcontrol, a sudden explosive episode, and then quiet again for about two years until the next episode. The pattern has been found in males and females (Davis, 1971; Davis & Sines, 1971; Persons & Marks, 1971).

   b. Caldwell (1972) saw the **4-3** person as a socially correct role-player who periodically breaks out into antisocial behavior.

3. Gilberstadt and Duker (1965) found the **4-3** pattern in a VA hospital male population. A person with this pattern tended to be sensitive to rejection and had poorly controlled anger with temper outbursts. Suicide attempts and alcoholism occurred when this anger turned inward.

4. However, a more recent study (Gynther, Altman, & Warbin, 1973b) has failed to replicate the findings of antisocial and violent behavior for the **4-3** pattern.

5. Megargee and Bohn (1979) found a group of incarcerated criminals with this **4-3** combination (Group Easy). This pattern might have been produced by a fake good tendency. These criminals were the best adjusted and best controlled of the ten groups of prisoners that they had studied. These prisoners had a relatively easy time of it in the prison and the lowest recidivism rate.

6. Hutton, Miner, Blades, and Langfeldt (1992) found a group of offenders in a forensic psychiatric hospital that resembled Megargee and Bohn's (1979) Easy codetype. These individuals were older than the average patient and their most frequent committing offense was child molestation.

Their most common Axis II diagnoses were borderline, narcissistic, or histrionic personality disorder. These individuals had the lowest rate of physical aggression in the institution.

7. Erickson et al. (1987) found that while there was no MMPI profile that typically represented sex offenders, the **4-3/3-4** profile was the modal codetype for incestuous biological fathers in their population. (See also the study's findings for the **4-2** and **4-7** codetypes.)

---

**4-3-5̅** (**5** scale T = 45 or below)

1. This pattern may be found for a woman who is hostile and aggressive. She represses anger, but she is unable to prevent her feelings from being acted out. Consequently, she resorts to masochistic behavior, which is intended to provoke rage in others. She then can pity herself for being mistreated (Carson, 1969).

---

**4-5** See also the **5-4** codetype, p. 208.

1. Men with this pattern may be nonconforming but are not likely to act out in obviously delinquent ways. However, their low tolerance for frustration can lead to brief periods of problem behavior (Graham, 1977).

2. An elevation on scale **5** may act as a suppressor of the acting out behavior that usually would be seen from the high scale **4.**

3. Tanner (1990a) found 12 individuals with this rare codetype in a group of psychiatric patients; eleven of them were male. These individuals were usually single, divorced, or separated. They resented any demands placed upon them, while they wanted nurturance for themselves. A high incidence of polydrug abuse and a history of criminal arrests were likely if the **4** scale was higher than the **5** scale. Most of the individuals had good verbal skills and initially seemed to want therapy; however, they were

very likely to terminate early. The most frequent diagnoses of these patients were passive-aggressive or dependent personality.

4.  Adolescents in treatment with this **4-5/5-4** pattern (Marks et al., 1974) were seen by their therapists as in better shape than the typical adolescent patient. They had greater ego-resiliency, were adaptive, and were organized. They also tended to be heavy drug users. The Marks, Seeman, and Haller book should be consulted for further information concerning this profile type.

5.  Outpatient psychiatric males with **4-5** frequently had interpersonal problems, especially breaking up with a girlfriend (King & Kelley, 1977b).

6.  Male college students with this combination tend to have home conflicts, insomnia, restlessness, and worry (Drake & Oetting, 1959).

## 4-5-9

1.  For men with this pattern, the high **5** score may be an indication that the **4-9** behavior is suppressed. Therefore, the person may not be acting out directly.

    When the **4-5-9** pattern is present in a male college student, the underachievement, which may be seen with the **4-9** pattern, is not manifested. The **5** scale acts as a suppressor (Drake, 1962).

## 4-6   See also the **4-6-5** codetype, p. 183.

1.  These people may be hostile, resentful, and suspicious. People with this pattern tend to transfer blame for their problems onto others (Carson, 1969). They may be litigious and threaten to initiate law suits.

2. These two scales potentiate each other. These people typically have poor impulse control, explosiveness, and a propensity towards violence (Trimboli & Kilgore, 1983).

3. Seriously disruptive relationships with the opposite sex may exist, such as divorce (Dahlstrom et al., 1972).

4. These people tend to have poor work records (Dahlstrom et al., 1972; Guthrie, 1949).

5. Alcoholism or poor judgment may be associated with this pattern.

6. People with this pattern tend to convert everything into anger (Caldwell, 1974).

7. They may demand a great deal of attention for themselves but resent giving any to other people (Graham, 1977).

8. They tend to be poor risks for counseling (Carson, 1969).

9. Marks et al. (1974) found the **4-6/6-4** pattern in a university hospital and outpatient clinic. It tended to be found for females who were described as self-centered, hostile, tense, defensive, and irritable. They usually refused to admit their difficulties and, therefore, did not deal with them. They frequently used rationalization as a primary defense mechanism. The Marks, Seeman, and Haller book should be consulted for further information concerning this pattern.

10. In one study of women with this profile plus a low **5** scale (Walters & Solomon, 1982), the women were indecisive and demanding of love and attention.

11. Goldwater and Duffy (1990) found that 72% of the women in a psychiatric unit with this profile and a low **5** scale (at least 30 points below the **4** and **6** scales, or the Scarlet O'Hara V), had been sexually abused as a child, or had had an alcoholic caretaker. Only 19% of the women who had other profile codetypes had had an alcoholic caretaker, and none of them had been sexually abused. The authors

suggest that this codetype for women should lead to an investigation of possible sexual abuse.

12. VA hospital males with this profile tended to be socially maladjusted with women. They were confused, resentful, and evasive (Hovey & Lewis, 1967).

13. Adolescents in treatment with this **4-6/6-4** pattern (Marks et al., 1974) were referred because they were defiant, disobedient, tense, restless, and negative. Their relationships with their parents were poor. They demanded attention and undercontrolled their impulses. About one-half of the group were involved with drugs. The Marks, Seeman, and Haller book should be consulted for further information concerning this profile.

14. For college students with this profile, men tended to be aggressive and belligerent with conflicts with their fathers. Women were rebellious towards their homes, restless, and lacking skills with the opposite sex (Drake & Oetting, 1959).

## 4-6-2

1. Hostility and depression often form a cyclical pattern with this profile. The expressions of hostility often lead to guilt; then anger reoccurs because of resenting the guilt feelings (Lachar, 1974).

2. Marks et al. (1974) found the **4-6-2/6-4-2** pattern in a university hospital and outpatient clinic. The pattern was primarily found for females. A woman with this pattern tended to be acting out, depressed, critical, and skeptical. The Marks, Seeman, and Haller book should be consulted for further information concerning this profile.

## 4-6-5̄ See 4-6 point 10.

1. Wives who are in marriage counseling have a higher proportion of this profile pattern than do wives from the general population (Arnold, 1970; Ollendick et al., 1983).

## 4-6-8

1. A person with a **4-6-8** pattern may be brought in for help by someone else. He/she usually has symptoms of seeing anger. Prognosis is poor because the person tends to want his/her problems solved by having other people change (Caldwell, 1972).

2. This is an adverse pattern for most short-term therapy.

3. Anderson and Holcomb (1983) have found this pattern as one of five in a group of accused murderers. This group of murderers had paranoid personalities or were sociopaths with bad judgment. They also were the group with the highest intelligence.

## 4-6-9

1. This is one of the most dangerous profiles for the potential to act out against others (Trimboli & Kilgore, 1983).

2. This pattern is found in people who suddenly are violent (Carson, 1969). This is especially true if scale **8** is elevated also.

## 4-7

1. People with this pattern tend to have repeated patterns of acting out and then being sorry for the acting out. While they may be very remorseful about acting out, this remorse is not usually sufficient to prevent them from acting out again (Dahlstrom et al., 1972).

2. These people have both excessive insensitivity and excessive concern about their actions. This may be cyclical (Lachar, 1974).

3. These people may respond to therapeutic support, but they are unlikely to make long-term changes in their personality (Graham, 1977).

4. Erickson et al. (1987) found this codetype to be the most common one for incestuous stepfathers in a group of convicted sex offenders; however, the authors cautioned that many other profile codetypes also were found for this group of offenders.

   (See also this study's findings for the **4-2** and **4-3** codetypes.)

5. Adolescents in treatment with this profile **4-7/7-4** (Marks et al., 1974) acted out, were provocative, resentful, and basically insecure. They had many friends but few close ones. The Marks, Seeman, and Haller book should be consulted for further information concerning this pattern.

6. Kelley and King (1979a) found the **4-7/7-4** profile code in a college counseling center. Clients with this profile were immature, moody, and reported feelings of inferiority, ruminations, and gastrointestinal problems.

### 4-7-2

1. Marks et al. (1974) found the **2-7-4/2-4-7/4-7-2** pattern in a university hospital and outpatient clinic. People with this pattern tended to be depressed and to have many worries. They were likely to be described as passive-aggressive, generally tearful, full of fear, nervous, and irritable. The Marks, Seeman, and Haller book should be consulted for further information concerning this profile.

### 4-8 See also the **8-4** codetype, p. 256.

1. People with this pattern may be unpredictable, impulsive, and odd in appearance and behavior (Dahlstrom et al., 1972; Hovey & Lewis, 1967).

2. People with this pattern tend to distrust others and have problems with close relationships (Caldwell, 1972).

3. These people tend to see the world as threatening, and they respond by either withdrawing or lashing out in anger. They may have serious concerns about their masculinity or femininity (Graham, 1977).

4. They tend to get into trouble because they have poor judgment as to when and how to fight out, rather than because they crave the excitement of trouble as people with the **4-9** pattern do.

5. One study (Lewandowski & Graham, 1972) has found that hospitalized psychiatric patients with this pattern have more unusual thoughts than other psychiatric patients and also are younger than the other patients.

6. This pattern is found frequently in people with suicidal ideation (Caldwell, 1972). Check MMPI-2 items 150, 506, 520, and 524 for endorsement of these items concerning suicidal thinking.

7. The person with the high **4** and **8** scales and a low **9** scale may be the black sheep of the family and constantly in trouble (Caldwell, 1972).

8. Gynther, Altman, and Sletten (1973) found that psychiatric inpatients with the **4-8/8-4** pattern had a history of antisocial behavior such as promiscuity or deserting their families.

9. VA hospital males were likely to be argumentative, unpredictable, odd, delinquent, and asocial (Hovey & Lewis, 1967).

10. Adolescents in treatment with the **4-8/8-4** pattern (Marks et al., 1974) were immature and extremely narcissistic. Only 16% showed any improvement in therapy. These adolescents were argumentative, resentful, and acting out. Those with the **4-8** pattern were more deviant and difficult

in therapy than those with the **8-4** pattern. The Marks, Seeman, and Haller book should be consulted for further information concerning this pattern.

11. Crimes committed by persons with this profile often are senseless, poorly planned, and poorly executed. They may include some of the more savage and vicious forms of sexual and homicidal assault (Pothast, 1956).

12. Anderson and Holcomb (1983) found this pattern as one of five in a group of murderers. Men with this pattern were most clearly identified by others as having severe mental problems. They tended to kill as the result of insults or slights. They were least likely to be drunk when they killed. Their profile pattern resembles Megargee and Bohn's (1979) Howe pattern.

13 This profile was one of those found for extrafamilial child molesters and offenders against adult women in a group of convicted sex offenders (Erickson et al., 1987); however, the authors caution that many other profile codetypes also were found for this group of offenders.

14. In a study of drug abusers (Patalano, 1980), this was the most frequent two-point code for Black abusers. The **4-9/9-4** code was the most frequent code for whites.

15. Caldwell (1972) found in one MMPI study of prostitutes and call girls that all of them had the **4-8** combination.

16. Thirteen out of 81 women seeking counseling for issues related to incest had the **4-8/8-4** codetype (Richey, 1991), and this was the most frequent codetype for this group of clients. In contrast, a control group of 90 women seeking counseling for issues other than incest had only three women with this codetype.

17. College men with this pattern tended to be indecisive, unhappy, worrying, and confused. They had conflicts with their fathers and were aggressive and belligerent.

Females also had conflicts at home, were depressed, and had headaches. They also lacked skills with the opposite sex (Drake & Oetting, 1959).

18. The mean profile for 13 bulimic undergraduate college students was a **4-8** codetype with a small elevation on the **7** scale and a high elevation of the **F** scale (Parmer, 1991).

## 4-8-F

1. These elevations tend to be obtained by potential juvenile delinquents (Hathaway & Monachesi, 1958).

2. They also are found in emotionally disturbed adolescents.

3. When these elevations occur with a low **2** scale, the person is usually an aggressive, punitive individual who likes to arouse anxiety and guilt in others (Carson, 1969).

   Such people may end up in jobs where their behavior is socially approved, e.g., law enforcer, school disciplinarian, or overzealous clergyman.

## 4-8-2

1. This profile indicates a person who is distressed while at the same time hostile and distrustful. The person tends to be isolated and potentially suicidal (Lachar, 1974).

2. Marks et al. (1974) found the **4-8-2/8-4-2/8-2-4** pattern in a university hospital and outpatient clinic. A person with this profile tended to be distrustful of others, keeping them at a distance. The person usually was described as depressed, tense, irritable, and hostile. The Marks, Seeman, and Haller book should be consulted for further information concerning this profile.

## 4-8-9

1. A person with a **4-8-9** profile may have a history of repeated aggression in situations where others get hurt. These people typically do not realize how they hurt others (Caldwell, 1972).

2. When a male has this profile, he may be violent but has charisma and vitality (Caldwell, 1972).

3. Highly aggressive males have the **4-8-9** scales as high points (Butcher, 1965).

4. When the **2** scale also is elevated (but not necessarily the next highest scale after the **4, 8,** and **9**), people talk about depression and tend to manipulate others so that they can get their own way (Caldwell, 1972).

## 4-9 See also the **9-4** codetype, p. 276.

1. People with their highest scale elevations on the **4** and **9** scales tend to be angry and arousal seekers. They must maintain excitement and will stir things up to get it. In contrast to people with high **4-8** scales (when poor judgment may get the person into trouble), the high **4-9** person seems to be seeking the excitement of the trouble.

2. The **9** scale activates and energizes the feelings shown by the **4** scale.

3. A marked disregard for social standards and values may exist (Graham, 1977). If this is true, the **Re** scale also will tend to be low.

4. The **4-9** pattern tends to characterize the following people:

a. Juvenile delinquents.

   (1) However, accompanying high scores on scales **2, 5, 7,** and **0** act as inhibitors of the delinquent behavior (Carkhuff, Barnette, & McCall, 1965).

   (2) This pattern may disappear with age.

b. Convicts.

c. Heroin addicts (Craig, 1984a). In one study, 21% had the **4-9/9-4** profile.

d. School and college underachievers. This is especially true for males if the **5** scale is low, whereas high **5** acts as a suppressor to the underachievement tendency of the **4-9** pattern (Drake & Oetting, 1959).

e. Student in trouble for college misconduct (Nyman & LeMay, 1967).

f. Female college students with interpersonal difficulties but fewer intrapsychic problems (King & Kelley, 1977a).

5. Lewandowski and Graham (1972) found that patients with an elevated **4-9** profile were younger at their first hospitalization than other patients. They also were irritable, angry, and easily annoyed. They became upset quickly if things did not suit them.

6. Gilberstadt and Duker (1965) found the **4-9** pattern in a VA hospital male population. A man with this pattern tended to be self-centered, moody, and irritable. He tended to be superficially friendly, but he had a low frustration tolerance.

7. In another study of VA hospital males, patients with this pattern were energetic, ambitious, and lively. They were emotionally unstable with asocial tendencies. They were impulsive and had difficulty controlling their impulses (Hovey & Lewis, 1967).

8. Marks et al. (1974) found the **4-9** pattern in a university hospital and outpatient clinic. A person with this pattern tended to be self-centered, under-controlled, insecure, irritable, and hostile. The Marks, Seeman, and Haller book should be consulted for further information concerning this profile.

9. Two studies (Gynther et al., 1973a; Gynther, Altman, & Sletten, 1973) also have found antisocial behavior such as excessive fighting and attempts to harm others for this pattern, **4-9/9-4**. Men with this pattern also tended to have a history of alcoholic benders. This description may not apply to Blacks who have a **4-9** profile.

10. Adolescents in treatment with the **4-9/9-4** pattern (Marks et al., 1974) were referred because of being defiant, disobedient, provocative, and truant from school. They usually had constant conflict with parents. However, they had many friends and were well liked by them. They were typically drug users. The Marks, Seeman, and Haller book should be consulted for further information concerning this pattern.

11. Megargee and Bohn (1979) found four profiles with this codetype for a group of incarcerated criminals.

   a. This was the most common two-point code for Group Able (83% of the group). The men in this group were happy-go-lucky and outgoing. They were charming, popular, and manipulative. They created a popular impression but were likely to get into trouble again when they got out of prison.

      (1) One of four MMPI cluster profiles found in a sample of incarcerated homicide offenders had elevations on these two scales, with the **9** scale slightly lower than 70 T-score points (Kalichman, 1988). (The other profile clusters were a within-normal-limits profile, a spike **4** profile, and a **4-2** profile.) Individuals in the **4-9** cluster were more likely to have committed another violent crime, such

as rape or assault, at the time of the homicide than the people in the other three profile clusters. They also were the most likely to have been convicted of a previous violent offense and least likely to have known their victim. This profile type is similar to Margargee and Bohn's (1979) Able codetype.

(2) Hutton et al. (1993) also found a group of men in their forensic psychiatric population that fit Megargee and Bohn's (1979) Able codetype. These individuals had more education than the average patient, and they had the highest proportion of assault with a deadly weapon. They were typically diagnosed as nonpsychotic.

b. Group Foxtrot also had this **4-9/9-4** combination (69% of the group) but also tended to be elevated on the **8** scale. Their criminal behavior seemed to be symptomatic of pervasive psychopathology. They had extensive criminal records and were one of the most violent groups. They had poor prison adjustment and the highest recidivism rate (Megargee & Bohn, 1979).

(1) Hutton et al. (1993) found a group of men who fit Megargee and Bohn's (1979) Foxtrot codetype. These individuals were younger than the average patient. This group had a high proportion of Black and Hispanic patients and also had a high proportion of offenders convicted of murder and robbery. They were most frequently committed to the psychiatric hospital because of major mental disorders.

12. This pattern was found in a group of male alcoholics. Also found were the **2-1-3, 2-4-7,** and **8-7-6** codetypes (Conley, 1981). In contrast to the other combinations, the **4-9** profile did not change with treatment.

13. College students with high points on these scales have lower grade point averages and higher dropout rates than

would be expected according to their ability (Barger & Hall, 1964).

14. College counselees with these high points were rated difficult to deal with (aggressive and opinionated) by their counselors. Male clients also had conflicts with their fathers. Female clients had home conflicts, had vague goals, lacked academic drive and were socially extroverted (Drake & Oetting, 1959).

## 4-0

1. Nine cases of this rare two-point code were found by Tanner (1990b) in a psychiatric population. All but one of these individuals were women. They were angry, hostile people who blamed others for their misfortune. They had poor social judgment and were impulsive and difficult to work with. The most common diagnoses were passive-aggressive or dependent personality disorder.

2. Adolescents in treatment with the **4-0/0-4** pattern (Marks et al., 1974) were suspicious and distrustful. They were resentful and prone to acting out. They also were shy and had few friends. The Marks, Seeman, and Haller book should be consulted for further information concerning this pattern.

**6-4-2** See the **4-6-2** pattern, p. 183.

**8-2-4** See p. 255.

**8-4-2** See the **4-8-2** pattern, p. 188.

# SUMMARY OF 4 SCALE INTERPRETATIONS

| T-score MMPI-2 | MMPI | Interpretations |
|---|---|---|
| <40 | <45 | Persons with these scores tend to be conventional. They usually are able to tolerate routine and like to be peaceable. They may lack interest in heterosexual activity. |
| 40-60 | 45-60 | The majority of people score in this range. People scoring at this level seldom show dissatisfaction with authority figures, and they tend to go along with society as it is presently constituted. |
| 60-65 | 60-70 | With college educated persons, this level usually indicates concern about the social problems of the world. It is a common level for social workers, psychologists, and others in the helping professions. People with scores in this range tend to be appropriate in their use of anger. |
| >65 | >70 | Persons at this level tend to be angry and fighting out. If the **5** scale is above or within the 5 T-score points of the **4** scale for men, this fighting out will be more covert than overt. People at the lower end of this elevation may have a situational crisis such as marital discord. In this latter instance, the elevation tends to go down after the problem is resolved. Other people with scores at this elevation may be unable to profit from their experiences, both good and bad. These people may not be in actual trouble with authority figures but instead may associate with persons who are. Adolescents usually outgrow this difficulty, but at age 40, such an elevation, if it is one of the highest scales, can be considered a long-standing trait and is probably very difficult to change. The key to success with these people is to try to channel the drive indicated by the high **4** into socially acceptable behavior. |

**Relation to Supplementary Scales**

**Do** scale—if the **4** scale is elevated and the **Do** scale also is elevated, the person frequently will be seen as domineering.

**Re scale**—if the **4** scale is elevated and the **Re** scale is below 50, the person may be rebellious.

# HARRIS AND LINGOES SUBSCALES FOR SCALE 4

| Subscales | Interpretation |
|---|---|
| Pd 1  Familial Discord (9 items) | This person is dissatisfied with immediate family. |
| Pd 2  Authority Conflicts (8 items) | He/she is resentful of authority and/or reports problems with the law. |
| Pd 3  Social imperturbability (6 items) | This individual feels socially competent and confident in social situations. |
| Pd 4  Social Alienation (13 items) | He/she feels misunderstood by others and feels estranged from others. |
| Pd 5  Self-alienation (12 items) | This person feels uncomfortable with self. |

# — NOTES —

# SCALE 5

## (Mf, Masculine-Feminine Interests Scale)

Scale **5** is one of the scales that has been affected the most by the change from the MMPI to the MMPI-2. Four items were deleted from the scale and six were rewritten, but it is the T-score distribution of the scale that has shown the most change. This change is not due to the conversion of linear T-scores to uniform T-scores since this was not done to scale **5** or to scale **0**. The T-score changes happened partially because of the reduction in number of items but mainly because the new normative group's endorsement of scale **5** items changed with more men answering items in the "feminine" direction than the original 1930 normative group. This has had the effect of lowering men's T-scores on this scale by approximately 10 T-score points (Strassberg, 1991). (See Table 3.1, pp. 42-43.)

On the other hand, women's **5** scale scores have not been changed, presumably since endorsement rates have not changed so dramatically between the old and new norm groups. See Table 3.2, p. 42, for the T-score changes on the women's profile. Dahlstrom (1992) has found that men's two-point codes with this scale were dramatically reduced in number when 1,138 male MMPIs were rescored using MMPI-2 norms. (See Table 4.1, p. 86.) Instead of 24% of the profiles having a two-point code involving scale **5** on the MMPI, only 12.5% of the MMPI-2 profiles had similar elevations involving this scale. For women on the other hand, the number of profiles involving the **5** scale as part of a two-point code was elevated from 4% with the original MMPI to 15% with the MMPI-2. (See Table 4.2, p. 87.) It must be remembered that the profiles in Dahlstrom's study (1992) came from a normal population, and the elevations reported are the highest scales in the profile but not necessarily clinically elevated.

I (JD) have found results similar to Dahlstrom's in my work with men's scale **5** on the MMPI-2. Typically, MMPI-2 profiles show the **5** scale to be much lower than on the original MMPI, and where there are two profiles available to compare on the same individual, the difference between the two **5** scales averages around 10 T-score points. Most of the men I test however, still score above 50 on the test, reflecting their college education and their interests in reading, art, and other aesthetic pursuits.

Women's MMPI-2 profiles do not appear to be as different from their original MMPI profiles as do the men's. Most of the women I test still have **5** scales below 50 T-score points and many of them are around 40. These women are not usually passive individuals as can be seen from their scores on the **Do** (Dominance) scale (p. 340) and their elevations on the **GM** (Gender Role-Masculine) scale (p. 384). The women who are passive also may have **5** scale scores around 40, but they also are lower on the **Do** scale and typically have elevated (>50) **GF** (Gender Role-Feminine) scale scores but not elevated (>50) **GM** scores.

These changes on the **5** scale show the necessity of scoring the MMPI-2 raw scores onto MMPI profiles so that the research reported in this section can be used most appropriately. This information is based primarily on data using the original MMPI T-scores and, therefore, can be misused if the differences between the T-scores on the original MMPI and the MMPI-2 are not taken into consideration.

Scale **5** is probably the most misunderstood of all the clinical scales for three reasons. The first reason is the scale's name, "Masculinity-Femininity." The implication is that this scale can determine if one is more or less masculine or feminine. The problem in today's society is that the definitions of masculinity and femininity are changing rapidly, and the current ones may not be very much like the original definitions used when this scale was constructed.

A second difficulty with the scale is the frequent assumption that it can detect males who are actual or latent homosexuals. Such an assumption is not warranted. Some males with homosexual preferences do receive elevations on this scale, but many false positives and false negatives exist. This scale just does not do an adequate job of identifying male homosexuality.

The third difficulty with this scale is purely mechanical. Actually two **5** scales exist, one for males and one for females, and each scale has its own interpretations.

## Males

Kunce and Anderson (1976, 1984) have hypothesized that role-flexibility is the underlying dimension of scale **5**. When this scale is elevated for males, it indicates an individual who can enjoy a wide range of interests and who will be perceived as interesting, complex, tolerant, and insightful. This scale tends to be moderately elevated among adjusted members of many occupational groups, such as social scientists (including psychologists), authors, physicians, artists, ministers, and teachers. Under stress, the individual with a moderately high score may show role adjustment difficulties.

Hovey and Lewis (1967) found that individuals with moderate elevations on scale **5** were sensitive, curious, socially perceptive, and tolerant. They were unlikely to show delinquent behavior and understood themselves and others fairly well.

Scores between 45 and 55 (MMPI) and 40 and 50 (MMPI-2) on this scale indicate that a man is interested in traditional masculine activities. Between 50 and 55 (MMPI) and 45 and 50 (MMPI-2) seems to be the typical range for noncollege educated males and for college educated males interested in majors such as engineering and agriculture. When this score goes lower than a T of 45 (MMPI) or 40 (MMPI-2), the man tends to adopt the attitudes of the legendary he-man, particularly in the treatment of females (examples: "love them and leave them" and "a woman's place is in the home"). In fact, some of these men appear to score conquests by carving notches on the bedpost (particularly so if their **4** scale is elevated).

As the elevation on this scale increases to above 60 (MMPI) or 55 (MMPI-2), one of two types of behavior may be observed.

One is an interest in aesthetics such as art, music, and literature. This interest tends to increase with education. The second type of behavior that can emerge is passivity. By passivity, we mean a preference for working through things in a covert and indirect manner, rather than in an overt and direct manner. The question of which of these two behaviors is indicated by the **5** scale is best determined by consulting other scales (particularly the supplementary scales **Dy** and **St**). High **Dy** (dependency) plus high **5** usually indicates passivity. High **St** (status) plus high **5** usually is indicative of aesthetic or achievement interests. When both the **Dy** and **St** scales are elevated above 60 T-score points, the relative heights of the two scales can indicate how much passivity and/or aesthetic or achievement interests are being shown by the **5** scale.

Above a T of 80 (MMPI) or 75 (MMPI-2), both an appreciation for aesthetics and passivity usually are present. With persons actively involved in the arts, however, the passivity may not be present.

While the **5** scale is the most frequent high point on male college student profiles, with scale **9** a close second, for male noncollege clients this is not a frequent high point. They rarely score above 60 on this scale (55, MMPI-2); in fact, their typical score is around 44 (50, MMPI-2).

**Females**

In the counseling center and mental health clinic populations, the usual maximum scale **5** score for women is 50; very rarely do we see scores above this level. Those few women we have seen who do score above 50 tend to be uninterested in being seen as feminine. They may or may not have masculine interests, but they definitely are not interested in appearing or behaving as other women do. They usually like to think of themselves as unique or different from women in general.

Another group of women who score in this range are teenage girls who are in some kind of trouble with the law or their families. They frequently seem to be unsure of what they are like as females and, therefore, score above the usual range of T-scores for females.

T-scores between 35 and 50 are typical and indicate interest in traditional feminine pursuits. This does not mean that the woman has no interest in a career outside the home but, instead, that she may prefer both career and the traditional activities connected with being a woman. As the score on this scale goes below 35, a seductive, helpless coyness usually begins to emerge if the **Dy** scale (see p. 335) is also above 50 T-score points. As the **Dy** scale goes above 50 and the **5** scale goes below 35, the amount of helplessness typically increases. The woman with these scores is not always actually helpless, but she may be using this approach to get others, particularly males, to help her.

## GENERAL INFORMATION

1. The **5** scale of 60 items (56 items, MMPI-2) contains questions concerning aesthetic interests, vocational choices, and passivity (Carson, 1969).

2. The same scale is used for both sexes, but high raw scores are elevations for men and low points for women.

3. The scale on the MMPI is highly correlated with education (Colligan et al., 1984).

   However, Gulas (1973) has indicated that the MMPI **5** scale may be more correlated with IQ, educational aspiration, and/or socioeconomic status than with years of education, per se.

4. Butcher and Pope (1992) have shown that for the MMPI-2 **5** scale, adjustments for educational level do not need to be made as they had to be for the original MMPI **5** scale; however, these authors still advocate caution when interpreting the **5** scale scores of men with very low or very high educational levels.

5. The **5** scale frequently is elevated for men but not for women.

6. Caldwell has hypothesized that the **5** scale may measure caring for others on the feminine end of the scale (high **5** for men, low **5** for women) with relationships meaning a great deal, and practical, survival, self-caring on the masculine end of the scale (low **5** for men, high **5** for women). People at the feminine end value emotions, feelings, and aesthetics, and are introspective. People at the masculine end value action and pragmatism (Caldwell, 1985).

7. Volentine (1981) has found that the femininity measures of the *Bem Sex Role Inventory* were more strongly related to scale **5** than the masculinity measures. Scale **5,** therefore, may be interpreted more accurately as a measure of femininity rather than a measure of masculinity.

8. For males, high **5** tends to negate the overt acting out behavior indicated by elevations on certain scales such as **4, 6,** and **9.** Passive-aggressive behavior may be seen instead.

9. With females, if a large number of questions are left unanswered, the scale is elevated.

10. In a study of a normal population, scores on scale **5** were lower for older men and higher for older women, perhaps reflecting somewhat lower educational levels for the older age groups (Colligan et al., 1984).

11. For a normal population, the mean score on this scale for the MMPI was 46 for women and 58 for men (Colligan et al., 1984).

12. Test-retest reliabilities for this scale on the MMPI-2 are .82 for men and .73 for women. Indeed this scale frequently remains the same even when the rest of the profile changes dramatically.

13. VA hospital males with this scale as a high point were likely to be peaceable and not show any delinquent behavior. They also tended to be sensitive, dependent, and submissive (Hovey & Lewis, 1967).

14. Cernovsky (1985b) has found that in a group of 97 male chronic alcoholics, the MMPI **5** scale was significantly related to intelligence, with higher scorers having better intellectual skills.

# HIGH SCORES

## Moderate Elevations—Male

(T = 55 through 65, MMPI-2)

(T = 60 through 70, MMPI)

1. This elevation is characteristic of males having a wide range of interests, especially aesthetic ones.

2. Kunce and Anderson (1976) have hypothesized that when this scale is in the moderate range, it may measure role-flexibility. A person who is role-flexible can enjoy a wide range of interests and may be perceived as interesting, colorful, complex, innerdirected, insightful, tolerant, and possibly dramatic.

3. Trimboli and Kilgore (1983) have expressed the belief that moderate elevations on this scale for men may reflect some capacity for sublimation, an adaptive defense mechanism.

4. Males scoring in this range on the scale are not necessarily passive, but they do tend to dislike physical violence (Caldwell, 1985).

5. Moderate elevations on scale **5** tend to be characteristic of college males. The **5** scale tends to be one of the two most frequent high points for male college students. The other frequent high point is scale **9.**

6. Gulas (1973) found that the two most frequently elevated scales (two-point code groups) in a study of 609 college males were (from most frequent to least frequent) **3-5/5-3, 5-9/9-5, 2-5/5-2, 5-7/7-5, 5-8/8-5,** and **5-6/6-5.** These two-point patterns were *not* necessarily above a T-score of 70.

## Moderate Elevations—Female

(T = 50 through 55, MMPI and MMPI-2)

1. Women with this elevation on the **5** scale may enjoy sports and/or outdoor activities.

2. They also tend to be uninterested in typical feminine sex roles.

3. They may prefer mechanical, computational, and scientific pursuits, and tend not to prefer literary pursuits (Carkhuff et al., 1965).

4. Scale **5** moderate elevations are frequent for females who drop out of school (Barger & Hall, 1964).

5. This elevation may be shown by girls in their late teens and by women from atypical cultural backgrounds (Carson, 1969).

6. Scale **5** is frequently elevated for girls in trouble with their families or the law.

## Marked Elevations—Male

(T = 65 or above, MMPI-2)
(T = 70 or above, MMPI)

The behaviors for this elevation are most clearly seen when the scale is the highest of the clinical scales.

1. Trimboli and Kilgore (1983) have expressed the belief that men with elevations at this level will tend to use the defense mechanism of suppression.

2. This elevation is characteristic of college males having a wide range of interests, especially aesthetic ones.

3. Scores in this range for blue-collar men tend to indicate passivity rather than aesthetic interests.

4. A high score suggests that the man does not identify with the culturally prescribed role for his sex (Carson, 1969).

5. Men with this elevation may tend to care too much about relationships.

6. Male homosexuals may show marked elevations on the **5** scale. However, since this is an obvious scale, males with same-sex preferences also can produce scores in the typical ranges by avoiding these obvious sex-oriented items.

## Marked Elevations—Females

(T = 55 or above, MMPI and MMPI-2)

1. As the elevation increases, the likelihood that aggressive behavior will be seen in women increases (Carson, 1969).

2. A high score suggests that the woman does not identify with the culturally prescribed role for her sex (Carson, 1969).

3. High scores in this range also may mean that the person is having trouble identifying with the feminine role.

4. Women with this elevation may become anxious if they are expected to adopt a feminine sexual role (Carson, 1969).

5. Trimboli and Kilgore (1983) have hypothesized that women with scores in this range may have difficulty appropriately channeling aggressive impulses.

# LOW SCORES

## Male

(T = 40 or below, MMPI-2)
(T = 50 or below, MMPI)

1. Low scores suggest strong identification with the prescribed masculine role (Carson, 1969).

2. Males with scores in this range may be described as easygoing, adventurous, and "coarse" (Carson, 1969).

3. Some males with low **5** scores may appear to be compulsive and inflexible about their masculinity (Carson, 1969).

4. Trimboli and Kilgore (1983) have hypothesized that men with scores in this range may have difficulty appropriately channeling aggressive impulses.

## Female

(T = 35 or below, MMPI-2 and MMPI)

1. Low scores suggest strong identification with the prescribed feminine role (Carson, 1969).

2. Females with very low **5** scale scores and high **Dy** (Dependency) scale scores (p. 335) may be passive, submissive, yielding, and demure, at times living caricatures of the feminine stereotype (Carson, 1969).

3. Caldwell (1985) has found that women with **5** scales this low are not caricatures of traditional femininity. They dress self-expressively to fit their mood. They are attracted to sensitive men with whom they can communicate.

4. Trimboli and Kilgore (1983) have hypothesized that women with **5** scales at this level will tend to use the defense mechanism of suppression.

5. These women tend to care too much about relationships. That may account for some lack of self-assertiveness in interpersonal relationships.

## CODETYPES

All scales in the codetype are at T-score of 65 or above (MMPI-2) or 70 or above (MMPI) and are listed in order from the highest to the lowest peaks. The scales in the codetype must be the highest clinical scales in the profile.

$\boxed{\text{1-2-3-}\overline{5}}$ See p. 96.

$\boxed{\text{1-5}}$ See p. 102.

$\boxed{\text{2-7-5-4}}$ See p. 128.

$\boxed{\text{3-4-5}}$ See p. 151.

$\boxed{\text{4-3-}\overline{5}}$ See p. 180.

$\boxed{\text{4-5}}$ See p. 180.

$\boxed{\text{4-5-9}}$ See p. 181.

$\boxed{\text{4-6-}\overline{5}}$ See p. 183.

$\boxed{\textbf{Spike 5}}$

1. A single elevation on this scale is very typical for college educated males.

$\boxed{\textbf{5-?}}$

1. An elevation on the **5** scale for females can result from the omission of items (elevated **?** scale), because a low raw score on scale **5** produces elevations on the women's profile.

$\boxed{\textbf{5-2}}$ See p. 123.

$\boxed{\textbf{5-4}}$ See also the **4-5** codetype, p. 180.

1. Males with this codetype may temper the anger shown by the high **4** scale. They may get their anger out covertly, perhaps even passive-aggressively.

2 This codetype may be associated with male sexual delinquents of the more passive type.

3. The **5-4** codetype is a common configuration for men who are nonconformists. They seem to delight in defying social conventions in their behavior and dress (Carson, 1969).

4. Women who are rebelling against the female role tend to have this combination (Carson, 1969). Their behavior becomes more atypical with increasing elevation of the **4** scale (Carson, 1969).

$\boxed{\bar{\textbf{5}}\textbf{-4}}$ (**5** Scale T = 40 or below, MMPI-2)
(**5** Scale T = 45 or below, MMPI)

1. Men with this combination tend to be flamboyantly masculine. In teenagers, this is often manifested in delinquent behavior (Carson, 1969).

2. Women with this combination may be hostile and angry, but they are unable to express these feelings directly. Therefore, they may provoke others to get angry at them. Then they can pity themselves, because they have been mistreated (Carson, 1969).

3. Women with this pattern may be passive-aggressive (Good & Brantner, 1974).

### 5-6

1. Adolescents in treatment with the **5-6/6-5** pattern (Marks et al., 1974) had more intellectual interests and valued wealth and material possessions more than other adolescents in treatment. They were irritable and acted out. They were sometimes suicidal and homicidal. The Marks, Seeman, and Haller book should be consulted for further information concerning this pattern.

### 5-7

1. Male college students with this profile usually were tense, indecisive, unhappy, worrying, and wanting reassurance (Drake & Oetting, 1959).

2. In another study of college clients, the men usually complained about academic problems and interpersonal difficulties, especially with their girlfriends (King & Kelley, 1977b).

### 5-8

1. For college students with this profile, men report being confused, unhappy, and having conflicts at home (Drake & Oetting, 1959).

### 5-8-9

1. When the **5-8-9** pattern is present, the lack of academic motivation seen for males with the high **8-9/9-8** profile is not manifested. The **5** scale acts as a suppressor (Drake & Oetting, 1959).

### 5-9

1. Tanner (1990a) found 11 men with this codetype in a psychiatric population. Most of them were brought in

by their families or referred by the courts or other agencies. They were hyperactive, mildly grandiose, and impulsive. These men tended to use alcohol to reduce anxiety and had a high incidence of violence when they were drinking. Men with the **5-9** codetype tended to have more severe pathology than men with the **9-5** codetype.

2.  Adolescents in treatment with the **5-9/9-5** pattern (Marks et al., 1974) were peaceable, rational, and ambitious. They had high aspirations and aesthetic interests. They also had relatively few school problems. However, emotional dependency and lack of self-assertiveness were problems for them, and many were drug users. The Marks, Seeman, and Haller book should be consulted for further information concerning this pattern.

3.  Male college counselees with the **5-9** pattern present problems concerning conflicts with their mothers, especially when scale **0** is low (Drake & Oetting, 1959).

## 5-0

1.  Tanner (1990b) found only three cases of this codetype in a group of psychiatric patients; however, they were very similar to each other. All of the patients were female, immature, anxious, and unconcerned about their appearance. They became pregnant while not married and were supported by welfare.

2.  Adolescents in treatment with the **5-0/0-5** pattern (Marks et al., 1974) had intellectual interests. However, they were slow to make friends and were shy, timid, and submissive. They had conflicts about sexuality and asserting themselves. They tended to overcontrol their impulses. The Marks, Seeman, and Haller book should be consulted for further information concerning this pattern.

3.  Male college counselees with the **5-0** pattern tend to show introverted behavior (Drake & Oetting, 1959).

# SUMMARY OF 5 SCALE INTERPRETATIONS
## FOR MALES

| T-score MMPI-2 | MMPI | Interpretations |
|---|---|---|
| < 35 | <45 | A man scoring in this range may be preoccupied with being tough and virile (the he-man syndrome). |
| 35-44 | 45-54 | A man scoring in this range usually is interested in traditional masculine pursuits such as sports, hunting, and outdoor life. The upper part of this range is where noncollege males, engineers, and men studying agriculture may score. |
| 45-70 | 55-80 | This level is typical for males with more than one year of college, particularly in the humanities and fine arts. This person usually has an interest in aesthetics. There also may be some passivity. This passivity is more likely as the scale gets closer to the top of this range of scores. The **Dy** and **St** scales (Dependency and Status) indicate how much dependency/passivity (**Dy**) may be present compared to the amount of aesthetic interest (**St**). |
| >70 | >80 | At this level, reference to the **Dy** and **St** scales is important because a **5** scale score in this range may indicate either great passivity, an unusual amount of interest in aesthetics or some combination of the two. |

## SUMMARY OF 5 SCALE INTERPRETATIONS
## FOR FEMALES

| T-Score MMPI-2 | MMPI | Interpretations |
|---|---|---|
| <35 | <35 | A woman scoring in this range may appear to be coy, seductive, and helpless (the southern belle syndrome). In this case, the **Dy** (Dependency) scale will be above 50 T-score points. The behavior may be a manipulative device, or the woman may be truly helpless. |
| 35-50 | 35-50 | The majority of women score in this range. A woman with a **5** scale in this range usually is comfortable with her feminine identity without necessarily being passive. The **Dy** scale score is a more accurate measure of the amount of passivity a woman has. |
| >50 | >50 | A woman scoring in this range may see herself as being unique and not like a typical woman. |

# SCALE 6

## (Pa, Paranoia Scale)

Although the **6** scale's T-score distribution has not been changed as much as other scales in the MMPI-2 conversion from linear T-scores to uniform T-scores (Strassberg, 1991) (See Tables 3.1 and 3.2, pp. 42-43.), the number of two-point codes involving the **6** scale has gone up (Dahlstrom, 1992; Walsh et al., 1990). This is most likely because other scales that are frequently part of two-point codes, such as scales **2, 4,** and **8,** have been lowered on the MMPI-2. (See Tables 4.1 and 4.2, pp. 86-87.) This means that the base rate of codetypes has changed for the MMPI-2, and this will need to be taken into consideration when interpreting the profile. With the original MMPI, it was unusual to see the **6** scale as one of the two highest scales for normal people under stress, and, when it did happen, the scale was frequently in the 70 to 75 T-score range and seemed to be the result of some recent trauma the test taker had suffered. It remains to be seen if this is also true when this scale is elevated on the MMPI-2.

The following interpretative material for the **6** scale is based upon it's meaning for the original MMPI and, therefore, needs to be used with caution for the MMPI-2.

Scale **6** measures three things. First, at the lower elevations (60-65, MMPI-2; 60-70, MMPI), typically the scale shows interpersonal sensitivity, usually of the kind "What are you thinking and feeling, and how can that affect me?" Second, when the **6** scale gets elevated into the clinical range (> 70, MMPI; > 65, MMPI-2), suspiciousness is usually added to the sensitivity. The motives of others are assumed to be malevolent, and, therefore, the client feels a need to watch out for others and what they can and will do to him/her. Very rarely is this scale clinically elevated without the sensitivity and/or suspiciousness being seen. Thus, these people typically are difficult persons with whom to work, because the suspiciousness and sensitivity towards others can include the therapist. We have had this suspiciousness and sensitivity take the form of questioning our credentials, checking whether the client will be fairly treated, and doubting the good intentions of others. In transactional analysis terms, this person exemplifies the "I'm O.K., you're not O.K." stance. If the suspiciousness is widespread, the **Pr** scale will be above 50 T-score points (See p. 353.). If the suspiciousness is confined to one or two people, usually someone close, the **Pr** scale will be below 50 T-score points.

The third element in scale **6** is much like a subtle spice and flavors the whole scale. This pervasive element is self-righteousness. A person with an elevation on this scale tends to have the feeling "I've done all this for you, and now look what you have done to me in return." Occasionally this statement actually is expressed, but more commonly this attitude is implied strongly.

Kunce and Anderson (1976, 1984) have hypothesized an underlying dimension for this scale that they call "inquiring." When other factors suggest good adjustment for an individual, this scale indicates an inquisitive and investigative orientation. The individual is likely to be curious, questioning, perceptive, and discriminating. Hovey and Lewis (1967) have found the positive characteristics connected with individuals with moderate elevations on the **6** scale to be that they are sensitive, kind, poised, and show clear thinking and initiative. These individuals are inclined to be progressive and have broad interests. When the individual is under stress, these positive characteristics become suspiciousness, hypersensitivity, and distorted perceptions.

Scale **6** is rarely elevated by itself; usually other scales also are elevated. In addition, this scale rarely is the highest peak on MMPI profiles but most likely the second or third highest point. This could change with the MMPI-2. The person may come for therapy because of some situational stress. Once this stress is alleviated successfully, the person typically will leave counseling with the paranoid behavior gone.

Scale **6** rarely goes below 40; again this may change for the MMPI-2 because this scale is 5 T-score points lower than the MMPI for the same raw score. When it is low, two interpretations are possible. The first is that the person really is a high **6,** sensitive and suspicious. Because the scale has somewhat obvious items, he/she has avoided marking these items in the scored direction and instead has answered them in the typical way to such an extent that he/she has overcompensated and is unusually low on this scale. These people are fairly easy to spot in therapy because the sensitivity/suspiciousness is not always easy to hide in this kind of intimate relationship.

The second interpretation for a low **6** scale is that the person is answering honestly. He/she tends to be a gullible type of person who is taken in occasionally by some others because he/she is not sensitive enough to perceive what others really are like.

## GENERAL INFORMATION

1. The 40 items of scale **6** reflect suspiciousness, interpersonal sensitivity, and self-righteousness.

2. Harris and Lingoes (1955) have divided the **6** scale into three subscales: ideas of external influence, poignancy, and moral virtue. The interpretation of these subscales are on p. 227.

3. This scale is made up of many obvious items. Thus, the paranoid person, who is typically interpersonally sensitive and suspicious, can mark the answers so as to show only what he/she wants you to see on this scale.

Therefore, a suspicious person can score low on scale **6.** In this instance, the person is too cautious, avoids obvious material, and overcompensates beyond normal limits.

4. This scale rarely produces false positives. People with elevations are suspicious and sensitive and readily show these characteristics (Carson, 1972).

5. Caldwell (1985) has hypothesized that people with this scale as one of their highest have a fear of attack. When the scale is quite elevated, a fear of physical attack is present. At lower elevations, the fear is of moral attack or judgment. This fear is frequently based upon a conditioning experience of having the person's integrity violated.

6. Trimboli and Kilgore (1983) have found that this is a character scale with the person typically using projection and externalization as defense mechanisms.

7. Hovanitz, Gynther, and Marks (1983) have found that both the subtle and obvious items (Weiner, 1948) on this scale predict various criteria. Their study found correlations between obvious items and ideas of persecution, and between subtle items and naivete. Therefore, both the subtle and obvious items of this scale are useful.

8. Schenkenberg et al. (1984) have found that younger psychiatric patients score higher on this scale than older psychiatric patients.

9. Hibbs et al. (1979) also have found the **6** scale to be higher for younger people.

   They also have found that Mexican American women score higher than Mexican American men and white men and women on this scale. They suggested that this may be a cultural effect.

10. In a study of a normal population, the men's mean score was 55 and the women's 56 (Colligan et al., 1984).

11. This scale is more elevated in profiles of wives in marriage counseling than in profiles of wives from the general population (Arnold, 1970; Ollendick et al., 1983).

12. MMPI-2 test-retest reliabilities for this scale are .67 for men and .58 for women (Butcher et al., 1989). These low reliabilities may reflect the fact that scale **6** is sensitive to changes in suspiciousness.

# HIGH SCORES

## Moderate Elevations

(T= 60 through 65, MMPI-2)
(T= 60 through 70, MMPI)

1. This elevation tends to characterize sensitive people (Carkhuff et al., 1965).

2. Kunce and Anderson (1976) have hypothesized that when this scale is in the moderate range (and there are not clinically elevated clinical scales except the **5** scale for men) it may measure inquisitiveness and investigative behavior.

3. College women clients with an elevation in this range tend to be sensitive specifically to physical defects in themselves (Loper, 1976).

## Marked Elevations

(T= 65 or above, MMPI-2)
(T= 70 or above, MMPI)

The behaviors mentioned for this elevation are most clearly seen when the scale is one of the highest of the clinical scales.

1. This elevation tends to characterize suspicious people.

   a. They feel that what is said or done around them is aimed specifically at them.

   b. They often interpret criticism of their ideas as criticism of themselves.

c. They usually feel that they are not getting what they deserve (Carson, 1969).

2. A person with a **6** scale score of 70 or above usually is more verbal about suspiciousness and feelings of injustice than someone with a moderate elevation on this scale.

3. People with elevations on this scale tend to have an anger that is focused on specific people (Trimboli & Kilgore, 1983).

4. The most minor rejection is remembered.

5. This elevation tends to characterize people who make mistakes costly to others (Carson, 1969). This seems to be an unconscious passive-aggressive way of coping with perceived injustice.

6. Trimboli and Kilgore (1983) have found that people with elevations on this scale tend to use the defense mechanisms of projection and externalization.

7. A relationship may be difficult to establish in therapy with these people because their marked suspiciousness and sensitivity could include the therapist.

   This suspiciousness towards the therapist may be along the dimensions of age or sex. "No young whippersnapper (the therapist) can help me." "I cannot trust a man, only a woman (therapist)."

8. In treatment, high scorers tend to be argumentative and rigid (Carson, 1969).

9. VA hospital males with this scale as high point tend to have long-standing resentment towards relatives. They are supersensitive to the opinions of others and are touchy and prone to blame others for their difficulties (Hovey & Lewis, 1967).

# LOW SCORES

(T= 40 or below, MMPI-2)

(T= 45 or below, MMPI)

1.  Low scores on this scale characterize people who are cheerful, conventional, and trusting.

2.  Women with low **6** scale scores on the MMPI-2 are unlikely to be sad, to have many fears, to be moody, to worry about the future, or to break down and cry easily (Keiller & Graham, 1993).

3.  A score of 45 or below on scale **6** may indicate a lack of personal sensitivity to others (Drake & Oetting, 1959).

4.  A suspicious person can score low on scale **6.** In this instance, the person is too cautious, avoids the obvious paranoid questions, and overcompensates beyond normal limits.

    The person resists revealing self in any way, because he/she feels a calamity will follow such a revelation (Carson, 1969).

5.  If this scale is below 45 and no other scale is below 45, the person may be really a high **6.** They also may have a little elevation on the **L** scale.

6.  Lewak (1993) reported an interesting case in which an extremely low **6** scale (T=30) was the only unusual feature on an MMPI taken for employment screening by a policeman who was subsequently found guilty of committing a series of rapes.

7.  These scores characterize college students who have problems related to underachievement or nonachievement. The necessity to deny hostility may drain off excess energy,

thus reducing the student's effectiveness (Anderson, 1956; Morgan, 1952).

In addition, difficulty with parents often exists. This difficulty may be related to repressed or denied hostility.

## CODETYPES

All scales in the codetypes are at a T-score of 65 or above (MMPI-2) or 70 or above (MMPI) and are listed in order from the highest to the lowest peaks. These scales in the codetypes must be the highest clinical scales on the profile.

| 1-6 | See p. 102.

| 4-6 | See p. 181.

| 4-6-2 | See p. 183.

| 4-6-5 | See p. 183.

| 4-6-8 | See p. 184.

| 4-6-9 | See p. 184.

| 4-9-6 | See p. 184.

| 5-6 | See p. 209.

| Spike 6 |

1. Paranoid symptoms are usually apparent when this scale is the only one elevated (Greene, 1991).

$\boxed{\text{6-2}}$ See the **2-6** codetype, p. 124.

$\boxed{\text{6-3}}$ See the **3-6** codetype, p. 152.

1. When the **6** scale is higher than the **3,** a hostile egocentric person who is struggling for power and prestige is likely. He/she tends not to recognize the hostility (Lachar, 1974).

$\boxed{\text{6-4}}$ See also the **4-6** codetype, p. 181.

1. Marks et al. (1974) found the **4-6/6-4** pattern in a university hospital and outpatient clinic. It was primarily a female pattern. These females were described as self-centered, hostile, tense, defensive, and irritable. They usually handled their difficulties by refusing to admit them, and frequently they used rationalization as a primary defense mechanism. The Marks, Seeman, and Haller book should be consulted for further information concerning this profile.

$\boxed{\text{6-4-2}}$

1. Marks et al. (1974) found the **4-6-2/6-4-2** pattern in a university hospital and outpatient clinic. It was primarily a female pattern. A woman with this pattern tended to be acting out, depressed, critical, and skeptical. The Marks, Seeman, and Haller book should be consulted for further information concerning this profile.

$\boxed{\text{6-5}}$

1. Tanner (1990a) found 8 cases (7 male) with this profile codetype in a psychiatric center. These individuals were aloof and guarded. They also were impulsive, abrasive, irritable, and easily angered. A minority showed flattened affect, inappropriate laughter, ideas of persecution, and obvious hallucinations which they denied. The most frequent diagnoses were personality disorder and/or psychoses. They were not usually amenable to treatment.

1. People with this codetype are anxious, worried, suspicious individuals. They tend to keep people at a distance and to have poor social judgment (Greene, 1991).

2. Counselors rated college men with this pattern plus no elevation of scale **5** as nonresponsive and had difficulty relating to them. These clients also had problems at home and were confused and worried. College women were restless and had conflicts with their siblings (Drake & Oetting, 1959).

3. Kelley and King (1979a) found the **6-7/7-6** codetype primarily for women clients in one college counseling center. Although they tended to have genito-urinary problems, crying spells, and feelings of inferiority, and were described as rigid, they did not have any consistent diagnosis or pattern of pathology.

**6-7-8-9**

1. This pattern suggests behavioral difficulties, especially among college freshmen women (Osborne, Sander, & Young, 1956).

These women tend to approach problems with animation, are sensitive, and feel that they are unduly controlled, limited, and mistreated.

**6-8** See also the **8-6** codetype, p. 257.

1. These people could have marginal psychological adjustment. They tend to have intense feelings of inferiority and insecurity. They are suspicious and distrustful of others and avoid deep emotional ties (Graham, 1977).

2. Relationships with others are unstable and characterized by resentment (Dahlstrom & Welsh, 1960).

3. They may present a wide variety of complaints that shift from one time to the next (Dahlstrom & Welsh, 1960).

4.  If these people can get verbally angry with the therapist, they tend to get better rapidly (Caldwell, 1974).

5.  One study (Lewandowski & Graham, 1972) has found that patients with the **6-8** pattern have spent more time in a neuropsychiatric hospital than other patients. They tended to be unfriendly with others; to have less social interests; to be more emotionally withdrawn, conceptually disorganized, and suspicious; and to have more hallucinatory behavior and unusual thought content.

6.  Another study reported in two references (Altman, Gynther, Warbin, & Sletten, 1972; Gynther, Altman, & Sletten, 1973) has found patients in a mental hospital with this **6-8/8-6** pattern often seem unfriendly and angry for no apparent reason. They also have thought disorders, hallucinations, delusions, hostility, and lack of insight. Poor judgment was typical. Of those patients labeled psychotic, schizophrenia was the most frequent diagnosis, especially paranoid schizophrenia. For the **6-8** profile, the delusions are apt to be delusions of grandeur. For the **8-6** profile, the affect is apt to be blunted.

7.  Marks et al. (1974) found the **8-6/6-8** pattern in a university hospital and outpatient clinic. They found this pattern primarily for females who were having unconventional, delusional thoughts. These women also were suspicious. The Marks, Seeman, and Haller book should be consulted for further information concerning this profile.

8.  Black psychiatric patients show this configuration significantly more than white psychiatric patients matched on age, sex, hospital status, socioeconomic status, and duration of illness (Costello & Tiffany, 1972).

9.  In a study comparing Hispanic, Black, and white schizophrenics, Velasquez and Callahan (1990b) found that Black schizophrenics had elevations on the **6** and **8** scales, whereas white and Hispanic schizophrenics had elevations on the **8** and **2** scales.

10. VA hospital males with this pattern tended to be ruminative and thinking in unusual ways. They had paranoid thinking

verging on the delusional. They also had precarious psychological and emotional adjustment and tended to be pre-psychotic (Hovey & Lewis, 1967).

11. Adolescents in treatment with the **6-8/8-6** pattern (Marks et al., 1974) were referred because of bizarre behavior. They had violent tempers and tended to be below average intellectually. They frequently used drugs. The Marks, Seeman, and Haller book should be consulted for further information concerning this profile.

12. For college students with this pattern, men tended to be indecisive, unhappy, and confused; women were restless, depressed, and had conflicts with parents and siblings. They also lacked skills with the opposite sex (Drake & Oetting, 1959).

## 6-9

1. This is not a common profile pattern; however, when present, it may indicate paranoid grandiosity (Lachar, 1974).

2. These people tend to be angry, rational, and insistent about why they do things. They tend to give much moral justification for whatever they do (Caldwell, 1972).

3. They have difficulty with criticism; therefore, they use projection frequently as a defense mechanism (Caldwell, 1972).

4. They are vulnerable to threat and feel anxious and tense much of the time. They may alternate between overcontrol and emotional outbursts (Graham, 1977).

5. VA hospitalized men with this pattern tended to be tense and overreact to possible danger. They seemed to be unable to express their emotions in an adaptive way (Hovey & Lewis, 1967).

6. Marks et al. (1974) found the **9-6/6-9** pattern in a university hospital and outpatient clinic. It was found primarily for females who were agitated, tense, excitable,

suspiciousness, and hostile. The Marks, Seeman, and Haller book should be consulted for further information concerning this profile.

7. In another study reported in two references, Gynther et al. (1973d) and Gynther, Altman, and Sletten (1973), patients with this codetype **6-9/9-6** were found to be excited, hostile, loud, and grandiose, with little likelihood of having depressive symptoms.

8. For college students with this pattern, men tended to be aggressive or belligerent, especially if the **0** scale was low. Women were restless (Drake & Oetting, 1959).

### 6-0

1. Tanner (1990b) found seven cases (all women) with this codetype in a psychiatric center. These women presented themselves as helpless victims with no responsibility for their problems. They were suspicious, guarded, and uncomfortable around people. They saw their hostility as self-defense.

2. Women counselees with this pattern have feelings of inferiority in regard to some physical feature and shyness (Drake & Oetting, 1959).

3. Individuals with these elevations tend to be quite paranoid and may be psychotic, although they do not show the fragmentation of thought processes typically seen with schizophrenia (Trimboli & Kilgore, 1983).

**8-6** See p. 257.

**8-6-7-F** See p. 259.

**8-7-6** See p. 260.

# SUMMARY OF 6 SCALE INTERPRETATIONS

| T-score MMPI-2 | MMPI | Interpretations |
|---|---|---|
| <40 | <45 | A person may score in this range for two reasons. First, the person may be gullible and taken in by other people because he/she is not suspicious enough of other people. Second, the person may have a low score on this scale because he/she is really very sensitive and suspicious but has been able to guess which questions would reveal this and has answered them in the opposite way, thus showing low on the scale. This latter interpretation is likely if this is the only clinical scale below 40. |
| 40-60 | 45-60 | The majority of people score in this range. |
| 60-65 | 60-70 | People who score in this range tend to be interpersonally sensitive to what others think of them. |
| >65 | >70 | In addition to sensitivity, suspiciousness is usually present when this scale is elevated. The client may assume that other people are after him/her. Righteous indignation also is usually present. |

**Relationship to Supplementary Scales**

When the **6** scale is elevated, the **Pr** scale indicates how widespread the suspiciousness is. When **Pr** is 50 or below, the suspiciousness may only be directed towards one person. When the **Pr** is more elevated, an entire group of individuals may be included.

# HARRIS AND LINGOES SUBSCALES FOR SCALE 6

| Subscales | Interpretation |
| --- | --- |
| Pa 1  Persecutory Ideas (17 items) | This individual tends to see the world and/or other people as threatening. He/she blames others for problems. |
| Pa 2  Poignancy (9 items) | This person sees self as very sensitive and high-strung. |
| Pa 3  Naivete (9 items) | He/she denies distrust of other people. He/she claims high moral values. |

# SCALE 7

## (Pt, Psychasthenia Scale)

This scale has been lowered about 7 T-score points for males in the conversion from the MMPI to MMPI-2, but female T-scores have not been similarly affected (Strassberg, 1991. See Tables 3.1 and 3.2, pp. 42-43.). Dahlstrom, however, in his comparison of MMPI and MMPI-2 two-point codetypes (1992), reported that for both men and women the number of two-point codes involving the **7** scale were slightly higher for the MMPI-2 than they were for the MMPI. (See Tables 4.1 and 4.2, pp. 86-87.) This may be due to the fact that the other scales that are usually found in two-point codes, namely scales **2, 4,** and **8,** have been lowered to a much greater extent than the **7** scale, leaving the **7** scale more likely to be one of the two highest elevations.

While this difference in codetype frequency is not as dramatic for the **7** scale as it is for some other scales, it does mean that some caution is necessary when using data derived from the MMPI, which has a different codetype frequency.

Scale **7** measures anxiety, usually of a long-term nature. The scale may be elevated during times of situational stress (state anxiety), but tends to measure situational stress plus a type of living that includes worrying a great deal (trait anxiety). The state anxiety component in the MMPI is most likely measured by scale **A** of the supplementary scales, while the trait anxiety is most likely measured by scale **7.** For further comments about the relationship between the two scales, see the **A** scale general information section (p. 306).

Scale **7** is one of the most frequent high points on profiles of clients in college counseling centers and mental health clinics. On the MMPI, this scale is usually elevated with scale **2** and/or scale **8**; however, both scales **2** and **8** are lowered on the MMPI-2 so it remains to be seen whether this relationship between the three scales will remain in this new test. A special relationship exists between scales **7** and **8.** When they are both elevated, special note is to be made as to which scale is the higher. When scale **7** is higher than scale **8,** especially by 10 points or more, the person usually has a better prognosis than when scale **8** is higher because the person is still fighting his/her problem and is highly anxious about it. When the **8** scale is higher, mental confusion keeps the person from focusing on solutions to his/her problems; therefore, therapy usually is not as productive as it is when scale **7** is higher.

At the lower elevations of scale **7** (T = 60 through 70 on the MMPI, or 60 through 65 on MMPI-2 and no other clinical scales are clinically elevated except perhaps the **5** scale for men), a person generally is punctual in meeting important assignments and deadlines and does not feel anxious. However, when a fear (actual or imagined) exists of not meeting an obligation, an anxious agitation emerges until the obligation is fulfilled. People with scale **7** at this level usually feel they cannot put off until tomorrow what they should do today without some dire consequences happening. As a result of their compulsivity, these people tend to make higher grades and faster promotions than others do. Of additional interest is the fact that people with these lower elevations on the **7** scale tend to be great intellectualizers.

Under the pressure of over-obligation, where deadlines or tasks cannot be met, scale **7** may begin to elevate for people who originally scored in the lower elevations of the scale. When T = 70 on MMPI or 65 on MMPI-2, the anxiety usually is evident to others but not necessarily to the person. A fear of failure or of making the wrong decision may appear also.

As the elevation of scale **7** increases, an element of omnipotence begins to emerge in that the person tends to adopt the attitude that he/she must not fail for fear of hurting others. Also, as this elevation increases, anxiety causes a loss of productivity, further raising fears of failure, and thereby raising more anxiety, ad infinitum.

Kunce and Anderson (1976, 1984) have hypothesized an underlying dimension of organization for this scale that in the normal individual with moderate elevations is shown as the ability to organize and to be punctual and methodical. Because they are systematic and convergent thinkers, these individuals make good managers and mechanics. Other occupations with moderately high scale **7** scores are chemists, carpenters, math science teachers, and bankers (Kunce & Callis 1969). For people with **7** scale elevations, stress produces such maladaptive behavior as worry, indecision, and obsession with minutia.

Persons with a low scale **7** (T = 45 or below, MMPI; T = 40 or below, MMPI-2) generally are secure with themselves and quite stable. These people are reported to be persistent and success-oriented by other authors. However, our experience has been that these people do not appear to take deadlines and work obligations as seriously as others because they are less anxious about them; therefore, these persons may give the impression of not caring about what others want to have done. This attitude may make employers uneasy. We hypothesize that some people with low scale **7** scores were at one time in the clinically elevated range, but the anxiety was so bothersome that they decided to become nonworriers and overcompensated into the low range of the scale.

## GENERAL INFORMATION

1.  Scale **7** consists of 48 items having to do with anxiety and dread, low self-confidence, undue sensitivity, and moodiness (Dahlstrom et al., 1972).

2.  This scale shows general characterological anxiety. Variations in the anxiety depend upon what other scale is elevated along with **7**.

    a.  For example, when scale **2** is elevated with scale **7**, depression and indecisiveness are associated with the worries and anxieties.

b. When scale **8** is the second member of the high pair, confusion and disorganized thinking appear with the anxiety.

3. Elevations on this scale may indicate magical thinking, rumination, and ritualistic behaviors (Trimboli & Kilgore, 1983).

4. Caldwell (1985) has hypothesized that this scale, when it is one of the person's highest, may reflect a fear of the unexpected, the unpredictable, and, therefore, these people do not like newness. As children they tended to be teased unmercifully and unpredictably by their siblings, which led to their fears.

5. Scale **7** may be indicating high level intellectualizing as a defense rather than compulsivity (Caldwell, 1972).

6. Schenkenberg et al. (1984) have found than do younger psychiatric patients score higher on this scale than older psychiatric patients.

7. Scales **7** and **8** are highly correlated (.84), but diagnosis and prognosis depend upon their relative heights.

a. When scale **7** is higher than scale **8,** regardless of the height of scale **8,** the person is still trying to fight his/her problem and is using defenses somewhat effectively.

b. When both scales are elevated above 75 and scale **8** is higher, the problem is likely to be more severe because the person is so confused.

8. MMPI-2 test-retest reliabilities are high—.89 for men and .88 for women—indicating that this scale does not fluctuate drastically over time (Butcher et al., 1989.)

9. Bowler et al., in two studies (1989, 1992), have found that scale **7** can be significantly elevated by organic solvent toxicity. In addition, scales **1, 2, 3,** and **8** can be similarly affected.

# HIGH SCORES

## Moderate Elevations

(T = 60 through 65, MMPI-2)

(T = 60 through 70, MMPI)

1. Kunce and Anderson (1976) have hypothesized that when this scale is in the moderate range (and there are no other markedly elevated clinical scales except perhaps the **5** scale for men), scale **7** may measure the ability to organize and to be punctual, decisive, and methodical.

## Marked Elevations

(T = 65 or above, MMPI-2)

(T = 70 or above, MMPI)

The behaviors mentioned for this elevation are seen most clearly when the scale is the highest of the clinical scales.

1. Single peaks on scale **7** are not particularly frequent; elevations for this scale tend to occur with elevations on other scales (Dahlstrom et al., 1972).

2. People with an elevation in this range on scale **7** tend to be worried, tense, indecisive, and unable to concentrate.

3. They tend to have a low threshold for anxiety and characteristically overreact with anxiety to new situations.

4. They tend not to change much. The basic personality pattern is difficult to change, but insight and relief from general stress may lead to improved adjustment. Our experience has been that even with counseling, the elevation usually remains in the moderate elevation range.

5. Individuals having marked elevations on this scale almost always exhibit extreme obsessionalism. That is, they go over the same thoughts again and again.

However, some compulsive people have no elevation on this scale, presumably because their compulsivity is working for them and it wards off any feelings of insecurity and concern about their own worth.

6.  VA hospital males with an elevation on this scale tend to be obsessive-compulsive and overreact to problems. They have a low threshold for anxiety (Hovey & Lewis, 1967).

7.  College counselees with this elevation tend to be characterized by obsessive-compulsive ruminations and introspection (Dahlstrom et al., 1972).

    a.  The problems with which these students are concerned are usually poor study habits and poor interpersonal relationships.

    b.  These counselees tend to remain in therapy over an extended period of time.

    c.  They tend to become more dependent upon the therapist the longer they see him/her, particularly when they are starting to make changes.

    d.  They tend to improve slowly.

8.  Binge eating severity among obese women may be related to elevations on scale **7** (Kolotkin, Revis, Kirkley, & Janick, 1987). While MMPI scales accounted for 29% of the variance in binge scores, scale **7** alone accounted for 23% of the total variance.


### LOW SCORES

(T = 40 or below, MMPI-2)

(T = 45 or below, MMPI)


1.  This person tends to be non-anxious, comfortable, and stable. He/she may seem to be lazy or non-motivated

because he/she does not respond to situations with the usual amount of anxiety.

2. Keller and Butcher (1991) have found that people with low MMPI-2 scores on this scale are not likely to put themselves down, to have many fears, to worry about things, or to get nervous or jittery. They are likely to be self-confident and cheerful.

3. In some cases, a person with a low **7** scale score may once have been a worrier but decided this style of life was too painful and so became even less anxious than people in general.

## CODETYPES

All scales in the combinations are at a T-score of 65 or above (MMPI-2) or 70 or above (MMPI) and are listed in order from the highest to the lowest peaks. The scales in the codetypes must be the highest clinical scales on the profile.

| **1-2-3-7** | See p. 96.

| **1-3-7** | See p. 100.

| **2-3-1-7** | See p. 119.

| **2-4-7** | See p. 122.

| **2-7-3** | See p. 127.

$\boxed{\textbf{2-7-3-1}}$ See p. 127.

$\boxed{\textbf{2-7-4}}$ See p. 127.

$\boxed{\textbf{2-7-4-3}}$ See the **2-7-4** pattern, point 2, p. 127.

$\boxed{\textbf{2-7-5-4}}$ See p. 128.

$\boxed{\textbf{2-7-8}}$ See p. 129.

$\boxed{\textbf{2-7-8-0}}$ See p. 130.

$\boxed{\textbf{2-8-7}}$ See p. 134.

$\boxed{\textbf{4-7-2}}$ See p. 185.

$\boxed{\textbf{5-7}}$ See p. 209.

$\boxed{\textbf{6-7-8-9}}$ See p. 222.

$\boxed{\textbf{Spike 7}}$

1. This is a rare single elevation. A person with this elevation typically is obsessive-compulsive and/or phobic.

$\boxed{\textbf{7-1}}$ See the **1-7** codetype, p. 103.

$\boxed{\textbf{7-2}}$ See also the **2-7** codetype, p. 124.

1. With the **7-2** profile, less depression but more anxiety and agitation is present than with the **2-7** profile (Guthrie, 1949).

**7-2-4**

1. Alfano et al. (1987) found six MMPI codetypes in a VA inpatient population of alcoholic males. The authors called the group of men with this codetype the "guilty drinkers." These men would be expected to have tension and excitable anxiety, phobic features, fear, and worry. In addition, passive-aggressive personality trait features with depression could be expected.

**7-2-8**

1. Balogh et al. (1993), in a study of college students, found that for this codetype it made a difference which of the three scales was the highest. When scales **2** or **8** were the highest, the test takers were likely to have schizotypal characteristics. When scale **7** was the highest scale, they were not.

**7-3** See the **3-7** codetype, p. 153.

**7-4** See the **4-7** codetype, p. 184.

**7-4-2** See the **7-2-4** codetype above.

**7-6** See the **6-7** codetype, p. 222.

**7-8** See also the **8-7** codetype, p. 259.

1. People with the **7-8** combination tend to be introverted, with worry, irritability, nervousness, and apathy present.

2. These people are in a great deal of turmoil and are not hesitant to admit to problems. They have feelings of insecurity, inadequacy, and inferiority, and they tend to be indecisive. They may feel inadequate in the traditional sex role (Graham, 1977).

3. If scale **7** is 10 T-score points higher than scale **8,** the tendency is to see anxiety and indecisiveness as the predominant features. If scale **8** is higher than scale **7,**

the tendency is to see mental confusion as the predominant feature.

4. When the **7** scale is the highest scale, the test taker is still worried about the confusion and turmoil that he or she is experiencing. When the **8** scale is the highest, especially when it is higher by 10 T-score points or more, the person has adjusted to the confusion and feelings of alienation, and this may be an indication of serious psychopathology. In addition, because the person is less worried, intervention would be more difficult (Greene, 1991).

5. Gynther, Altman, and Sletten (1973) have found that psychiatric inpatients with this pattern, **7-8/8-7,** may have bizarre speech. Depersonalization also is present at times.

6. Gilberstadt and Duker (1965) have found this **7-8-(2-1-3-4)** pattern in a VA hospital male population, Scales **1, 2, 3,** and **4** are elevated above 70 but are not necessarily the next highest scales after **7** and **8.** A man with this profile tended to be shy, be fearful, feel inadequate, and have difficulty concentrating.

7. Adolescents in treatment with the **7-8/8-7** pattern (Marks et al., 1974) were worriers. They were shy, anxious, and inhibited. Many had deviant thoughts and behavior. The **7** scale does not seem to suppress the **8** scale behaviors as it does for adults. The Marks, Seeman, and Haller book should be consulted for further information concerning this pattern.

8. VA hospital males are excessively introspective, socially maladjusted, and have chronic feelings of anxiety (Hovey & Lewis, 1967).

9. For college clients with this profile, men tend to be introverted, self-conscious, or socially insecure. They are tense, indecisive, and confused. They may have conflicts with their mothers and siblings. Women clients lack self-

confidence, are indecisive, and are socially insecure. They also may be exhausted and nervous.

10. Kelley and King (1980) have found with the **7-8/8-7** profile in a college client population that males have delusions, flat affect, and an extensive family history of schizophrenia and alcoholism. These males were more disturbed than the **7-8-2/8-7-2** males. (See the **7-8-2** combination, below.)

Females, although diagnosed as schizophrenic-latent type, as were the males, lacked the overt psychotic features the males showed. In addition to having flat affect and disrupted thought processes, they abused drugs.

## 7-8-2

1. Kelley and King (1980) found that the **7-8-2/8-7-2** profile group in a college client population had different descriptors depending upon the sex of the client. Males in this group had many features in common with **7-8/8-7** males. Both codetypes had depression, interpersonal problems, and at least one physical complaint. They also had disrupted thought processes, ideas of reference, suicidal ideations, and obsessions. They were typically diagnosed as schizophrenic-latent type. The **7-8-2/8-7-2** males in addition had social withdrawal.

Females were less disturbed than the males. Females only had interpersonal problems and suicidal ideation. Their most likely diagnosis was adjustment reaction.

## 7-9

1. People with a **7-9** codetype tend to present many unconnected thoughts and talk compulsively about them.

2. These people may alternate between grandiosity and self-condemnation.

3. Adolescents in treatment with the **7-9/9-7** pattern (Marks et al., 1974) were seen as worrying and vulnerable to

threat—real or imagined. They were basically insecure and had strong needs for attention. At the same time, they were conflicted over emotional dependency. The Marks, Seeman, and Haller book should be consulted for further information concerning this pattern.

4. Kelley and King (1979a) found the **7-9/9-7** codetype primarily for men in their college counseling center population. Males with this codetype had lost weight, and were tense, nervous, and suspicious. Their judgments were poor and their thoughts disrupted. They were typically diagnosed as schizophrenic.

### 7-0

1. Although this pattern is uncommon, when it is present, the person has a serious generalized social inadequacy (Lachar, 1974).

2. Adolescents in treatment with the **7-0/0-7** pattern (Marks et al., 1974) typically were referred because of shyness and extreme sensitivity. They tended to blame themselves excessively and were overcontrolled. The Marks, Seeman, and Haller book should be consulted for further information concerning this pattern.

3. Social problems are found in college students with the **7** and **0** scales as the two highest points in a profile (Drake & Oetting, 1959).

   a. These students tend to be nonverbal and lack confidence and social skills.

   b. College counselors rate these clients as "shy."

   c. They also are tense, are confused, worry a great deal, and suffer from insomnia.

### 8-6-7-F
See p. 259.

### 8-7-2
See p. 260.

# SUMMARY OF 7 SCALE INTERPRETATIONS

| T-score MMPI-2 | MMPI | Interpretations |
|---|---|---|
| <40 | <45 | These people are non-worriers and may be secure with themselves and quite stable emotionally. They may appear to be somewhat lazy and non-task oriented. |
| 40-60 | 45-60 | The majority of people score in this range. |
| 60-65 | 60-70 | If no clinical scales are elevated except perhaps scale **5** for men, people in this range generally are punctual in fulfilling obligations or worry if they are not punctual. This is especially true if the **A** scale is below 50. They usually prefer to get things done ahead of time. They tend to be seen as conscientious workers. They usually do not see themselves as anxious. |
| >65 | >70 | At this level, some agitation may develop. The person tends to become more overtly anxious and fidgety. A fear of failure may become prominent. As this scale elevates, the person may become less productive because of his/her worrying. |

# SCALE 8

## (Sc, Schizophrenia Scale)

Scale **8** is one of the clinical scales that has been significantly lowered in the transition from the MMPI to the MMPI-2, especially for men (Strassberg, 1991). (See Tables 3.1 and 3.2, pp. 42-43.) On the average, this scale is 10 T-score points lower for men on the MMPI-2 and 5 T-score points lower for women.

These differences do not seem to affect the number of two-point codes involving scale **8** that are found on the MMPI-2 (Dahlstrom, 1992). (See Tables 4.1 and 4.2, pp. 86-87.) This is due, in part, to the lowering of the marked elevation range to 65 T-score points on the MMPI-2 instead of the 70 used on the original MMPI, thus compensating for some of the lowering of this scale on the MMPI-2. The **8** scale codetypes that will be affected by this change between the two versions of the MMPI will be those involving the other clinical scales that are affected even more by the conversion to the MMPI-2. Those **8** scale codetypes that include scales that also have been lowered drastically by this conversion, namely scales **2, 4,** and **7,** should be found less frequently for the MMPI-2; and those **8** scale codetypes that include scales that have been raised by the conversion of the MMPI to the MMPI-2, namely scales **1, 6,** and **0,** should be found more frequently on the MMPI-2. Indeed that is what Dahlstrom (1992) seems to have found in his analysis of the comparability of the two-point codetypes for the MMPI and MMPI-2.

This differential effect on the two-point codes involving scale **8** is another reason to score MMPI-2 raw scores for the clinical scales onto the MMPI profile sheets so that the interpretation for the profile can be based upon the configuration of the original MMPI, which is what the majority of the codetype research is based upon. Until data derived from the MMPI-2 are available, using the MMPI-2 profile with MMPI derived data could lead a clinician to misread the profile. Because the **8** scale is one of the clinical scales most frequently elevated, and it's interpretation can lead to momentous decisions regarding the test taker, it is imperative to be as accurate as possible in interpreting it. When the conversion of MMPI-2 raw scores to MMPI T-scores is done, then the interpretations given in the rest of this section on the **8** scale can be used with some confidence.

Scale **8** measures mental confusion; the higher the elevation, the more confused the person is. At the lower elevations (60 through 70, MMPI; 60 through 65, MMPI-2), scale **8** may mean different thinking of one kind or another, especially in college counseling clients. We have found avant-garde or highly creative people sometimes scoring in this range. They tend to think differently than people usually do, and they have a moderately elevated **8** scale; however, they do not think so differently that they are out of touch with people.

When scale **8** is between 70 and 80 (MMPI) or 65 and 80 (MMPI-2), usually difficulties appear in the client's logic so that it does not hold together well over a period of time. The counselor may find that the client seemingly makes sense for short periods of time during the counseling session but does not when the total session is analyzed.

With a T above 80, the client may start using terms in an idiosyncratic manner. The person can deteriorate to a point where the meaning of words is not the same for him/her as for the rest of the world. This results in much confused communication between the client and other persons. Besides confused communication, this scale also may reflect confusion in perceiving people and situations. As a consequence, the person with a scale **8** elevated above a T of 80 usually has poor judgment and may get into difficulty because of it.

Elevations on the **8** scale may be the result of a chronic disorientation or a temporary disorientation. The prognosis obviously is better when the elevation is because of a temporary disorientation, usually the result of situational pressures. Because the person has not been confused in the past, usually with some therapy and a lessening of the stress, the person returns to a non-confused state. On the other hand, chronic disorientation is much harder to change. The person who has had it for a long period of time must learn an entirely new way of thinking in order to get rid of the confusion.

Elevations on scale **8** above 90 usually are due to situational stress rather than chronic disorientation. We have found that people with identity crises ("Who am I, what am I?") frequently score in this range. We also have found that warm, supportive, somewhat directive counseling is the best approach to use until the confusion ends. The client usually cannot take nondirective counseling very well because it is too ambiguous. As a matter of fact, for most clients with scale **8** elevations above 80, we have found the more directive and less ambiguous types of therapy to be the most helpful. They provide some direction out of the confusion the person is experiencing.

Kunce and Anderson (1976, 1984) have hypothesized imagination as the underlying dimension on scale **8.** Thus, when people are functioning well, moderate elevations suggest an individual who is spontaneous, advant-garde, and creative. These individuals are good at imagining what could be. Thoughts and feelings from the preconscious that would frighten others can be molded by these individuals into novel, usable forms. Researchers working with creative persons have found that they earn elevated scores on this scale, for example, architects, (MacKinnon, 1962) and writers (Barron, 1969). High ego strength seems to be required if scale **8** characteristics are to work in a positive direction. Stress can turn these positive traits into idiosyncratic and bizarre behavior.

Persons with low scale **8** scores (45 or below) tend to see themselves as pragmatic realists with little interest in contemplation, theory, and/or philosophy. These people may have difficulty letting their minds imagine possibilities. They also tend to have difficulty with persons who are unable to perceive life as they do. They tend to like a lot of structure in their lives.

When the scale is elevated with scale **0** (social introversion), the problems with the confusion shown in the **8** scale elevation tend to become greater because of the person's isolation from others. These two scales frequently are elevated together, because the confusion the person is feeling tends to foster withdrawal from others, which increases the confusion because of a lack of contact with others, which leads to more isolation, and so forth.

# GENERAL INFORMATION

1. Scale **8** consists of 78 items dealing with social alienation, peculiar perceptions, complaints of family alienation, and difficulties in concentration and impulse control.

2. This scale indicates a person's distortion of the world. He/she perceives things differently from others, and often reacts to things in unusual ways.

3. Harris and Lingoes (1955) have subjectively developed subscales for the **8** scale. These are social alienation; emotional alienation; lack of ego mastery-cognitive; lack of ego mastery-conative; lack of ego mastery-defect of inhibition and control; and sensory motor dissociation. The interpretation of these subscales is on p. 265.

4. The higher the score on the **8** scale, the more shared verbal symbolism is lost and the odder and more disorganized thinking becomes.

   A low **0** scale appears to have some controlling effect on this disorganized thinking.

5. This scale is related to self-identity. The higher the scale, the more the person may be having difficulty in this area (Lachar, 1974).

6. Caldwell (1985) has hypothesized that this scale, when it is one of the highest for people, is based upon a childhood conditioning experience of hostility that was inescapable and unrelenting.

7. The score may be elevated by anxiety, identity crisis, or sudden personal dislocation such as divorce or culture shock.

8.  Schenkenberg et al. (1984) have found that younger psychiatric patients score higher on this scale than older psychiatric patients.

9.  Blacks tend to have the **8** scale elevated (Costello & Tiffany, 1972; Gynther, Fowler, & Erdberg, 1971).

    In a prison population, Blacks tend to score higher than whites on this scale (as well as scales **F** and **9**) (Holland, 1979).

10. MMPI-2 test-retest reliabilities are .87 for men and .80 for women. This scale tends to remain stable over time, except when people receive psychological help or when the elevations are due to situations identified in point **7** (Butcher et al., 1989).

11. Scales **7** and **8** are highly correlated (.84) (Butcher et. al., 1989) (Lough & Green, 1950), but diagnosis and prognosis depend upon their relative heights.

    a.  When scale **7** is higher than scale **8,** regardless of the height of scale **8,** the person is still trying to fight his/her problems and is using defenses somewhat effectively.

    b.  When both scales are elevated above 75 and scale **8** is higher, the problem is likely to be more severe because the person is not fighting the problem as much as when scale **7** is higher.

12. A series of studies has found that this scale is affected by various types of physical problems.

    a.  Gass (1991) found that patients with seizure disorders and patients with other neurologic disorders had higher **8** scale elevations than cardiac patients. He suggested using caution in interpreting psychopathology when neurological disorders are present since the elevations on the **8** scale may be due, at least in part, to the neurologic symptoms.

b.  In another study, Gass (1992) found 21 MMPI-2 items that reflect neurologic symptoms. Eight of them are on the **8** scale. These items are 31(T), 106(F), 147(T), 168(T), 177(F), 182(T), 229(T), and 247(T). In a group of 110 patients with cerebrovascular disease (CVD), Gass found that, on an average, two or three of these items were endorsed, thereby raising this scale five T-score points. Scales **1, 2,** and **3** also are affected by the inclusion of these items.

Gass recommended scoring a cerebrovascular patient's MMPI-2 profile twice, once in the standard manner and again after eliminating the pathologically endorsed CVD items. He felt that the adjusted MMPI-2 profile would give a more accurate estimate of the psychological functioning for this type of patient.

c.  Bowler et al., in two studies (Bowler et al., 1989; Bowler et al., 1992), have found that the **8** scale can be significantly elevated by organic solvent toxicity (Bowler et al., 1992). In addition, scales **1, 2, 3** and **7** can be similarly affected (Bowler et al., 1989).

d.  Moore, McFall, Kivlahan, and Capestany (1989) have found that chronic pain patients may earn elevated **8** scale scores because they report bizarre sensory experiences, somatic symptoms, depression, and inertia as part of their chronic pain experience.

## HIGH SCORES

### Moderate Elevations

(T = 60 through 65, MMPI-2)

(T = 60 through 70, MMPI)

1.  Kunce and Anderson (1976) have hypothesized that when this scale is in the moderate range (and there are not elevated clinical scales except perhaps the **5** scale for men), it may measure the ability to think divergently and act creatively.

2. Some college students with this elevation may be highly creative or avant-garde.

3. This elevation may characterize relatively well adjusted college males who have internal conflicts and are at odds with themselves.

4. Academic nonachievers are significantly higher than academic achievers on this scale.

### Marked Elevations

(T = 65 or above, MMPI-2)

(T = 70 or above, MMPI)

The behaviors mentioned for this elevation are most clearly seen when the scale is the highest of the clinical scales on a profile.

1. People with a T-score above 70 on the **8** scale tend to feel alienated and remote from their general social environment. They may have questions about their identity.

2. In the lower part of this range, people may appear to be in contact with reality, but others frequently have difficulty following their logic.

3. They may feel they are lacking something that is fundamental to relating successfully to others.

4. Adolescents frequently score in this 70 or above range. If they are intelligent, the high **8** score may indicate creative thinking. If they have low intelligence, the high **8** score may indicate poor school performance (Good & Brantner, 1974).

5. These elevations may indicate people who are confused, vague in goals, lacking in knowledge or information, and/ or lacking in academic motivation.

6. Patients who are clinically diagnosed as schizophrenic usually get T-scores up to 80. Above this T-score range,

people do not seem to be psychotic, but rather severely neurotic or under acute stress.

7.  When trying to differentiate between patients with schizophrenia and those with major depression, Ben-Porath et al. (1991) found that both groups had similar scores on the **8** scale, but male depressives were higher on the **2** scale and lower on the **9** and **F** scales than schizophrenic patients. Female depressives were also higher on the **2** scale and lower on the **F** scale, and in addition were higher on the **7** scale.

8.  One study (Glosz & Grant, 1981) has found that the lower the **8** scale is within the elevated range, the shorter the stay in a psychiatric hospital. Also, the higher the **2** scale elevation, the shorter the stay in the hospital.

9.  Chronicity of the patient's problems who were in therapy in a counseling center was predicted by combining T-scores for scales **8 + 9 + R + Dy + Do - 3 - Es - Cn** (Anderson & Kunce, 1984). For patients with index scores above 157, 60% had bizarre ideation. For those with index scores between 136 and 150, only 10% had bizarre ideation.

10. VA hospital males with this scale as a high point have trouble being accepted by their peers. They may be somewhat eccentric and interpersonally isolated. They also may be disoriented and have strange attitudes and beliefs (Hovey & Lewis, 1967).

11. Alfano et al. (1987) found six MMPI codetypes in a VA inpatient population of alcoholic males. One group of 16 men had the **8** scale highly elevated (T=100). In addition, all of the other clinical scales also were elevated but to a much lesser extent. This psychotic-appearing profile is typical in alcoholic populations, and usually the men in it have the poorest social histories and the worst consequences of drinking.

12. Disturbed criminal groups frequently have elevations on this scale.

a.  Roman and Gerbing (1989), in a study of 340 male forensic state hospital patients, found seven MMPI cluster profiles. The **8** scale was the highest clinical scale in 41% of the profiles. Scale **4** was the highest or second highest scale in 32% of the profiles.

b.  Megargee and Bohn (1979) found a group of criminals with many clinical scale elevations, most frequently (57%) scale **8.** They labeled this group of criminals "How." The individuals in this group were the most disturbed compared to the other groups of the study, and this disturbance extended into all areas of functioning. They were confused, anxious, irrational, and aggressive. Megargee and Bohn saw many of them as needing mental health treatment.

c.  DiFrancesca and Meloy (1989) found criminals with the How codetype in their study to be quite variable in their thinking impairment. Some had no formal thought disorders while others had severe thought disorders. Less variability was found in the individuals' affective disorders. They were clearly disturbed and readily admitted to feeling badly. These authors felt that an affective disorder or organic impairment had to be ruled out before a schizophrenic diagnosis was made for these criminals.

d.  Hutton et al. (1993) found a group of criminals in a forensic psychiatric population that closely resembled the How codetype. This group of criminals was the most disturbed of all the groups that Hutton et al. studied. This group had the greatest number of prior prison terms and were most likely to have major mental disorders.

e.  A study by Hall et al. (1986) of men who had committed sex offenses against children showed that these men typically had an MMPI profile that showed general psychological disturbance with the **4** and **8** scales as the most frequent elevations.

f. Another study by Hall et al. (1992) contrasting child sexual and nonsexual offenders found three profile clusters that did not differentiate on the basis of the crimes committed. Cluster 1 was a **4-9** profile, Cluster 2 was a **4-8/8-4** profile, and Cluster 3 had an elevated **8** scale.

13. For nonhospitalized patients, elevations on this scale were associated with the following (Anderson & Kunce, 1984):

    a. feeling isolated (73%),

    b. heterosexual relationship difficulties (57%), and/or

    c. stressful home life (53%).

    For this nonhospitalized group of patients, the majority did not have severe psychopathology. Instead, many times the elevated scores reflected stressful identity or personal crises.

14. Richey (1991) found three profile groups as a result of a cluster analysis of the MMPIs of 81 women who were being treated for issues related to incest. The largest of these profile groups (41 women), which the author labeled the "overwhelmed group," had elevations on all of the clinical scales except scales **5** and **9**. The highest clinical scale of this profile was the **8** scale, and the next highest elevations were scales **4** and **2**. The other two profiles found in this cluster analysis were a within-normal-limits profile (20 women) and a **4-8** profile (20 women).

15. Keller and Butcher (1991) found an **8** scale MMPI-2 codetype for men in a chronic pain population. This elevation seemed to be accompanied by a generally elevated profile. The men in this codetype frequently had a history of schizophrenia or another unspecified psychosis that may have contributed to their problems with chronic pain.

16. College counselees with scale **8** peaks present problems with peer relationships and people's acceptance of them. Sexual preoccupation is frequent, along with sexual confusion and bizarre fantasies (Mello & Guthrie, 1958).

    a. They tend to persist in treatment even though their response to treatment is quite variable.

    b. They do not have the psychotic features seen in older people with high scales.

17. For another group of college counselees, males were indecisive, unhappy, and confused. Women were depressed, had conflicts with parents or siblings, and lacked skills with the opposite sex (Drake & Oetting, 1959).

## LOW SCORES

(T = 40 or below, MMPI-2)

(T = 45 or below, MMPI)

1. People with a score of 45 or below on the **8** scale may appear unimaginative, rigid, noncreative, or restrained (Hovey & Lewis, 1967).

## CODETYPES

All scales in the combinations are at a T-score of 65 or above (MMPI-2) or 70 or above (MMPI) and are listed in order from the highest to the lowest peaks. The scales in the combinations must be the highest clinical scales on the profile.

**1-3-8** See p. 100.

**1-3-8-2** See the **1-3-8** pattern, point 4, p. 101.

2-4-8 See p. 122.

2-7-8 See p. 129.

2-7-8-0 See p. 130.

2-8-1-3 See p. 133.

4-6-8 See p. 184.

4-8-F See p. 188.

4-8-2 See the **8-2-4** codetype, p. 255.

4-8-9 See p. 189.

5-8-9 See p. 209.

6-7-8-9 See p. 222.

7-8-2 See p. 239.

Spike 8

1. These people usually relate poorly to others and may seem unusual or odd.

2. Occasionally an intelligent and creative person will have a spike **8** in the lower ranges of the marked elevation (Greene, 1991).

8-1 See the **1-8** codetype, p. 103.

8-1-2-3

1. Gilberstadt and Duker (1965) found the **8-1-2-3-(7-4-6-0)** pattern in a VA hospital male population. Scales **7,**

**4, 6,** and **0** are elevated above 70, but they are not necessarily the next highest scales after scales **8, 1, 2,** and **3.** A man with this profile typically was inadequate in all areas of his life. He usually had confused thinking and flat affect.

---

| **8-2** | See also the **2-8** codetype, p. 131, especially point 8.

1. Marks et al. (1974) found this **2-8/8-2** pattern in a university hospital and outpatient clinic. People with this pattern were usually anxious, depressed, and tearful. They tended to keep people at a distance and were afraid of emotional involvement. They tended to fear loss of control and reported periods of dizziness or forgetfulness. The Marks, Seeman, and Haller book should be consulted for further information concerning this profile.

2. In a study comparing Hispanic, Black, and white schizophrenics, Velasquez and Callahan (1990b) found that Black schizophrenics had elevations on the **6** and **8** scales, whereas white and Hispanic schizophrenics had elevations on the **8** and **2** scales.

| **8-2-1-3** | See the **2-8-1-3** codetype, p. 133.

| **8-2-4** |

1. Marks et al. (1974) found this **4-8-2/8-4-2/8-2-4** pattern in a university hospital and outpatient clinic. A person with this profile tended to be distrustful of others, keeping them at a distance. He/she usually was described as depressed, tense, irritable, and hostile. The Marks, Seeman, and Haller book should be consulted for further information concerning this profile.

2. Gilberstadt and Duker (1965) also found an **8-2-4-(7)** pattern in a VA hospital male population. Scale **7** is elevated,

but it is not necessarily the next highest scale after **8**, **2**, and **4**. They found that a person with this profile was immature and had confused and hostile thinking. He tended to be irritable, tense, and restless. The Gilberstadt and Duker book should be consulted for further information concerning this pattern.

**8-2-7** See the **2-8-7** codetype, p. 134.

1. Balogh et al. (1993) in a study of college students found that it made a difference as to which of the three scales was the highest for this codetype. When scales **2** or **8** were the highest, the test takers were more likely to have schizotypal characteristics. When scale **7** was the highest scale, they did not.

**8-3** See also the **3-8** codetype, p. 153.

1. This pattern combines a moderate amount of distress, plus some somatic complaints, especially headaches and insomnia (Lachar, 1974).

2. Marks et al. (1974) found the **8-3/3-8** pattern in a university and outpatient clinic. The pattern usually was for a woman who was having difficulties with thinking and concentrating. She usually was seen by others as apathetic, immature, and dependent. The Marks, Seeman, and Haller book should be consulted for further information concerning this profile.

**8-4** See also the **4-8** codetype, p. 185.

1. Velasquez, Callahan, and Carrillo (1989) found an elevated **8-4** profile common for Hispanic sex offenders.

**8-4-2** See the **8-2-4** codetype, point 1, p. 255.

**8-5**

1. The inhibition suggested by the **5** scale and the fragmentation suggested by the **8** scale may lead to an

isolated, destructive act by an individual who is typically overcontrolled (Trimboli & Kilgore, 1983).

2. Tanner (1990a) found 13 cases of this codetype in a psychiatric clinic; 77% of them were male. These patients typically came from strife-ridden families with mental illness and physical abuse common. Despite poor relations with their parents, these patients were often living at home. Marriage was rare for these individuals, and they seemed to be asexual. They were immature and passive with sporadic work histories. Women with this pattern were more frankly psychotic.

**8-6** See also the **6-8** codetype, p. 222.

1. A person with this pattern is usually in a panic and has diffuse thinking. The person tends to break down when supports are gone (Caldwell, 1972).

2. Often these people do not marry, but if they do marry, they tend to show poor judgment in mate selection (Caldwell, 1972).

3. Women often have a little girl quality about them and look younger than they really are (Caldwell, 1972).

4. In a psychiatric hospital, this may be the profile of an assaultive person (Caldwell, 1972).

5. Marks et al. (1974) found this **8-6/6-8** pattern in a university hospital and outpatient clinic. They found this pattern primarily for females who were having unconventional, delusional thoughts. These women also were suspicious. The Marks, Seeman, and Haller book should be consulted for further information concerning this profile.

6. Gilberstadt and Duker (1965) found the **8-6-(7-2)** pattern in a VA hospital male population. Scales **7** and **2** are

elevated but are not necessarily the next highest scales after scales after **8** and **6.** A man with this pattern tended to have thinking disturbances, such as confusion and poor concentration. He tended to be shy and withdrawn.

7. Megargee and Bohn (1979) found a group of incarcerated criminals with the **6-8/8-6** profile (Group Charlie).

   These men tended to be antisocial, bitter, hostile, aggressive, and sensitive to perceived insults. They had extensive criminal records and ranked high in substance abuse. However, because they were socially isolated, they did not have a number of disciplinary write-ups.

8. Hutton et al. (1993) found a group of criminals in a forensic psychiatric population that closely resembled Group Charlie. These individuals were among the youngest criminals in their population. Probably because of their age, they usually were not married, had the lowest level of education, and were most likely to have been incarcerated as juveniles. They also had the highest conviction rate for theft. These individuals frequently were identified as being suicidal as well as having hallucinations. Their modal Axis II diagnosis was either antisocial personality disorder or one of the Cluster C category of personality disorders.

9. DiFrancesca and Meloy (1989) found Group Charlie criminals (Megargee & Bohn, 1979) in their study to have absent to mild thinking impairment in contrast to Group How criminals. (See the Marked Elevation section for a discussion of Group How.) The criminals in Group Charlie, however, were more angry, less depressed, more vigorous, and more constricted and defensive than the Group How criminals.

10. Anderson et al. (1979) have found this pattern as one of three profiles in a group of sex offenders. (The other two profiles were **4-9** and **2-4.**) These people often had sex offenses that blatantly degraded the victim. They showed

long-term socially maladaptive behavior. They tended to act out in self-defeating ways and showed chronic bad judgment. The **F** scale also was elevated for this profile.

11. In one study (Kurlychek & Jordan, 1980) of criminals judged responsible or not responsible for their crimes due to mental illness, those judged not responsible had the **8-6** code as the modal codetype (30% of the cases). However, this study had a small number of subjects.

### 8-6-7-F

1. Anderson and Holcomb (1983) found two of their five MMPI codetypes for murderers to have this configuration.

   a. Murderers with the most elevated **8-6-7-F** codetype came from the most disturbed background. They were confused, immature, and perhaps mentally deficient. They tended to have killed strangers.

   b. Murderers with the lower **8-6-7-F** profile were more likely (88%) to be considered to have no mental disorder despite their profile elevation. However, 47% had had previous psychiatric evaluations or treatment. They were most likely on drugs or drinking at the time of their crimes. They also tended to kill strangers. They fit Megargee and Bohn's (1979) Group Charlie.

### 8-7  See the **7-8** codetype, p. 237.

1. Panic plus withdrawal may be present for a person with the **8-7** pattern (Caldwell, 1972).

2. The **8-7** pattern may indicate long-standing feelings of inadequacy, inferiority, and insecurity. Very frequently the person feels himself/herself to be the inferior member of the family (Caldwell, 1972).

3. These people tend to be passive-dependent. If they are, the **Dy** scale will be above 50 T-score points.

4. A clear cut psychosis with great turmoil is likely (Lachar, 1974).

5. Prognosis for therapy is poor, because these people do not form stable, mature, or warm relationships easily. They usually do not integrate what they learn or profit from their own experiences.

6. This profile indicates more serious problems than a **7-8** profile does. There may have been mental hospitalization and/or therapy.

7. With a high **F** scale and an **8-7** pattern, the person may feel unreal (Caldwell, 1972).

8. With a high **0** scale and an **8-7** pattern, social withdrawal may exist (Caldwell, 1972).

9. With a low **0** scale and an **8-7** pattern, inappropriate behavior may exist (Caldwell, 1972).

### 8-7-2

1. Marks et al. (1974) found this **2-7-8/8-7-2** pattern in a university hospital and outpatient clinic. A person with this pattern typically was described as tense, anxious, and depressed, with confused thinking and much self-doubt. The Marks, Seeman, and Haller book should be consulted for further information concerning this pattern.

### 8-7-6

1. This pattern was found in a group of male alcoholics. Also found were the **2-1-3, 2-4-7,** and **4-9** combinations (Conley, 1981).

**8-9** See also the **9-8** codetype, p. 278.

1. This is usually a serious pattern, indicating severe psychological disturbances. The person may be confused, disoriented, overly verbal, and under tremendous pressure (Caldwell, 1972).

2. People with this pattern are hyperactive and emotionally labile. They may have a high need to achieve but perform poorly. They tend to be uncomfortable in heterosexual relationships, and poor sexual adjustment is common (Graham, 1977).

3. These people's problems may center around lack of achievement or impending failure (Caldwell, 1972).

4. This pattern may indicate an identity crisis in which the person does not know who or what he/she is (Caldwell, 1972).

   a. Onset of the crisis is usually sudden.

   b. The crisis does not usually last long when the person receives counseling.

5. Other scales usually are elevated with this pattern.

6. Therapy is difficult with these people, because they have a hard time settling down to anything long enough to deal with it (Carson, 1969).

7. Psychiatric inpatients with **8-9/9-8** pattern are more likely to have hostile-paranoid excitement than patients in general. They also have frequent ratings for flight of ideas, loud voice, labile mood, and unrealistic hostility. They may be quite erratic and have considerable confusion and perplexity. Onset of this behavior frequently is rapid; however, there may have been behavior problems in school.

For the **8-9** profile, increased speech and activity typically are found. With the **9-8** profile, the patient may not know why he/she is hospitalized (Altman, Warbin, Sletten, & Gynther, 1973).

8. Marks et al. (1974) found this **8-9/9-8** pattern in a university hospital and outpatient clinic. They found the pattern usually for females who were characterized by delusional thinking, rumination, anxiety, and agitation. The Marks, Seeman, and Haller book should be consulted for further information concerning this profile.

9. Gilberstadt and Duker (1965) found this **8-9** pattern in a VA hospital male population. A person with this profile tended to be hyperactive and to have confused thinking. He also tended to be tense and suspicious.

10. VA hospital males with this profile are hyperactive and overideational. They are likely to have persecutory hallucinations and delusions and react to them aggressively (Hovey & Lewis, 1967).

11. Adolescents in treatment with the **8-9/9-8** pattern (Marks et al., 1974) tended to act out and resent authority figures. Those with the **8-9** pattern were tearful and cried openly. Those with the **9-8** pattern were more demanding. Both groups had rapid talking and movement. This pattern tended to be correlated with serious psychopathology. The Marks, Seeman, and Haller book should be consulted for further information concerning this pattern.

12. Megargee and Bohn (1979) found a relatively small group (Group Jupiter) of incarcerated criminals with the **8-9/9-8** profile combination. These men tended to do better than one would expect from their backgrounds, which were poor. A larger percentage of Blacks were in this group (60%) than in the other groups, and perhaps some of the scale elevations came from that fact. They had a high incidence of drug abuse but low violence and

generally did well in prison. However, when they did get into trouble, they had a higher percentage of assaults than the other groups. They had one of the lowest recidivism rates.

13. College male counselees with this pattern were unhappy, confused, and worrying. Females were restless, depressed, confused, lacking in skills with the opposite sex, and in conflict with parents and siblings (Drake & Oetting, 1959).

**8-0** See also the **0-8** codetype, p. 289.

1. Tanner (1990b) found 8 cases with this codetype in a psychiatric center. All but one of these individuals were female. They were all middle-aged with multiple psychiatric hospitalizations for psychotic diagnoses. They had memory deficits and trouble concentrating. They complained about their nerves and were likely to have hallucinations and delusions. Despite their histories, most were married.

2. Marked withdrawal and people avoidance are most likely with this pattern (Lachar, 1974).

3. VA hospital males with this combination are worried, confused, and indecisive (Hovey & Lewis, 1967).

4. College counselees with this pattern tend to be nervous and nonverbal, as well as introverted and shy. They tend to be poor communicators in counseling sessions (Drake & Oetting, 1959).

# SUMMARY OF 8 SCALE INTERPRETATIONS

| T-Score MMPI-2 | MMPI | Interpretations |
|---|---|---|
| <40 | <45 | These people tend to see themselves as realists and usually are not interested in contemplation, theory, or philosophy. They may be unimaginative and like structure and routine in their lives. |
| 40-60 | 45-60 | The majority of people score in this range. |
| 60-65 | 60-70 | Persons with scores in this range may think somewhat differently than other people. These may be avant-garde or highly creative individuals. |
| 65-80 | 70-80 | At this level, difficulties in logical thinking may develop. To follow the person's train of thought over a period of time may be difficult. |
| 80-90 | 80-90 | People start seeming very confused. Communication usually becomes quite difficult. The person also may have trouble perceiving people and situations accurately and thus may have poor judgment. |
| >90 | >90 | People at this level usually are suffering from some kind of identity crisis, not knowing who or what they are. This elevation is usually the result of situational stress. |

# HARRIS AND LINGOES SUBSCALES FOR SCALE 8

| Subscales | Interpretation |
|---|---|
| Sc 1 Social Alienation (21 items) | These people feel alienated from family and others. They report feeling lonely and misunderstood. |
| Sc 2 Emotional Alienation (11 items) | This individual experiences self as strange and alien. |
| Sc 3 Lack of Ego Mastery, Cognitive (10 items) | He/she reports unusual thoughts and strange ideas. He/she also reports problems with thinking clearly. |
| Sc 4 Lack of Ego Mastery, Conative (14 items) | This person reports problems coping with life and may show depression and despair. |
| Sc 5 Lack of Ego Mastery, Defective Inhibition (11 items) | He/she feels not in control of emotions and may report ups and downs. |
| Sc 6 Bizarre Sensory Experiences (20 items) | This individual reports unusual sensory experiences. |

# SCALE 9

## (Ma, Mania Scale)

Scale **9** has been lowered about 5 T-score points in the transition from the MMPI to the MMPI-2 (Strassberg, 1991). (See Tables 3.1 and 3.2, pp. 42-43.) Perhaps as a result of this, Dahlstrom (1992) has found that two-point codetypes involving this scale are found less frequently in MMPI-2 profiles than in MMPI profiles. (See Tables 4.1 and 4.2, pp. 86-87.) Given the frequency with which the **9** scale appears in codetypes for college populations and for nonpsychiatric populations, it is important to interpret this scale accurately. We recommend that the MMPI-2 raw scores be plotted on the original MMPI profile so that the research about this scale that is based upon the old MMPI norms can be used most effectively.

Scale **9** measures psychic energy; that is, the higher the elevation, the more energetic a person is, and the more he/ she feels compelled to act using that energy. Another element that seems to occur with an elevation on this scale is an increase in diversity and multiplicity of thoughts. As with some of the other scales, elevations must be interpreted in light of the population involved.

In college populations, particularly with graduate school students, moderate elevations are typical and indicate mental activity, probably with accompanying physical energy. As the scale increases into the marked elevation range, a concomitant increase in psychic energy often presents difficulties. The person may begin to "spin his wheels," become over-involved and overcommitted, and get fewer things completed. A good phrase for a person with a score over 80 is "running around like a chicken with its head cut off."

Scale **9** is one of the most common elevations on the MMPI, especially with college populations. This scale and scale **5** for men are the most frequent peaks on college profiles.

Kunce and Anderson (1976, 1984) have hypothesized zest as the underlying dimension for scale **9.** In the cases where a person is well adjusted, the appropriate descriptors for the individual with a moderately high elevation would be enthusiastic, eager, talkative, and versatile. He/she has a drive to be involved and to get others involved in activities. Hovey and Lewis (1967) find that while these people may be expansive and hyperactive, they also may be quite friendly and happy.

Members of a large number of occupations have moderately high scores on scale **9.** For example, social scientists, physicians, writers, and radio announcers have characteristics consistent with those outlined above. When placed under stress, the maladaptive behavior of these individuals can be superficiality, unreliability, and noncompletion of tasks.

Low scale **9** scores with a college population are unusual, especially with graduate students. When this occurs, several interpretations might be made.

1.  If these people are succeeding in college with little difficulty and scale **2** is not elevated, they may be directing all their available energy into academic pursuits. In other words, they are succeeding in college even with low energy because they have directed what energy they have into academic activities.

2.  If these people are succeeding in college with little difficulty and scale **2** is moderately elevated, they could have been tired when they took the inventory, or they could be at the bottom of a mood swing (such as a post-exam letdown).

3.  If these people are not succeeding in college, they probably have limited energy available, which they are either channeling into a single nonacademic pursuit such as a job, emotional concerns, or social activities, or they are dissipating their limited energy into too many areas.

The typical level on scale **9** for noncollege educated people is near 50, which is adequate for usual occupational and recreational pursuits. As the scale increases to 60, a need for activity is manifested. If this need for activity is not fulfilled (particularly on the job), an agitation may set in with a mild dissatisfaction about life in general. Where opportunities for the release of this energy occur, no difficulty usually is noted. As the elevation increases, usually not enough opportunity exists to release all of the energy. As a result, fantasy may become a part of the person's life, while the activity also increases (usually not directed too wisely). If people with clinically elevated **9** scores also have scale **2** scores below 45, they may report becoming depressed if they cannot be highly active.

A low scale **9** score in a noncollege population usually evidences itself in lethargy. The person tends to feel chronically tired, has difficulty getting out of bed, and may have poor job performance.

For both college and noncollege populations, an elevation on the **9** scale tends to energize the behavior or problems seen in elevations on the other clinical scales. For example, if scale **4** also is elevated with scale **9,** the fighting out of scale **4** usually is accentuated and tends to become overt behavior rather than covert thinking about fighting out.

## GENERAL INFORMATION

1. The 49 items on this scale measure self-centeredness, grandiosity, and irritability.

2. Scale **9** also seems to measure sensation seeking, high activity level, self-confidence, competitiveness, impatience, personal invulnerability, and contemptuousness of timidity and weakness (Lachar, 1974).

3. Harris and Lingoes (1955) have subjectively divided the **9** scale into four subscales. These are amorality, psycho-motor acceleration, imperturbability, and ego inflation. The interpretations of these subscales are shown on p. 280.

4. This is a psychic energy scale. When other scales are elevated, they tell the direction in which the energy will be expended. For example, a high **4-9** combination may mean the person is overtly fighting someone or something, whereas a high **2-9** combination may mean the person is an agitated depressive.

5. When this scale is clinically elevated, the person may be overactive, have maladaptive hyperactivity, be irritable, and/or have insufficient restraints on his/her behavior.

6. High scores on scale **9** probably do not indicate classic textbook manics, because manics will not sit still long enough to take the MMPI.

7. Trimboli and Kilgore (1983) in their research consider this a character scale.

8. Caldwell (1985) has hypothesized that this scale, when it is one of the highest, measures a fear of future frustration of wants. People with this scale elevated cannot relax because they believe their future depends upon their activity level.

9. Hovanitz and Gynther (1980) have found that the **9** scale's subtle and obvious items (Weiner, 1948) are equally useful in predicting manic behavior; however, the subtle items predict certain criteria that are not predicted by the obvious scales.

   Snyder and Graham (1984) also have found this to be true.

10. Scores on scale **9** are lower for older people in a nonpsychiatric population, perhaps as an indication of lower energy levels (Colligan et al., 1984).

11. Schenkenberg et al. (1984) also have found that younger psychiatric patients score higher on this scale than older psychiatric patients.

12.  Hibbs et al. (1979) have found that men have significantly higher **9** scores than women (as well as higher **1** scale scores). They suggest that this may be due to a sex-role sanctioning of acting-out behavior.

13.  In a study of a normal population, the average men's score on this scale was 55 (Colligan et al., 1984).

14.  Education is positively correlated with scale **9.**

15.  This scale on the MMPI-2 has the most items requiring an above 8th-grade reading level, so interpretation of this scale for persons with low reading ability should be made cautiously (Paolo, Ryan, & Smith, 1991).

16.  A study of 600 small-town police officers over a 13-year period, by Bartol (1991) to find out which ones were likely to be terminated for poor performance, produced an "immaturity index" made up of a combination of scales **4, 9,** and **L** raw scores. A cutoff score of 49 was a good predictor of termination. High **3** and **K** scores added to the accuracy of this measure.

17.  Huesmann et al. (1978) have proposed an MMPI measure of aggressive acting out that consists of adding the T-scores of the **F, 4,** and **9** scales. This composite was found to be useful in a college population for identifying individuals with higher self-ratings on a hostility inventory (Schill et al., 1986). The composite did a better job of identifying these individuals than considering elevations on the **4** and **9** scales separately or the two scales together.

18.  For a prison population, Blacks tend to score higher than whites on this scale (as well as scales **F** and **8**) (Holland, 1979).

19.  MMPI-2 test-retest reliabilities for this scale are .83 for men and .68 for women (Butcher et al., 1989).

# HIGH SCORES

## Moderate Elevations

(T = 60 through 65, MMPI-2)

(T = 60 through 70, MMPI)

1. A person with a moderate elevation tends to be gregarious (Carson, 1969).

2. Kunce and Anderson (1976) have hypothesized that when this scale is in the moderate range (and there are no other elevated clinical scales except perhaps the **5** scale for men), it may measure zestfulness and enthusiasm.

3. If the person with a **9** scale at this level is on a boring job (such as an assembly line), he/she may fantasize a lot.

4. Scale **9** tends to be one of the two most frequent high points for college students. The other is scale **5** for college males.

5. A moderate elevation on the **9** scale usually is desirable for college students, particularly graduate students, indicating energy enough to carry projects through.

## Marked Elevations

(T = 65 or above, MMPI-2)

(T = 70 or above, MMPI)

The behaviors mentioned for this elevation are most clearly seen when the scale is one of the highest of the clinical scales in the profile.

1. As scale **9** goes up, people tend to become increasingly involved in activities but less efficient in what they are doing. They may start "spinning their wheels."

2. Three features characterize a high scorer on this scale— overactivity, emotional excitement, and flight of ideas.

3. The mood of the person with a marked elevation on this scale may be good-humored euphoria, but on occasion he/she can become irritable with outbursts of temper.

4. Elevations on this scale may reflect the use of the defense mechanisms of denial and acting-out. The latter defense mechanism is especially seen when the **4** scale also is elevated (Trimboli & Kilgore, 1983).

5. The following groups of people tend to have marked elevations on scale **9**:

   a. Juvenile delinquents (in conjunction with a high **4** scale),

   b. Highly aggressive boys (not necessarily labeled as delinquent), and

   c. College underachievers.

6. A high **9** and low **0** combination is called the "socializer" pattern, whereas a high **0** and low **9** combination is called the "nonsocializer" pattern (Good & Brantner, 1974).

7. This scale (as well as the **4** scale) was significantly elevated for clients in a residential treatment program for cocaine addiction (Walfish et al., 1990).

8. VA hospital males with this scale elevated were expansive, hyperactive, grandiose, and talkative (Hovey & Lewis, 1967).

9. When scale **9** is the peak score in college counselees, other traits the person has are expressed in a more energetic fashion than when the **9** scale is low.

10. In a college population, some females with the spike **9** profile were considered normal, but other women with the profile had a past history of criminal activity and barbituate abuse. They were also antisocial. Males were also antisocial, impulsive, irritable, and tended to use drugs (Kelley & King, 1979a).

# LOW SCORES

(T = 40 or below, MMPI-2)

(T = 45 or below, MMPI)

1.  People with low scale **9** scores tend to have low energy and a low activity level. They can be difficult to motivate and may be apathetic.

2.  Keiller and Graham (1993) have found that individuals with low MMPI-2 scores on this scale are not likely to stir up excitement, to be too talkative, or to swear and curse.

3.  This level of **9** may indicate a severe mood disturbance that includes apathy and feelings of emptiness. This can be true even if the **2** scale is not elevated (Trimboli & Kilgore, 1983).

4.  Some individuals have learned to channel their limited energy into their most important projects and therefore get them done without unduly taxing themselves.

5.  When this scale is near a T of 45 (MMPI) or 40 (MMPI-2), it may indicate that the person is tired or temporarily ill (for example, has a cold).

6.  At the lowest levels of this scale, people may be depressed, even if scale **2** is not elevated (Carson, 1969).

7.  Male college counselees with scale **9** at a low level are perceived as dependent and wanting reassurance. Women counselees are perceived as shy, especially if the **0** scale is elevated above 55 (Drake & Oetting, 1959).

# CODETYPES

All scales in these combinations are at a T-score of 65 or above (MMPI-2) or 70 or above (MMPI) and are listed in order from the highest to the lowest peaks. The scales in the codetypes must be the highest clinical scales on the profile.

**1-3-9** See p. 101.

**4-5-9** See p. 181.

**4-6-9** See p. 184.

**4-8-9** See p. 189.

**5-8-9** See p. 209.

**6-7-8-9** See p. 222.

**Spike 9**

1. These individuals are energetic and talkative and do not tire easily. They may have poor impulse control.

2. Gilberstadt and Duker (1965) found this pattern in a VA hosptial male population. Those men with only scale **9** elevated were hyperactive and talkative people who were involved in many projects. They frequently had previous attacks of depression.

**9-1** See also the **1-9** codetype, p. 104.

1. Medical patients with the **9-1** codetype who were seen by a physician were all in acute distress. They seldom were manic, but they were tense, restless, and ambitious. They were frustrated by their failure to reach their high levels of aspiration. Physical complaints for men centered around the gastrointestinal tract and headaches (Guthrie, 1949).

**9-2** See also the **2-9** codetype, p. 134.

1. The **9-2** codetype tends to typify people for whom activity is no longer effective in warding off their depression. These people may be seen as agitated depressives (Dahlstrom et al., 1972).

2. Activity may alternate with fatigue (Caldwell, 1972).

3. These people may set it up so they will fail when they feel they cannot succeed (Caldwell, 1972).

**9-3** See the **3-9** codetype, p. 154.

**9-4** See also the **4-9** codetype, p. 189.

1. People with this codetype may use acting out as a defense mechanism (Trimboli & Kilgore, 1983).

2. Patients with the **9-4** pattern seen by a physician showed the general effects of tension and fatigue. These effects followed periods of great overactivity (Guthrie, 1949).

a. These patients had poor family adjustment and problems centering around their sexual adjustments.

b. They did not stay in treatment long; therefore, they could only be treated superficially.

3. The **9-4** codetype is the most common one found in entering college freshman (nine percent of the men's profiles and eight percent of the women's) (Fowler & Coyle, 1969).

---

**9-5** See the **5-9** codetype, p. 209.

1. Tanner (1990a) found 11 men with this codetype in a psychiatric population. Most of them were brought in by their families or referred by the courts or other agencies. They were hyperactive, mildly grandiose, and impulsive. These men tended to use alcohol to reduce anxiety and had a high incidence of violence when they were drinking. Men with the **5-9** codetype tended to have more severe pathology than men with the **9-5** codetype.

---

**9-6** See the **6-9** codetype, p. 224.

1. Marks et al. (1974) found the **9-6/6-9** pattern in a university hospital and outpatient clinic. The profile primarily was found for females who were agitated, tense, excitable, suspicious, and hostile. The Marks, Seeman, and Haller book should be consulted for further information concerning this profile.

---

**9-7** See the **7-9** codetype, p. 239.

**9-8** See also the **8-9** codetype, p. 261.

1. The **9-8** pattern is more likely found in mental hospital populations than in nonhospitalized populations. It indicates more serious problems than the **9-4** combination.

   The **F** scale elevation tends to vary with the severity of these people's condition. The higher the **F** scale with the **9-8** pattern, the more serious the condition tends to be.

2. Marks et al. (1974) found the **8-9/9-8** pattern in a university hospital and outpatient clinic. The pattern occurred mostly with women characterized by delusional thinking, ruminations, anxiety, and agitation. The Marks, Seeman, and Haller book should be consulted for further information concerning this profile.

**9-0**

1. In college counselees, when the **9-0** pattern occurred, the behavior shown by the **0** scale seemed to dominate in that the people were socially shy and withdrawn even though agitated (Drake & Oetting, 1959).

# SUMMARY OF 9 SCALE INTERPRETATIONS

| T-score MMPI-2 | MMPI | Interpretations |
|---|---|---|
| <40 | <45 | People may have scores in this range of scale **9** for two reasons. One, they may have been tired when they took the test; or two, they may have a limited amount of energy. |
| 40-60 | 45-60 | This range of scores is typical and indicates an average amount of energy. College students tend to score in the upper range of these scores. |
| 60-65 | 60-70 | Persons with these scores tend to be quite active and have many projects that they usually complete. This range is typical for graduate students. |
| >65 | >70 | People in this range seem to have an excess of energy. They may take on more projects than they can complete. They may fantasize a lot if they cannot keep busy. With a low **2** scale, people may report that if they cannot keep busy, they tend to become depressed. |

# HARRIS AND LINGOES SUBSCALES FOR SCALE 9

| Subscales | Interpretation |
| --- | --- |
| Ma1 Amorality (6 items) | This person is callous towards others and feels justified in this. |
| Ma2 Psychomotor Acceleration (11 items) | He/she is hyperactive and emotionally labile. |
| Ma3 Imperturbability (8 items) | This individual is confident and does not care what others think. |
| Ma4 Ego Inflation (9 items) | He/she feels very important if not grandiose. |

# SCALE 0

## (Si, Social Introversion-Extroversion Scale)

Scale **0** has had one item deleted in the MMPI-2. It was not converted to uniform T-scores since it is not considered a true clinical scale by the revisers of the MMPI; therefore, its distribution has not been lowered as many of the other clinical scales have been (Strassberg, 1991). (See Tables 3.1 and 3.2, pp. 42-43.) In general, studies comparing MMPI-2s and MMPIs given to the same individual (Strassberg, 1991; Ward, 1991) have found that T-scores for this scale are basically the same for the two versions of the test at the 70 T-score level. As the T-score elevations increase however, the MMPI-2 scores are increasingly higher than the MMPI scores for men but not for women. Thus, instead of the **0** scale being on average 5 T-score points lower for the MMPI-2 as people might expect, the scale remains at the same T-score level or is even higher.

This means that the likelihood of the **0** scale being part of a two-point code on an MMPI-2 profile for a male is greater than it is on an MMPI profile, and indeed that is what has been found by Dahlstrom (1992) in his study rescoring MMPI profiles onto MMPI-2 profile forms. (See Tables 4.1 and 4.2, pp. 86-87.) The number of male profiles with the **0** scale as one of the two highest scales increased from 5% of the male MMPI profiles to 11% of the male MMPI-2 profiles. The female profiles were not similarly changed but remained approximately the same for the two versions of the test.

Scale **0** measures a person's preference for being alone (high **0**) or being with others (low **0**). The difficulty in working with this scale is in avoiding the value judgments implied in the scale's title (social introversion). We have found it best not to use the scale name when interpreting the MMPI to clients because the tendency in our culture is to think that extroversion is good whereas introversion is bad. This is not true, of course. Each type of social adjustment has its advantages and disadvantages, depending upon the context in which it is operating.

Persons with a moderately elevated scale **0** prefer to be by themselves or with a few select friends. This fact usually does not mean that they cannot interact with others; it only means that this is not their preference. One advantage of this preference in college is that these people are able to isolate themselves from others so that assignments, studying, and reading can be done. One disadvantage of **0** scores in this range for college students is that people with these scores may not be socially adept. Because they prefer to be by themselves, they tend not to be at ease with many people and may not know current music or slang. One procedure I have found helpful in working with people having scale **0** in this range is to have them join one activity of their choice, so they can keep social ties, while not overwhelming them with people. The **0** scale may elevate to this range as a person becomes older.

Persons with scale **0** scores in the marked elevation range tend to be people who are withdrawing from others, not because of an inherently introverted nature, but because they either have been hurt in some way or the problems indicated by other clincial scale elevations are overwhelming them, and consequently they are isolating themselves. In these situations, the **0** scale accentuates the problems seen in other clinical elevations because the person withdraws from people who might be helpful. People with **0** scale scores in this range frequently do not enter counseling because of their aversion to being with others. If they do become clients, the reason is because their problems are overwhelming them.

A real difficulty with an elevated scale **0** in conjunction with an elevated scale **8** is that these two scales tend to accentuate each other. As people become confused (high **8**), they also tend to isolate themselves. And, as they become more isolated, they tend to become more confused because they lack contact with others.

People with low scale **0** scores prefer to be with people as opposed to being alone. They tend to be socially adept and involved with people. An advantage of the low **0** score for these people is that they remain in touch with the world when there is psychological difficulty. This level of the **0** scale particularly is helpful when people have an elevated scale **8** and are confused. The primary disadvantage for persons with this level of the **0** scale is that they may have difficulty being alone. Thus, in college, they usually would rather go to a party than study by themselves. These people also tend to have difficulty in occupations where they are not involved with people.

Kunce and Anderson (1976, 1984) have hypothesized autonomy as the underlying dimension of this scale. Well functioning individuals with moderate elevations will be independent and resourceful. When a person becomes stressed, this may turn into a withdrawal from social interactions.

We find most college students (non-clients) scoring in the low range on the **0** scale, with the average for this group being near 45.

An interesting use of the **0** scale is to note its location for each of the persons in marital counseling. Good and Brantner (1974) have suggested that the behavior shown on the **0** scale can be an important factor in marital conflict if one of the couple is moderately elevated or higher on the scale and the other person is low on this scale. When the **0** scale scorers are that much apart, one of the couple is more of a socializer than the other, and this may be one cause of their marital difficulty.

## GENERAL INFORMATION

1. Scale **0** consists of 70 items (69 items, MMPI-2) concerning uneasiness in social situations, insecurities, worries, and lack of social participation.

2. The higher the scale, the more the person prefers being by himself/herself; the lower the scale the more the person seeks social contacts.

3. College students tend to be in the low range on this scale.

4. Trimboli and Kilgore (1983) in their research saw this as a character scale.

5. New content homogeneous subscales have been developed for the **0** scale (Ben-Porath, Hostetler, Butcher, & Graham, 1989). These new subscales are Shyness/Self-Consciousness, Social Avoidance, and Alienation—Self and Others.

6. As a high point, scale **0** is most frequently paired with scales **2, 7,** and **8.**

7. This scale is negatively correlated to education (Colligan et al., 1984).

8. MMPI-2 test-retest reliabilities for the scale are .92 for men and .91 for women (Butcher et al., 1989).

9. In a study comparing males who had committed incest with males who were non-incestuous child sexual molesters, the profiles were relatively similar except that the **0** scale was much higher for the incestuous males (Panton, 1979).

10. Husband and wife profile pairs, in which at least 15 T-score points difference exists on this scale, were found more often for couples in marriage counseling than for couples from the general population (Arnold, 1970; Ollendick et al., 1983).

11. Students in a college counseling center with higher MMPI **0** scale scores tended to remain in therapy longer than students with lower **0** scores (Elliott et al., 1987). The authors hypothesized that this may be due to the students with the higher **0** scales having less of a support system.

## HIGH SCORES

### Moderate Elevations

(T = 60 through 65, MMPI-2)

(T = 60 through 70, MMPI)

1. A moderate elevation on this scale indicates that an individual feels more comfortable alone or in a small group whose members are well known.

2. Kunce and Anderson (1976) have hypothesized that when this scale is in the moderate range (and there are no other elevated clinical scales except the **5** scale for men), it may measure personal autonomy, self-direction, and perhaps self-actualization.

3. It indicates less participation in activities.

4. College people with this elevation tend to be more introverted than the typical college student, because the median score for college students is around 45.

## Marked Elevations

(T = 65 or above, MMPI-2)

(T = 70 or above, MMPI)

The behaviors mentioned for this elevation are seen most clearly when the scale is one of the highest of the clinical scales on the profile.

1. People with marked elevations tend to be withdrawn and anxious around people (Carson, 1969). They are also shy and socially insecure. A person with a **0** scale at this level may have an attachment deficit (cannot connect with others).

2. Elevations on this scale may reflect the use of avoidance and withdrawal, which may be accompanied by suspiciousness (Trimboli & Kilgore, 1983).

3. Other scales when combined with scale **0** often give an indication of the type and seriousness of the social adjustment problems.

   An elevation of this scale tends to suppress the acting-out behavior typically seen with high **4** and **9** scale elevations; however, it may enhance the ruminating behavior seen with the high **2** and **7** scales, and especially may enhance the ruminating behavior seen with the high **8** scale.

4. A high **0** and low **9** scale combination is called the "non-socializer" pattern, while the high **9** and low **0** combination is called the "socializer" pattern (Good & Brantner, 1974).

## LOW SCORES

(T = 40 or below, MMPI-2)

(T = 45 or below, MMPI)

1. Low scores indicate socially extroverted persons who are poised and confident in social and group situations.

2. Caldwell (1977) has hypothesized that a low score on this scale may show a liking to be in front of people or a certain amount of exhibitionism.

3. Carson (1985) reported that people with very low **0** scores may have an excessive dependency upon being attractive to others.

4. Scores of 45 or below seem to be indicative of an adequate social adjustment even when other clinical scales are high, particularly scales **2, 7,** and **8,** which usually are associated with serious problems (Graham, Schroeder, & Lilly, 1971).

5. With women, low scale **0** scores seem to be associated with good social adjustment including parental relationships. With men, however, the social adjustment does not necessarily mean freedom from parental conflicts (Drake & Oetting, 1959).

6. This elevation seems to be related to social aggressiveness in some men (Drake & Oetting, 1959).

7. These scores tend to be typical of college students.

   Gulas (1973) found the **0** scale to be the most frequent (39%) low point for a group of college males, N = 60.

8. Low scale **0** scores typify college students who underachieve because of their tendency to be involved in many social activities (Cottle, 1953).

9. Below a T of 30, persons may show a certain flightiness and superficiality in their relationships. These individuals have well developed social techniques and many social contacts, but they do not tend to establish relationships of real intimacy.

10. Venn (1988) has found that in a population of men who took the MMPI as part of employment screening, 17 of them who scored low on both the **2** scale (T-score = 41) and the **0** scale (T-score = 37) showed high incidences of arrest, personal injury, impulsivity, recklessness, deceitfulness, and other indicators of pathology. They showed these characteristics even though they did not have elevations on the **4** scale or the **9** scale.

## CODETYPES

All scales in these combinations are at a T-score of 65 or above (MMPI-2) or 70 or above (MMPI) and are listed in order from the highest to the lowest peaks. These scales in the codetypes must be the highest clinical scales on the profile.

| **2-7-8-0** | See p. 130.

| **Spike 0** |

1. These people are frequently shy and easily embarrassed in social situations. This usually has been true for their whole life.

2. Kelley and King (1979a) have found a spike **0** profile in a college counseling center population. These clients typically came in for religious problems and/or marital difficulties.

They were not withdrawn but did date infrequently. They were typically diagnosed as adjustment reaction (most often marital adjustment).

---

**0-2** See also the **2-0** codetype, p. 135.

1. Tanner (1990b) found 19 cases with this codetype in a psychiatric clinic. They were typically single or divorced women who had poor social skills. They were very depressed and dissatisfied with themselves. They were also insecure and had strong feelings of inadequacy. The most frequent diagnoses for these women were depression and inadequate or schizoid personality disorder. These patients showed little improvement over time.

2. In college counselees, men with a **0-2** combination typically appear unhappy and tense, worry a great deal, and lack effective social skills, paritcularly with members of the opposite sex (Drake & Oetting, 1959).

3. College women also show the same presenting picture as college men, with the addition of depression, lack of self-confidence, and (when scale **1** is low point) feelings of physical inferiority (Drake & Oetting, 1959).

---

**0-4** See the **4-0** codetype, p. 193.

**0-5** See the **5-0** codetype, p. 210.

**0-6** See the **6-0** codetype, p. 225.

**0-7** See the **7-0** codetype, p. 240.

**0-8** See also the **8-0** codetype, p. 263.

1.  Counselees with a high **0-8** combination tend to be shy and have problems communicating with the counselor.

2.  Women counselees with a high **0-8** combination may vacillate between conflicts with mother and conflicts with father (Drake & Oetting, 1959).

3.  Women counselees tend to be non-relaters and have serious problems, especially when scale **5** is the low point of the pattern (Drake & Oetting, 1959).

**0-9** See the **9-0** combination, p. 278.

# SUMMARY OF 0 SCALE INTERPRETATIONS

| T-score | | Interpretations |
| MMPI-2 | MMPI | |
| --- | --- | --- |
| <40 | <45 | A person with a score in this range prefers to be with others and not by himself/herself. The typical range for college students for this scale is between 40 and 45. |
| 40-60 | 45-60 | The majority of people score in this range. |
| 60-65 | 60-70 | At this level, the person prefers to be alone or with one or two good friends. |
| >65 | >70 | A score in this range may indicate that the person's problems are causing active withdrawal from others. |

# SUPPLEMENTARY SCALES

The MMPI, as it originally was developed, included only the standard validity and clinical scales. However, over a period of time, more than 550 additional scales have been proposed by various individuals. In previous editions of this book we have discussed 12 of these scales, which we labeled "research scales." In this chapter we will be updating information about these research scales, which we now call "supplementary scales," and we will talk about new supplementary scales that have been added to the MMPI-2 by the revisors of the test. We will finish this introduction with a brief discussion of content scales for both the MMPI and MMPI-2.

Six of the eleven supplementary scales that we recommended be used for MMPI interpretations in previous editions of this book remain in the new MMPI-2. These six scales are **A** (Anxiety), **R** (Repression), **Es** (Ego Strength), **Do** (Dominance), **Re** (Social Responsibility), and **MAC** (MacAndrew Addiction Scale). The other five scales that we recommended, **Lb** (Low Back Pain), **Dy** (Dependency), **Pr** (Prejudice), **St** (Status), and **Cn** (Control), were dropped from the MMPI-2 but are still available for the MMPI.

The six scales that have remained as supplementary scales on the MMPI-2 have been differentially affected by the change from the MMPI to the MMPI-2. Two types of changes have been made, one in scale length and the other in T-score distribution. Four of the six scales are relatively unchanged in length. The **A** and **MAC** scales have had no items dropped, although four of the **MAC** items have been rewritten. The **Re** scale has had two items dropped (6% of the scale items), and the **R** and **Do** scales have lost three items each (8% and 11% of the scale items, respectively). The **Es** scale has lost 25% of its items or 16 out of 68 items.

In addition to these changes due to losing some items, the T-score conversions for these six scales also have been changed. Tables 5.1 and 5.2, pp. 293-296, show the old and new T-scores for the same raw scores of these six scales. Some of the differences between the two sets of T-scores are most likely due to the shortening of some of the scales, for example, the changes in the **Es** scale. Other T-score changes are more difficult to explain. For example, the **A** scale, which has not been shortened, has T-scores approximately 5 T-score points higher on the MMPI-2 than the original MMPI for the same raw scores. On the original MMPI, a test taker had to endorse 28 **A** scale items to reach 70 T-score points or clinical significance. On the MMPI-2, if the test taker endorses 28 items, he or she will score 75 T-score points, or 10 points above the line indicating clinical significance.

The other supplementary scales that have been retained on the MMPI-2 also have been affected by the T-score changes but not as much as the **A** scale. The T-score changes for each of the six retained scales as well as the possible implications of those changes for interpreting these scales will be discussed in the introductory section for each of the scales.

The five supplementary scales that have not been kept for the MMPI-2 by the test revisors are still sufficiently intact to be scored if a clinician should so desire. These scales also are shorter on the MMPI-2, although not to any greater extent than the **Es** scale that was kept on the MMPI-2. The new scale lengths and the percentage of shrinkage is as follows: **Lb** scale, reduced by 4 items (16%); **Dy** scale, reduced by 9 items (16%); **Pr** scale, reduced by 2 items (6%); **St** scale, reduced by 8 items (24%); and the **Cn** scale, reduced by 9 items (18%).

## TABLE 5.1

### MMPI and MMPI-2 T-Scores for Six Supplementary Scales for Men

| | A scale (0 items omitted) | | | R scale (3 items omitted) | | | Es scale (16 items omitted) | | | MAC scale (0 items omitted) | | | Do scale (3 items omitted) | | | Re scale (2 items omitted) | | |
|---|---|---|---|---|---|---|---|---|---|---|---|---|---|---|---|---|---|---|
| R.S. | a | b | c | a | b | c | a | b | c | a | b | c | a | b | c | a | b | c |
| 1 | 36 | 37 | 1 | 20 | | | | | | | | | | | | | | |
| 2 | 37 | 39 | 2 | 22 | | | | | | | | | | | | | | |
| 3 | 38 | 40 | 2 | 24 | | | | | | | | | | | | | | |
| 4 | 40 | 42 | 2 | 26 | | | | | | | | | | | | | | |
| 5 | 41 | 43 | 2 | 28 | | | | | | | | | | | | | | |
| 6 | 42 | 44 | 2 | 30 | 30 | 0 | | | | | | | | | | | | |
| 7 | 44 | 46 | 2 | 32 | 32 | 0 | | | | | | | | | | | | |
| 8 | 45 | 47 | 2 | 34 | 34 | 0 | | | | | | | | | | | | |
| 9 | 46 | 49 | 3 | 36 | 36 | 0 | | | | | | | | | | | | |
| 10 | 47 | 50 | 3 | 38 | 39 | 1 | | | | | | | 37 | 30 | -7 | | | |
| 11 | 49 | 51 | 2 | 40 | 41 | 1 | | | | | | | 39 | 31 | -8 | | | |
| 12 | 50 | 53 | 3 | 42 | 43 | 1 | | | | | | | 42 | 34 | -8 | 30 | 30 | 0 |
| 13 | 51 | 54 | 3 | 45 | 45 | 0 | | | | | | | 45 | 38 | -7 | 33 | 32 | -1 |
| 14 | 52 | 56 | 4 | 47 | 47 | 0 | | | | | | | 48 | 41 | -7 | 35 | 34 | -1 |
| 15 | 54 | 57 | 3 | 49 | 50 | 1 | | | | | | | 51 | 45 | -6 | 37 | 37 | 0 |
| 16 | 55 | 58 | 3 | 51 | 52 | 1 | | | | | | | 54 | 48 | -6 | 40 | 39 | -1 |
| 17 | 56 | 60 | 4 | 53 | 54 | 1 | | | | | | | 57 | 51 | -6 | 42 | 42 | 0 |
| 18 | 57 | 61 | 4 | 55 | 56 | 1 | | | | | | | 59 | 55 | -4 | 45 | 45 | 0 |
| 19 | 59 | 63 | 4 | 57 | 58 | 1 | | | | | | | 62 | 58 | -4 | 47 | 47 | 0 |
| 20 | 60 | 64 | 4 | 59 | 61 | 2 | | | | | | | 65 | 61 | -4 | 50 | 50 | 0 |
| 21 | 61 | 65 | 4 | 61 | 63 | 2 | | | | 47 | 48 | | 68 | 65 | -3 | 52 | 52 | 0 |
| 22 | 62 | 67 | 5 | 63 | 65 | 2 | | | | 50 | 51 | 1 | 70 | 68 | -2 | 54 | 55 | 1 |
| 23 | 64 | 68 | 4 | 66 | 67 | 1 | | | | 53 | 53 | 0 | 73 | 72 | -1 | 57 | 57 | 0 |
| 24 | 65 | 70 | 5 | 68 | 69 | 1 | | | | 56 | 5 | -1 | 76 | 75 | -1 | 59 | 60 | 1 |
| 25 | 66 | 71 | 5 | 70 | 72 | 2 | | | | 59 | 58 | -1 | 79 | 78 | -1 | 62 | 63 | 1 |
| 26 | 67 | 73 | 6 | 72 | 74 | 2 | | | | 61 | 60 | -1 | | | | 64 | 65 | 1 |
| 27 | 69 | 74 | 5 | 74 | 76 | 2 | | | | 64 | 62 | -2 | | | | 66 | 68 | 2 |

R.S. = raw score

a = MMPI T-score

b = MMPI-2 T-score

c = T-score differences between MMPI & MMPI-2 (Minus numbers indicate MMPI-2 lower than MMPI.)

**TABLE 5.1** continued

| R.S. | A scale (0 items omitted) | | | R scale (3 items omitted) | | | Es scale (16 items omitted) | | | MAC scale (0 items omitted) | | | Do scale (3 items omitted) | | | Re scale (2 items omitted) | | |
|---|---|---|---|---|---|---|---|---|---|---|---|---|---|---|---|---|---|---|
| | a | b | c | a | b | c | a | b | c | a | b | c | a | b | c | a | b | c |
| 28 | 70 | 75 | 5 | 76 | 78 | 2 | 24 | 30 | 6 | 67 | 65 | -2 | | | | 69 | 70 | 1 |
| 29 | 71 | 77 | 6 | 78 | 81 | 3 | 25 | 31 | 6 | 70 | 67 | -3 | | | | 71 | 73 | 2 |
| 30 | 72 | 78 | 6 | 80 | 83 | 3 | 27 | 34 | 7 | 73 | 69 | -4 | | | | 74 | 76 | 2 |
| 31 | 74 | 80 | 6 | 82 | 85 | 3 | 29 | 36 | 7 | 76 | 72 | -4 | | | | | | |
| 32 | 75 | 81 | 6 | 84 | 87 | 3 | 30 | 38 | 8 | 79 | 74 | -5 | | | | | | |
| 33 | 76 | 82 | 6 | 86 | 89 | 3 | 32 | 40 | 8 | 81 | 76 | -5 | | | | | | |
| 34 | 77 | 84 | 7 | 88 | 92 | 4 | 33 | 42 | 9 | 84 | 78 | -6 | | | | | | |
| 35 | 79 | 85 | 6 | 91 | 94 | 3 | 35 | 45 | 10 | 87 | 81 | -6 | | | | | | |
| 36 | 80 | 87 | 7 | 93 | 96 | 3 | 37 | 47 | 10 | 90 | 83 | -7 | | | | | | |
| 37 | 81 | 88 | 7 | 95 | 98 | 3 | 38 | 49 | 11 | 93 | 85 | -8 | | | | | | |
| 38 | 82 | 89 | 7 | | | | 40 | 51 | 11 | 96 | 88 | -8 | | | | | | |
| 39 | 84 | 91 | 7 | | | | 41 | 54 | 13 | 99 | 90 | -9 | | | | | | |
| 40 | | | | | | | 43 | 56 | 13 | 101 | 92 | -9 | | | | | | |
| 41 | | | | | | | 45 | 58 | 13 | 104 | 95 | -9 | | | | | | |
| 42 | | | | | | | 46 | 60 | 14 | 107 | 97 | -10 | | | | | | |
| 43 | | | | | | | 48 | 63 | 15 | 110 | 99 | -11 | | | | | | |
| 44 | | | | | | | 49 | 65 | 16 | 113 | 102 | -11 | | | | | | |
| 45 | | | | | | | 51 | 67 | 16 | 116 | 106 | -12 | | | | | | |
| 46 | | | | | | | 53 | 69 | 16 | 119 | 104 | -12 | | | | | | |
| 47 | | | | | | | 54 | 72 | 18 | | | | | | | | | |
| 48 | | | | | | | 56 | 74 | 18 | | | | | | | | | |
| 49 | | | | | | | 58 | 76 | 18 | | | | | | | | | |
| 50 | | | | | | | 59 | 78 | 19 | | | | | | | | | |
| 51 | | | | | | | 61 | 81 | 20 | | | | | | | | | |
| 52 | | | | | | | 62 | 83 | 21 | | | | | | | | | |

R.S. = raw score

a = MMPI T-score

b = MMPI-2 T-score

c = T-score differences between MMPI & MMPI-2 (Minus numbers indicate MMPI-2 lower than MMPI.)

## TABLE 5.2
## MMPI and MMPI-2 T-scores for
## Six Supplementary Scales for Women

| R.S. | A scale (0 items omitted) | | | R scale (3 items omitted) | | | Es scale (16 items omitted) | | | MAC scale (0 items omitted) | | | Do scale (3 items omitted) | | | Re scale (2 items omitted) | | |
|---|---|---|---|---|---|---|---|---|---|---|---|---|---|---|---|---|---|---|
| | a | b | c | a | b | c | a | b | c | a | b | c | a | b | c | a | b | c |
| 1 | 34 | 37 | 3 | | | | | | | | | | | | | | | |
| 2 | 35 | 38 | 3 | | | | | | | | | | | | | | | |
| 3 | 36 | 39 | 3 | | | | | | | | | | | | | | | |
| 4 | 37 | 40 | 3 | | | | | | | | | | | | | | | |
| 5 | 38 | 42 | 4 | | | | | | | | | | | | | | | |
| 6 | 40 | 43 | 3 | | | | | | | | | | | | | | | |
| 7 | 41 | 44 | 3 | | | | | | | | | | | | | | | |
| 8 | 42 | 45 | 3 | | | | | | | | | | | | | | | |
| 9 | 43 | 47 | 3 | 29 | 31 | 2 | | | | | | | | | | | | |
| 10 | 44 | 48 | 4 | 32 | 33 | 1 | | | | | | | 37 | 30 | -7 | | | |
| 11 | 46 | 49 | 3 | 34 | 36 | 2 | | | | | | | 39 | 32 | -7 | | | |
| 12 | 47 | 50 | 3 | 36 | 39 | 3 | | | | | | | 42 | 35 | -7 | | | |
| 13 | 48 | 52 | 4 | 39 | 41 | 2 | | | | | | | 45 | 39 | -6 | | | |
| 14 | 49 | 53 | 4 | 41 | 44 | 3 | | | | | | | 48 | 42 | -6 | 30 | 30 | 0 |
| 15 | 50 | 54 | 4 | 44 | 46 | 2 | | | | | | | 51 | 46 | -5 | 33 | 32 | -1 |
| 16 | 51 | 56 | 5 | 46 | 49 | 3 | | | | | | | 53 | 49 | -4 | 35 | 35 | 0 |
| 17 | 53 | 57 | 4 | 48 | 52 | 4 | | | | | | | 56 | 53 | -3 | 38 | 38 | 0 |
| 18 | 54 | 58 | 4 | 51 | 54 | 3 | | | | | | | 59 | 56 | -3 | 41 | 41 | 0 |
| 19 | 55 | 59 | 4 | 53 | 57 | 4 | | | | | | | 62 | 59 | -3 | 43 | 44 | 1 |
| 20 | 56 | 61 | 5 | 55 | 60 | 5 | | | | | | | 65 | 63 | -2 | 46 | 47 | 1 |
| 21 | 57 | 62 | 5 | 58 | 62 | 4 | | | | 54 | 53 | -1 | 68 | 66 | -2 | 49 | 50 | 1 |
| 22 | 58 | 63 | 5 | 60 | 65 | 5 | | | | 57 | 56 | -1 | 70 | 70 | 0 | 51 | 53 | 2 |
| 23 | 60 | 64 | 4 | 62 | 67 | 5 | | | | 60 | 59 | -1 | 73 | 73 | 0 | 54 | 56 | 2 |
| 24 | 61 | 66 | 5 | 65 | 70 | 5 | | | | 63 | 62 | -1 | 76 | 77 | 1 | 57 | 59 | 2 |
| 25 | 62 | 67 | 5 | 67 | 73 | 6 | | | | 66 | 64 | -2 | 79 | 80 | 1 | 59 | 62 | 3 |
| 26 | 63 | 68 | 5 | 69 | 75 | 6 | | | | 69 | 67 | -2 | | | | 62 | 65 | 3 |

R.S. = raw score

a = MMPI T-score

b = MMPI-2 T-score

c = T-score differences between MMPI & MMPI-2 (Minus numbers indicate MMPI-2 lower than MMPI.)

**TABLE 5.2** continued

| R.S. | A scale (0 items omitted) | | | R scale (3 items omitted) | | | Es scale (16 items omitted) | | | MAC scale (0 items omitted) | | | Do scale (3 items omitted) | | | Re scale (2 items omitted) | | |
|---|---|---|---|---|---|---|---|---|---|---|---|---|---|---|---|---|---|---|
| | a | b | c | a | b | c | a | b | c | a | b | c | a | b | c | a | b | c |
| 27 | 64 | 69 | 5 | 72 | 78 | 6 | 29 | 35 | 6 | 71 | 70 | -1 | | | | 64 | 68 | 4 |
| 28 | 66 | 71 | 5 | 74 | 81 | 7 | 31 | 37 | 6 | 74 | 73 | -1 | | | | 67 | 71 | 4 |
| 29 | 67 | 72 | 5 | 76 | 83 | 7 | 32 | 39 | 7 | 77 | 75 | -2 | | | | 70 | 74 | 4 |
| 30 | 68 | 73 | 5 | 79 | 86 | 7 | 34 | 41 | 7 | 80 | 78 | -2 | | | | 72 | 77 | 5 |
| 31 | 69 | 75 | 6 | 81 | 88 | 7 | 36 | 43 | 7 | 83 | 81 | -2 | | | | | | |
| 32 | 70 | 76 | 6 | 84 | 91 | 7 | 37 | 45 | 8 | 86 | 85 | 2 | | | | | | |
| 33 | 71 | 77 | 6 | 86 | 94 | 8 | 39 | 47 | 8 | 89 | 86 | 3 | | | | | | |
| 34 | 73 | 78 | 5 | 88 | 96 | 8 | 41 | 49 | 8 | 91 | 89 | 2 | | | | | | |
| 35 | 74 | 80 | 6 | 91 | 99 | 8 | 42 | 51 | 9 | 94 | 92 | 2 | | | | | | |
| 36 | 75 | 81 | 6 | 93 | 102 | 9 | 43 | 53 | 10 | 97 | 94 | 3 | | | | | | |
| 37 | 76 | 82 | 6 | 95 | 104 | 10 | 45 | 55 | 10 | 100 | 97 | 3 | | | | | | |
| 38 | 77 | 83 | 6 | | | | 47 | 57 | 10 | 103 | 100 | -3 | | | | | | |
| 39 | 78 | 85 | 7 | | | | 48 | 59 | 11 | 106 | 103 | -3 | | | | | | |
| 40 | | | | | | | 50 | 61 | 11 | 109 | 105 | -4 | | | | | | |
| 41 | | | | | | | 51 | 64 | 13 | 111 | 108 | -3 | | | | | | |
| 42 | | | | | | | 53 | 66 | 13 | 114 | 111 | -3 | | | | | | |
| 43 | | | | | | | 54 | 68 | 14 | 117 | 114 | -3 | | | | | | |
| 44 | | | | | | | 56 | 70 | 14 | 120 | 116 | -4 | | | | | | |
| 45 | | | | | | | 58 | 72 | 14 | | | | | | | | | |
| 46 | | | | | | | 59 | 74 | 15 | | | | | | | | | |
| 47 | | | | | | | 61 | 76 | 15 | | | | | | | | | |
| 48 | | | | | | | 62 | 78 | 16 | | | | | | | | | |
| 49 | | | | | | | 64 | 80 | 16 | | | | | | | | | |
| 50 | | | | | | | 65 | 82 | 17 | | | | | | | | | |
| 51 | | | | | | | 67 | 84 | 17 | | | | | | | | | |
| 52 | | | | | | | 69 | 86 | 17 | | | | | | | | | |

R.S. = raw score

a = MMPI T-score

b = MMPI-2 T-score

c = T-score differences between MMPI & MMPI-2 (Minus numbers indicate MMPI-2 lower than MMPI.)

The MMPI-2 items that make up these five scales are shown in Table 5.3. The means and standard deviations for these scales are in Table 5.4, and the T-score conversions for them are in Tables 5.5 and 5.6. We still believe that all eleven supplementary scales, the six that are already included on the MMPI-2 and the five that are available through the tables in this book, are useful adjuncts to the interpretation of the validity and clinical scales on a profile, and strongly urge clinicians to continue using them.

We will talk about these eleven scales first in this chapter and then will describe and briefly discuss six supplementary scales that have been added to the MMPI-2. There are a total of 18 scales shown on the MMPI-2 supplementary scale profile; six of them have already been described above. Three of the remaining 12 scales are new validity scales—**F**ʙ, **TRIN,** and **VRIN**—and have been discussed in the validity scale section (Chapter III) of this book. Three of the MMPI-2 supplementary scales are new subscales for the **0** scale (Social Introversion-Extroversion) and have been discussed in the **0** scale section of the clinical scale chapter (IV). The remaining six supplementary scales, **O-H** (Overcontrolled Hostility), **Mt** (College Maladjustment), **GM** (Gender Role - Masculine), **GF** (Gender Role - Feminine), **PK** (Post-traumatic Stress Disorder - Keane), and **PS** (Post-traumatic Stress Disorder - Schlenger), are covered as additional MMPI-2 supplementary scales in this chapter.

Content scales for both the MMPI and MMPI-2 are discussed after the additional supplementary scale section. We find ourselves using the content scales as a way of gaining insight into the test taker's diagnosis of his or her problems. There are important limitations to the use of content scales however, which we will talk about in that section of the chapter. In the last part of this chapter, we briefly discuss the various sets of critical items that are available for the MMPI and MMPI-2.

Hand scoring keys are available for most of these supplementary scales from National Computer Systems, P.O. Box 1416, Minneapolis, MN 55440, 800-627-7271. Keys for the MMPI-2 versions of the **Lb, Dy, Pr, St,** and **Cn** scales may be made from the information given in Table 5.3.

## TABLE 5.3
## Composition of Supplementary Scales
## Not Included in the MMPI-2

| Scale | | MMPI-2 Item Numbers |
|-------|---|---------------------|
| **Lb** | T | 56, 100, 113, 218, 313. |
| | F | 3, 41, 98, 136, 141, 167, 176, 208, 243, 289, 297, 365, 398, 443, 449, 461. |
| **Dy** | T | 19, 21, 22, 38, 56, 70, 73, 87, 127, 129, 146, 153, 167, 175, 185, 190, 215, 219, 233, 243, 275, 277, 285, 289, 301, 305, 309, 326, 331, 338, 339, 348, 364, 368, 369, 390, 396, 398, 421, 446, 457. |
| | F | 10, 63, 95, 152, 157, 181, 239. |
| **Pr** | T | 32, 44, 71, 81, 94, 104, 110, 124, 145, 150, 158, 172, 227, 254, 275, 279, 283, 286, 305, 316, 346, 347, 358, 399, 418, 436, 463. |
| | F | 67, 163, 199. |
| **St** | T | 67, 105, 112, 137, 191, 207, 217, 222, 262, 263. |
| | F | 16, 124, 127, 167, 193, 243, 254, 268, 275, 291, 320, 334, 351, 395, 424, 435. |
| **Cn** | T | 7, 12, 29, 56, 84, 93, 103, 122, 134, 151, 169, 186, 203, 215, 218, 260, 267, 286, 301, 344, 347, 352, 390, 411, 423, 456, 469. |
| | F | 68, 80, 83, 100, 155, 159, 223, 227, 276, 283, 329, 355, 420, 455. |

**TABLE 5.4**
**Means and Standard Deviations for Supplementary Scales**
**Not Included in the MMPI-2**

| Scale | Total Sample (MMPI-2) N = 120 | | Males (MMPI-2) N = 44 | | Males (MMPI norm grp.) | | Females (MMPI-2) N = 76 | | Females (MMPI norm grp.) | |
|---|---|---|---|---|---|---|---|---|---|---|
| | Means | S.D. | Means | S.D. | Means | S.D. | Means | S.D. | Means | S.D. |
| **Lb** 8.40 (4/25 items lost, 16%) | 8.40 | 2.55 | 7.89 | 2.50 | 8.60 | 2.30 | 8.70 | 2.58 | 8.63 | 2.46 |
| **Dy** (9/57 items lost, 16%) | 17.20 | 8.87 | 15.57 | 9.10 | 18.27 | 8.83 | 18.15 | 8.74 | 22.64 | 9.23 |
| **Pr** (2/32 items lost, 6%) | 9.06 | 5.21 | 9.21 | 5.60 | 10.61 | 5.17 | 8.97 | 5.01 | 10.31 | 5.15 |
| **St** (8/34 items lost, 24%) | 17.63 | 3.01 | 17.34 | 2.76 | 15.39 | 3.90 | 17.79 | 3.15 | 14.56 | 3.46 |
| **Cn** (9/50 items lost, 18%) | 21.22 | 4.19 | 20.57 | 4.05 | 22.19 | 4.50 | 21.59 | 4.24 | 21.83 | 4.54 |

## TABLE 5.5
## MMPI and MMPI-2 T-scores for
## Five Supplementary Scales for Men

| R.S. | Lb scale (4 items omitted) | | | Dy scale (9 items omitted) | | | Pr scale (2 items omitted) | | | St scale (8 items omitted) | | | Cn scale (9 items omitted) | | |
|---|---|---|---|---|---|---|---|---|---|---|---|---|---|---|---|
| | a | b | c | a | b | c | a | b | c | a | b | c | a | b | c |
| 1 | | | | | | | | | | | | | | | |
| 2 | | | | | | | | | | | | | | | |
| 3 | 24 | 30 | 6 | | | | | | | | | | | | |
| 4 | 28 | 35 | 7 | | | | 36 | 40 | 4 | | | | | | |
| 5 | 32 | 40 | 8 | | | | 38 | 42 | 4 | | | | | | |
| 6 | 36 | 43 | 7 | 35 | 40 | 5 | 39 | 44 | 5 | | | | | | |
| 7 | 41 | 47 | 6 | 36 | 41 | 5 | 41 | 46 | 5 | | | | | | |
| 8 | 45 | 50 | 5 | 37 | 42 | 5 | 43 | 48 | 5 | | | | 7 | 20 | 13 |
| 9 | 49 | 55 | 6 | 39 | 43 | 4 | 45 | 50 | 5 | 31 | 20 | -11 | 9 | 23 | 14 |
| 10 | 53 | 60 | 7 | 40 | 44 | 4 | 47 | 51 | 4 | 33 | 23 | -10 | 12 | 25 | 13 |
| 11 | 57 | 63 | 6 | 41 | 45 | 4 | 49 | 53 | 4 | 35 | 26 | -9 | 14 | 28 | 14 |
| 12 | 62 | 67 | 5 | 42 | 46 | 4 | 51 | 55 | 4 | 38 | 30 | -8 | 17 | 30 | 13 |
| 13 | 66 | 70 | 4 | 43 | 47 | 4 | 52 | 56 | 4 | 40 | 35 | -5 | 20 | 32 | 12 |
| 14 | 70 | 75 | 5 | 44 | 48 | 4 | 54 | 58 | 4 | 42 | 40 | -2 | 22 | 34 | 12 |
| 15 | 74 | 80 | 6 | 45 | 49 | 4 | 56 | 59 | 3 | 44 | 43 | -1 | 25 | 36 | 11 |
| 16 | 78 | 85 | 7 | 46 | 50 | 4 | 58 | 60 | 2 | 46 | 46 | 0 | 27 | 38 | 11 |
| 17 | 83 | 90 | 7 | 47 | 51 | 4 | 60 | 63 | 3 | 49 | 50 | 1 | 30 | 40 | 10 |
| 18 | 87 | 93 | 6 | 48 | 52 | 4 | 62 | 65 | 3 | 51 | 53 | 2 | 32 | 43 | 11 |
| 19 | 91 | 97 | 6 | 50 | 53 | 3 | 63 | 67 | 4 | 53 | 56 | 3 | 35 | 45 | 10 |
| 20 | 95 | 100 | 5 | 51 | 54 | 3 | 65 | 70 | 5 | 55 | 60 | 5 | 38 | 48 | 10 |

R.S. = raw score

a = MMPI T-score

b = MMPI-2 T-score

c = T-score differences between MMPI & MMPI-2 (Minus numbers indicate MMPI-2 lower than MMPI.)

**TABLE 5.5** continued

| | Lb scale (4 items omitted) | | | Dy scale (9 items omitted) | | | Pr scale (2 items omitted) | | | St scale (8 items omitted) | | | Cn scale (9 items omitted) | | |
|------|---|---|---|----|----|---|----|----|---|----|----|----|----|-----|----|
| R.S. | a | b | c | a | b | c | a | b | c | a | b | c | a | b | c |
| 21 | | | | 52 | 55 | 3 | 67 | 72 | 5 | 57 | 63 | 6 | 40 | 50 | 10 |
| 22 | | | | 53 | 56 | 3 | 69 | 74 | 5 | 59 | 66 | 7 | 43 | 53 | 10 |
| 23 | | | | 54 | 57 | 3 | 71 | 75 | 4 | 62 | 70 | 8 | 45 | 55 | 10 |
| 24 | | | | 55 | 58 | 3 | 73 | 77 | 4 | 64 | 73 | 9 | 48 | 58 | 10 |
| 25 | | | | 56 | 60 | 4 | 75 | 79 | 4 | 66 | 76 | 10 | 50 | 60 | 10 |
| 26 | | | | 57 | 61 | 4 | 76 | 80 | 4 | 69 | 80 | 11 | 53 | 63 | 10 |
| 27 | | | | 58 | 62 | 4 | 78 | 82 | 4 | 71 | 83 | 12 | 55 | 65 | 10 |
| 28 | | | | 59 | 63 | 4 | 80 | 84 | 4 | 73 | 86 | 13 | 58 | 68 | 10 |
| 29 | | | | 61 | 64 | 3 | 82 | 85 | 3 | | | | 61 | 79 | 9 |
| 30 | | | | 62 | 65 | 3 | | | | | | | 63 | 73 | 10 |
| 31 | | | | 63 | 66 | 3 | | | | | | | 66 | 75 | 9 |
| 32 | | | | 64 | 67 | 3 | | | | | | | 68 | 78 | 10 |
| 33 | | | | 65 | 68 | 3 | | | | | | | 71 | 80 | 9 |
| 34 | | | | 66 | 70 | 4 | | | | | | | 73 | 83 | 10 |
| 35 | | | | 67 | 71 | 4 | | | | | | | 76 | 85 | 9 |
| 36 | | | | 68 | 72 | 4 | | | | | | | 79 | 88 | 9 |
| 37 | | | | 69 | 73 | 4 | | | | | | | 81 | 90 | 9 |
| 38 | | | | 70 | 74 | 4 | | | | | | | 84 | 93 | 9 |
| 39 | | | | 72 | 75 | 3 | | | | | | | 86 | 96 | 10 |
| 40 | | | | 73 | 76 | 3 | | | | | | | 86 | 96 | 10 |
| 41 | | | | 74 | 77 | 3 | | | | | | | 91 | 100 | 9 |
| 42 | | | | 75 | 78 | 3 | | | | | | | | | |
| 43 | | | | 76 | 80 | 4 | | | | | | | | | |

R.S. = raw score

a = MMPI T-score

b = MMPI-2 T-score

c = T-score differences between MMPI & MMPI-2 (Minus numbers indicate MMPI-2 lower than MMPI.)

## TABLE 5.6
## MMPI and MMPI-2 T-scores for
## Five Supplementary Scales for Women

| | Lb scale (4 items omitted) | | | Dy scale (9 items omitted) | | | Pr scale (2 items omitted) | | | St scale (8 items omitted) | | | Cn scale (9 items omitted) | | |
|------|----|----|----|----|----|----|----|----|----|----|----|----|----|----|----|
| R.S. | a | b | c | a | b | c | a | b | c | a | b | c | a | b | c |
| 1 | | 20 | | 25 | 30 | 5 | | | | | | | | | |
| 2 | 20 | 23 | 3 | 26 | 31 | 5 | | | | | | | | | |
| 3 | 24 | 26 | 2 | 27 | 33 | 6 | | | | | | | | | |
| 4 | 28 | 30 | 2 | 28 | 34 | 6 | 36 | 40 | 4 | | | | | | |
| 5 | 32 | 35 | 3 | 29 | 36 | 7 | 38 | 42 | 4 | | | | | | |
| 6 | 37 | 40 | 3 | 30 | 37 | 7 | 39 | 44 | 5 | | | | | | |
| 7 | 41 | 43 | 2 | 31 | 39 | 8 | 41 | 46 | 5 | | | | | | |
| 8 | 45 | 46 | 1 | 32 | 40 | 8 | 43 | 48 | 5 | 29 | 20 | -9 | | | |
| 9 | 49 | 50 | 1 | 34 | 41 | 7 | 45 | 50 | 5 | 31 | 23 | -7 | 6 | 20 | 14 |
| 10 | 53 | 55 | 2 | 35 | 42 | 7 | 47 | 52 | 5 | 33 | 26 | -7 | 9 | 23 | 14 |
| 11 | 57 | 60 | 3 | 36 | 43 | 7 | 49 | 54 | 5 | 35 | 30 | -5 | 11 | 25 | 14 |
| 12 | 62 | 63 | 1 | 37 | 44 | 7 | 51 | 56 | 5 | 38 | 33 | -5 | 14 | 28 | 14 |
| 13 | 66 | 66 | 0 | 38 | 45 | 7 | 52 | 58 | 6 | 40 | 35 | -5 | 17 | 30 | 13 |
| 14 | 70 | 70 | 0 | 39 | 46 | 7 | 54 | 60 | 6 | 42 | 38 | -4 | 19 | 33 | 14 |
| 15 | 74 | 75 | 1 | 40 | 47 | 7 | 56 | 63 | 7 | 44 | 40 | -4 | 22 | 35 | 13 |
| 16 | 78 | 80 | 2 | 41 | 48 | 7 | 58 | 65 | 7 | 46 | 43 | -3 | 25 | 38 | 13 |
| 17 | 83 | 83 | 0 | 42 | 49 | 7 | 60 | 68 | 8 | 49 | 46 | -3 | 27 | 40 | 13 |
| 18 | 87 | 86 | 1 | 43 | 50 | 7 | 62 | 70 | 8 | 51 | 50 | -1 | 30 | 43 | 13 |
| 19 | 91 | 90 | -1 | 44 | 52 | 8 | 63 | 72 | 9 | 53 | 53 | 0 | 32 | 45 | 13 |
| 20 | 95 | 95 | 0 | 45 | 53 | 8 | 65 | 74 | 9 | 55 | 57 | 2 | 35 | 48 | 13 |

R.S. = raw score

a = MMPI T-score

b = MMPI-2 T-score

c = T-score differences between MMPI & MMPI-2 (Minus numbers indicate MMPI-2 lower than MMPI.)

**TABLE 5.6** continued

| R.S. | Lb scale (4 items omitted) | | | Dy scale (9 items omitted) | | | Pr scale (2 items omitted) | | | St scale (8 items omitted) | | | Cn scale (9 items omitted) | | |
|---|---|---|---|---|---|---|---|---|---|---|---|---|---|---|---|
| | a | b | c | a | b | c | a | b | c | a | b | c | a | b | c |
| 21 | | | | 46 | 54 | 8 | 67 | 76 | 9 | 58 | 60 | 2 | 38 | 50 | 12 |
| 22 | | | | 47 | 55 | 8 | 69 | 78 | 9 | 60 | 63 | 3 | 40 | 52 | 12 |
| 23 | | | | 48 | 56 | 8 | 71 | 80 | 9 | 62 | 67 | 5 | 43 | 54 | 11 |
| 24 | | | | 49 | 57 | 8 | 73 | 81 | 8 | 64 | 70 | 6 | 45 | 56 | 11 |
| 25 | | | | 50 | 58 | 8 | 75 | 83 | 8 | 66 | 73 | 7 | 48 | 58 | 10 |
| 26 | | | | 51 | 59 | 8 | 76 | 85 | 9 | 69 | 77 | 8 | 51 | 60 | 9 |
| 27 | | | | 53 | 60 | 7 | 78 | 86 | 8 | | | | 53 | 63 | 10 |
| 28 | | | | 54 | 62 | 8 | 80 | 87 | 7 | | | | 56 | 65 | 9 |
| 29 | | | | 55 | 63 | 8 | 82 | 90 | 8 | | | | 58 | 68 | 10 |
| 30 | | | | 56 | 64 | 8 | | | | | | | 61 | 70 | 9 |
| 31 | | | | 57 | 65 | 8 | | | | | | | 64 | 72 | 8 |
| 32 | | | | 58 | 66 | 8 | | | | | | | 66 | 75 | 9 |
| 33 | | | | 59 | 67 | 8 | | | | | | | 69 | 78 | 9 |
| 34 | | | | 60 | 68 | 8 | | | | | | | 74 | 80 | 8 |
| 35 | | | | 61 | 69 | 8 | | | | | | | 74 | 82 | 8 |
| 36 | | | | 62 | 70 | 8 | | | | | | | 77 | 84 | 7 |
| 37 | | | | 63 | 72 | 9 | | | | | | | 79 | 86 | 7 |
| 38 | | | | 64 | 73 | 9 | | | | | | | 82 | 88 | 6 |
| 39 | | | | 65 | 74 | 9 | | | | | | | 85 | 90 | 5 |
| 40 | | | | 66 | 75 | 9 | | | | | | | | | |
| 41 | | | | 67 | 76 | 9 | | | | | | | | | |
| 42 | | | | 68 | 77 | 9 | | | | | | | | | |
| 43 | | | | 69 | 78 | 9 | | | | | | | | | |
| 44 | | | | 71 | 80 | 9 | | | | | | | | | |

R.S. = raw score

a = MMPI T-score

b = MMPI-2 T-score

c = T-score differences between MMPI & MMPI-2 (Minus numbers indicate MMPI-2 lower than MMPI.)

We find most of these supplementary scales to be tremendously helpful in interpreting the MMPI; however, little information is available about some of them. Consequently, this chapter is based primarily upon our work in various counseling and clinical settings (four university counseling centers, a community mental health center, a psychiatric clinic, and a drug treatment center).

In contrast to the clinical scales, elevations on the supplementary scales do not necessarily have negative connotations. In some instances, they have positive interpretations. To interpret these scales most accurately, each one must be dealt with individually, then in combination with other scales, and finally in light of the context in which it occurs. This last factor especially is important. For example, an elevation on scale **A** (which indicates conscious anxiety) may or may not have negative implications. Such an elevation is appropriate if the person is awaiting sentencing for a crime or if his/her mate has just died. Such an elevation may have a negative connotation if the person does not have an outside reason for worry, but instead has much free-floating anxiety. Conversely, a low scale **A** may be positive if the person is well balanced psychologically and is taking the MMPI as part of an experiment or for self-knowledge; but such a score generally would not be considered appropriate for a person in difficulty with the law. In general, then, these scales are most accurately interpreted when all the factors noted above are taken into consideration.

We use some of these scales in combination with each other such as scales **A** and **R**, **Dy** and **Do**, **Re** and **Pr**, and **Do** and **St**. These combinations will be dealt with specifically in the various scale sections.

We believe we also have identified two profiles for the supplementary scales, one indicating good mental health and the other indicating poor mental health. Good mental health seems to be indicated primarily by elevations (T = 55 or above) on **Es, Do,** and **St,** and low scores (T = 45 or below) on

**A, Dy,** and **Pr.** The poor mental health profile is indicated primarily by low scores (T = 45 or below) on **Es** and **Do,** and high scores (T = 55 or above) on **A, R, Dy,** and **Pr.**

In the Appendix are shown the intercorrelations among the validity, clinical, and selected supplementary scales for two groups of nonpsychiatric subjects. The figures reported in the light type are scale intercorrelations for over 50,000 medical outpatients at the Mayo Clinic (Swenson, Pearson, & Osborne, 1973). Psychiatric patients were excluded from this sample.

The second set of figures, reported in bold type, are intercorrelations for 847 profiles from people in the Muncie, Indiana, area. Many of these profiles came from students in graduate level courses in Counseling Psychology at Ball State University and their friends who took the test to help these students fulfill requirements for a testing course. As far as could be determined, none of the people in this sample was being counseled for psychological problems.

Pertinent intercorrelations for some of the supplementary scales is reported in the sections on the individual scales. Our hope is that these correlations will help clarify the relationships between various scales and the more familiar validity and clinical scales.

As a final note, some of these supplementary scales are not considered moderately elevated at 60 or markedly elevated at 65 (MMPI-2) or 70 (MMPI) as are the clinical scales. What is called high for each scale differs from these conventional classifications. Each scale section must be consulted to find out what is considered elevated for that scale.

# A SCALE

## (Conscious Anxiety Scale)

The **A** scale is one of the scales that has been retained as a supplementary scale on the MMPI-2. Although the number of items on the scale remains the same for the newest version of the **A** scale, the T-scores have been changed, effectively raising the T-scores approximately 5 T-score points for comparable raw scores. (See Tables 5.1 and 5.2, pp. 293-296.) This is most likely due to the fact that contemporary samples of normal individuals do not endorse as many of the items on this scale as the original Minnesota sample (Colligan & Offord, 1988). However, most of the information presented for the **A** scale in this chapter is derived from research conducted using the original MMPI T-scores; therefore, it is most appropriate to use the old T-scores instead of the new ones until data are available based upon the new MMPI-2 T-score distribution for this scale. We recommend scoring this scale on the original MMPI profile and using the T-scores from that profile to access the information presented in this section.

The **A** scale measures the amount of overt anxiety present when the test was taken. Scores on this scale frequently are elevated on profiles of clients seeking help for personal problems in college counseling centers and in mental health agencies. The higher the **A** score, the more anxiety the person is reporting. A low scale score indicates relative freedom from conscious anxiety. The **A** scale correlates highly with measures of anxiety for medical outpatients (.90 with scale **7**, Swenson et al., 1973).

An individual with a high **A** score is likely to have the following characteristics:

1.  self-doubt,
2.  difficulty in concentrating,
3.  a tendency to worry and brood,
4.  lack of energy, and
5.  a negative outlook on life.

A high **A** scale score with high clinical scale scores is an indication that the person is hurting enough to be a good therapy risk, unless the situation that provoked the high **A** has changed dramatically since the test taking, thereby lessening the pressure on the client. Clients with low **A** scale scores (below 50), but with many problems indicated on the clinical scales, are usually poor therapy risks because they are not highly anxious about their problems and/or have learned to live with them even though these problems have not been solved.

As was mentioned before, people with high **A** scores and high clinical scores tend to be good therapy risks. First, high **A** scorers tend to be very ready to admit to having psychological problems, and therefore, the clinical scales may be elevated because of this tendency and not because of having serious problems. Second, because high **A** scorers have much self-doubt, they may be more aware of a need to change their behavior and may be willing to work at doing so. Third, high **A** scorers may be cautious about showing unusual feeling and behavior. Such individuals do not want to be viewed as abnormal, and they may be in less trouble because of their cautious behavior.

In summation, a client who is highly anxious (high Scale **A**) and who generally feels maladjusted (high clinical scales) is more likely to seek help and work on changing than a client whose answers on the test indicate pathology (high clinicals) but who does not seem to be overtly anxious about his/her psychological adjustment (low **A** scale).

Scale **A** seems to represent short-term, situational anxiety, whereas scale **7** (the other anxiety scale on the MMPI-2 and MMPI) seems to represent long-term characterological anxiety, a way of dealing with life by ruminating and worrying a great deal. This rumination and worrying may go on all or most of the time, even when a specific worrisome situation is not present. High scale **7** people, in general then, tend to be chronic worriers, even when the worry is not immediately necessary.

Scale **A** usually shows anxiety in response to a particular situation and may be high when scale **7** is the average range

(45 through 60). A person with this combination (high **A** scale, average **7** scale) is usually worrying about a specific problem but does not have the chronic worrying shown by a high scale **7**. We have found that a typical reason for a person having this combination is because he/she is anxious about taking the test but is not typically an anxious person or worried about a large number of things.

In some cases, the **7** scale may be elevated without the **A** scale being above 60. In this instance, the person tends to be a chronic worrier, but at the time of taking the test he/she was not overtly worried about a specific situation.

An examination of items that make up the **A** scale in comparison with those that make up the **7** scale is useful in pointing out some of differences between these two scales. One group of items on both scales has to do with self-doubt. The **7** scale self-doubts seem to involve the total person more than those on the **A** scale. For example, "I certainly feel useless at times," is an item on scale **7**. The self-doubt of the individual with a high **A** scale score is more in regard to interactions with people such as, "I feel unable to tell anyone all about myself."

A second group of items that sets the **A** scale apart from the **7** scale has to do with phobias that are on the **7** scale but not on the **A** scale. A third set of items indicates that a high **7** scale individual is likely to have fits of excitement and anxiety, whereas the high **A** scale individual is more likely to report the presence of steady anxiety.

Despite these differences, scales **7** and **A** have much overlap and usually are seen as elevated together rather than one elevated and the other not. When these two scales are elevated, the anxiety is both chronic and situational.

Scales **A** and **R** have a unique relationship to each other. In addition to looking at them separately, they also should be looked at together and interpreted in light of each other. In your work with the **A** scale, as well as the individual **A** scale interpretations, we would suggest that you look at the **A** and **R** combinations, pp. 320-321.

# GENERAL INFORMATION

1.  The 39 items for the **A** scale can be divided into five clusters: items related to decreased thinking efficiency; items that refer to negative emotions such as anxiety and worry; items that reflect pessimism and loss of energy; items concerning interpersonal sensitivity; and items that suggest schizoid mentation (Colligan & Offord, 1988).

2.  Welsh (1956) factor analyzed the MMPI items, and from this analysis he derived the **A** scale as a measure of one of the two main MMPI factors. (Scale **R** measures the other factor.) This first factor has high positive loadings on scales **7** (.90) and **8** (.79), and a high negative loading on scale **K** (-.71) (Swenson et al., 1973).

3.  The **A** scale is strongly related to indices of overt anxiety and seems to measure tension, nervousness, and distress.

4.  The **A** scale measures general conscious anxiety of a situational nature, in contrast to scale **7,** which measures a more characterological, long-term anxiety.

5.  Welsh's **A** scale (1956) appears to be the most satisfactory single measure of conscious anxiety on the MMPI.

6.  High and low scores can be "good" or "bad," appropriate or inappropriate, helpful or a hindrance, depending upon the specific situation of the person.

    For example, if a person is facing a situational trauma and he/she is not very anxious about it (low to average **A** score), this lack of anxiety could be a hindrance to working through the trauma.

7.  Scores on this scale for a contemporary sample of men and women were significantly lower than scores for this scale in the original MMPI sample (Colligan & Offord, 1988).

8. Heppner and Anderson (1985) have found that ineffective problem solvers tend to be significantly higher on this scale than effective problem solvers.

9. The retest correlations for this scale in the MMPI-2 for a group of community adults was .91 (Butcher et al., 1989).

10. Items of the **A** scale tend to be of uniformly low social desirability (Wiggins & Rumrill, 1959).

11. Under ideal-self instructions ("Take this test trying to look as good as possible"), the one scale with the largest shift was the **A** scale; it became significantly lower (Parsons, Yourshaw, & Borstelmann, 1968).

12. In addition to interpreting the **A** scale alone, in certain instances the **A** scale should be considered in relationship to the **R** scale. See the **A** and **R** combination table, pp. 320-321.

## HIGH SCORES

(T = 65 or above, MMPI-2)
(T = 60 or above, MMPI)

See also the **A** and **R** combinations, pp. 320-321.

1. High **A** scores indicate that the person is overtly anxious. The higher the score, the more anxious the person is.

2. Men with high **A** scores have been described as lacking confidence in their own abilities and unable to make decisions without hesitation, vacillation, or delay (Block & Bailey, 1955).

   a. They tend to be suggestible and respond more to evaluations made of them by others than they do to their own self-evaluations. However, they may not act on others' evaluations but just worry about them.

b. These men tend to lack social poise and are upset easily in social situations.

c. They usually are pessimistic about their own professional future and advancement.

3. A high score on this scale can be achieved by a true response set bias since all but one of the **A** scale items are scored true. If this bias is present, the **TRIN** (True Response Inconsistency scale) also should be elevated (Greene, 1991).

## LOW SCORES

(T = 45 or below)

See also the **A** and **R** combinations, pp. 320-321.

1. Clients with low scores tend not to be consciously anxious.

2. This non-anxiety may be "good" (when nothing exists about which to be anxious) or "bad" (when the clinical scales indicate problems exist that should concern the person).

## CODETYPES

1. When **A** is high (55 or above) and **R** is high (55 or above), depression often is encountered with accompanying tenseness and nervousness as well as anxiety, insomnia, and undue sensitivity. Generalized neurasthenic features of fatigue, chronic tiredness, or exhaustion may be seen. These subjects are perceived as rigid by others and are chronic worriers. They suffer from feelings of inadequacy and a brooding preoccupation with their personal difficulties (Welsh, 1965).

2. For a summary of selected **A** and **R** scale combinations, see the chart on pp. 320-321.

# SUMMARY OF A SCALE INTERPRETATIONS

| T-score | | Interpretations |
| --- | --- | --- |
| MMPI-2 | MMPI | |
| <45 | <45 | This person is not consciously anxious. The average score for well functioning individuals is 45. |
| 45-65 | 45-60 | This person has minimal (lower scores) to mild (higher scores) conscious anxiety. The majority of people score below 50 T-score points. |
| >65 | >60 | This person has a high level of conscious anxiety, which may cause debilitation as the scale is elevated. The person may lack poise, and be easily upset, pessimistic, and not trusting of himself/herself. Such a person tends to be influenced by others' evaluations of him/her, although he/she may not always act overtly on these evaluations. |

# R SCALE

## (Conscious Repression Scale)

This scale is one that has been retained for the MMPI-2 as one of that test's supplementary scales. The scale has been shortened slightly; three items have been dropped making it now 37 items long. The T-score distribution has not been changed for this scale in the transition to the MMPI-2, which is in contrast to the changes that have been made for the **A** scale. (See Tables 5.1 and 5.2, pp. 293-296.)

The **R** scale measures conscious repression (or suppression to be more accurate). A person with a high score on this scale seems to be saying, "Some areas of my life are none of your business." Determining what areas are off limits is impossible until the client is asked. For example, one of our clients who had a high **R,** but an otherwise average profile, stated that he did not want to talk about his recent departure from the ministry of his church. He felt fairly comfortable about his decision, as was indicated by his test profile, but was still not ready to talk with others about his change in vocation.

While the high **A** scale seems to have some relationship to seeking help at a university counseling center, the **R** scale does not. Clients coming for help with personal problems tend to score above 55 T-score points on the **A** scale, whereas they average around 50 for the **R** scale. Normal college students tend to score below 45 T-score points on the **A** scale, whereas they average around 50 for the **R** scale (Anderson & Duckworth, 1969). Thus, the **R** scale seems to average around 50 T-score points regardless of personal adjustment.

Another unusual feature of the **R** scale is that it does not correlate above .50 with any of the other scales on the MMPI. (See the Appendix.) This is in spite of the fact that it is supposed to be a scale that accounts for the second largest amount of variance in the MMPI. (The **A** scale measures the largest amount [Welsh, 1956].)

The items in the scale are quite varied. A high score on the **R** scale suggests that the person

1. has health concerns,
2. denies feelings of anger,
3. is socially introverted,
4. denies being stimulated by people,
5. is not aggressive, and
6. lacks social dominance.

As has been mentioned previously, the **R** scale is not frequently elevated in clients seeking help at a college counseling center. Some clinical impressions, however, from a sample of 32 MMPIs from a college counseling center population, are as follows:

1. When the **R** scale was elevated 60 T-score points or higher and the **A** scale was 5 T-score points or more lower than the **R** scale, the client was likely to be seen as shy and guarded in his/her behavior or in his/her reactions to the interviewer. In some cases, these clients were even resistive to being in therapy or to having a psychological evaluation. In spite of the client's resistance to this particular situation, a history of dependency was likely. Physical complaints were common and of an unshakable nature. No comments are in the case notes of these people to indicate that they had any insight into their problems. People working with them found them quite unresponsive to psychological explanations for their problems.

2. On the other hand, when the **R** scale was elevated above 60 T-score points and the **A** scale was at least 5 T-score points or more higher, a much more pathological picture of the client was seen. The person not only was shy and guarded, but also typically complained of being isolated, being depressed, and having suicidal thoughts. In a disproportionate number of these cases, some attempt at suicide had been made, although some of these attempts seem to have been attention seeking. These people complained of difficulty in concentrating and had periods of confusion. Usually also a negative family history was

present, but this could be the result of a phenomenon that Chance (1957) reported in her investigation of individuals who had pleasant memories as opposed to those who had unpleasant memories. Those individuals with pleasant memories had **R** scores higher than their **A** scores. Those with unpleasant memories had **A** scores higher than their **R** scores.

3. When both the **R** and the **A** scales were above 60 T-score points and approximately equal to one another (within 5 T-score points), the person tended to be shy and guarded with feelings of isolation, depression, and some history of dependency upon others for support.

This analysis of these college student profiles would suggest that the interpretation of an elevated **R** scale is highly dependent upon its relationship with the **A** scale. A summation of the relationship between these two scales is found on pp. 320-321.

A low **R** score indicates a lack of conscious repression and perhaps a willingness to be open and self-disclosing to others. The **R** scale, as a conscious repression scale, contrasts with the **3** scale, which we see as an unconscious repression scale. One scale may be elevated without the other one being so. In the previous example of the ex-minister's non-willingness to talk about his departure from his church, the **R** scale was elevated whereas the **3** scale was not. He recognized the problem area (average **3** scale) but did not want to talk about it (high **R**). We have seen many situations where the opposite also was true: the clients used unconscious repression and denial a great deal (scale **3** high), but they were not consciously saying some areas were off limits (**R** scale average or below). These people are willing to talk about their problems if they recognize them, which they may not (high **3**).

Scale **R** also has points in common with the **K** and **Cn** scales. An elevated **K** scale indicates that the person feels everything is all right with his/her life. A person with this scale elevation may not be able to look at things that are not going well. An elevated **Cn** scale indicates that the person controls to whom his/her behavior is shown. Some profiles have all four of these points (**K, 3, R,** and **Cn**) above 65. When this pattern occurs, these people may be saying in many ways and on many scales that they tend to restrict themselves to talking about some subjects (**R**) that usually are positive (**K** and **3**), and that they will not expose themselves or their behavior to all people (**Cn**). The overall impression is that of a highly constricted person.

## GENERAL INFORMATION

1.  The **R** scale consists of 37 items (MMPI-2) or 40 items (MMPI) measuring health and physical symptoms; emotionality, violence, and activity; reactions to other people in social situations; social dominance, feelings of personal adequacy and personal appearance; and personal and vocational interests.

2.  Welch factor analyzed the MMPI (1956) and developed the **R** scale as a measure of the second factor in the MMPI. (The first factor is measured by scale **A**.)

3.  The **R** scale is moderately correlated with elevations on scales **2, 3, 5,** and **6,** and negatively correlated with scale **9** (Welsh, 1956).

4.  This scale appears to measure the use of denial and rationalization as coping behaviors and a lack of effective self-insight.

5.  The **R** scale measures conscious repression and denial, as contrasted with scale **3,** which tends to measure unconscious denial.

6.  High or low scores can be "good" or "bad," appropriate or inappropriate, helpful or a hindrance, depending upon the specific situation of the person.

    For example, if a person has lost a loved one, a high **R** score may indicate a situation that is therapeutic for a while, thus helping the person to keep going in daily life without collapsing.

7. The **R** scale is composed of items all marked false. A false response set, therefore, would elevate this scale. If a false response set is operating, the **TRIN** score (True Response Inconsistency scale) would be below 9 (Greene, 1991).

8. Scale **R** items are more heterogeneous and neutral in social desirability value as compared to scale **A** items, which are homogeneous and of low social desirability (Wiggins & Rumrill, 1959).

9. The retest correlation coefficients for this scale on the MMPI are .79 for men and .77 for women (Butcher et al., 1989).

10. Men and women in a contemporary normative sample scored higher on the **R** scale than the men and women in the original Minnesota sample (Colligan & Offord, 1988).

11. This scale seems to be correlated with age in that older individuals in a contemporary normative group scored higher than younger people on this scale (Colligan & Offord, 1988).

12. In addition to interpreting the **R** scale alone, the **R** scale should be considered in relationship to the **A** scale in certain instances shown in the **A** and **R** combination table, pp. 320-321.

## HIGH SCORES

(T = 60 or above)

See also the **A** and **R** combinations, pp. 320-321.

1. Clients scoring high on **R** seem to be saying that some areas of their lives exist that they do not want to talk about with others.

2. Graham (1977) reported that high **R** scale scorers may be plodders and unimaginative people.

3. In one study, high **R** males were seen as people who readily made concessions and sidestepped trouble or disagreeable situations rather than face unpleasantness of any sort (Block & Bailey, 1955).

   a. They appeared highly civilized, formal, and conventional.

   b. They seemed clear-thinking, but they were rated slow, painstaking, and thorough.

## LOW SCORES

(T = 45 or below)

See also the **A** and **R** combinations, pp. 320-321.

1. People with low **R** scores are not trying to consciously repress any topics covered on the MMPI.

2. They probably are willing to discuss with someone problem areas covered by the MMPI insofar as they recognize these problems.

3. Their willingness to discuss these areas with a counselor may depend upon whether they see the counselor as one in whom they can confide and whether they feel the subject matter is appropriate to their counseling goals.

## CODETYPES

| A-R |

1. For a summary of selected **A** and **R** scale combinations, see the summary on pp. 320-321.

# SUMMARY OF R SCALE INTERPRETATIONS

| T-score | | Interpretations |
| MMPI-2 | MMPI | |
| --- | --- | --- |
| <45 | | A person with a score in this range is not consciously repressing feelings or attitudes. The person is usually willing to discuss recognized problems that are perceived as relating to his/her counseling goals. |
| 45-60 | | This person has minimal (T = 45 to 50) to mild (T = 50 to 60) conscious repression of feelings. The person may feel reluctant to discuss some topics with the counselor. |
| >60 | | A person with a score in this range has a strong need to consciously repress feelings. The higher the T-score, the greater the need to repress. This person usually prefers to avoid unpleasant topics and situations. He/she may be seen as formal, logical, and cautious. |

# SUMMARY OF A AND R COMBINATION INTERPRETATIONS

| If the A Scale Score Is | If the R Scale Score Is | Interpretations |
| --- | --- | --- |
| <45 | <45 | This person is neither consciously anxious nor consciously repressing feelings. Three types of persons are in this category: |

1.  Persons taking the MMPI as part of an experiment or class assignment.

2.  Persons seeking counseling for vocational guidance.

3.  Clients who are unconcerned about their behavior, such as alcoholics and sociopaths. These people have a poor prognosis for change in therapy.

| If the A Scale Score Is | If the R Scale Score Is | Interpretations |
| --- | --- | --- |
| >60 | <45 | This person appears to be both anxious and open. This score combination usually is helpful for the counseling situation; the anxiety serves as motivation to work on problems, and the openness allows flexibility in both depth and breadth of subject areas. This combination is more common for people voluntarily seeking counseling for problems. |
| <45 | >60 | This person is not consciously anxious, but he/she is consciously repressing information. This person is difficult to work with in therapy, because he/she is limiting the areas of discussion and is not sufficiently anxious to work on his/her problems. This combination is common for three groups of people: |

1. Persons seeking vocational counseling. The person feels that exploring certain areas of his/her life is not relevant to the task.

2. Job applicants who hold back certain data from the prospective employer and who wish to present themselves in a good light.

3. People with health problems who are referred to therapy by their doctors. They do not see themselves as needing psychological help.

>60        >60        This person is both consciously anxious and consciously repressing talking about areas on the test; however, if the **R** scale is higher than the **A** scale, the person could be having difficulty admitting to the anxiety. The prognosis for successful therapy is indicated by the relative heights of the two scales. If the **A** scale is 5 or more T-score points higher than **R,** the person may overcome his/her repressive tendencies because of the greater anxiety. If the **R** scale is 5 or more T-score points higher than **A,** the person might terminate counseling rather than deal with his/ her anxiety.

# Es SCALE

## (Ego-Strength Scale)

The **Es** scale has been retained on the MMPI-2 as one of the supplementary scales. However, in the transition it has lost almost one-fourth of its items. The new scale now consists of 52 items compared with 68 items in the original MMPI **Es** scale. The T-score distribution for this scale also has been changed, most likely to reflect the change in number of items in the scale. (See Tables 5.1 and 5.2, pp. 293-296.) It remains to be seen how the loss of this many items will affect the scale. It is our initial impression that the scale is lower on the MMPI-2 than what we usually find on the original MMPI; however, this is only a clinical impression at this moment, based upon a small number of cases. Plotting this scale on the original MMPI profile and using this information for interpretation will not help since the scale has been changed so much. We urge you to be careful when interpreting this scale on the MMPI-2 until information is available that is based upon data derived from the new scale.

The ego-strength scale seems to be one of the best indicators of psychological health on the MMPI. The higher the **Es** scale, the more likely the person is able to bounce back from problems without becoming debilitated by them. The lower the **Es** scale, the more likely the person is to have difficulty coping with his/her problems. This scale, then, seems to be a measure of ego-resiliency.

The lower the **Es** scale, the more worthless the person usually feels. When the score is below a T of 30, the person may be having problems connected with employment. He/she may not be functioning well at work because of feelings of worthlessness.

Besides measuring the actual ability to bounce back from problems, the **Es** scale occasionally may measure how much a person feels he/she can recover from problems without measuring the actual ability to do so. Obviously, determining whether or not this second interpretation, rather than the first one, is true for a client is important in order to treat him/her most adequately.

Some characteristics also may exist with an elevated **Es** scale that would not be interpreted as positive. Barron (1956) found that high scorers sometimes had higher than average aggression and hostility. Further investigation showed that this was related to how pathological their early childhood was. Those who had the most difficulty as children were the most likely to be hostile as adults. That is, a high score on **Es** may show poor control over hostility along with general ego strength if the individual has had childhood experiences characterized by friction in the home, poor relations with parents, or a mother lacking in emotional warmth. Low scores on the **Es** scale did not always present a consistent picture in the way people handled hostility but, in general, people with low **Es** were submissive, rigid, and unadaptive.

Crumpton, Cantor, and Batiste (1960) did a factor analysis of the ego-strength scale. The five most important factors would suggest that a reconsideration of the label might be needed. Factors 1, 4, and 5 seemed to be related to absence of symptoms or denial of symptoms. Factor 1 was associated with the absence of physical symptomatology and phobic behavior. Factor 4 was the absence of symptoms related to anxiety, rumination, and distractibility, and Factor 5 seemed to be the denial of weakness in the face of distress. Factor 2 was related to moderate religious interests, such as attending church but the avoidance of more fundamentalist beliefs or behaviors. Factor 3 was correlated with lack of rebelliousness.

The authors (Crumpton et al., 1960) felt on the basis of this factor analysis that what is being measured is the absence of specific ego weaknesses and not the presence of ego strength.

Dahlstrom and Welsh (1960), on the other hand, seem to feel that ego strength is probably the best measure of personality control that we have on the test.

# GENERAL INFORMATION

1.  The **Es** scale of 52 items on MMPI-2 and 68 items on MMPI measures physiological stability and good health, a strong sense of reality, feelings of personal adequacy and vitality, and spontaneity and intelligence (Barron, 1953).

2.  Barron (1953) developed the **Es** scale to differentiate those individuals who showed a greater degree of improvement after psychotherapy from individuals with similar problems who did not improve.

    Some studies (Fowler, Teal, & Coyle, 1967; Getter & Sunderland, 1962) have found that the **Es** scores are unrelated to changes in treatment progress. These studies used change after hospitalization to measure the **Es** predictability, however, instead of the change after psychotherapy that Barron (1953) used.

3.  The **Es** scale elevation may show the length of time therapy will be needed by the client. The lower the **Es**, the longer the client/patient will need therapy.

    One study of nonschizophrenic inpatients (Young et al., 1980) has found that the higher the **Es** scale, the shorter the hospital stay.

4.  The **Es** scale seems to be a measure of ego-resiliency; that is, the ability to recover from environmental pressures and problems.

5.  Crumpton et al. (1960) have suggested in one study that what is measured by the **Es** scale is the absence of specific ego weaknesses and not the presence of ego strength.

6.  While the **Es** score originally was developed as an index of prognosis in therapy, it also can be used as a criterion

of improvement in therapy. That is, people in therapy originally may have low **Es** scores, but with psychological improvement the **Es** scores tend to rise.

Abnormally low **Es** scores may result from a large number of unanswered items (see the **?** score) giving the impression erroneously of greater "ego weakness" than may be present.

7. The retest correlation coefficients for this scale on the MMPI-2 are .78 for men and .83 for women (Butcher et al., 1989).

8. The **Es** scale has high negative correlations with scales **2** (-.51), **0** (-.51), **A** (-.68), **Dy** (-.64), and **Pr** (-.53) for a group of normal people (see the Appendix). The **Es** scale has high positive correlations with **Do** (.60) and **St** (.54) for the same group.

9. Among normals, the **Es** scale seems to measure an underlying belief in self-adequacy along with a tolerant, balanced attitude (Harmon, 1980).

10. Arnold (1970) has found that marital conflict is more likely to occur if the Ego-strength scores for the couple are below 50 or if a difference exists of more than 15 points between the two T-scores.

11. Heppner and Anderson (1985) have found that self-appraised ineffective problem solvers tend to be significantly lower than effective problem solvers on this scale.

12. This scale has considerable item overlap with the **PK** scale (Post-traumatic Stress Disorder-Keane) and the **PS** scale (Post-traumatic Stress Disorder-Schlenger) in the MMPI-2, although the items are scored in the opposite directions (Greene, 1991).

13. The **Es** scale is positively related to intelligence and to education (Tamkin & Klett, 1957).

14. Some studies (Tamkin & Klett, 1957) have found no correlation between age and **Es** score, but others (Getter & Sunderland, 1962) have found that older people tend to have lower **Es** scores.

15. The **Es** scores for college students average between 55 and 65 (Anderson & Duckworth, 1969).

# HIGH SCORES

(T = 55 or above)

1. High scores usually indicate an ability to deal with environmental pressures.

2. Occasionally, high scores are indications that people feel they can deal adequately with pressures when they really cannot.

   Dahlstrom et al. (1972) have suggested that when a person has a high **Es** score and is having problems shown by clinical scale elevations but is denying them, the high **Es** score may not be indicating a favorable response to treatment. If the person, however, has a high **Es** score and admits to having difficulties, the **Es** score probably indicates a favorable response to treatment.

3. Because people with high **Es** scores see themselves as competent, these people will see psychotherapy as useful only if they believe the therapist is more competent than they are.

4. People with **Es** scores in this range can be confronted in therapy without falling apart psychologically.

5. The high score indicates that the person may be able to work within the cultural, social, and personal limits of his/her society.

6. A high score may indicate that a person can deal effectively with others, gain their acceptance, and create favorable impressions on them.

7. Anderson and Kunce (1984) have found that for clients who have markedly elevated **8** scale scores, elevations on **Es** and **Cn** scales may indicate those who are aware of pathological feelings and their potential for acting out impulsively, but their conscious awareness and adequate level of ego strength **(Es)** may enable them to better control their behavior **(Cn)**.

8. High scores tend to be typical of college students. The usual score for such students is near 60 (Anderson & Duckworth, 1969).

## LOW SCORES

(T = 45 or below)

1. Low scores may indicate less self-restraint and environmental mastery than average scores do.

2. The person with a score in this range frequently perceives situations as stressful when others do not. Therefore, he/she is chronically under more stress than the person with a high **Es** score.

3. Occasionally, low scores are indications that people feel they cannot deal adequately with problems when they really can.

4. Low scores may occur when the person is feeling he/she needs help in therapy (the "cry for help" syndrome). A person who feels this way typically has a high **F** score as well as the low **Es** score.

5. Extraordinarily low scores usually indicate a perceived or real inability to cope with everyday occurrences.

6. Cernovsky (1984) has found in one study that alcohol use was related to the average profile elevation of the clinical scales more clearly for people with low **Es** scores than for those with high **Es** scores. In other words, those people with high average profiles and low **Es** were more likely to have alcohol abuse than those people with high average profiles and high **Es** scores.

7. In one study, self-appraised ineffective problem solvers were significantly lower on **Es** (Heppner & Anderson, 1985).

## CODETYPES

| **Es-Do-St** | (T = 55 or above)

1. This codetype tends to be typical of college students and well adjusted individuals.

| **Es-Do-St** | (T = 45 or below) plus **Dy** (T = 55 or above)

1. These people feel they are not worth much and do not expect much out of life. They also feel they must rely on others to make decisions for them.

# SUMMARY OF Es SCALE INTERPRETATIONS

| T-score MMPI-2    MMPI | Interpretations |
|---|---|
| <35 | A person with this score tends to have a very poor self-concept and usually feels helpless to act in bettering his/her situation. This person often frustrates the counselor by having good intentions but not acting on them. The person needs ego building before he/she is able to deal with problems. |
| 35-45 | This person tends to have a poor self-concept. |
| 45-60 | This person usually has enough ego strength to deal with life's stresses and minor setbacks. For a college student, an **Es** score in the lower part of this range may indicate that he/she is not as confident of his/her abilities as other college students are. |
| >60 | This person is or feels that he/she is resilient and able to recover from most setbacks. If a client has emotional difficulties indicated by elevated clinical scales and recognizes this, he/she usually will make a good response to treatment. If he/she has emotional problems and does not recognize this, the client may not have a favorable response to treatment and indeed may be resistive to suggestions of the necessity of treatment. This level is typical for college students. Usually, scales **9, Do,** and **St** also are elevated. |

# Lb SCALE

## (Low Back Pain Scale)

The **Lb** scale has not been kept as one of the supplementary scales for the MMPI-2. This is most likely due to the lack of research about the scale. The scale is still available for the MMPI-2 with the loss of only four of its original 25 items. The MMPI-2 item numbers that make up this scale are shown in Table 5.3 (p. 298). The means and standard deviations for this scale on the MMPI-2 are given in Table 5.4. Finally, Tables 5.5 and 5.6 give T-score conversions for the scale when it is used with the MMPI-2. Caution is urged when these T-score tables are used since they were derived from a small group of 120 college students and therefore may not be generalizable to the general population.

In the first edition of this book (1975), the suggestion was made not to use the **Lb** scale because I (Duckworth) had not been able to discover any useful interpretation of it for college counseling centers or mental health clinic populations. In the process of analyzing the scale according to the content of the items since that printing, we feel we have some leads on the possible interpretation of high scores (above 60 T-score points) for this scale.

In the original study by Hanvik (1951), this scale was developed to differentiate between those people with organic low back pain and those with functional low back pain (no organic reason for the pain). The scale has 21 items on the MMPI-2 and 25 items on the MMPI, 12 of which are claims to being unflappable, seldom angry, and always in control of feelings; for example, answering false to "It makes me angry to have people try to hurry me."

Endorsement of these items alone, however, would not make an elevation on the scale. It is the additional endorsement of items that indicates that all is not what it seems to be in this person's professed Eden that raises the score to interpretable levels (above 60 T-score points): "I wish I could be as happy as others seem to be (true)"; "I have periods of restlessness when I cannot sit long in a chair (true)." An additional four items indicate the presence of physical complaints, and several items that deny religious beliefs also are included.

The message that the individual seems to be giving is that "I'm a wonderful person. I love people, and they never annoy me, but for some reason I am uncomfortable and not as happy as I should be."

Dynamically, we have a picture of an individual who at one level of awareness feels comfortable with the demands that others place on him/her but who at another more unconscious level is saying "get off my back." Considerable psychic energy may be going into maintaining a friendly facade.

These personality characteristics are true even if no physical complaints are present. While this seems similar to a conversion reaction, which is more likely shown by an elevated **3** scale, an elevation on the **Lb** scale represents a more specific reaction to stress than a conversion reaction. Basically, **Lb** is only a denial of anger/irritation without any physical conversion, while the **3** scale involves denial in many areas plus a physiological conversion. When the stress is gone, we hypothesize that the **Lb** score will come down below 60 T-score points whereas the **3** scale will not become lower.

We predict that if **Lb** is elevated and the **3** scale is not, the possibility of an isolated conversion reaction exists. If both the **Lb** scale and scale **3** are up, a more general conversion syndrome exists.

In summary, the **Lb** scale seems to be measuring a person's ability to maintain a friendly, calm facade while feeling frustration and discontentment/anger at a preconscious level. We hypothesize that this "conversion" is less entrenched as a characterological trait than the conversion reaction shown by the **3** scale; therefore, we believe the **Lb** scale will be more mobile, rising and falling more readily than the **3** scale, while showing many of the same characteristics.

# GENERAL INFORMATION

1.  In Hanvik's (1951) original study, the **Lb** scale of 21 items (MMPI-2) or 25 items (MMPI) differentiated between two groups, each of 30 patients, one group with diagnosed organic low back pain (low **Lb**) and the other group with back pain but no clearcut organic reason for the pain (high **Lb**).

2.  The correlation of **Lb** with other scales is minimal.

    a.  Hanvik (1951) found the **Lb** scale to correlate highly with scales **1** and **3**; however, we have found **Lb** to have a correlation only of .32 with scale **1** and .39 with scale **3** in a group of 847 normals (Appendix). Swenson et al. (1973) for a group of 50,000 medical patients found a .21 correlation between **Lb** and scale **1** and a .26 correlation for **Lb** and scale **3** (Appendix).

    b.  The scale does correlate .45 with an anxiety score, .45 with a neurotic score, and .41 with a subtle hysteria scale in Swenson, Pearson, and Osborne's medical population (1973). The correlations with other scales however are minimal.

    c.  In our population of 847 normals (Appendix), the **Lb** scale does not correlate above .40 with any other scale on the MMPI.

3.  Swenson et al. (1973) found that the **Lb** scale varied little according to age.

4.  The mean T-score on this scale was 54 for a medical population (Swenson et al., 1973). This also is the mean T-score found in a group of counseling center clients (N = 406) (Anderson & Duckworth, 1969) who had no clinical scales above 70 T-score points with the possible exception of the **5** scale.

# HIGH SCORES

## (T = 60 or above)

1. A person with a **Lb** score in this range may be feeling anger/irritation but not want to acknowledge it or perhaps the amount of angry feelings.

2. If these people are aware of the anger/irritation, they may feel that they should not have it.

   a. The person may think his/her needs are not that important.

   b. The person may think he/she is selfish to have the anger/irritation.

3. One study of college students has found that clients with psychosomatic disorders scored higher on **Lb** than clients without psychosomatic disorders (Klein & Cross, 1984).

4. In this same study, women who reported problems with their mothers were more likely to have psychomatic disorders.

5. Klein and Cross (1984) suggested that psychotherapists ask college female clients who have **Lb** above 60 about their relationships with their mothers. In this study, almost one-half of the women who reported frequent problems with their mothers had psychosomatic disorders, whereas only 12% of the women who did not report these problems had psychosomatic disorders.

# SUMMARY OF Lb SCALE INTERPRETATIONS

| T-score | Interpretations |
|---------|-----------------|
| <60 | The interpretation is unknown at the present time. |
| >60 | People with scores in this range may see themselves as not angry and in control of their feelings. Underneath they may be irritated and unhappy with what is happening. They may recognize that they are uncomfortable but they may not recognize the depth of their unhappiness or anger. |
| | They like to see themselves as "nice" and they believe that anger is not nice. |
| | They may have this elevation because they feel they cannot do anything about the situation that makes them angry. |
| | They may feel they "should" not be angry, their needs are not that important, or it seems selfish to have them. |

# Dy SCALE

## (Dependency Scale)

The **Dy** scale has not been kept as one of the supplementary scales for the MMPI-2; however, it is still possible to score it on the MMPI-2 with the loss of nine out of the original 57 items. A table listing the item numbers for this scale on the MMPI-2 is in Table 5.3 (p. 298), and the T-score conversion tables for this new scale are in Tables 5.5 and 5.6 (pp. 300-303). We feel that it is important to have this scale for the MMPI-2, given the use we make of it in comparison to the **Do** (Dominance) scale. The **Do** scale is available as one of the MMPI-2 supplementary scales and, therefore, having the **Dy** scale as well will allow the comparisons between these two scales to continue. We would urge caution, however, in the use of the new T-score tables that we have devised for this scale since they are based upon a small sample of 120 college students.

The dependency scale is a fairly easy one to interpret. The higher the scale score, the more the person would like to or actually is psychologically leaning on others. The lower the scale, the more independent the person usually is.

Most mentally healthy persons will have their **Dy** scales below a T-score of 50, whereas the typical client's profile has the **Dy** scale above a T-score of 55. As the client becomes better able to cope with his/her problems, the **Dy** scale typically will be reduced below 50, thus becoming like the **Dy** scales in the healthy profiles.

Benefits can be obtained by interpreting the **Dy** scale in conjunction with the **Do** (Dominance) scale; therefore, we have included a summary table of **Dy-Do** combinations, pp. 344-345.

In general, when dependency is high, dominance is low and vice versa, but occasionally both scales will be elevated above a T-score of 50. When this happens, an important procedure is to note which of the two scales is the highest. When **Do** is higher than **Dy,** while both are above 50, persons will seem independent and liking to take charge of their lives but will frequently remain in bad relationships because their dependency needs are being met in the relationship.

If the **Dy** is higher than the **Do,** people seem to be ambivalent about whether or not they want to take charge of their own lives. This ambivalence tends to come out as passive-aggressive or passive-demanding behavior. These people may ask others to help them make decisions for them (dependency), but then they become aggressive about or critical of the decision that is made (dominance). Persons with this **Dy-Do** combination are especially difficult to deal with in therapy because the therapist may be one of the people the client is passive-aggressive or passive-demanding toward. The prognosis for these clients is not as good as it is for other clients (even those with high **Dy** and low **Do**), because the ambivalence usually gets in the way of therapy unless it is handled adroitly by the therapist.

## GENERAL INFORMATION

1. Navran (1954) developed the **Dy** scale of 57 items (48 items on the MMPI-2) to identify people who are highly dependent upon others.

2. Navran developed the scale by asking 16 judges to specify, independently, MMPI items they felt reflected dependency. The resulting 157 items were tested and cross-validated on neuropsychiatric patients, and a scale of 57 items was derived.

3. One study (Birtchnell & Kennard, 1983) has found that the **Dy** scale

   a. is related to the sex of the individual. Women choose more **Dy** items than men.

b.   is not related to age. More **Dy** items are not chosen as one gets older.

c.   is related to psychiatric pathology; the more severe the symptoms, the higher the **Dy** score.

d.   is related to depression. A .60 correlation exists between **Dy** and scale **2**. (For normal subjects, the correlation is .54. See the Appendix.)

e.   is related to anxiety. A .72 correlation exists between **Dy** and scale **7**. (For normal subjects, the correlation is .56. See the Appendix.)

f.   is positively correlated to poor quality marriages.

g.   is negatively correlated to the **Do** scale. (For normal subjects, the correlation is -.63. See the Appendix.)

h.   is higher for women with dominant husbands.

4.   Another study (Nacev, 1980) found the **Dy** score to be negatively correlated with the **Es** scale (-.62). In this same study, elevation of the **Dy** scale was not found to be a predictor of patients' attendance in psychotherapy for an adult, nonpsychiatric outpatient population.

5.   Heppner and Anderson (1985) have found that self-appraised ineffective problem solvers tend to be significantly higher on this scale than effective problem solvers.

6.   The mean for this scale is low (44 T-score points) for college students (Anderson & Duckworth, 1969).

7.   In addition to interpreting the **Dy** scale alone, the **Dy** scale can be considered in relationship to the **Do** (dominance) scale, in certain instances shown in the **Dy** and **Do** combination summary, pp. 344-345.

# HIGH SCORES

## (T = 55 or above)

See also the **Dy** and **Do** combinations, pp. 344-345.

1. High scores tend to indicate that the person is dependent and somewhat passive.

2. Graham (1977) felt that this scale might be a good measure of self-reported dependency; however, other people might not judge the person as dependent.

3. Birtchnell and Kennard (1983) have found that high **Dy** scores are related to being female, having high depression (**2** scale) and anxiety (**7** scale) scores, having early loss or separation experiences, and having a poor quality marriage and a dominant marital partner.

# LOW SCORES

## (T = 50 or below)

See also the **Dy** and **Do** combinations, pp. 344-345.

1. Persons with low scores tend to be independent of others.

2. This level tends to be typical for college students, with the mean score being 44 T-score points (Anderson & Duckworth, 1969).

# CODETYPES

| **Dy-Do** |

1. For a summary of selected **Dy-Do** scale combinations, see pp. 344-345.

# SUMMARY OF **Dy** SCALE INTERPRETATIONS

| T-score<br>MMPI-2 & MMPI | Interpretations |
|---|---|
| <50 | This person tends to be independent of others; this can be either from choice or necessity. The mean score for college students is 44. |
| 50-55 | A person at this level feels a need to be somewhat dependent. |
| >55 | This person has a strong need to be dependent at this time; the higher the elevation, the more dependent the person feels. Such a score may be either characterological or situational. These persons also may be passive. This is the typical range of scores for clients coming in voluntarily for help.<br><br>See pp. 344-345 for **Dy-Do** combinations. |

# Do SCALE

## (Dominance Scale)

The **Do** scale has been kept as one of the supplementary scales of the MMPI-2. In the process of changing from the MMPI to the MMPI-2, the scale lost three out of its 28 items. The T-score distribution also has been changed; see Tables 5.1 and 5.2, pp. 293-296. This new distribution seems to lower the **Do** score more than the loss of items would warrant, except at the upper elevations of the scale. For example, test takers have a **Do** scale of 51 T-score points when they endorse 15 items on the original MMPI. On the MMPI-2, the same number of item endorsements would convert to a lower T-score of 45 in spite of having fewer items available to endorse. Caution needs to be used, therefore, in interpreting the MMPI-2 **Do** scale in exactly the same manner as would be done with the original MMPI **Do** scale.

The **Do** scale is a fairly simple measure of a person's ability to take charge of his/her own life. The higher this scale, the more the person is saying that he/she is able to take charge of his/her own life. The **Do** scale may show domineering behavior when the scale is very high (above 70) and the **4** scale is above 70 T-score points. Even then, the person may not always show domineering behavior. The presence of the behavior seems to depend upon certain other scales being elevated with the **Do**; if the **5** scale is elevated 5 or more T-score points above the **4** scale for men or is below 40 T-score points for women, it may temper the domineering behavior.

The lower the **Do** scale, the more the person is saying he/she does not want to take charge of his/her life. The lower **Do** score usually is accompanied by an elevation on the **Dy** scale. When this happens, the person usually wants other people to take over his/her life and wants to be dependent upon them.

In addition to interpreting this scale alone, its relationship with the **Dy** scale should be considered. We have found an elevation on the **Do** scale (when **Dy** is below 50) to be a good sign of progress in therapy. Also, elevations above a T-score of 60 on **Es, Do,** and **St** usually are signs of a healthy person. The **Dy-Do** relationships are summarized on pp. 344-345.

## GENERAL INFORMATION

1. The **Do** scale of 25 items (MMPI-2) or 28 items (MMPI) was developed by Gough, McClosky, and Meehl (1951) and measures poise, self-assurance, resourcefulness, efficiency, and perseverance.

2. The scale was developed by the "peer group nomination technique." One hundred college and 124 high school students were asked to nominate members of their group whom they considered to be the most and least dominant. Those items on the MMPI that differentiated between the two groups were used for the **Do** scale.

3. This scale seems to measure a person's ability to take charge of his/her own life.

4. The **Do** scale has been shown to be successful in predicting staff ratings and peer nominations for dominance and in identifying outstanding leaders in high school programs (Dahlstrom & Welsh, 1960).

5. In one study (Birtchnell & Kennard, 1983), no significant relationship was found between elevation on **Do** and age or sex.

6. The retest correlation coefficients for the **Do** scale on the MMPI-2 are .84 for men and .86 for women (Butcher et al., 1989).

7. Heppner and Anderson (1985) have found that ineffective problem solvers tend to be significantly lower on this scale than effective problem solvers.

8. College students tend to score high on this scale with a mean of 60 T-score points (Anderson & Duckworth, 1969).

9. A group of college achievers scored higher than nonachievers on this scale (Morgan, 1952).

10. An elevated score on the **Do** scale has been found to be significantly related to middle management success.

11. In addition to interpreting this scale alone, in certain instances shown in the **Dy** and **Do** combination summary, pp. 344-345, and discussed in the opening paragraphs of **Dy** scale, the **Do** scale is to be considered in relationship to the **Dy** scale.

## HIGH SCORES

(T = 55 or above, MMPI-2)

(T = 60 or above, MMPI)

See also the **Dy** and **Do** combinations, pp. 344-345.

1. High scorers tend to be people who take charge of their lives.

2. When the person has a **Do** score above 65 and a **4** scale in the clinically elevated range, he/she may be seen as domineering.

## LOW SCORES

(T = 45 or below, MMPI-2)

(T = 50 or below, MMPI)

See also the **Dy** and **Do** combinations, pp. 344-345.

1. A person with a low **Do** score usually would like others to take charge of his/her life.

# CODETYPES

**Es-Do-St**    See p. 328.

**Es-Do-St**    (T = 45 or below) See p. 328.

**Dy-Do**

1.  For a summary of selected **Dy-Do** scale combinations, see pp. 344-345.

## SUMMARY OF Do SCALE INTERPRETATIONS

| T-score MMPI-2 | MMPI | Interpretations |
|---|---|---|
| <45 | <50 | A person with a score in this range prefers to have others take charge of his/her life at this time. This level is typical for clients in therapy. |
| 45-55 | 50-60 | A person with a score at this level is able to control much of his/her life and at the same time is able to be dependent upon others periodically. This range is typical for people who do not have a college education. |
| >55 | >60 | This person tends to take charge of his/her own life. He/she is able to meet deadlines, plan, and organize his/her life. At higher levels, a person may be seen by others as imposing or domineering if his/her **4** scale score is also elevated. The mean for college students is a T-score of 60 on the original MMPI.

See **Dy-Do** combinations, pp. 344-345. |

# SUMMARY OF Dy AND Do COMBINATION INTERPRETATIONS

| If the Dy Scale Score Is | If the Do Scale Score Is | Interpretations |
|---|---|---|
| <50 | <45 | This is a rare combination. |
| <50 | >50 | This person likes to control his/her life and feels comfortable doing it. |
| <45 | >55 | This person may be a leader since leaders usually fall in this category. This combination is usual for well adjusted college students. |
| >60 | <45 | This person feels unable to take charge of his/her life and feels that others must be relied upon at this time. The individual may feel more comfortable being a follower or in a semi-dependent position and may be unable to make major decisions. When the ego-strength (Es) and status (St) scales also are low, the person may feel worthless. Most likely, the person feels the need to lean on someone and will use either the therapist or another person for this purpose. These clients rarely miss appointments and usually try hard to please the therapist. |
| >50 | >50 | People with this combination may seem ambivalent about whether to be dependent or dominant. This is especially true if the two scales are close together in elevation.<br><br>When the Do is 5 points or more above the Dy, the person appears more dominant than dependent but may stay in bad relationships because of the dependency needs. |

When the **Dy** is 5 points or more above the **Do,** the person may be passive-aggressive; that is, the person controls through weakness. The person appears to be dependent but is actually in charge of the situation. This person usually manipulates others (including the counselor) by appearing to be dependent, when in fact the person is determining the course of his/her own behavior and the counseling sessions.

# Re SCALE
## (Social Responsibility Scale)

The **Re** scale has been kept as one of the MMPI-2 supplementary scales by the MMPI-2 test revisors. In the conversion from the MMPI to the MMPI-2, two of the original 32 items were lost. The T-score distribution of the new version of this scale is compared to the old T-score distribution in Tables 5.1 and 5.2, pp. 293-296. As can be seen from these tables, the two distributions are quite similar; therefore, the new **Re** scale should look quite similar to the old scale on the new MMPI-2 profile.

The **Re** scale originally was developed to determine the social responsibility of a person. That is, persons receiving high scores on this scale were seen as socially responsible, willing to accept the consequences of their behavior, trustworthy, and dependable, while persons receiving low scores were seen as socially irresponsible. We have noted, however, that persons receiving low scores could be equally as socially responsible as persons receiving elevated scores. Instead of social responsibility then, we feel this scale measures the acceptance (high score) or rejection (low score) of a previously held value system.

For persons under age 25, an elevation on this scale above 50 indicates that they accept in general the value system of their parents. A score in the 40 through 50 range usually indicates that the person is questioning the parental value system (a typical procedure for college students and for those mental health clients going through a traumatic life change). Scores below 40 usually indicate that the person is not just questioning but actually is rejecting the parental value system.

One caution must be noted. Many people tend to presume that a person is showing acceptance or rejection of white middle-class values by his/her score on the **Re** scale. What this scale seems to be showing for this below 25 age group is acceptance or rejection of the parental values that may or may not be those of the white, middle-class. For example, Black ghetto-reared college students may receive low scores on this scale because they are rejecting the ghetto values with which they were reared and now are accepting white middle-class values. Thus, to tell accurately what values are being accepted or rejected for young people, one must know the person's background.

For persons above the age of 25, interpretation of this scale is based upon the person's present value system, which may or may not be similar to his/her parents. Persons with elevations on the **Re** scale above 50 tend to accept their present value system and intend to continue using it. Persons with scores of 40 through 50 are questioning their present value system, and those below 40 are rejecting their most recently held value system. An illustration of this is a 40-year-old male with a **Re** score of 35. He had been reared with one value system (his parents'), which he had rejected in his early 20s. Now at age 40, he was reevaluating his own value system and felt that the values of his parents (those rejected 20 years previously) now were more valid for him than those he had held more recently.

For people of all ages, the higher the **Re** scale, the more rigid a person seems to be in his/her acceptance of values and the less willing to explore other values.

As one examines items and intercorrelations of this scale with other scales, a consistent picture of a person with a high score emerges.

High scorers report that they had little trouble with authorities as they were growing up. They answer false to such items as "In school I was sometimes sent to the principal for cutting up" and "My parents have objected to the kind of people I went around with." This self-report receives some support from **Re**'s scale -.48 correlation with the obvious Psychopathic Deviate Scale (Swenson et al., 1973).

Part of their comfort with authorities may be based on the fact that they seldom admit to taking risks. Seven of the 32 items on this scale indicate a lack of interest in creating excitement. They answer true to "I have never done anything dangerous for the thrill of it" and false to "I enjoy a race or game better when I bet on it."

This conservative approach to life does not appear to be related to fear but rather to a lack of interest in this kind of stimulating situation because they report that they feel comfortable with a variety of other situations that could produce anxiety. They answer true to "I do not dread seeing a doctor about a sickness or injury" and "I usually work things out for myself rather than get someone to show me how."

The items concerning not taking risks seem to support the presence of a control factor in high **Re** people's behavior. This also is supported by a correlation of -.53 with Impulsivity and -.50 with Neurotic Under-control scales (Swenson et al., 1973).

High scorers on **Re** also report that they expect others to be positive in their behavior. They answer false to "A large number of people are guilty of bad sexual conduct" and "I have often found people jealous of my good ideas, just because they had not thought of them first." This also is supported by **Re** scale correlation of -.49 with the **Pr** scale and .52 with the **K** scale (Appendix).

This would seem to be one scale on which a certain type of good student would get high scores. This would be the student who reports liking school since **Re** correlates .61 with academic achievement, .51 with intellectual efficiency, .51 with intellectual quotient, and .51 with teaching potential (Swenson et al., 1973).

All of these factors together indicate someone who is confident, even-tempered, non-pretentious, comfortable with authority, and competent in academic areas, with little need to pursue adventure.

While high scorers have many strong points, several defects are possible. They may be unimaginative and noncreative. This is particularly likely to be true if scales **7** and **8** are below 45 T-score points. Their lives may be controlled by a considerable number of "ought to's" with which they are comfortable but which could annoy other people who have to work with them. That is, they may expect others to live up to their standards and be as comfortable with them as they are. Consequently, they may have difficulty understanding why others cannot or will not perform as they do.

In addition to interpreting the **Re** scale alone, in certain instances shown in the **Re** and **Pr** combination summary, pp. 358-359, considering the **Re** scale in relationship to the **Pr** (prejudice or rigid thinking) scale is helpful. At first glance, the **Re** and **Pr** scales would appear to be positively correlated; that is, those who question their previous values (low **Re**) also would be open to alternative viewpoints (low **Pr**). Similarly, those who wholeheartedly accept their previous values (high **Re**) would not be open to alternate viewpoints (high **Pr**). Certainly these combinations do appear; however, other combinations also appear. Specifically, at least one segment of people who are questioning their previous values (low **Re**) (they usually consider themselves to be "liberal" thinkers) are not tolerant of others (high **Pr**), particularly others who accept the more traditional American value system. Apparently, these people are not as liberal as they believe themselves to be, at least about others who believe differently than they do.

Conversely, some people who accept their middle-class background with all its implications (high **Re**) also are able to listen to alternative beliefs held by others (low **Pr**). These people appear to have taken a position for themselves, but they are able to allow others to have their own positions.

If, however, the **Re** scale is above 65 T-score points and the **Pr** is low, the person's tolerance may be a willingness to let others express their beliefs as long as the others are responsible with these beliefs.

Interestingly, the **Re** scale tends to be correlated with age; the older the person, the higher the **Re** scale tends to be. We usually find the **Re** scale low for college students as they question how they were reared and some of the values of their parents.

# GENERAL INFORMATION

1.  The **Re** 32-item scale (30 items, MMPI-2) was developed by Gough (1952) to measure social responsibility.

2.  Social responsibility was defined by Gough as the willingness to accept the consequences of one's own behavior, dependability, trustworthiness, and sense of obligation to the group.

3.  Gough used the "peer nomination" method with this scale, asking college and high school students to choose the most and least responsible members of their groups. The MMPI items that differentiated between these two groups were the basis for the scale.

4.  Instead of measuring social responsibility, the **Re** scale seems to measure how much the person accepts the values with which he/she was reared. Persons below age 25 who score high on this scale tend to accept their parents' values. When people question or reject the values of their parents, they usually score low on the **Re** scale.

    Persons above age 25 who score low on this scale may be rejecting their most recently held value systems, which may or may not be the same as their parents.

5.  Test-retest reliability coefficients for this scale in the MMPI-2 are .85 for men and .74 for women.

6.  Heppner and Anderson (1985) have found that ineffective problem solvers were significantly lower on this scale than effective problem solvers.

7.  In addition to interpreting this scale alone, consideration of the **Re** scale in relationship to the **Pr** scale is helpful. See the **Re** and **Pr** combination summary, pp. 358-359.

8.  The **Re** scale has differentiated "responsible" from "irresponsible" people (school disciplinary problems, people nominated for responsibility, and good school citizenship) (Dahlstrom & Welsh, 1960).

9.  A group of college achievers scored higher than nonachievers on this scale (Morgan, 1952).

# HIGH SCORES

See also the **Re** and **Pr** combination, pp. 358-359.

1.  People under the age of 25 who score high on the **Re** scale tend to accept their parents' values.

    Persons over the age of 25 accept their present value system, which may or may not be the same as their parents'.

2.  Persons with high **Re** scores tend to have positions of leadership and responsibility.

# LOW SCORES

(T = 40 or below)

See also the **Re** and **Pr** combinations, pp. 358-359.

1.  When people under the age of 25 reject their parents' values, they tend to score low on the **Re** scale.

    Persons over the age of 25 scoring in this range tend to reject their present value system, which may or may not be the same as their parents'.

2.  Low scorers may have substituted a new religion, philosophy, or political outlook for their old values.

# CODETYPES

**Re-Pr**

1.  For a summary of selected **Re** and **Pr** scale combinations, see pp. 358-359.

# SUMMARY OF Re SCALE INTERPRETATIONS

| T-score MMPI-2 & MMPI | Interpretations | |
|---|---|---|
| | Below Age 25 | Over Age 25 |
| <40 | This person tends to deny the value system of his/her parents. Such a person may have substituted another value system for the paternal one. | This person tends to deny his/her most recently held value system (which may be different from the parents'). |
| 40-50 | People in this range tend to question their parents' values. They may be exploring alternative viewpoints. Their values seem to be in flux. | People in this range tend to be questioning their most recently held value system and are usually exploring different values. |
| 50-65 | People with scores in this range tend to accept their parents' values. The higher the score in this range, the more the person has accepted these values. | A person with a score in this range tends to accept his/her present value system. The higher the score, the more the person has accepted these values. |
| >65 | The higher a score is above 65, the more rigid a person seems to be in his/her acceptance of values and the less willing to explore other values. | |

**Relationship to Clinical scales:** If the **4** scale is above 70 T-score points and the **Re** scale is below 50, the person may be rebellious.

# Pr SCALE
## (Prejudice Scale)

The **Pr** scale was not retained as one of the MMPI-2 supplementary scales but it is relatively intact in the new test. Only two of the 34 items that make up this scale have been eliminated on the MMPI-2. The items in this scale on the MMPI-2 are listed in Table 5.3, p. 298, and the T-score conversion tables for this scale for men and women are shown on pp. 300-303. We urge caution in using these new conversion tables, however, because they are based upon only 120 college students. The new T-scores shown on pp. 300-303 are higher for the MMPI-2 in spite of the smaller number of items that make up the scale. This may be due to the norm group used, college students, who may have lower prejudice scale scores than the original Minnesota norm group.

The **Pr** scale was designed originally to measure anti-Semitic prejudice. While the scale does measure prejudice, it appears to be concerned with the much broader concept of rigidity in thinking. That is, elevations on this scale seem to indicate that a person is able to accept only concepts and values similar to his/her own and rejects alternative ways of thinking. Elevations on this scale also may identify persons who are not secure with their present value systems and therefore must shut out alternative viewpoints.

People with low **Pr** scores usually are able to tolerate opinions different from their own. These lower scores also can indicate a person who is secure with his/her values and therefore is able to allow others to have theirs. Thus, the **Pr** scale seems to indicate a person's willingness to accept or to look at alternative viewpoints.

The **Pr** scale consists of 32 items (34 items, MMPI). The largest number of them (12 items) reflects negative, cynical, and contemptuous attitudes toward the motivations of others. "I can't blame anyone for trying to grab everything he can get in this world." Nine items covering foreboding or unreasonable fears are included. "Sometimes I feel as if I must injure either myself or someone else."

Seven items indicate uncertainty of self and social skills. "I refuse to play some games because I am not good at them." The remaining are miscellaneous items, e.g., "I feel there is only one true religion."

Evidence exists that prejudice may be a general response tendency that influences the individual's reactions to a variety of situations and persons. English (1971) has pointed out that a sizable majority of studies seems to confirm the belief that prejudice is a general pervasive attitudinal characteristic of some individuals. These people tend to reject any group they consider significantly different from their own, particularly those with ethnic, racial, or religious differences.

Some interesting correlations were found by Gough (1951) in his original study. Low scorers had an average IQ of 111, whereas high scorers had an average IQ of 98. A later correlation was found (1951) between **Pr** and Intellectual Quotient of -.70, and **Pr** and Intellectual Efficiency of -.63. Further support for this negative relationship between intellectual ability and prejudice comes from research with college students who have a mean score of 40 on **Pr** (Anderson & Duckworth, 1969).

Social class also is related to prejudice. Again, in Gough's original study (1951), the socioeconomic status (SES) scale he used correlated -.60 with **Pr**, with higher SES students scoring lower on the **Pr** scale. Thus, an elevated score is not unusual for an individual of lower social status or for one of more limited intellectual potential; but an elevated score for someone of better than average intelligence, such as a college student, needs to be looked at in another way.

Therapists should explore the possibility that their more intelligent clients with high **Pr** scores may be in a period of poor expectations; that is, these clients may have some doubts as to whether or not they can cope with the problems that are bothering them. They may have a pervasive sour grapes attitude that could be temporary and subject to therapeutic intervention. The possibility exists that some resistance to therapy may occur because these clients tend to be blaming others for what has gone wrong in their lives. They also may be very resistive to accepting new ideas during the counseling session.

In addition to interpreting this scale by itself, it should be interpreted in combination with the **Re** scale. The summary of the various combinations of **Re** and **Pr** is found on pp. 358-359.

## GENERAL INFORMATION

1. The MMPI-2 **Pr** 32-item scale (34 items, MMPI) was devised by Gough (1951) to differentiate those high school students who scored high on an anti-Semitism test (were most prejudiced) from those who scored low.

2. The scale seems to measure the much broader area of rigidity in thinking, with people who are more rigid scoring high on the scale.

3. Heppner and Anderson (1985) have found that self-appraised ineffective problem solvers tended to be significantly higher on this scale than effective problem solvers.

4. In addition to interpreting this scale alone, considering the **Pr** scale's relationship to the **Re** scale is helpful in certain instances shown in the **Re** and **Pr** combination summary, pp. 358-359.

5. The **Pr** scale correlates positively with the California F Scale (Jensen, 1957).

6. College students tend to score in the low range on this scale with a mean of 40 T-score points (Anderson & Duckworth, 1969).

# HIGH SCORES

## (T = 55 or above)

See also the **Re** and **Pr** Combinations, pp. 358-359.

1.  High scorers on this scale tend to be rigid and not willing to look at others' points of view.

2.  They may not be willing to question their own value systems.

3.  The higher the score, the more rigid and adamant these people usually are about their beliefs.

4.  This rigidity can either be a permanent attitude ("I am always correct") or the result of situational stress ("I need to maintain my present position so that I don't become disoriented").

5.  High scorers in college may have poor academic achievement.

6.  High scorers are more likely to come from the lower social classes (Gough, 1951).

7.  They also are likely to have lower IQ scores (Jensen, 1957).

# LOW SCORES

## (T = 45 or below)

See also the **Re** and **Pr** combinations, pp. 358-359.

1.  Low scorers tend to be open to alternative points of view.

2.  The person usually has a positive view of the world and tends to be effective in coping with his/her life.

3.  A score in the 45 or below range is helpful in counseling, because the client is receptive to opinions different from his/her own.

# CODETYPES

## Re-Pr

1. For a summary of selected **Re** and **Pr** scale combinations, see pp. 358-359.

## SUMMARY OF Pr SCALE INTERPRETATIONS

| T-score | Interpretations |
| --- | --- |
| <45 | Persons in this range usually are seen as open-minded and willing to entertain opinions contrary to their own. They are likely to have a positive outlook on life. College students tend to score in this range. |
| 45-55 | The majority of people score in this range. |
| >55 | Persons with elevations on this scale usually are rigid in their beliefs. That is, they are not open to considering alternative points of view or questioning their own value systems. As the score increases, the person becomes more rigid and restricted in his/her thinking. He/she also tends to be cynical and distrustful of other people and of the world in general. |

**Relationship to Clinical Scales:** If a person has an elevated score on scale **6** (Paranoia), the higher the **Pr** scale is above 50 the more encompassing the suspiciousness. For example, a recently divorced woman client with a **6** scale at 70 and a **Pr** of 50 may be only suspicious of her ex-husband, whereas a recently divorced woman client with a **6** scale of 70 and a **Pr** of 65 may be suspicious of all men.

# SUMMARY OF Re AND Pr SCALE
# COMBINATION INTERPRETATIONS

| If Re is | and Pr is | Interpretations |
|----------|-----------|-----------------|
| <40 | <50 | A person with this combination usually has rejected a previously held value system and has adopted a new one. He/she is willing to let others express their beliefs, however, and can tolerate being around people with different opinions. |
| | >50 | People with this combination usually have rejected a previously held value system and have adopted a new one. They also tend to be rigid about their new beliefs and cannot tolerate others who have beliefs different from theirs. |
| 40-50 | <50 | People with this combination usually are questioning their value system and are open to exploring other people's ideas and values. |
| | >50 | People with this combination are usually questioning their own beliefs and may not be able to tolerate others around them who are not also in the process of questioning their beliefs. |
| 50-65 | <50 | A person with this combination tends to accept the value system with which he/she was reared but is still able to associate with people who have different value systems. |
| | >50 | People with this combination usually are accepting of the value system with which they were reared but have a difficult time accepting other people who believe differently than they do. |

| | | |
|---|---|---|
| >65 | <50 | A person with this combination may be rigid in his/her beliefs and value system but is willing to let others express different beliefs as long as they are seen as "good" people and carry out their responsibilities. |
| | >50 | A person with this combination may be rigid in his/her beliefs and value system. He/she also is intolerant of others who have different beliefs. He/she is likely to reject things that are "different." |

# St SCALE

## (Status Scale)

The **St** scale was not retained as one of the MMPI-2 supplementary scales by the revisors of the MMPI; however, many of the items are still available in the new test. The new MMPI-2 **St** scale has 26 items compared to 34 for the scale on the old MMPI. The items that make up the MMPI-2 **St** scale are shown in Table 5.3, p. 298, and the T-score conversions for this new version of the scale are shown on pp. 300-303. Caution is urged when using these conversion tables, because they are based upon a small number (120) of college students.

The **St** scale was developed originally to distinguish those people who had high socioeconomic status from those who had low socioeconomic status. Instead of measuring the socioeconomic status the person has, we believe this scale is measuring the socioeconomic status the person desires. It also may be measuring a liking for some of the finer things of life (books, art, music, clothes, and nice surroundings) that go along with higher socioeconomic status. This last interpretation of a high status score is especially true when the **5** scale is elevated above 55 for males and is below 45 for females. In many respects, the **5** and **St** scales are measuring some of the same aspects of a person's life.

When the **5** scale is low for males or high for females, a high **St** score then may be measuring the strivings of a person to better himself/herself, to achieve recognition, and to improve his/her way of life. It also may be measuring an emphasis that the person has on acquiring some of the materialistic trappings of a better life, i.e., a nicer home, a better car, or more material goods. When the **5** scale indicates that a person does not have many aesthetic interests, then the elevated **St** scale seems to be measuring a desire for upward mobility and recognition.

Many times an MMPI profile has problem areas indicated on it, and the **St** scale is elevated. This elevation may be a good sign, because the client is saying he/she desires some of the better things of life and may be willing to improve in order to achieve them. An elevation on the **St** scale may be showing why a person is striving to remain in college or in a good job when everything is collapsing around him/her.

We also find this scale to be a very useful one to look at in marriage counseling. If the **St** scale is at approximately the same level for both people, usually no problem exists in this area. If one of the couple's **St** scores is high while the other's is low or average, then this may be an indication of a problem area. One of the couple desires a high status while the other one does not and indeed may see no reason for striving in this way. A frequent occurrence with married couples coming in for counseling is to have a wife scoring high on **St** and the husband not. She wants to better their life (usually by him getting a better job) while he is content where he is. A compounding factor may be that the wife feels unable to specify her ambitions because "a wife should not criticize her husband's work if he's happy with it." Frequently, we have been able to persuade the wife to find a job with high status herself or to go back to school for further education to satisfy her status needs without necessarily disturbing the husband with his lesser status needs.

The **St** scale frequently is elevated above 60 T-score points with the **Es** and **Do** scales. This shows a very normal pattern for college students and people with good psychological functioning.

People with low **St** scores tend to fall into three groups. The first is composed of those people who work in low status jobs, are from a low socioeconomic status background, and are reasonably content with their lot in life. In fact, these people may become uncomfortable in high status situations. The second group of people with low **St** scores is made up of those who have achieved middle status positions but who feel that their upward mobility is ended. The third group of people with low **St** scores is made up of those who also have low **Es** and **Do** scores and high **Dy** scores. These people usually feel that they are not worth much and therefore should not expect much from life, including high status. When counseling persons in this third group, we have found that it is usually necessary to build their self-concept before other counseling can be done.

To explore further the implications of the low **St** score, we took a group of college counseling center clients (N = 16) with a low **St** score and examined the case notes for these clients. Some marked consistencies were found among the clients. Almost all of them had disturbed profiles; that is, three or more of the clinical scales were above 70 T-score points. All these clients reported dissatisfaction with themselves and how they were adjusting to their environment. Often the dissatisfaction centered around an inability to make decisions or to deal in a comfortable fashion with people.

All of the case notes for these people reported inappropriate social behavior. The clients did not always interpret it as such, but the case notes indicated that the behavior was unusual for the situations in which clients found themselves. For example, "The client came in and kept his finger in a page of a book he was reading. He would go back to reading after finishing a sentence." And again, "She appeared to come on very strongly as one who desired much closeness and friendship. Whenever anyone came close to her, however, she would turn her back to them psychologically and refuse to acknowledge them. At this point she would react with surprise and anger when they became upset with her."

Another common behavior for these clients was resistance to counseling; that is, they found it difficult to talk, avoided subjects, and frequently missed sessions. A close corollary to this was the large number of these clients who terminated counseling either by becoming no-shows or by quitting before the counselor felt that they had reached maximum benefit. As a result, these clients generally had poor outcomes, although several of them made great gains in terms of changing their behavior. To a lesser extent, some of them seemed to be easily influenced by others.

In summation, this group of individuals in a college counseling center with low social status scores were people who generally had disturbed profiles, were dissatisfied with themselves, and were engaged in some inappropriate social behavior. In spite of their stated desire to change some of the above, they generally were resistive to counseling and were likely to terminate counseling before the counselor felt that any real progress had been made.

These generally unfavorable implications of the low status score are borne out in the favorable implications found for the high status scores for a group of normal persons not coming in for counseling. The status scale correlates highly with the following MMPI scales: **O** (-.61), **Es** (.54), **Ca** (-.51), **Dy** (-.53), and **Do** (.61) (Appendix).

## GENERAL INFORMATION

1. The **St** scale of 34 items (26, MMPI-2) was developed by Gough (1948) to distinguish between two groups of high school students, those with high socioeconomic status and those with low socioeconomic status.

2. These 34 items can be grouped as follows: literacy and aesthetic interests; social poise, security, and confidence in self and others; denial of fear and anxiety; broadminded attitudes toward moral, religious, and sexual matters; and positive, dogmatic, and self-righteous opinions (Gough, 1948).

3. A significant positive correlation exists between this scale and the **K** scale.

4. Gough (1949) has found an interesting relationship when objective status measures (such as amount of money earned) are compared to the **St** scale score. Persons of low objective status, but upwardly mobile, tend to score relatively higher on the **St** scale than on the objective status measures.

The reverse is true of people tending toward downward mobility.

5. Heppner and Anderson (1985) have found that ineffective problem solvers were significantly lower on this scale than effective problem solvers.

## HIGH SCORES

(T = 55 or above)

1. High scores tend to indicate a desire for the better things of life that are associated with education and/or upper socioeconomic status.

2. A person with a high **St** score, as compared to a person with a low **St** score, seems to have greater reserve in connection with personal affairs and problems, fewer somatic complaints, more satisfactory overall adjustment, greater intelligence, higher scholastic aptitude, and less social introversion (Gough, 1949).

3. College students typically score high on the **St** scale, with the mean being between 55 and 60 (Anderson & Duckworth, 1969).

4. A person with **St** scores in this range may be dissatisfied if his/her job is not of high status.

5. If a wife has an **St** score in the high range but her husband does not, she may be dissatisfied because he does not want or strive for higher status.

6. If a person has an **St** score in this range and is coming in for help for serious problems, the elevated **St** score can indicate good motivation for counseling. The client may be willing to work very diligently on these problems in order to achieve higher status.

# LOW SCORES

## (T = 40 or below)

1. People with scores of 40 or below tend to have status desires similar to people from the lower socioeconomic levels.

2. These groups of people tend to have low **St** scores.

   a. Those who work in low status jobs, are from a low socioeconomic background, and are reasonably content with their status.

   b. Those who are in middle status positions and feel that they have gone as high as they can.

   c. Those who also have low **Es** and **Do** scores and high **Dy** scores. These people usually have low self-esteem and low self-confidence and feel they do not deserve any higher status.

   These people may be unmarried, may stay in a bad marriage, or may have been in a series of bad marriages.

3. If a person with a score in this range is in college, the motivation to remain in college may be lacking unless family pressure helps to keep him/her there.

## CODETYPES

Es-Do-St (T = 55 or above) See p. 328.

E̅s̅-D̅o̅-S̅t̅ (T = 45 or below) See p. 328.

# SUMMARY OF St SCALE INTERPRETATIONS

| T-score MMPI-2 & MMPI | Interpretations |
|---|---|
| <40 | These people have status desires similar to people from the lower socioeconomic levels. They usually have low achievement needs and do not expect or strive for a higher status. If these people are from a lower socioeconomic group, they tend to be reasonably content with their lives. If they are from a middle socioeconomic group, they may feel their upward mobility is ended and not be so contented with their lives. When this scale is low and the **Es** and **Do** scores are also low, people may have extremely poor self-esteem and no self-confidence. They may feel that they do not deserve a better life. These people may be unmarried, may stay in a bad marriage, or may have contracted sequential bad marriages. If people with these scores are in college, they may not really want to be there but may remain in college through family pressure. |
| 40-55 | These people have status desires similar to the general, noncollege population. |
| 55-60 | People at this level have status desires similar to those of the general college graduate. They tend to like having some of the nicer things in life, such as good books and a nice home. They may be dissatisfied if their jobs lack status or if the financial rewards are insufficient to provide the material that goes with status. |
| >60 | People at this level have status desires similar to those of a graduate student or someone from a high socioeconomic level. They usually have high achievement needs and especially like to be recognized for doing a good job at work or school. They may be dissatisfied if they do not have some of the nicer things in life, such as good books or nice homes. They may complain of job dissatisfaction if their status needs are not met by their jobs. |

# Cn SCALE

## (Control Scale)

The **Cn** scale was not retained as a MMPI-2 supplementary scale by the revisors of the test. However, it is still available in the new test, having lost only nine out of the 50 items on the original MMPI. The items that make up the MMPI-2 version of this scale are given in Table 5.3, page 298, and T-score conversion tables are given for men and women on pp. 300-303. Caution is urged when using these tables, because they are based upon a small sample (120) of college students.

The control scale is an especially useful one on the MMPI. An elevated **Cn** scale can be a clue as to how much of the behavior indicated by elevations on the clinical scales will be exhibited in the presence of other people. If the **Cn** scale is elevated with other clinical scale elevations indicating some problems, the client has some ability to control his/her problem behavior and to show only what he/she wishes others to observe. While these others may not always be the people the counselor wishes would or would not see the client's behavior, the elevation on **Cn** does indicate a strength, because the client has the ability to control problem behavior to some extent. A problem occasionally occurs when the client chooses to hide certain or all problem behavior from the counselor as well as from others.

When the **Cn** scale is above 55 with no clinical elevations on the clinical scales, the client may appear somewhat reserved and nonemotional. This behavior is especially true the higher the **Cn** scale. Many people with this combination have grown up in an environment where emotions were not readily expressed or encouraged. Some of these people may express the wish that they could be freer with other people or at least more expressive of their emotions. In these instances, a sign of therapeutic progress may be a lowering of the **Cn** scale. Elevations on the **Cn** scale can, thus, indicate client strength (when the clinical scales are high) or potential problems (when the clinical scales are low).

A low **Cn** score means that the person tends to show the behavior indicated by his/her clinical scale score elevations. If the clinical scores are not elevated, the person has no behavior that needs to be controlled. This does not mean, however, that the person cannot control his/her behavior if the clinical scales should become elevated. However if a person has the clinical scales elevated, a low **Cn** score does mean that the behavior indicated by the elevated clinical scale scores is not being controlled by the person, and the clinical scale behavior is exhibited in the presence of others.

Elevations on the **Cn** scale, especially when accompanied by elevations on the **K, 3,** and **R** scales, may indicate a type of person who is constricted in many ways. For further discussion of these scales, see the **R** scale commentary, page 315.

The important thing to remember in interpreting the **Cn** scale is to look at the accompanying clinical scales and to use their elevations in combination with **Cn** scale placement to get the most accurate interpretation of the **Cn** scale.

A rather wide combination of items make up the **Cn** scale. The items can be divided into seven major categories:

1.  The first group of items appears to be an awareness of and an admission to base impulses and behavior. "I sometimes feel like swearing." "I gossip a little at times." This may lead to an openness in counseling interviews, which counselors like.

2.  A second group of items indicates that the individual is uncomfortable at the conscious level. "I sometimes feel that I am about to go to pieces." "I wish I could be as happy as others seem to be." In a college population, people with elevated clinical scales and high **Cn** scores report uncomfortable feelings but seem to see their cause as being situational; that is, a bad marriage situation, lack of vocational choice, or inability to set appropriate goals because of the university structure.

3.  A group of manic items is the third major category. "When I get bored I like to stir up some excitement." "At times my thoughts have raced ahead faster than I could speak them." This suggests that a rather high activity level exists for the person with a high **Cn** scale score.

4.  Some religious items are included as a fourth group. They appear to be a rejection of some of the more fundamentalistic beliefs such as miracles and the accuracy of prophets.

5.  A fifth group of items concerns the denial of certain symptoms, such as the use of alcohol or having fainting spells.

6.  Some items referring to family relations compose a sixth group. People with a high **Cn** scale report their relations are poor. They answer false to "I love my mother" and to "Members of my family and my close relatives get along quite well."

7.  A final group of items deals with the expectations of others. In this area, some would say that people with high **Cn** scores simply are being realistic because they agree with an item such as "People generally demand more respect for their own rights than they are willing to allow for others."

These groups of items seem to indicate that people with high **Cn** scores tend to be very aware of their feelings, especially their feelings of discomfort and impulsivity. A hypothesis we would like to suggest is that persons with a high control scale may have a set to admit that these impulses exist, and this may raise the pathological scales unduly high. The **Cn** scale then may be picking up a response bias. People with a high control scale and high clinical scales may overemphasize the pathological feelings they do have and, therefore, may not truly be as disturbed as individuals with high clinical scales but lower control scales.

# GENERAL INFORMATION

1.  Cuadra (1953) developed the 50-item **Cn** scale (41 items, MMPI-2) as a measure of personality control.

2.  After identifying 30 pairs of similar MMPI clinical scale profiles, where one person of the pair was hospitalized and the other was not, Cuadra isolated the MMPI items that differentiated these two groups and developed the **Cn** scale.

# HIGH SCORES

(T = 60 or above)

1.  A person with a high **Cn** score may have a measure of personal control that can prevent problem behavior (as shown by elevations on clinical scales) from being exhibited in the presence of others.

2.  People who have high **Cn** scores without elevations on clinical scales may appear to be overcontrolled and somewhat unemotional. Their lack of clinical scale elevations would seem to indicate that no need exists for the amount of personal control shown by the elevation on the **Cn** scale.

3.  Anderson and Kunce (1984) have found that for clients who have markedly elevated **8** scale scores, elevations on **Es** and **Cn** scales may indicate clients who are aware of pathological feelings and their potential for acting out impulsively, but their conscious awareness **(Cn)** and adequate level of ego strength **(Es)** may enable them to better control their behavior.

# LOW SCORES

(T = 50 or below)

1. A person with a low **Cn** score, but with elevated clinical scale scores, readily shows the behavior indicated by the clinical scale elevations.

2. A person with a low **Cn** score and no elevated clinical scale scores has no behavior that needs to be controlled, and the **Cn** score reflects this.

These combinations do not mean that the person is unable to control his/her behavior should clinical scales go above 70. If clinical scales do go above 70, the **Cn** scale also may rise.

# SUMMARY OF Cn SCALE INTERPRETATIONS

| If the Highest Clinical Scale is | | and **Cn** is | Interpretations |
|---|---|---|---|
| MMPI-2 | MMPI | | |
| <65 | <70 | <50 | This combination of scores is usual for persons with minor or no psychological problems. |
| | | 50-60 | This person may appear to be somewhat unemotional. He/she may tend to mask feelings. The person is usually aware of keeping some emotions hidden and may have good reasons for doing so. |
| | | >60 | The person tends to be overcontrolled, objective, and detached. He/she tends to suppress outward expression of inner feelings and impulses and probably has difficulty expressing warmth. |
| >65 | >70 | <50 | The person cannot keep the impulses and/or behavior shown by the clinical scale elevations from being observed by others. |
| | | 50-60 | The person has some control over the amount of behavior that is shown but not as much as when **Cn** is above 60. |

| >60 | The person is able to conceal and control the impulses and behavior indicated by the clinical scale elevation; although, if the person chooses to do so, the impulses and behavior may be revealed. If the person chooses not to show the behavior indicated by clinical scales, he/she may fantasize about them. |

---

# MAC SCALE

The **MAC** scale is one of the supplementary scales that has been retained on the MMPI-2. It has been relabeled the **MAC-R** to reflect the fact that four items were rewritten. The scale remains the same length, however, 49 items. The T-score conversions for the **MAC-R** on the MMPI-2 (see Tables 5.1 and 5.2, pp. 293-296). show that clinical significance is not reached until the **MAC** raw score reaches 28 for men and 26 for women. This change from the raw score of 24 suggested by MacAndrew (1965) reflects some of the concerns that have been expressed (Gottesman & Prescott, 1989; Greene, 1991; Greene & Garvin, 1988) that the original cutoff score of 24 is not appropriate for all populations. For example, the cutoff score of 24 tends to overdiagnose Blacks as alcoholic (Graham & Mayo, 1985; Walters, Greene, Jeffrey, Kruzich, & Haskin, 1983). Greene (1991) has an excellent review of the research about the **MAC** scale and the problems that have been found with it.

The MacAndrew Addiction scale **(MAC)** was developed by Craig MacAndrew (1965), originally to differentiate male psychiatric outpatients who were in treatment for alcohol abuse from male nonsubstance-abusing psychiatric outpatients. Fifty-one MMPI items were identified that made such a differentiation. Two of the 51 items were excluded from the scale since they were too obvious in asking about alcohol symptoms, leaving 49 items. A cutoff score of 24 and above was used by MacAndrew to identify alcoholics, and this score correctly classified 81.5% of his population.

Since 1965, this 49-item scale has been cross validated many times and with many different populations—VA hospital inpatients (Burke & Marcus, 1977), general hospital inpatients (de Groot & Adamson, 1973), and nonpsychiatric outpatients (Lachar, Berman, Grissell, & Schoof, 1976; Rhodes, 1969). In these studies and others, again approximately 85% of the alcoholics were correctly identified, whereas 15% of them were classified falsely as nonalcoholic. MacAndrew (1981) has hypothesized that these 15% false negatives are not primary alcoholics but really "reactive" or secondary alcoholics. He described these people as "neurotics who also happen to drink too much" and believed that they do so to remove themselves from the pain of their daily living.

This is in contrast to the primary alcoholic who is reward-seeking rather than punishment-avoidant as the secondary alcoholic is. Primary alcoholics are described by Finney, Smith, Skeeters, and Auvenshire (1971) as "bold, uninhibited, self-confident, sociable people who mix well with others. They show rebellious urges and resentment of authorities. They tell of carousing, gambling, playing hookey, and generally 'cutting up.' Yet their answers show that they are drawn to religion" (p. 1058). Burke (1983) also saw the **MAC** scale as a measure of the impulsivity, the pressure for action, and the acting-out potential that lead to alcoholism and probably also to the misuse of other substances.

Female alcoholics also have been studied but much less frequently than male alcoholics. In general, females' MacAndrew scores are lower than the males'. Authors of one study (Svanum, Levitt, & McAdoo, 1982) have found 23 and above as the most accurate cutoff score for their population of female alcoholics. In work that I (JD) have done with nonpsychiatric clients, I also have found that women in general score lower than men on the **MAC** scale. The females' average score was 19, whereas the males' average score was 21 (Duckworth, 1983).

After the **MAC** scale was used with alcoholics for a period of time, drug abusers were tested (Burke & Marcus, 1977; Kranitz, 1972; Lachar et al., 1976; Sutker, Archer, Brantley, & Kilpatrick, 1979), and the scale was found to differentiate them from nondrug abusers with approximately the same degree of accuracy as was found in the differentiation of alcoholics from nonalcoholics. The scale accurately classified heroin and polydrug abusers in these studies; however, Caldwell (1985) has reported that the scale does not pick up cocaine abuse in the population he has tested (medical center inpatients and outpatients). It also does not differentiate recreational marijuana users in the population with whom these authors work (college students).

In college and mental health settings, the scale may need to be used somewhat differently than it is in a psychiatric population. If people are having trouble with alcohol or drug use, we find the cutoff scores that MacAndrew and others have used, 24 and above for men and 23 and above for women, to be useful. However, if people are not having trouble with drinking or drug abuse, we have felt safer in labeling men addictive only when their scores are 28 or above and women when their scores are 26 or above. When men and women score this high, most of them recognize the "pull" of alcohol or drugs, but they have not been having problems with addiction because they have worked very hard at controlling themselves. Many of these people seem to be motivated by the "horrible example" of an alcoholic parent or parents, and they use this example to limit their drinking or drug use.

People in college and mental health settings who have scores of 24 through 27 on this scale also may report some of this "pull" of alcohol or drugs, but much less frequently than the people with scores of 28 or more. We also have found many people in this range who have never tried alcohol or drugs because of religious beliefs. Possibly if they did not have those beliefs and had tried drinking and/or drugs, they might indeed be alcoholic or drug abusers.

The meaning of a low score on the MacAndrew scale (below 15) is currently unknown. However, Caldwell (1985) has hypothesized that people scoring 10 raw score points or below cannot tolerate alcohol. People in general score from 15 through 22 raw score points on this scale.

We have found that the score on this scale does not tend to change over time. Duckworth has found that on retesting people after a six-month period, the MacAndrew score typically changed 2 raw score points or less. Indeed, so stable is this scale that it has been found not to change with successful treatment for alcoholism (Galluci, Kay, & Thornby, 1989; Huber & Danahy, 1975). MacAndrew also has noted (1981) that the **MAC** scores of alcoholics do not change with treatment or even after prolonged substance abuse. He also found that the **MAC** scores are not related to age or race. What the scale does seem to measure is a fundamental character dimension. He endorses Finney's (1971) description of the primary alcoholic noted earlier as the personality characteristics measured by elevations on the **MAC** scale.

## GENERAL INFORMATION

1. This 49-item scale measures the potential for addiction to alcohol and/or drugs.

2. Schwartz and Graham (1979) factor analyzed the scale and found it measures impulsivity, high energy level, interpersonal shallowness, and general psychological maladjustment.

3. Test-retest reliability coefficients are high for the **MAC** on the original MMPI, but they are not so high for the MMPI-2 **MAC.**

   a. Scores do not change significantly with successful treatment for addiction.

   b. Over a 6-month period, **MAC** scores for subjects did not change significantly (Duckworth, 1983).

   c. The retest reliability coefficients for this scale on the MMPI-2 are .62 for men and .78 for women (Butcher et al., 1989).

4. Schwartz and Graham (1979) have found the scale correlates .55 with scale **9** (impulsivity and energy) and -.62 with scale **R** (repression). In another study of therapy clients (Duckworth, 1983), the scale correlated with **K,** -.34; **9,** .39; **R,** -.38; **Re,** -50; and **Pr,** .36.

5. It has not correlated with race in some studies (Lachar et al., 1976; Page & Bozler, 1982; Uecker, Boutilier, &

Richardson, 1980); however, Walters et al., (1983) found that this scale did not discriminate between Black alcoholics and Black nonalcoholics in an active duty military sample.

6.  There is not a single, optimal cutting score for all populations. Cutoff scores of 24 to 29 have been used in different studies to achieve the maximum hit rate (Greene, 1991).

7.  Populations where using 24 as a cutoff score may be particularly inappropriate are

    a.  nonwhite groups, especially Blacks;

    b.  psychiatric patients, especially Blacks; and

    c.  medical patients, especially those with seizure disorders.

8.  The scale does correlate with age (Appledorf & Hunley, 1975; Duckworth, 1983; Friedrich & Loftsgard, 1978; MacAndrew, 1965; Uecker et al., 1980).

9.  The average range of scores for a group of nonaddictive normals (N = 433) was from 15 through 23 (Duckworth, 1983):

    The mean score for women was 19.

    The mean score for men was 21.

10. Colligan and Offord (1987) have found that the **MAC** score identified approximately 40% of the men and 20% of the women in a contemporary normative sample as at risk for alcoholism (>24 raw score point on the **MAC**). These authors suggested that clinicians take a conservative approach in their interpretation of scores from the **MAC** scale.

11. The scale seems to show discrimination between substance abusers and nonabusers as early as late adolescence (MacAndrew, 1979b).

12. The scale may be predictive of future alcoholism as early as entrance to college. Hoffman, Loper, and Kammeier (1974) found the mean **MAC** scale scores of 25 hospitalized alcoholics were not significantly different than their average scores at the time of their entrance to college, some 13 years earlier when they were also in the addictive range.

13. MacAndrew has hypothesized that alcoholics who are not elevated on the **MAC** scale may be introverted, neurotic persons who use alcohol to self-medicate (1981).

14. Suicide prone alcoholics are likely to be those who are using alcohol but not scoring in the addictive range on the scale (MacAndrew, 1981).

15. Graham and Strenger (1988) found no one MMPI profile type characteristic of alcoholics. Consistently, however, scale **4** was one of the high points on the profile. Reflecting this elevation, alcoholics have a tendency to be impulsive, to resent authority, to have low frustration tolerance, and to have poorly controlled anger.

16. Craig (1984b) has found that drug addicts with a co-existing alcohol problem have higher **MAC** scores than addicts without a current alcohol problem.

17. Otto, Lang, Megargee, and Rosenblatt (1988) have found that the Positive Malingering scale (**Mp**) (Cofer, Chance, & Judson, 1949) in combination with the **MAC** scale accurately identified 37 out of 40 alcoholics who were asked to conceal their alcoholism on the MMPI. These authors suggested using the **Mp** and the **MAC** scales together to accurately detect alcoholics who are trying to look good on the MMPI.

18. Cernovsky (1985a) found that an elevated **R** scale (>60) may serve as a warning sign of possible false negatives

in screening for addictions. Kennedy and McPeake (1987), however, were unable to replicate Cernovsky's findings.

19. Almost 50% of seizure disorder patients had significant **MAC** scores (>24) in one study (Bornstein, Rosenberger, Harkness-Kling, & Suga, 1989). These authors suggested that caution should be used when administering the **MAC** to seizure disorder patients. They believe that there is some content bias in the **MAC** scale when applied to patients with seizure disorders.

20. Another study of patients with epilepsy found that over 49% of the patients were falsely classified as alcoholic by the **MAC** scale (Steenman, Hermann, Wyler, & Richey, 1988). A similarity of experiential and behavior characteristics between seizure patients and substance abusers was suggested as a possible reason for the findings.

21. Researchers have found that the scale can be administered as a separate test of 49 items with no significant difference in the **MAC** score than the score obtained when the scale is administered embedded in the total MMPI (Duckworth, 1983; MacAndrew, 1979a).

## HIGH SCORES

(28 and above for males, MMPI-2)

(24 and above for males, MMPI)

(26 and above for females, MMPI-2)

(23 and above for females, MMPI)

1. The cutoff scores of 24 and above for men and 23 and above for women for both the MMPI and MMPI-2 work best for people self-referred or brought in by others for substance abuse problems.

2. For people who are having psychological difficulties, but substance abuse is not one of them, scores of 24 through 27 raw score points for men and 23 through 25 raw score points for women may not indicate current substance abuse but a potential for it if psychological pressure should be increased.

   a. Some people in this range may recognize the "pull" of substance abuse but work hard at controlling it because of the example of an addicted parent.

   b. Others may have religious beliefs that keep them from using alcohol or drugs.

3. The higher the raw score above 28 for men and 26 for women, and the more psychological pressure the person is under, the greater the likelihood that there will be substance abuse.

4. Clopton, Weiner, and Davis (1980) found 27 and above to be the best cutoff score for their sample of psychiatric inpatients.

5. Alcoholics who score in the addictive range on this scale (primary alcoholics) report four times as many symptoms of "brain dysfunction" in childhood as do alcoholics who do not score in the addictive range (secondary alcoholics) (MacAndrew, 1981).

6. In one study by Greene, Arredondo, and Davis (1990), alcoholics and psychiatric inpatients scored slightly higher on the MMPI-2 **MAC** scale than they did on the original **MAC** scale.

7. Allen, Faden, Miller, and Rawlings (1991) found that alcoholics with high **MAC** scores were more extraverted and sensation-seeking than alcoholics with non-elevated **MAC** scores. Alcoholics with low **MAC** scores were less

interested in gaining attention from others and had lower needs for variety, stimulation, and immediate pleasure.

## LOW SCORES

(below 24 for males
and 23 for females)

1.  Individuals who were alcoholics but had low **MAC** scores were less outgoing and gregarious than alcoholics with high **MAC** scores (Svanum & Ehrmann, 1992). They tended to be solitary drinkers and were not likely to have acting-out behavior.

2.  Kennedy and McPeake (1987) found that alcoholics with **MAC** scores below 23 were repressed, conventional, moody, restless, and dissatisfied. The modal two-point code for this group was **2-7**, with 32% of the individuals receiving this code. This group of low scoring **MAC** patients were quite homogeneous compared to the more heterogeneous high **MAC** group of alcoholics.

3.  People with low **MAC** scales may be individuals who try to avoid punishment (Graham & Strenger, 1988).

# SUMMARY OF MAC SCALE INTERPRETATIONS

| Raw Score MMPI-2 & MMPI | Interpretations |
|---|---|
| 0-15 (Men & Women) | A person scoring in this range may not be able to tolerate alcohol. |
| 16-22 (Women) <br> 16-23 (Men) | This is the average range of scores for people in general. If people are substance abusers and score in this range, they may be secondary alcoholics; that is, their alcoholism is secondary to their personal problems and it is used to avoid the pain they feel. Suicide prone alcoholics come from this group. Approximately 15% of diagnosed alcoholics are secondary alcoholics. |
| 23-25 (Women) <br> 24-27 (Men) | If the person is self- or other-referred because of substance abuse problems, the **MAC** score confirms the diagnosis. If the person has psychological problems but substance abuse is not one of them, he/she may not be abusing alcohol. |
| >26 (Women) <br> >28 (Men) | For people without any psychological problems of addictions, this score may be a false positive (labeling people addictive when they are not). Scores in this range indicate addictive potential that may be acted upon (in alcoholics and drug abusers) or not (for those who recognize the addictive potential but control it, perhaps through abstinence). The higher the **MAC** scale and the more psychological pressure the person is under, the greater the likelihood of substance abuse. |

# ADDITIONAL MMPI-2
# SUPPLEMENTARY SCALES

Besides the six MMPI-2 supplementary scales that have already been discussed in this chapter, **A, R, Es, Do, Re,** and **MAC-R,** six other scales also are scored on the supplementary scale profile of the MMPI-2. These six scales are **O-H, Mt, GM, GF, PK,** and **PS.** They will be discussed briefly in this section.

The **O-H** scale (Overcontrolled-Hostility, Megargee & Mendelsohn, 1962) and the **Mt** scale (College Maladjustment, Kleinmuntz, 1961) have been available as scales for a long time and are discussed at length in Greene's 1991 book on the MMPI and MMPI-2 (Greene, 1991). We have not found these two scales to be useful for our MMPI-2 interpretations because the **O-H** scale is applicable to a very small group of individuals and the **Mt** scale gives test information that is available on another scale that is routinely scored. The **O-H** scale was developed to detect individuals who overcontrol their hostility until they have a sudden aggressive episode. While this scale has done a good job when applied to the criminal population, using the scale for other groups of individuals may lead to a misdiagnosis. For example, Graham (1978) has found that Blacks and females score higher on this scale than the original group of overcontrolled criminals used to develop this scale; therefore, Blacks and women are likely to be misdiagnosed as having overcontrolled hostility when this may not be true.

The **Mt** scale was designed to detect general maladjustment in college students. It has a very high correlation with the **A** scale, which picks up general maladjustment for a much broader group of clients. This scale, therefore, does not seem to offer any new information.

The **GM** (Gender Role - Masculine) and **GF** (Gender Role - Feminine) scales have been developed for the MMPI-2 by

Peterson (Peterson & Dahlstrom, 1992). Items were selected for inclusion in these scales if they were endorsed by at least 70% of one sex and there was at least a 10% difference in rate of endorsement between the two sexes. The endorsement frequencies used for the scales' construction were obtained from the MMPI-2 national restandardization sample. Peterson hoped to create independent, unipolar measures of masculinity (**GM**) and feminity (**GF**). She hypothesized that based upon elevations of those two scales, individuals could be classified as androgynous (high **GM**, high **GF**), masculine (high **GM**, low **GF**), feminine (high **GF**, low **GM**), or undifferentiated (low **GM**, low **GF**).

A stereotypic characterization of each gender seems to have been produced by Peterson's method of selecting scale items (Greene, 1991). While there is not much research about these two scales, Gentry & Meyer (1990) have found in one study that the **GM** scale has a high correlation with measures of self-esteem and an equally negative correlation with measures of psychopathology. On the other hand, these researchers also found that the **GF** scale was not correlated with either measures of self-esteem or psychopathology. Thus, it seems that the **GM** and **GF** scales may be measuring something other than masculinity and femininity.

We have found in our work with these scales that the **GM** scale does seem to be correlated with good mental health. Typically our graduate students, both men and women, score 50 or above on this scale. On the other hand, their scores on the **GF** scale are quite varied. Until further research is done on these two scales, we prefer to use the **GM** scale as a general measure of psychological health and defer the interpretation of the **GF** scale until more is known about its meaning.

The **PK** and **PS** supplementary scales (Keane et al., 1984; Schlenger & Kulka, 1987) were designed to diagnose Post-traumatic Stress Disorder (PTSD). Green (1991) suggested extreme caution in using these scales for this purpose since both scales have very high correlations with the **A** scale and, therefore, may be yet another measure of general maladjustment. We have found that our clients who have post-traumatic stress may or may not have elevated **PK** and **PS** scales. The clients who we see with PTSD typically cycle in and out of intense distress. When they are in the distressed phase of their cycles, they usually have elevations on **PK** and **PS.** When they are not in this phase of their cycles, they do not. We believe, therefore, that these scales should not be used to diagnose PTSD since there are times when individuals with PTSD do not elevate on them.

After a trial period with these six MMPI-2 supplementary scales, we find ourselves reluctant to use them frequently. Three of the scales (**Mt, PK,** and **PS**) are so correlated with the **A** scale that they seem to be redundant. One of the scales (**O-H**) may misdiagnose Blacks and women, and the **GM** scale seems to be yet another measure of psychological health.

Besides these six scales that have been available for the MMPI-2 since it was published in 1989, three other scales have recently been added to the MMPI-2 computer reports that are available from National Computer Systems. These new scales are the Addiction Potential Scale (**APS**), the Addiction Admission Scale (**AAS**), and the Marital Distress Scale (**MDS**).

The Addiction Potential Scale (**APS**) was designed by Weed, Butcher, Ben-Porath, and McKenna (1992) as a measure of the personality factors that correlate with addictive disorders. The scale was developed by the method that MacAndrew used to develop his addiction scale, the **MAC** (MacAndrew, 1965). MacAndrew identified MMPI items that differentiated alcohol and drug users from groups of psychiatric patients and normals. These items became the **MAC** scale. The **APS** scale has been developed using this same method but is made up of MMPI-2 items that differentiate between these groups of patients. This new scale has 39 items instead of the 49 in the original **MAC** scale. Cross-validation studies (Greene, Week, Butcher, Arredondo, & Davis, 1992; Shondrick et al., 1992; Weed et al., 1992) have shown the **APS** to be superior to the **MAC** and the **MAC-R** (the MMPI-2 **MAC** scale) in identifying groups of substance abusers.

The Addiction Admission Scale (**AAS**) was also developed by Weed et al. (1992) to measure a test taker's willingness to acknowledge problems with alcohol and/or drugs. It also was found to do a better job than the **MAC** scale in identifying alcohol and drug abusers when used with individuals who were already in alcohol and drug treatment programs (Greene et al., 1992, Weed et al., 1992) or when used with individuals who were being evaluated because of legal problems (Shondrick et al., 1992). Shondrick et al. (1992) pointed out, however, that individuals in their study were undergoing evaluations that could have had a significant impact on their legal proceedings. These researchers felt that it was possible that their subjects were more willing to admit to problems with alcohol and/or drugs than people who are in more typical settings such as mental health centers. Because the **AAS** scale is measuring the individual's willingness to acknowledge addiction problems, the most appropriate way to use the scale may be as a measure of the individual's openness to treatment for his/her addictions.

The Marital Distress Scale (**MDS**) was developed by Hjemboe and Butcher (1991) to assess marital stress. This 15-item scale was created by selecting MMPI-2 items that highly correlated with an outside measure of marital distress, the Spanier Dyadic Adjustment scale. There may be some indication of marital distress when the scale is between 60 and 64 T-score points on the MMPI-2, and there is a strong indication of distress when the scale is above 65 T-score points (Butcher & Williams, 1992). Preliminary research (Hjemboe & Butcher, 1991) indicates that the **MDS** scale does a better job of measuring marital distress than either the **4** scale or the MMPI-2 **FAM** (Family Problems) content scale.

These new supplementary scales, the **APS, AAS,** and **MDS** are of such recent origin that very little is known about them except for the studies that have been mentioned; therefore, interpretations given for each of these scales need to be tentative until further corroborative research is available.

# CONTENT SCALES

Scales reflecting major content areas have been developed for both the MMPI (Wiggins, 1966) and the MMPI-2 (Butcher et al., 1989). The Wiggins content scales are 13 relatively independent, nonoverlapping, homogeneous scales that are made up of MMPI items with obvious content. These 13 scales and their meanings are shown in Table 5.7. The items that made up these 13 scales are available in Dahlstrom, Welsh, and Dahlstrom (1972). Elevations on these scales can be taken as indications of the test takers' diagnoses of their problems (Wiggins, 1966). Since the items are obvious, individuals taking the test can also deliberately elevate or lower the scales by choosing whether to answer the items or not. Therefore, these scales are vulnerable to both faking bad and faking good distortions. Further information regarding the Wiggins content scales and their interpretation is available in a monograph by Nichols (1987). This is an excellent source of information regarding these scales and their relationship to the clinical scales of the MMPI.

If you should wish to continue to use the original Wiggins content scales with the MMPI-2, it is possible to do so with some modifications (Levitt, 1990). The Religious Fundamentalism scale (**REL**) is no longer available because of the elimination of most religious items in the MMPI-2, and the Health Concerns (**HEA**) and Feminine Interest (**FEM**) scales also have had some items eliminated, but the rest of the scales are relatively intact.

There are also content scales for the MMPI-2 (Butcher et al., 1989). These content scales and their meanings are shown in Table 5.8. These 15 scales, in contrast to the Wiggins scales, are not independent of each other and do have items that overlap. For example, the Obsessiveness (**OBS**), Cynicism (**CYN**), Work Interference (**WRK**), and Negative Treatment Indicators (**TRT**) scales have almost one-half of their items in common with other content scales. In spite of scale names that are quite similar, there is very little item overlap between the MMPI-2 and Wiggins content scales. Items that make up these new content scales can be found in the *MMPI-2 Manual* (Butcher et al., 1989), or the book by Butcher (1990) that deals exclusively with the MMPI-2 content scales. The new MMPI-2 content scales are also subject to conscious distortion; therefore, caution is advised in using these scales as accurate indications of an individual's problems (Caldwell, 1991).

We use the MMPI and MMPI-2 content scales to find out what clients see as the problems that need to be dealt with in their therapy. We usually begin therapy by talking about those self-diagnosed problems. We find that this helps clients feel understood because we are dealing with issues that they feel are relevant to their well-being. If the clinical scales show problems that are not indicated on the content scales, we wait to talk about those problems until we have established rapport by discussing the client's self-diagnosed problems. We find that we have more success in getting clients to deal with issues shown on the clinical scales if we put off discussing those areas until after two or three sessions of talking about problems shown by the content scale elevations. Thus, using the content scales and the information contained in them can add a useful dimension to your work with the MMPI and/or MMPI-2.

**TABLE 5.7**
**Wiggins Content Scales**

| SCALE | NAME | MEANING |
|---|---|---|
| HEA | Poor Health | The person is concerned about health. |
| DEP | Depression | He/she is depressed. |
| ORG | Organic Symptoms | This individual has problems with symptoms that may be organic in nature, such as headaches and loss of consciousness. |
| FAM | Family Problems | He/she reports an unhappy home life, which may be current as well as in family of origin. |
| AUT | Authority Conflict | Others are seen as unscrupulous and dishonest. Life is a jungle. |
| FEM | Feminine Interests | This person likes many different types of activities, including those that are considered feminine. |
| REL | Religious Fundamentalism | He/she has religious beliefs that are fundamentalist and/or conservative. |
| HOS | Manifest Hostility | This individual is angry, competitive, and uncooperative. |
| MOR | Poor Morale | This person has little self-confidence and is sensitive. |
| PHO | Phobias | He/she reports fears of a phobic nature. |
| PSY | Psychoticism | This person reports psychotic symptoms such as feelings of unreality and loss of control. |
| HYP | Hypomania | He/she has excessive excitement and restlessness. |
| SOC | Social Maladjustment | This individual is shy, uneasy in social situations, reserved. |

## TABLE 5.8
## MMPI-2 Content Scales

| SCALE | NAME | MEANING |
|-------|------|---------|

### Internal Problems

| | | |
|-------|------|---------|
| ANX | Anxiety | This person reports feelings of anxiety and nervousness. |
| FRS | Fears | He/she has many specific fears. |
| OBS | Obsessiveness | This individual has difficulty making decisions and worries excessively. |
| DEP | Depression | He/she has depressed mood and thoughts. |
| HEA | Health Concerns | This person reports many physical symptoms. |
| BIZ | Bizarre Mentation | He/she has strange thoughts and experiences. |

### External Problems

| | | |
|-------|------|---------|
| ANG | Anger | This individual reports being irritable and angry, may lose control and smash objects, etc. |
| CYN | Cynicism | He/she expects other people to lie, cheat, and steal and trusts nobody. |
| ASP | Antisocial Practices | This person reports antisocial behaviors such as stealing and other problem behaviors. |
| TPA | Type A Behavior | He/she is hard driving, impatient, and work-oriented. |

## Negative Self-View

LSE     Low Self-Esteem     This individual has a low self-opinion and lacks self-confidence.

## General Problem Areas

SOD     Social Discomfort     He/she is shy and uneasy around others.

FAM     Family Problems     This person reports difficulties within current family.

WRK     Work Interference     He/she has many problems that interfere with work, such as being tired and working under a great deal of tension.

TRT     Negative Treatment Indicators     This individual has attitudes that interfere with successful therapy. He/she does not want to discuss problems and is pessimistic about the worth of therapy.

CHAPTER

# SAMPLE MMPI
# INTERPRETATIONS

This chapter presents two different methods of interpreting MMPI/MMPI-2 profiles using the supplementary scales as well as the validity and clinical scales. The first section of the chapter was written by Jane Duckworth, and the second section was written by Wayne Anderson. In interpreting the MMPI-2 and MMPI, many similarities as well as many differences occur for the two methods. Both approaches are presented to show different ways of doing interpretations.

# MMPI INTERPRETATIONS

Jane Duckworth

When I interpret a MMPI, I usually am focusing my attention on two things: (1) what are the current *behaviors* and *feelings* of the individual who took the test, and (2) what are the *underlying reasons* for these behaviors and feelings. If the person is coming in for counseling and/or therapy, I also am interested in *what type of treatment* might prove most effective for the individual.

Some limitations of the applicability of the way I do MMPI interpretations do exist. I have worked mainly with bright people, both young (students) and old (faculty), at a university counseling center. If a choice of interpretations is possible, I tend to err on the side of the optimistic one. I have found that the high points of a profile for these two groups do not always have the dire implications that are attached to them in the MMPI interpretations derived from clinical populations. True, the behavior and feelings of these counseling center clients may be maladaptive, but because of the client's intelligence and residence in an environment geared to trying new things, the manifestations of the maladaptive behavior and feelings usually are milder, and the likelihood of positive change is much greater than with clients in clinical populations. If the profile being interpreted is from a different population than that found in a counseling center, you need to check to see if the optimistic approach I use is applicable.

Another difference between the way I do interpretations and the way some others do them is that I operate from a philosophy that emphasizes looking for the strengths within a client and building on those while minimizing maladaptive behavior. I tend to ignore maladaptive behavior if it is not causing the client or the people around him/her a great deal of trouble, and I reinforce or try to build upon the adaptive behavior the client is exhibiting. A further difference in the way I do interpretations is that while I am aware of the underlying dynamics of the client's behavior as shown on the test profile, my main focus in the interpretation is on the client's behavior and the way his/her feelings affect that behavior.

My impression is that this interpretative approach emphasizing client strengths rather than weaknesses, focusing on behavior and feelings rather than underlying dynamics, is becoming more applicable to mental health centers and private clinic populations than it used to be. As state outpatient mental health systems become prevalent and therapy is more available and less stigmatized, my feeling is that more "normal" people (nonneurotic, nonpsychotic) are coming for help with everyday problems such as dealing with their children or marriage. Clients in these agencies resemble the ones seen in college counseling centers more than they resemble patients in mental institutions, and the approaches stressed in this chapter tend to be applicable to them.

The following are some general guidelines I use for interpreting the original MMPI. Since this test is still being used by many clinicians, I feel that it is still useful to discuss how I interpret this version of the MMPI and to show a sample MMPI interpretation. After this is done, I will discuss how I interpret the MMPI-2 and show a sample MMPI-2 interpretation.

## INTERPRETING THE MMPI

When working with the MMPI, I divide the interpretation into three parts covering the validity, clinical, and supplementary scales. I deal with each section separately at first and then look at them together. In general, I do not pay attention to scales appearing between 45 and 60 T-score points, except for certain supplementary scales (**Dy, Do, Re, Pr,** and **St**), because scales in this middle range do not tend to indicate unique behavior. I start by individually interpreting the very highest scales in each section and then work down to the scales closest to 60 T-score points. After this, I look at the scales that are the farthest below 45 T-score points. In most MMPI profiles, many more high points occur than low points.

I start an MMPI interpretation by looking at the validity scales and use them as an indication of the general test-taking attitude of the individual; for example, is the client saying he/she is feeling good (high **K**) or bad (high **F**) about life on the day he/she took the test? The higher these validity scales are above 60 T-score points, the more likely the person is to be emphasizing that particular feeling and maybe even exaggerating it: "I feel like I'm overwhelmed with problems" (high **F**); "Life is absolutely beautiful, nothing is the slightest bit wrong with what's happening" (high **K**). In the validity scale section of this book (Chapter III) are some typical combinations of validity scales and their interpretations.

After getting a general idea about the mood of the person taking the test, I then proceed to the clinical scales and interpret them individually from the highest scale above 60 down to the one closest to 60 T-score points. I look then at the lowest scales below 45 and interpret them and then move up to the scales closest to 45 T-score points. If several scales are above 70 T-score points, I tend to downplay the scales between 60 and 70 T-score points, because these may be elevated due to the heightened emotional state of the client.

If no scales are above 70, except perhaps the **5** scale for men, then the scales within the 60-70 T-score range can be very useful for indicating behavior that is present but not necessarily a problem as it might be if the scale were above 70. Instead, the behavior may be a way of dealing with life that is adaptive rather than maladaptive. The summary at the end of each clinical scale section indicates the wealth of information that can be obtained from MMPI scale scores in this usually ignored 60-70 T-score range.

After looking at the various high and low points of the clinical scales, I move to the MMPI supplementary scales (**A, R, Es, Lb, Dy, Do, Re, Pr, St, Cn, MAC**) and follow the same procedure used with the clinical scales. I start interpreting the highest scales and work down to those scales closest to 60 T-score points. I then interpret the lowest scales and work up to the scales closest to 45 T-score points. I do not ignore the scales between 60 and 70 T-score points within this supplementary scale group even if a number of scales are above 70. I find that all elevations above 60 on these scales are useful regardless of their relative height.

After noting the high and low scales for the clinical and supplementary scale sections, I then start the much more difficult process of considering the scales in combinations and balancing the information from one scale against the information from another. I do not ignore inconsistencies in the individual scale interpretations but rather try to determine under what conditions these two behaviors could exist in the same person at the same time. This situation is where the supplementary scales are of the greatest use. They can help refine the information presented in the clinical scale elevations so that the most accurate interpretation of the clinical scales can be given. A high **2** scale may not indicate self-deprecation, for example, if the ego-strength scale **(Es)** is above 50 T-score points. Summaries showing refinements of the clinical scales by the supplementary scales are at the end of the appropriate clinical scales (Chapter IV).

In addition to the refinements already mentioned, the supplementary scales indicate strengths that a client may have that temper predictions made from the clinical scales. The control scale **(Cn)**, if elevated above 60 T-score points, indicates ability of the client to control the outward manifestation of his/her maladaptive behavior shown on the elevated clinical scales. A client may have a **2-7-8** profile, but if he/she also has a **Cn** scale above 60, that person probably has some control over who sees the depression, anxiety, and confusion indicated by the clinical scales. He/she also may be able to temper the amount of these behaviors shown. These supplementary scale refinements provide important information for the most accurate interpretation of the clinical scales.

In addition to examining these refinements of the clinical scale information, the practitioner should consider the clinical scales in their various combinations. I have found two-point combinations to be the most useful. Occasionally, three-point combinations are helpful but, in general, they do not add more information than what is found in the two-point combinations.

When all this information on a profile has been gathered, the interpretations can be made. When I do an interpretation, I try to say something first about the *test-taking attitude* of the person so that the rest of the information given in the report can be interpreted in light of how the client was feeling at the time. I proceed then with the body of the report and start by mentioning those *behaviors and feelings* most likely to be overtly shown and expressed by the client, using the two or three highest clinical scale elevations as my clues. In reference to the **2-7-8** profile mentioned previously, for example, I might say, "Mr. R. is most likely to be reporting severe depression and would appear to be highly anxious and confused."

Next I bring in the *refinements* to the clinical scales that I may have learned from the supplementary scales or from the clinical scale combinations. If the **2-7-8** profile has an **Es** scale above 45, I would say, "The depression shown by Mr. R. does not, however, include the self-deprecation typically seen in these cases."

After describing as accurately as I can the behavior and feelings shown by the client, I then proceed to hypotheses, if I have any, concerning why these behaviors and feelings may be present. An interpretation for a woman with a high **2-4-6** in the midst of a divorce might be, "The depression, anger, and confusion shown by this woman seem most likely to be her reaction to the pending divorce. It would be helpful to verify this reaction by seeing if her anger is directed specifically toward her husband and the situation she is in or whether it is generalized to many other people and situations."

Following these hypotheses, I then go to *strengths* I may see in the profile. These strengths may be revealed by the supplementary scales or sometimes by lower clinical scales elevations.

The report is closed with some predictions concerning *prognosis* and *implications for therapy*. For a **2-8** profile, statements such as the following might be made. "Miss R. should be amenable to therapy because of the amount of psychological pain she is feeling. However, I recommend that therapy progress slowly and with as many simple, specific suggestions as possible because of the amount of psychological confusion the client is experiencing."

With these points in mind, let's look at Figure 6.1, a profile of Mr. J.R. The following is a typical interpretation for a person with such a profile.

The client, Mr. R., is a 34-year-old white male with a master's degree in art. He is on the faculty of a small, midwestern college. Mr. R. is coming for therapy because he is upset about his marriage and also because his family doctor has suggested that some of the tenseness he has been experiencing may be because of psychological problems.

The man is doing well as an art professor at the college, but he reports not feeling really good about what is happening in his life. He has the feeling, he says, that something must be better somewhere. He has focused on his wife as the cause of much unhappiness because she is "too placid" and, he feels, not interested in discussing anything other than everyday events.

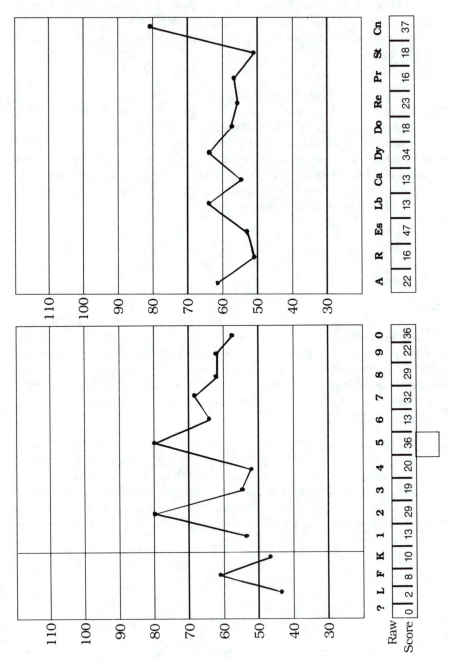

**Figure 6.1.** MMPI profile of Mr. J.R.

*MMPI & MMPI-2*

The following is an example of a work sheet and summary (interpretation) as they might be for Mr. R. When the MMPI interpretation is sent to someone, the work sheet material about the individual scales is not sent. Only the summary, without the scale identifications (material in parentheses in the summary), is sent as the interpretation.

## MMPI INTERPRETATION WORKSHEET

### Validity Scales

**F** = 62 | Slight elevation; perhaps is feeling a small amount of psychological pain.

**L** = 43 | A typical score for a person with his educational level. He is willing to admit to some common human faults. Not of much significance unless the **L** score is high.

### Clinical Scales

**2** = 80 | Depression may include self-deprecation. Check **Es** score in supplementary scale section for clues as to whether self-deprecation is involved.

**5** = 80 | Aesthetic interests and possible passivity. Very likely this scale is at least partially elevated because this man is an artist and highly educated. Need to check **Dy-Do** in the supplementary scale section to see if passivity also is involved in this elevation.

**7** = 69 | Anxiety, but at a minimum level (below 70). This anxiety will more likely be seen as occasional tenseness rather than overt anxiety.

**6** = 67 | Some interpersonal sensitivity without the general suspiciousness seen when the scale is above 70.

| | |
|---|---|
| **8** = 64 | At this level, the scale may show creativity or belonging to an atypical group. Because this person is an artist, the creativity interpretation is the most likely. |
| **9** = 63 | An abundance of psychological energy. This is a typical level for a productive person. |
| **0** = 60 | Borderline for interpretation. This scale may indicate preferences for being by himself, but it does not indicate problems with being around others. |

## Supplementary Scales

| | |
|---|---|
| Control **Cn** = 81 | Great ability to control who sees the behavior shown on the elevated clinical scales. Because **Cn** is very high and clinical scores are not greatly elevated, this person may be too controlled at times. |
| Low back pain **Lb** = 66 | May be saying, "I'm a wonderful person. I love people, and they never annoy me, but for some reason I am uncomfortable and not as happy as I should be." |
| Dependency **Dy** = 66 | Psychological dependency. He would like to lean on others at times and have them take care of him. |
| Anxiety **A** = 62 | Some situational anxiety. This score is at about the level to be expected when the **7** scale is between 60 and 70 T-score points. |
| **Dy-Do** combination | This is sometimes looked at when a small point spread exists (less than 10 T-score points) |

| | |
|---|---|
| **Dy** = 66<br>**Do** = 59 | or both scales are above 50 T-score points. For this person, it indicates the psychological dependency already mentioned, combined with a strong underlying desire to take charge of his own life. This ambivalence can create problems for this man and those close to him because he may act one way one time and the opposite way very shortly afterwards. Another way this combination may be shown is by passive-aggressive behavior. This man may subtly ask others to take care of him and then subvert that helping by complaining about the results or subverting the effectiveness of them in some way. |

### Refinements

| | |
|---|---|
| **F** elevation compared to clinical scales | When the **F** scale elevation is only between 60 and 70 T-score points, but the clinicals (excluding scales **5** and **9**) are above 70 T-score points, the person is not complaining as much on the **F** scale as he is on the clinical scales. This may be because he is used to feeling the depression shown by the elevated **2** scale. He reports being definitely depressed (the elevation on **2**), but he is not greatly worried about it (lower **F** scale). |
| **2** scale compared to **Es** scale | Mr. R. is feeling depressed but is not self-deprecating. He feels life is somewhat unpleasant (high **2**) but does not necessarily see himself as the cause or as unworthy of a better existence (**Es** above 50). |
| **5** scale compared | While showing aesthetic interests, this scale (**5**) also may be showing some passivity (**Dy** |

to **Dy** and
**Do**

= 66). However, this passivity is tempered by some feelings of dominance and/or passive-aggressiveness (**Do** = 59 and **Dy** - **Do** spread).

## Summary
(Scale identifications are added for clarity. In a report they would not be included.)

This profile depicts a person who was feeling somewhat bad at the time he took the test (**F** scale). He most likely was complaining about feeling depressed (**2**) and perhaps some tenseness (**7**). He is liable to have some passive-aggressive tendencies (**5** and **Dy-Do**) that could be directed at those closest to him, because he has a tendency to be quite sensitive to how others feel about him (**6**).

He has much control (**Cn**) over his behavior, and he can keep people from seeing his depression and tenseness if he wishes. However, this control is at such a high level that he may use it in the therapy situation to keep important feelings and behavior from the therapist as well as from others in the outside world.

Another problem in working with this client could be that he may not have some of the necessary insight into why he is so unhappy (**Lb**). He may feel that he tries hard and loves people, but things still do not feel right nor is he happy.

These feelings of unhappiness and depression probably have been around for a long time, so that the client is not as worried about them as others with similar feelings might be (difference between **F** elevation and the clinical elevations). The prognosis for therapy is mixed. On the one hand, this client does report depression and tenseness and a general feeling of malaise; but, on the other hand, he is not exceptionally worried about these feelings and has such control over the expression of them that he may not be willing or able to show them in their full ramifications to the therapist. Add to this the possibility of some passive-aggressive behavior as the therapist gets closer and the interpersonal sensitivity of the client, and it can be seen that some potential problems are at hand.

This type of client tends to work well with a therapist who goes slowly and helps deal with the overt signs of discomfort before starting to delve into the underlying dynamics. Frequently a client of this type does well with a woman or a very empathetic man because of the perceived help this type of counselor/ therapist can give. This client wants someone to lean on and usually will respond quickly to therapist warmth. What the client does not see and what may take longer to deal with are his underlying aggressiveness and sensitivity. The possibility exists that the client will terminate therapy once the pain is gone but before the more hidden dynamics are dealt with.

# INTERPRETING THE MMPI-2

I find that I am still in the process of refining my method of interpreting the MMPI-2. I am more confident of my interpretation of an elevated clinical profile when it shows clearly defined one- or two-point elevations; that is, the one or two highest clinical scales are at least 5 T-score points above the next highest clinical scale. When the profile is not clearly defined, or is very close to the 65 T-score level (only two to three T-score points higher), I rescore the profile onto an MMPI profile using the MMPI-2 raw scores. If the MMPI profile configuration is different than that shown on the MMPI-2, I use the MMPI profile for my interpretation since most research for clinical scale elevations is based upon the original MMPI profile. When the MMPI profile and the MMPI-2 profile are the same, as they are for the sample MMPI-2 (see p. 408) being interpreted in this chapter, then I use the MMPI-2 T-scores for my interpretation.

Besides rescoring elevated MMPI-2 clinical scales if they are not clearly defined or are close to 65 T-score points, there are two additional modifications that I have made in my clinical scale interpretation procedure for the MMPI-2 that are not present in my interpretation of the original MMPI. One of these changes is that I am now using the Harris and Lingoes subscales and the MMPI-2 **0** scale subscales (Ben-Porath et al., 1989) to refine the interpretations that I make of elevated clinical scales. The second change that I have made is that I am very cautious in interpreting an MMPI-2 profile if all the clinical scale elevations except the **5** scale for men are in the moderate range, i. e., between 60 and 65 T-score points. When the MMPI-2 profile is moderately elevated, I usually rescore the MMPI-2 clinical scales onto the original MMPI profile form and then interpret the MMPI profile, but I am still hesitant to make definitive statements about this profile because some of the scales have lost some items.

After considering the clinical scale elevations, I then look at the MMPI-2 supplementary scales. I interpret only those supplementary scales that are 65 T-score points or above.

I only look at the low points for these scales (below 40 T-score points) when they occur for the MMPI-2 supplementary scales that were also available for the MMPI, namely the **Es, Do,** and **Re** scales, since I am not sure what low points mean for the other MMPI-2 supplementary scales. I use the supplementary scales that I have transferred to the MMPI-2, namely the **Lb, Dy, Pr, St,** and **Cn** scales, very cautiously. This is because the T-scores that I have developed for these scales are based upon a small sample of college students and, therefore, may not be applicable to the general population.

After I have gathered information from the clinical and supplementary scales in the manner described above, I then go about the process of interpreting the MMPI-2 in a similar manner to my interpreting the original MMPI. I first indicate the test-taking attitude of the person based upon the validity scale elevations, and then I talk about the behaviors and feelings of the person that are indicated by the various clinical scale elevations. I follow this by discussing refinements to the clinical scale interpretations that need to be considered based upon information derived from clinical subscales and/ or supplementary scales.

After this has been done, I try to indicate any strengths that I may see in the profile and close with some predictions concerning prognosis and implications for therapy. With this procedure in mind, let's look at Figure 6.2, the MMPI-2 profile of Mrs. X.

Mrs. X is a 35-year-old woman who is coming into counseling because of marital problems. Besides the marital issues that the client has presented, the counselor reports the client as having a long-term pattern of being the "victim" in her relationships. The counselor wants testing done with Mrs. X so that the counselor can get a better idea as to how Mrs. X is dealing with her current marital problems and what the dynamics are that lead to Mrs. X being a victim in many of her interpersonal relationships. Mrs. X has had one year of college and is currently working in a low level clerical job at a local business. She and her husband are living together, but Mrs. X reports that her husband is very distant. He denies that he is acting any differently towards her. The husband is not interested in any type of counseling.

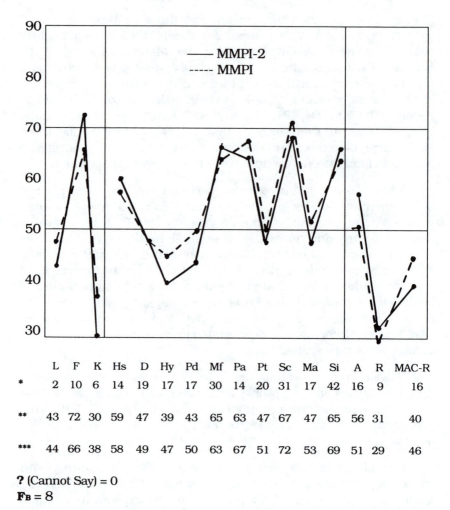

|   | L | F | K | Hs | D | Hy | Pd | Mf | Pa | Pt | Sc | Ma | Si | A | R | MAC-R |
|---|---|---|---|---|---|----|----|----|----|----|----|----|----|---|---|-------|
| * | 2 | 10 | 6 | 14 | 19 | 17 | 17 | 30 | 14 | 20 | 31 | 17 | 42 | 16 | 9 | 16 |
| ** | 43 | 72 | 30 | 59 | 47 | 39 | 43 | 65 | 63 | 47 | 67 | 47 | 65 | 56 | 31 | 40 |
| *** | 44 | 66 | 38 | 58 | 49 | 47 | 50 | 63 | 67 | 51 | 72 | 53 | 69 | 51 | 29 | 46 |

**?** (Cannot Say) = 0
**F**B = 8

\*   Raw score
\*\*   MMPI-2 T-score
\*\*\*   MMPI T-score

---

**Figure 6.2.**   MMPI-2 profile of Mrs. X.

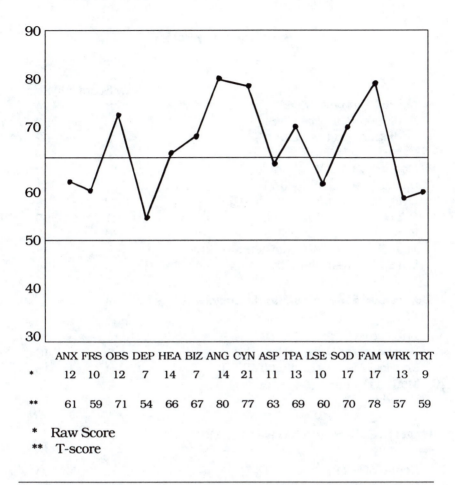

|   | ANX | FRS | OBS | DEP | HEA | BIZ | ANG | CYN | ASP | TPA | LSE | SOD | FAM | WRK | TRT |
|---|-----|-----|-----|-----|-----|-----|-----|-----|-----|-----|-----|-----|-----|-----|-----|
| * | 12 | 10 | 12 | 7 | 14 | 7 | 14 | 21 | 11 | 13 | 10 | 17 | 17 | 13 | 9 |
| ** | 61 | 59 | 71 | 54 | 66 | 67 | 80 | 77 | 63 | 69 | 60 | 70 | 78 | 57 | 59 |

\* Raw Score
\*\* T-score

---

**Figure 6.3.** MMPI-2 content scales for Mrs. X.

## Supplementary Scales

| | Raw Score | T-Score |
|---|---|---|
| Marital Distress (**MDS**) | 8 | 74 |
| Addiction Potential (**APS**) | 23 | 50 |
| Addiction Admission (**AAS**) | 5 | 67 |
| Ego Strength (**Es**) | 24 | 30 |
| Dominance (**Do**) | 14 | 42 |
| Social Responsibility (**Re**) | 18 | 41 |
| Overcontrolled Hostility (**O-H**) | 13 | 48 |
| PTSD - Keane (**PK**) | 21 | 69 |
| PTSD - Schlenger (**PS**) | 26 | 66 |
| True Response Inconsistency (**TRIN**) | 8 | 58F |
| Variable Response Inconsistency (**VRIN**) | 6 | 54 |

### Depression Subscales (Harris-Lingoes):

| | | |
|---|---|---|
| Subjective Depression (**D1**) | 11 | 58 |
| Psychomotor Retardation (**D2**) | 5 | 46 |
| Physical Malfunctioning (**D3**) | 3 | 48 |
| Mental Dullness (**D4**) | 4 | 57 |
| Brooding (**D5**) | 2 | 47 |

### Hysteria Subscales (Harris-Lingoes):

| | | |
|---|---|---|
| Denial of Social Anxiety (**Hy1**) | 0 | 30 |
| Need for Affection (**Hy2**) | 1 | 30 |
| Lassitude-Malaise (**Hy3**) | 6 | 63 |
| Somatic Complaints (**Hy4**) | 6 | 61 |
| Inhibition of Aggression (**Hy5**) | 2 | 39 |

### Psychopathic Deviate Subscales (Harris Lingoes):

| | | |
|---|---|---|
| Familial Discord (**Pd1**) | 5 | 68 |
| Authority Problems (**Pd2**) | 2 | 47 |
| Social Imperturbability (**Pd3**) | 0 | 31 |
| Social Alienation (**Pd4**) | 6 | 60 |
| Self-alienation (**Pd5**) | 5 | 58 |

### Paranoia Subscales (Harris-Lingoes):

| | | |
|---|---|---|
| Persecutory Ideas (**Pa1**) | 5 | 69 |
| Poignancy (**Pa2**) | 5 | 65 |
| Naivete (**Pa3**) | 3 | 41 |

### Schizophrenia Subscales (Harris-Lingoes):

| | | |
|---|---|---|
| Social Alienation (**Sc1**) | 8 | 69 |
| Emotional Alienation (**Sc2**) | 2 | 58 |
| Lack of Ego Mastery, Cognitive (**Sc3**) | 1 | 49 |
| Lack of Ego Mastery, Conative (**Sc4**) | 2 | 49 |
| Lack of Ego Mastery, Def. Inhib. (**Sc5**) | 5 | 72 |
| Bizarre Sensory Experiences (**Sc6**) | 9 | 81 |

### Hypomania Subscales (Harris-Lingoes):

| | | |
|---|---|---|
| Amorality (**Ma1**) | 0 | 37 |
| Psychomotor Acceleration (**Ma2**) | 7 | 60 |
| Imperturbability (**Ma3**) | 1 | 37 |
| Ego Inflation (**Ma4**) | 4 | 56 |

### Social Introversion Subscales (Ben-Porath, Hostetler, Butcher, & Graham):

| | | |
|---|---|---|
| Shyness / Self-consciousness (**Si1**) | 13 | 71 |
| Social Avoidance (**Si2**) | 6 | 65 |
| Alienation—Self and Others (**Si3**) | 11 | 66 |

## Additional Supplementary Scales

(These scales were scored from the MMPI-2 answer sheet using the item numbers listed for the scales in Table 5.3., p. 298. The T-scores were derived using Table 5.5., p. 300).

| | Raw Score | T-score |
|---|---|---|
| Low Back Pain | 11 | 60 |
| Dependency | 32 | 66 |
| Prejudice | 16 | 65 |
| Status | 12 | 33 |
| Control | 22 | 52 |

*Ch VI Sample MMPI Interpretations 411*

# MMPI-2 INTERPRETATION WORKSHEET

## Validity Scales

**F** = 72 — Feels as if life is not going along well. May have some unusual or bizarre feelings.

**K** = 30 — Is being brutally honest and reporting many personal faults. (**Es** = 30 also shows lack of self-esteem.)

**L** = 43 — Is willing to admit to common human faults.

## Clinical Scales

**8** = 67 — Is feeling depersonalized and estranged (**Sc6**). Also feels at the mercy of her emotions (**Sc5**) and alienated from others (**Sc1**).

**5** = 65 — Does not have typical feminine interests. May not want to see herself as a typical woman. May have some feelings alien to her gender (**Sc**) or some identity confusion.

**0** = 65 — Is shy, self-conscious, and alienated from herself and others (**Si1, Si2**). She avoids mingling with people (**Si3**).

**6** = 63 — Is sensitive to others' opinions of her. May feel that an intimate other cannot be trusted (**Pa1**).

## Supplementary Scales

**MDS** = 74 — Reports severe marital distress.

**PTSD-K** = 69
**PTSD-S** = 66
**A** = 65 — Feels overwhelmed with emotions and stress.

*MMPI & MMPI-2*

| | |
|---|---|
| **AAS** = 67 | Reports abusing alcohol or drugs although **MAC-R** and **APS** are not elevated. (Is this part of her overemphasizing personal faults?) |
| **Dy** = 66 | Needs relationships to support her. May stay in a bad relationship because of her neediness. |
| **Pr** = 65 | Feels more comfortable around others who are like her. Her personal sensitivity (**6** scale) is most likely limited to how one or two individuals think of her. |
| **Es** = 30 | Has unusually low ego-strength. Feels unable to cope. Believes she has inadequate skills to deal with her problems. |
| **Re** = 41 | Is unconventional, questioning society's rules and regulations. (Her **5** scale also shows unconventional gender identity.) |
| **Do** = 42 | Feels unable to run her own life. Would like to lean on someone. (**Dy** also shows this.) |

### Content Scales

| | |
|---|---|
| **ANG** = 80 | Has intense feelings of anger, which she recognizes. |
| **FAM** = 78 | Reports considerable familial discord. (Her marriage problems.) |
| **CYN** = 77 | Believes other people will lie and cheat. Does not trust other people (her husband?). |
| **OBS** = 71 | Has difficulty making decisions and reports worrying excessively. |
| **SOD** = 70 | Is uncomfortable around others, shy. |
| **TPA** = 69 | Is driven and easily angered when frustrated. |

| | |
|---|---|
| **BIZ** = 67 | Reports having strange thoughts and experiences. |
| **HEA** = 66 | Has some health concerns. |

### Refinements

| | |
|---|---|
| Clinical scales compared to content scales | Mrs. X has only one clinical scale elevated (**8**) but reports many problems on the content scales. This may be a manifestation of her tendency to overemphasize her personal inadequacies (low **K**) and her belief that she is not capable of handling her problems (low **Es**). |
| **5** scale compared to low **Re** | She sees herself as different than other women (**5**) and somewhat bizarre (**Sc**). She rejects society's standards (low **Re**) but still doesn't feel good about herself (low **Es**). |

### Summary

(Scale identifications are added for clarity.
In a report they would not be included.)

When Mrs. X took the MMPI-2, she felt badly about her situation (**F**) and was stressing how many personal inadequacies she had (low **K**, low **Es**). Her test shows that she is confused, feels alienated from others, and is experiencing some bizarre feelings and/or sensations (**8, 0**). She sees herself as an unconventional woman (**5**), and, while she rejects society's norms in general (low **Re**), she may still blame herself for the problems she is experiencing in her interpersonal relationships because of her unconventionality and because she has a tendency to blame herself for anything that goes wrong (low **Es**).

She reports problems with anger (**ANG**), suspiciousness (**CYN, 6**), and a lack of personal control (**ANG, TPA**). These problems with anger, suspiciousness, and lack of control are in marked contrast to her dependence on other people (**Dy**). Because of this dependence, it is highly unlikely that she will confront others with the anger and suspiciousness that she has. She is much more likely to take the blame for her problems onto herself and see them as due to her confusion, her bizarre perceptions of others, and her inadequate coping skills (low **Es**). She is experiencing a great deal of tension right now because she recognizes her anger and her tension but believes she has no way to deal with them overtly without jeopardizing her relationships with the very people she so desperately needs (high **Dy**).

This type of client tends to work well with a therapist who helps her deal with the tensions caused by the conflict between her anger and suspiciousness and her dependency. She needs help perceiving reality and sorting through what are her responsibilities and problems and what are other people's responsibilities and problems. She also needs help in recognizing the personal strengths that she has and using them to start dealing with her problems. This client seems to be a victim because (1) she does not believe she perceives things realistically, (2) she does not see herself as capable or worthwhile, and (3) she is very dependent upon other people.

With an increase in her ego-strength through therapy and with help in sorting out what is reality, she could become more confident and assertive in her relationships and therefore less likely to be a victim of them.

Making these personal changes will take a while because Mrs. X's ego-strength is so low. It will take some time to convince her that she has abilities that she can use to cope with her problems. She also will need help to see that some of her perceptions are not as bizarre as she seems to perceive them to be (just barely elevated **8** scale contrasted to **BIZ** content scale elevation). With time and support, Mrs. X should be able to make the changes necessary to make her long-term pattern of being a victim into one of coping with the problems in her marriage as an adequate, competent woman.

# MMPI INTERPRETATIONS

Wayne Anderson

It was with some trepidation that I approached using the MMPI-2. I had had 35 years of experience with the MMPI and had developed a clinical sense about the interaction between the clinical scales and the ways in which the supplementary scales modified the clinical scales' interpretation. In a sense, profiles talked to me and let me make predictions about present and future behavior that could be verified. At first I was fearful that my interpretive base and clinical insights would not transfer to the MMPI-2. It was several years before I felt I knew enough about the revised test to use it in place of the MMPI.

I was eventually reassured that the goal of the authors of the revision to have continuity of the MMPI-2 with the MMPI had been achieved with some important exceptions. For example, according to a study by Edwards, Morrison, and Weissman (1993), correlations between raw scores on the MMPI and MMPI-2 are well into the 90s. This means that dropping, adding, and rewriting items had no major impact on the way in which the items were answered. These authors also report T-scores correlations between the two tests in the 90s.

There were, however, some problems for me in making the change. I could not assume a direct correspondence between code or profile types between the two tests. Despite the high correlations between scales on the two tests, another change that took place in renorming made me cautious about using MMPI two-point code interpretations for the MMPI-2. On the original MMPI, individual clinical scales differ in the percentage of the population that falls above a T-score of 70. The MMPI-2 was developed with uniform T-scores so that the percentage of the population falling above a particular T-score is directly comparable. If the individual has a T-score of 75 on two scales, that individual is also at the same percentage of the population on both scales. While this makes the test easier to interpret at one level, it introduced a new problem. This new standardization in some cases changes the high-point code on the test, and in others it changes the relationship between scales in a codetype. Since codetypes are so important to most psychologists who use the MMPI, this could be a serious defect in terms of using previous MMPI research for interpreting the new MMPI-2.

There is disagreement about how cautious one needs to be in using MMPI interpretations with the MMPI-2, particularly as regards the two-point codetypes. The authors of the revision appear to feel the least need for caution in using these interpretations. Others are inclined to be more guarded.

Edwards, Morrison, and Weissman's (1993) study of 200 outpatients reaffirms that the MMPI-2 maintains the raw score equivalence with the MMPI, but they also found problems of comparability at the level of T-score comparisons. They concluded that with well defined profiles for women comparability is quite good, but for men there are likely to be problems because there are more discrepancies. For example, the authors found 9 and 10 T-score point differences between the two forms for men on scales **2, 4, 5,** and **8,** which suggests that MMPI-2 scores characterize some men as less significantly depressed, impulsive, or disturbed than the MMPI scores. Further evidence for caution in using MMPI interpretations for MMPI-2 profiles comes from Dahlstrom (1992). He prepared tables showing the frequencies and percentages of each two-point high-point pair earned by men and by women on the restandardization sample. From his tables Dahlstrom concluded that some code pairs change relatively little from MMPI to MMPI-2 and others are more drastically affected. (See Tables 4.1 and 4.2., pp. 86-87.)

Munley (1991) has had similar findings to Dahlstrom. He concluded that scales **1, 2, 3, 6,** and **7** will equal or exceed their original frequency as high-point scales and that scales **4, 8,** and **9** have been reduced in high-point codes for male and female psychiatric patients.

My conclusion from these various studies is that in spite of the changes in codetype frequencies, the test modifications, such as dropped and rewritten items, do not change the basic nature of the interpretations that can be given to individual clinical scales. As others (e.g., Chojnacki & Walsh 1992; Munley, 1991) have pointed out, this has important implications. If the source of changes in test profiles had been the result of dropped, added, or rewritten items, then the reliability and validity of the scales on the MMPI-2 would have been suspect. If, as appears to be the case, profile changes are due to changes in the T-score distributions on the MMPI-2 profile, then most of the material developed for the MMPI can be used in working with the MMPI-2.

Because the interpretation problems come from changes in relationships among MMPI-2 scales, the test interpreter needs to be aware of ways to restore relationships among scales so that the two- and three-point codes will be the same as they were on the MMPI. Based on studies I have been discussing, several approaches seem possible:

1.  If there are well defined codetypes with 5 points between the codetype and the next highest clinical scale or group of scales (about 30% of the profiles), you are fairly safe in using the codetype interpretations generated from the MMPI, particularly for female profiles.

2.  If you are in doubt about an MMPI-2 profile, you can do one of two things.

    a.  Use Appendix K of the MMPI-2 manual to convert MMPI-2 raw scores into MMPI T-scores.

    b.  Replot the MMPI-2 raw scores on the MMPI profile.

Interpreting an MMPI-2 profile often takes a considerable amount of time, because the clinician needs to think through the many possibilities for how a scale might be interpreted. With practice, however, an interpretation can be done quite quickly. As the standard characteristics associated with an MMPI-2 profile configuration become known, spotting inconsistencies and outstanding characteristics becomes second nature. Even with experience it pays the clinician to review the information given in this book occasionally, because even an experienced clinician needs to be reminded of interpretation possibilities that may have been forgotten.

## Interpretation

A general procedure I use for developing an MMPI-2 interpretation is as follows:

1. Check the validity scores to find out what the attitude of the client was toward taking the test; that is, was the client being open, being defensive, or admitting to thoughts and behavior of an unusual nature? A frequent profile in a client population is a high **F** (>70) and low **K** (<45). This would influence me to develop a different interpretation than if there were an **F** of 45 and a **K** of 70. In the first case, I would suspect that the client might be exaggerating symptoms and thus creating an undue elevation on the clinical scale scores. In the second case, the client might be striving to present a normal picture and would be much less likely to be open about personal defects.

   I also pay attention to elevated **L** scale scores and modify my interpretation if other profile characteristics exist. For example, a high **Re** (Social Responsibility) scale indicates to me that a high **L** reflects the client's overly high standards and is not a conscious falsification of his or her behavior. I would recommend the reader give special attention to the patterns of **L, F,** and **K,** which are discussed in our chapter on validity scales (Chapter III).

2. Next I establish the basic characteristics of the high clinical scales both by themselves and in combination with each other. For example, if a high **4** scale (>65) occurs with the next highest clinical scale 5 T-score points or more below, I use the interpretation for the **4** scale. If the profile has both the **4** and **9** scales elevated with the two being

within 5 T-score points, I use the **4-9** two-point code interpretation.

3. Having established the interpretation of the most elevated clinical scales, I am now in a position to consider what modifications are suggested by other scales. First, I check those clinical scales that also are elevated but at a somewhat lower level than the very highest ones. If the **4** scale is at 80 T-score points and the **8** scale is at 70, for example, the **8** scale adds a bad judgment element to the interpretation. The person with this kind of profile may engage in bizarre actions, interpret incorrectly what another person is expecting or asking of him/her (**8**), as well as act out in some way (**4**). The **8** scale in this case indicates the likelihood of more negative behavior than just the **4** scale by itself.

On the other hand, some scales may be positive modifiers of highly elevated scales; that is, elevations on them would allow the test administrator to interpret the higher scales more positively than usual. An example would be a man's profile where the **5** scale is elevated (above 60) with the **4** scale (above 65). The **5** scale acts as a suppressor of the acting out usually associated with a high **4**. Sometimes the positive interpretation is relative; for example, a **7-8** profile with an **A** scale above 60 T-score points indicates a disturbed person. This person usually is very uncomfortable, and characteristics of maladjustment typically are present. However, this is a more positive pattern than if the **7** and **8** are high and the **A** scale is low (below 50 T-score points), because this combination would suggest the possibility of a more chronic adjustment problem and one that is less likely to change as a result of therapy.

Beginning users of the MMPI sometimes make the mistake of interpreting each scale individually without regard for the rest of the profile. The clinician needs to keep in mind that clinical scale elevations modify and change each other's interpretation. That is, an elevated scale will not indicate the same characteristics when other scales or combinations of scales are also elevated. We have attempted to show how scales modify each other in the previous chapters of this book.

4.  The next point in doing an MMPI-2 assessment is to consider the low scales (those below 45 T-score points) on the profile and to look at the high scale and low scale interpretations together for additional insights. An example would be that an individual with a low **4** and an elevated **0** scale would likely be someone who is not only shy and withdrawn (**0** scale) but also someone who is probably sexually inexperienced (**4** scale). A female profile with a low **5** and a high **4** would suggest that this is an individual who uses sex as a way of manipulating and controlling men. A low **2** with a high **9** on a profile would suggest an unusually buoyant, outgoing individual who may not be appropriately responsive to the problems of other people.

5.  I have always found that supplemental scales add important information beyond that given by the clinical scales. On the MMPI, I was particularly fond of **A, R,** and **Es** and, despite the limited research on some of the other supplementary scales, felt they were very useful in painting a more complete picture of the client or patient. The MMPI-2 gives many new supplemental scales, and I am still exploring their usefulness.

6.  Having completed the first five stages of interpretation, the more creative aspect of interpreting the MMPI can be done; that is, interpreting the inconsistencies. Much of what I have discussed up to this point can be done in a more or less routine manner. This step requires experience with the test and some knowledge of the relationships between scales. One asks, what are the inconsistencies in this test, which scales do not relate to one another in a logical or usual manner? The clinician must think through possible reasons as to why these unusual relations exist. For example, what can be made out of a profile in which **2** and **9** are both above 70? What can one make of a high **Es** and a low **K**?

Occasionally one will have an MMPI-2 profile about which a consistent report can be written, but when talking to the client the report does not match with either the client's overt behavior or with what the client evidently believes about himself or herself. I have found no good explanation for this situation. It is rather rare but it does occur, and the clinician should come to expect it occasionally. Some deeper level at which the interpretation is true may exist, but a client should not be forced to fit a particular interpretation if the assessor and the client do not view it as applicable.

As examples of how I interpret the MMPI, three sample interpretations will be given.

## PROFILE #1 (MMPI-2)

This client is an 18-year-old male college student who was referred for treatment evaluation after being arrested for making harassing phone calls to a young woman he had known for years. When arrested he said, "I don't understand why I did."

The elevated **F** with low **K** suggests the client is anxious and wants to be helped or at least wants to convey the image of someone who needs help. While the **F** score is over the critical 65 T-score, I would still treat the profile as reflective of his personality; but in my mind I would lower the clinical scores somewhat.

Elevation on the **6** scale is unusual in a college population and may be partly a reaction to having been arrested. The two-point code **6-8** is a particularly pathological one, especially when the **4** is as high as it is. (On the MMPI-1 this pattern would be an **8-6-4**, but the interpretation would remain the same.)

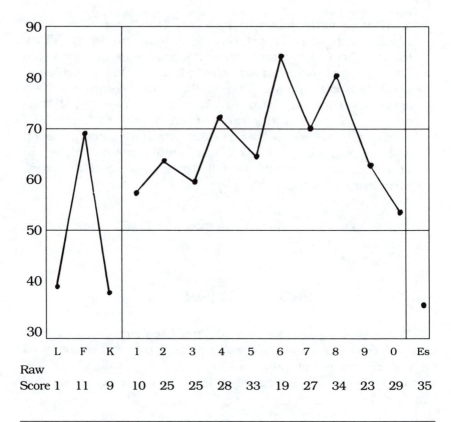

**Figure 6.4.** MMPI-2 profile of basic scales and supplementary scale for Profile #1.

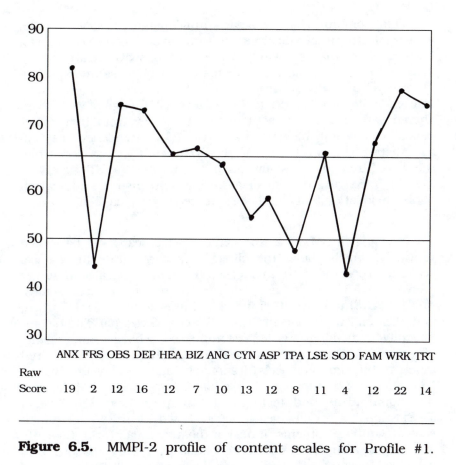

**Figure 6.5.** MMPI-2 profile of content scales for Profile #1.

This configuration of scales indicates an angry, hostile, antisocial individual who is overly sensitive to perceived insults. It is unlikely that he will have any deep social relationships. This will be partly the result of his suspiciousness and distrust of others, but also reflects the fact that he is likely to be unfriendly to others and to have unusual thoughts that when shared with others cause them to back away from him. Other people who know him are likely to report that they see him as creepy. The pathology of this pattern is increased when the Ego Strength is as low as it is in this case (T-score 35). The high **8** with the low ego-strength is also an indication of bizarre ideation that could be expressed in unusual behavior.

In using the MMPI-2, the content scales can now be scored routinely, which allows the clinician to corroborate the clinical scale interpretation. In this case, the content scales that are above the 65 T-score are supportive of the clinical scales. Anxiety **(ANX)** indicates this individual feels nervous and worried, and has difficulty concentrating. Obsessiveness **(OBS)** indicates difficulty in making decisions, compulsive behavior, and rigidity of thinking. Depression **(DEP)** shows this student is tired much of the time and feels despondent and pessimistic. Bizarre Mentation **(BIZ)** supports the clinical hypothesis that he has delusional ideas and feelings of unreality. Low Self-Esteem **(LSE)** supports the low self-concept shown by the Ego Strength scale. Family Problems **(FAM)** indicates anger and hostility toward the family, probably because of family discord and perceived lack of affection. Work Interference **(WRK)** indicates that this client's attitude and behavior interfere with his work performance. And finally, Negative Treatment Indicators **(TRT)** indicate he has a negative attitude toward doctors and mental health treatment.

A summary of the above elevations would lead us to say that this individual is a poor problem solver who feels misunderstood by others and does not believe that he is capable of making any significant changes in his life. He is not likely to understand why he did what he did or appreciate the impact of his behavior upon the target victim.

Although I would not have high therapeutic aspirations for this client, there are some things a therapist might do that would be of help. (1) The therapist could use techniques to build the client's ego strength and self-esteem. (2) If he can be helped to feel better about himself, it will build a groundwork for interpersonal skills training so that the client can recognize what his impact is upon others. (3) Because this client is in trouble with the law, he needs help in cognitively recognizing and controlling his inappropriate behavior.

The therapist should recognize that there is the potential for aggressive acting out and listen carefully for any indications that action is planned against the client's victim.

## PROFILE #2 (MMPI-2)

This client is a 24-year-old male who works at a local nonprofit organization. He sought therapy because of anxiety attacks, crying spells, and a belief that he has mouth cancer. His dentist has not been able to reassure him that no disease exists.

The validity scores indicate that his test-taking attitude was good and that the profile should be a reflection of his present functioning and concerns.

The clinical scales are unusual in that a single elevation on **7** is rare. When **7** is elevated, we usually have greater elevations on **2** or **8** than we see here. With an elevation this high, we would expect this client to be a worried, tense, indecisive individual who has difficulty concentrating.

Knowing that he has been on his job for only six weeks and that he is planning to be married in the near future helps us make some sense of this elevation. Persons with an elevated **7** tend to have difficulty adjusting to change and characteristically overreact with anxiety to new situations.

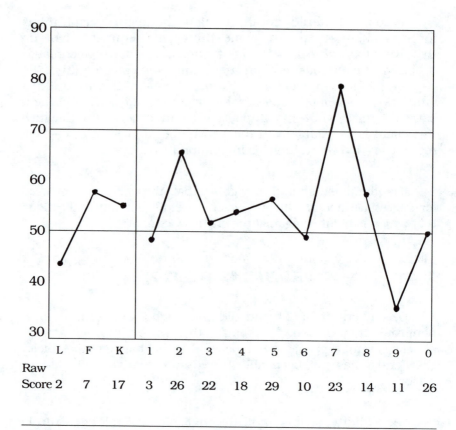

**Figure 6.6.** MMPI-2 profile of basic scales for Profile #2.

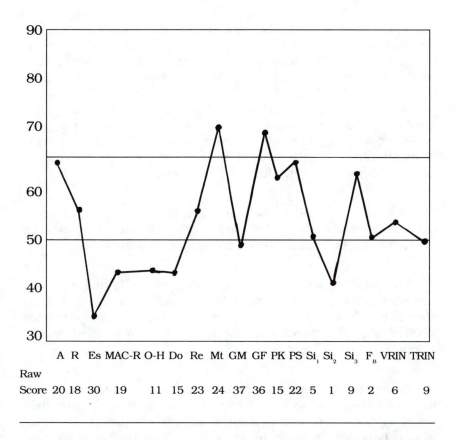

**Figure 6.7.** MMPI-2 profile of supplementary scales for Profile #2.

The moderate elevation of **2** would support the above observations that this is an anxious individual who overreacts to stress and who probably anticipates problems before they occur. A client with a **2-7** profile is usually seen as a good candidate for psychotherapy but because the **7** scale is considerably higher than **2** in this case, there is a poorer prognosis for major change in psychotherapy. People with single point high **7**s become more comfortable and feel relief from therapy, but they tend to keep the same personality pattern; that is, they continue to be obsessive.

The low **9** is also unusual and indicates an individual who has a low energy and activity level. This low score suggests the client may be apathetic and have feelings of emptiness.

The supplementary scales add additional information about this client. The low **Es** score and elevations on **2** and **7** suggest an individual who feels he must rely on others to make decisions for him since he is not likely to trust his own problem-solving ability.

While the **R** is high enough to indicate an individual who will hold back on certain topics, the **A** score is higher than the **R** by 5 T-score points, and this suggests that this individual is uncomfortable enough to work on his problems in therapy. This discomfort, however, is not likely to be high enough to override the other indications given above that he is unlikely to make major changes in his personality as a result of psychotherapy.

## PROFILE #3 (MMPI)

The individual shown in Profile #3 is a 21-year-old female college student. The validity scores indicate the classic "cry for help" pattern. The high **F** and low **K** scales suggest that this women is exaggerating her symptoms, probably to insure that the therapist will see her problems as serious enough to demand attention.

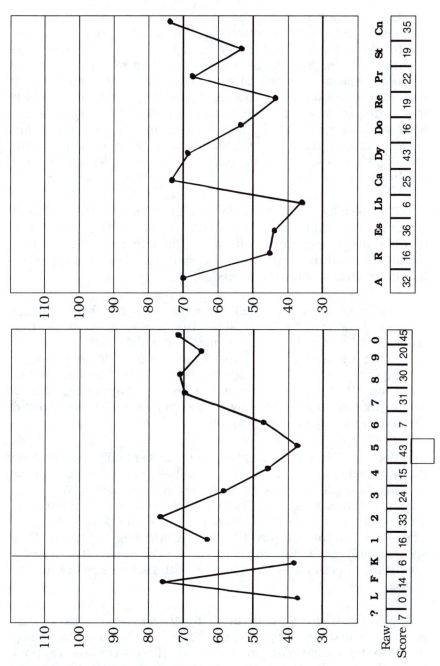

**Figure 6.8.** MMPI profile for Profile #3.

On the clinical scales the elevated **2** scale indicates gloom, sadness, and dissatisfaction with life, but because of the height of the **7** and **8** scales, we need to consider a modification of the **2** scale. The three scores together suggest a tense, anxious, depressed individual who may exhibit confused thinking and much self-doubt. A not unusual score concurrent with this pattern is a low **5** scale, which in college women intensifies what we have just said about tenseness, anxiety, and depression and brings in the strong possibility of lack of skills with the opposite sex. Study problems also are indicated for this combination of scales.

The elevated **0** scale adds emphasis to the shyness and introversion symptoms and again supports the possibility of difficulty in relations with the opposite sex. The general maladjustment indicated by the pattern also is supported by the elevations on the **A** (Anxiety).

The high **Pr** (Prejudice) scale is unusual for a college student; however, as the rest of the profile is elevated, this scale may be a reflection of some of the difficulties the client is having in adjusting at this time. This scale may reflect a temporary negative attitude toward others because of her situation; that is, because of her own unhappiness, she is feeling that no one is any good, and her prejudice is extended to almost all groups and individuals.

The low **Es** (Ego-strength) score is certainly not a good therapy indicator, but the **F-K** combination suggests she is hurting enough to want to work on her problems. We know she is voluntarily seeking help and is young and intelligent, all factors which improve her chances of doing well in therapy. The elevation of the **Cn** (Control) scale also suggests that she probably is holding together at least in public. The therapy potential, therefore, is much better than the low **Es** would suggest.

A factor that will help in doing therapy with this woman is the elevated **Dy** (Dependency) scale, which shows a strong need to be dependent on someone. If appropriate rapport is established by the therapist, this woman should stay as a client. The therapist will need to keep in the mind that this client will have some tendency toward passivity and wanting the therapist to set the direction and pace of therapy. While using the dependency therapeutically, the therapist should encourage the client to take responsibility for herself and her behavior.

In summary, this test indicates a client who is depressed, tense, and having trouble relating to others. She probably is concerned about relationships with men and has a generally negative attitude toward people. Both negative and positive signs are present for her as a therapy risk, although I would suggest that signs for positive prognosis are stronger at this time.

## INTERPRETING THE MMPI TO THE CLIENT

A number of reasons exist for doing an MMPI interpretation.

1.  a mental health agency may need a diagnostic statement for treatment planning,

2.  the court may need an evaluation to aid in decision making,

3.  a rehabilitation agency may need to know a client's potential for a training program,

4.  a company may be screening personnel for a sensitive position,

5.  a therapist may need some guidance as to appropriate therapy intervention, or

6.  a client may wish to know more about himself or herself.

What is brought into focus by the test interpreter will be different in each of these situations, and even the language in which the results are reported is likely to vary.

Most of what has been written about interpreting the MMPI is for its use in the preparation of diagnostic reports in clinical settings (reasons 1 and 2 above). Most of the rest of the written material concerns interpretations of the MMPI for screening purposes (reasons 3 and 4 above). The prediction of success in some jobs and/or training programs can be improved by using critical scales or specific profile patterns.

However, interpretations of the MMPI also may be used either as hypotheses for the therapist to test out in therapy (reason 5) or in a discussion of the test results with the client (reason 6). I want to comment upon this last reason for doing an MMPI/MMPI-2 assessment in this last section, because relatively little has been written about it. In a previous edition of this book, we made some comments about the therapeutic value of doing test interpretations with clients, and recently there has been some research to indicate the value of such a procedure (Finn, & Tonsager, 1992). We want to continue to encourage therapists to give test results to clients using some of the appropriate cautions mentioned here. We also would refer you to an excellent book by Lewak (Lewak, Marks, & Nelson, 1990), which is most useful in this endeavor.

In interpreting the MMPI to clients, keep certain points in mind:

1.  As a therapist interpreting the MMPI/MMPI-2, you are trying to create some viable and useful hypotheses about the client and the client's behavior. You are looking for ideas about problem areas and behaviors that may be causing the client difficulties with others, and you are looking for ideas about dynamics that interfere with effective living, such as life patterns that may be restrictive of growth. One of the goals of a therapist is to increase the client's awareness of self and of his/her behavior so that control over the behavior may be increased.

2.  Because you will be talking directly to the client, there is an opportunity to verify the accuracy of your hypotheses about the client. If you are wrong about

*MMPI & MMPI-2*

a particular hypothesis, you should be able to determine the error in discussion with the client. Most of the time, interpretations should be given to the client as tentative possibilities and not as finalities. Rejection by the client of an interpretation may not invalidate an hypothesis, or on the other hand, ready acceptance on the part of the client of an interpretation does not always indicate that the hypothesis is valid. For an individual with a high **1-3** scale combination to reject the hypothesis that he/she may have psychological factors in his/her physical problems is to be expected given the dynamics of the high **1-3** combination. In this case the client's rejection does not invalidate the hypothesis.

3. Frequently, as a test interpreter, you can arrive at some generalities about the client and client's behavior, but the client must be given an opportunity to provide the specifics. For example, a client with an elevated **2** scale will have the interpretation made that he/she is depressed. The client should then be able to be more specific about why he/she feels depressed and in what areas of life this is being felt.

4. When several likely interpretations for an elevated score exist, explain to the client that more than one possibility exists and allow the client to sort out which interpretation is the most accurate. For example, an elevated **2-7** combination indicating depression and anxiety may be the result of current difficulties such as vocational or marital dissatisfactions. On the other hand, it may be the result of a long-standing chronic condition. The client should be able to indicate which of these two interpretations is more accurate or even whether parts of both interpretations are applicable.

5. Of necessity, you must be aware of the norms for the particular client population with whom you are working. This is particularly true for the supplementary scales with college students, where the average scores may not be those given on the profile. An "average"

score of 50 T-score points on scale **A** in a college population, for example, is actually elevated for that population because a score of 40 is the average for this particular group (Anderson & Duckworth, 1969). It remains to be established what the average score will be in different contexts for the content scales.

The need to know special group norms is especially important in interpreting profiles for individuals from different cultural or ethnic backgrounds. The interpretations of profiles of Northern Europeans tend to be similar to profiles found in the United States. However, profiles for people from other countries may look elevated when in fact the individual's adjustment is quite normal for his cultural group (Butcher & Pancheri, 1976).

6.  When working with a new population, you should remember that the interpretation of profiles may vary depending upon the group with whom you are working. A profile that looks like that of a relatively acute schizophrenic in a mental hospital population may indicate an identity crisis in a college student population. The difference in potential for successful treatment is great; therefore, the possibilities of what a particular profile means for a population need to be checked with much care.

7.  Some counselors interpreting an MMPI to a client worry that the client will see the height of some of the scores on the profile and become upset. Keep in mind that the client does not know what scale height means. If you treat an interpretation calmly, the client will most likely react the same way.

What is important is for a client to have a meaningful interpretation at a level that is appropriate for the client's present needs. Part of the problem of giving an adequate interpretation revolves around the language the counselor may use in discussing the profile. The interpreter should stay away from using such terms as "schizophrenic," "emotionally disturbed," "passive-aggressive," and as much as possible go back to behavioral references. Such phrases as "You often feel cut off from other people," "People really don't seem to understand you or your intentions," "You find yourself brooding a lot," or "There are times when things feel unreal to you," are statements that will be less threatening and more meaningful to clients. Most clients accept these interpretations quite readily because they describe behavior that the client has reported and is very close to what the client already feels. These statements then form the basis of discussion of the problems and reassure the client that the test interpreter is an individual who really understands him or her in a way that others do not.

8. Finally, you should not interpret too much material in one session. The client should be given ample time to deal with, elaborate upon, or give examples of the behavior that you are presenting. The approach to the client should not be one of an expert laying out or dissecting the client's personality, but rather of two people trying to understand what makes one of the two behave or feel the way he or she does.

We hope that this chapter showing two different methods of interpretation using both MMPI and MMPI-2 profiles and four types of scales (validity, clinical, supplementary, and content) will be helpful in demonstrating the possibilities available in developing a test interpretation that fits the personal style of the clinician.

# ETHNIC AND CROSS-CULTURAL DIFFERENCES ON THE MMPI-2

Wayne Anderson

Because race is so difficult to define and is so loaded with emotional connotations, I find it more profitable to speak in terms of cross-cultural and ethnic differences as I examine the studies done using the MMPI and MMPI-2 with major minority groups in the U.S. I believe that subcultures, especially those that have characteristics that set them apart from the majority U.S. white culture, have different experiences and different expectations for what is seen as normal. If the subculture is isolated enough, its members probably will answer some MMPI questions in clinical directions without having the pathology those answers imply in the standardization sample. In trying to understand some of the conflicting research findings on ethnic groups, I will be concerned with the concept of **acculturation**, defined as, "the process, witting or unwitting, whereby individuals assume the behavior patterns of an in-group sufficiently to be accepted into the group, or to get along in it without friction" (English & English, 1959).

In this first section I examine the research on MMPI differences between Anglo-Americans and Afro-Americans, Hispanics, and Native Americans. Some suggestions will be given at the end of this section for interpreting MMPI profiles from these minority groups. In the second section of this chapter is a brief overview of some national differences on the MMPI.

The original MMPI norms were developed on a mostly U.S. midwestern sample in the 1930s. A need for new norms arose not only because this original group was not representative of the country's population, but for several other reasons. First, individuals had changed the way they make self-reports; that is, the average individual now taking the MMPI admits to engaging in more behavior that once was considered aberrant. Second, as American culture has changed over time, attitudes toward sex, women, race, war, and morality also have changed. Many would put 1968 as the critical year for the revolution in American values, because it was the focal point of many of these changes: nonsupportive attitudes towards a war, the increase in the acceptability of drug use, Black protests, the strengthening of the women's movement, and a change in sexual standards. These differences between the 1930s and now were the bases for doing a revision of the MMPI normative group.

The MMPI-2 provides us with an up-to-date standardization sample that includes minority members. Including minorities in the norm group, however, does not mean that the norms automatically apply to minority groups. The change in the norms resulting from the inclusion of minorities is slight because they make up such a small percentage of the new standardization sample; therefore, the test norms still do not reflect many minorities' particular situational differences or cultural heritage.

Ethnic group differences in response to MMPI and MMPI-2 items depend upon a number of variables. A prime variable is the fact that ethnic group membership in America is highly correlated with social class. The research cited in the following pages will show that social classes have differences in their attitude toward a number of variables including locus of control and planning for the future. In addition, members of the lower class are more likely to be exposed to factors that can influence personality development in a negative way, such as physical abuse, poor diet, and/or mentally ill or alcoholic parents (Srole, Langner, Michael, Opler, & Rennie, 1962). These factors are likely to be reflected in the individual's responses to the MMPI items. In addition to this, language factors in some circumstances can make for a significant difference in response patterns.

Controversy exists about a number of issues that need to be explored by all clinicians who are in a position to interpret tests that have been administered to members of minority groups. Questions being debated by authors in the field, and which continue to be debated despite the development of a more representative sample for the MMPI-2, include the following:

1.  Are there significant differences between Anglo-Americans and members of other groups such as Afro-Americans, Hispanics, and Native Americans on the MMPI and MMPI-2?

2.  If differences do exist, are they due to test bias and socioeconomic class factors or do they measure some real differences in behavior between minorities and Anglo-Americans?

3.  If differences exist, are new norms needed for these various cultural groups?

4.  Without separate norms, how should a clinician approach interpreting MMPIs from minority clients?

In the following section, I will be using "Black" instead of "Afro-American."


## OVERVIEW

The first question that clinicians must consider, "Are there significant ethnic differences on the MMPI and MMPI-2?" is not an easy one to answer since the research findings seem to be contradictory. Pritchard and Rosenblatt (1980) have shown in their research that there are no significant differences in mean scale scores between the MMPI profiles of Blacks and whites taken from the same clinical population. In their analysis of all the studies on Black-white differences, which these authors found acceptable, no MMPI scales were found for which significant racial differences occurred more frequently than nonsignificant differences.

Pritchard and Rosenblatt (1980) concluded that little, if any, evidence exists that Blacks score substantially higher or lower than whites on the MMPI scales. They also believed that if a researcher finds differences between elevations of Blacks and whites in a particular population, this may reflect actual differences in pathology. Dahlstrom, Lachar, and Dahlstrom (1986) also hypothesized that large scale research would support the view that the MMPI is not racially biased and that one does not need to be concerned about ethnic differences since those differences that are found are due to pathology or other variables.

Leona Dahlstrom (1986) suggested one of these variables when she wrote that to understand ethnic differences we need to isolate behavior and attitudes related to the mental health difficulties experienced by minorities. She believed there is the possibility that differences in performance of minority groups on the MMPI may reflect genuine differences minorities face in their daily lives.

An intermediate stance is taken by Greene (1987) in his review of the literature on ethnic differences on the MMPI. He found that ethnic differences do exist on the MMPI but that when variables such as education, age, and social class were controlled, then these ethnic differences were unlikely to be found. He concluded from his review that clinicians and researchers need to be aware of the multitude of factors that can affect MMPI performance besides race. Greene's conclusions are very similar to those of Dahlstrom and Welsh (1960) who concluded that the findings ". . .are the sort that would be expected from known effects of socioeconomic inequities" (p. 273).

On the opposite side of the question of race differences on the MMPI is Gynther (Gynther, 1972, 1989; Gynther & Green, 1980) who has stated that not only do racial differences exist but that these differences need to be taken into consideration in making judgments about people. He also felt that the conclusions a researcher draws about the presence and nature of ethnic group differences is probably influenced by where the researcher stands on a liberal-conservative or democratic-authoritarian dimension.

I tend to agree with Greene (1987) and take an intermediate approach to this question. I believe that caution is needed when working with minority groups and that getting closure too soon and saying there are no differences for minority groups on the MMPI may be doing more injustice to members of minority groups than to approach their responses "as if" there were some cultural differences that influenced their responses to the MMPI. As will be shown, the level of integration some subgroups, particularly Afro-Americans and Hispanics, have into the mainstream culture is still an open question. The clinician can not assume from the present research that the world view, and the resultant interpretations placed on the meaning of MMPI items, is the same among all ethnic groups taking the test. My experience and reading of the research in this area indicates that, for some groups, differences exist in how items are interpreted because of cultural norms. As a result, the question the test user must ask is, "How acculturated into the white culture is this particular individual or group who is being tested?" When the individual is acculturated, use the usual interpretation for the MMPI. When the individual is not acculturated, do not use the typical interpretation for the test. Under some circumstances, good adjustment or at least survival for some minority group members may lie in adopting a worldview that is at variance with that of the larger community. The clinician needs to have some criteria that he/she can use to guess who those individuals are.

The first step will be to examine the research on two ethnic groups for which there are a significant number of studies, namely Afro-Americans and Hispanics. For each of these reviews, an examination will be made of the research that has been done on normal populations within that ethnic group. Next, the research that has been done on more deviant individuals including substance abusers will be examined. Then each review will be finished with some suggestions about how to interpret the MMPI for that particular group.

## AFRO-AMERICANS

### Normals

In Costello's (1977) attempt to create a test of Black identity, he used 32 MMPI items that differentiated Black from white outpatients and cross validated the scale on a group of police officers. The 32 items that he found appear to be representative of the same areas as Jones (1978) found to be relevant a year later. For example, Costello found that Blacks were more likely to say, "I am entirely self-confident" and "I am a very important person." They also answered items in a direction that indicated a cynical attitude toward other people's motivations.

In a study using a pool of 361 items from the MMPI and California Psychological Inventory (CPI) with 226 Black and white college students, Jones (1978) found significant differences at the .001 level on 84 of the items and significant differences at the .01 level on another 91 items. After doing a cluster analysis Jones stated that, "In decreasing order of importance of race differences, Blacks reported themselves as more dominant and poised socially. They also were more fundamentalist in their religious beliefs, concerned with impulse management, self-critical, psychologically tough, cynical and power oriented, conventional in moral attitudes, and conformist than whites" (page 248).

These different rates of answering items may reflect some different underlying factors, and this is indicated in a factor analysis that was done of MMPI items using a sample of 20,860 subjects: 18,148 white and 2,712 Black. Using a seven-factor solution, Beck, McRae, Henrichs, Sneider, Horwitz, Rennier, Thomas, and Hedlund (1989) found five factors that showed up for both Blacks and whites but not necessarily with the same weights. These factors were Neurotic Symptoms, Somatization, Psychopathy, Feminine Interests, and Suspicious Cynicism. The other two factors were different for the two races: Whites had an Optimism and a Family Rapport factor while Blacks had a Paranoia and an unnamed factor.

The paranoia factor found in the Beck et al. study (1989) could be the result of the social conditions under which some Afro-Americans have to function. Grier and Cobbs (1968) in *Black Rage* indicate that the personality of Blacks is affected when they come from areas where there is a major degree of prejudice. "For his own survival, then, he must develop a cultural paranoia in which every white man is a potential enemy unless proved otherwise, and every social system is set against him unless he personally finds out differently" (p. 149).

Two groups of Afro-Americans are most likely to respond differently to MMPI items that reflect pathology, yet be within normal limits of adjustment in their subgroup: (1) those who have been isolated from the main stream of American culture, and (2) those who are still in a process of being assimilated into the main culture.

An example of an isolated group is reported in a study by Gynther, Fowler, and Erdberg (1971). They tested a group of 88 Afro-Americans from a rural community in Alabama and found **8-6** and **8-9** codes most frequent for males and **6-8, 8-6,** and **8-9** codes for women. An example of a different worldview is that 58% of the subjects answered true to "Evil spirits possess me at times." Without knowing the nature of these individuals' backgrounds, 84 of the 88 would have been diagnosed as psychotic based on their MMPI profiles.

Doob (1960) has hypothesized that a group in transition from one culture to another is under unusual strains and therefore should be more discontent, aggressive, and interpersonally sensitive than groups that are not in transition. MMPIs from people who are experiencing prejudice or who are in transition could be elevated reflecting the strains being experienced. Therefore, caution should be used in attributing psychopathology to individuals who are going through these transition periods.

In their review of 11 studies that had been done on normals, Gynther and Green (1980) found that Blacks and whites scored similarly on all scales except **F, 8,** and **9.** On these three scales, Blacks scored significantly higher than whites by 5 to 10 T-score points. Dana and Whatley (1991) have found in their review of the literature that even with socioeconomic status controlled, item and scale differences continue to exist between Blacks and whites on the MMPI, especially on scales **F, 8,** and **9.** Because these are scales that are frequently used to make assertions about serious pathology, Blacks will frequently be misclassified as pathological.

So far I have been speaking of differences in T-scores that show up on scales of the MMPI. The reader needs to recognize the possibility that even when T-scores on an MMPI scale are similar for different cultural groups, the way the items are answered to achieve that score may be different suggesting that the behavioral correlates of the scale score may not be the same. That is, a T-score of 70 on the Overcontrolled Hostility scale may not mean the same thing for an Afro-American as it would for a white American.

Greene's (1987) review of Black-white differences on the MMPI found few studies that gave behavioral correlates for the clinical scales, but on the few that did, at least three of the seven studies found Black-white differences. While Pritchard and Rosenblatt (1980) have previously criticized these studies, Greene still recommended looking for clinical correlates for the Black-white differences found in the MMPI.

I agree with Gynther's position (1989) that when using the test for screening or with "normal" populations it might be better to err on the side of under-interpretation of elevated scores for Blacks, particularly moderate elevations (T-scores 65-75) on scales **F, 8,** and **9.** Also, I suggest that the Overcontrolled Hostility scale probably should not be used with Blacks as an indicator of psychopathology (Hutton et al., 1992).

## Deviant Populations

Significant MMPI scale differences may exist in deviant populations for Afro-Americans and whites. This is indicated by a number of studies, although other studies suggest that these differences maybe due to other variables besides race. Gynther and Green (1980) found that Blacks tested in psychiatric settings scored higher on some MMPI scales than whites, but these differences were not as great as they were for Blacks and whites in a normal population.

Hutton et al. (1992) found for 412 forensic psychiatric inpatients that Blacks had scores 5 T-score points higher on the Overcontrolled-Hostility scale **(O-H)** than whites. Forty-three percent of the Blacks scored in the clinically elevated range on this scale, but their elevated scores appeared to be unrelated to criminal charges, psychiatric diagnosis, years of education, or incidents of physical assault in the hospital. None of the descriptors of the overcontrolled-hostile personality fit the Black patients, indicating that they were likely to be incorrectly labeled by the MMPI as having overcontrolled-hostility.

Elion and Megargee (1975), after working with criminal offenders of various types, concluded that scale **4** is valid for Blacks only if clinicians "mentally subtract" 5 points from the **4** scale T-score to correct for racial bias.

Penk, Robinowitz, Black, Dolan, Bell, Dorsett, Ames, and Noriega (1989) reviewed literature that showed that Black Vietnam era noncombat veterans scored lower than white noncombat veterans on MMPI scales **2, 3, 4, 7,** and higher on **9,** whereas Blacks with heavy combat exposure scored significantly higher than white heavy combat veterans on **F, 1, 3, 6,** and **8.** To test whether or not the higher T-scores were due to the level of combat the individual was exposed to or were the result of minority status, Penk et al. (1989) compared a group of Hispanic and white Vietnam veterans with a Black sample. They found no differences for veterans with no-combat or light combat, but significant differences between Black heavy combat veterans and Hispanics and whites on scales **1, 2, 3, 4, 6, 7,** and **8.**

These authors suggested that the Black sample's higher scores might have been related to the turmoil that was going on in Black communities during the Vietnam era and the Black troops' loss of faith in their reasons for being in combat. An alternative explanation is that there may have been more Blacks assigned to hazardous duty, which resulted in a disproportionately higher number of Black casualties. This would increase the tendency toward paranoid reactions on the part of the Black combat veterans.

In another study, Hispanic, Black, and white schizophrenics were compared. The most frequent high-point code for Hispanic and white patients was **8-2,** but for Blacks it was more likely to be **8-6** (Velasquez & Callahan, 1990b). This again seems to point to a paranoia factor in Blacks' responses.

Butcher, Braswell, and Raney (1983) found similar results in a sample of Native American, Black, and white inpatients. Blacks had higher scores on scales **F, 6, 8,** and **9** even when the sample was controlled for social status. Butcher et al. (1983) believed there could be many reasons for these racial differences. For example, who gets referred for treatment may differ from one culture to another since behavior that is accepted or at least ignored in one culture may lead to hospitalization in another. Certain problem behaviors also may have a higher base rate in one group than in another group because different prevailing social conditions predispose its members to different psychological problems.

Another approach to the problem of Black-white differences is the belief that differences between ethnic groups may not exist except as the result of moderator variables. Authors who advocate this believe that, if the moderator variables are controlled, ethnic differences will drop out. For example, Johnson and Brems (1990) matched a small inpatient psychiatric sample of Blacks and whites on age, gender, and Axis I and Axis II diagnoses and found no significant differences between Blacks' and whites' MMPI profiles or in their two-point codes. These authors concluded that MMPI differences identified in previous studies may be attributable to moderator variables. As a result, they recommend that psychologists consider personal history, educational level, intelligence, age, socioeconomic status, and gender when interpreting ethnic minorities' MMPIs.

In another study where relevant variables were also matched, Bertelson, Marks, and May (1982) matched Black and white psychiatric patients on a number of crucial variables: race, sex, socioeconomic status, age, and number of years of schooling. When these variables were matched, these authors did not find any scale elevations that could be attributed to race.

Holcomb, Adams, and Ponder (1984) believe that intelligence is another variable that influences scores on the MMPI. These authors found that a group of Black accused murderers had lower intelligence scores than white murderers, and significantly higher scores than the white accused murderers on the **F** and **9** scales, but they did not differ on the **8** scale. These differences on the MMPI scales disappeared when the effects of nonverbal intelligence were removed statistically.

I would argue that even when Blacks and whites get similar scores on an MMPI scale, they may not reflect similar behavior. Smith and Graham in a study done in 1981 found that high scores on the **F** scale for white patients were associated with psychopathology, including emotional withdrawal, hallucinations, and thought disorder; however, for Black patients this was not true. Their conclusion was that elevated scores on the **F** scale did not have the same pathological implications for Black patients as they did for white patients.

## Substance Abusers

One study (Robyak, Prange & Sands, 1988) found that a group of Black alcoholics had MMPI profiles similar to whites', but they differed in terms of the perceived benefits of using alcohol, the negative physiological consequences of alcohol abuse, and the amount of alcohol they drank each day. Whites were more likely than Blacks to use alcohol to control feelings of tension, depression, and worry.

In another study, Black alcoholics scored significantly higher than white alcoholics on the **F, 1,** and **9** scales of the MMPI. The elevation on scale **1** is consistent with findings of Megargee and Carbonell (1991) of a group of young adult male prison inmates and their use of sick call. Blacks were more frequent users of sick call than whites and showed a tendency to somaticize their psychological distress.

## Implications from Research

Based upon the studies that we have reviewed in this chapter, it seems highly unlikely to me that any of the differences that have been found for Blacks and whites on the MMPI are innate. For example, many of the studies that I have reviewed, such as White's (1974), indicate that highly acculturated Blacks score similarly to whites on the MMPI. It seems much more important to focus upon specific social or environmental facts that the clinician needs to keep in mind when interpreting an MMPI-2 for an Afro-American.

This is consistent with the McDonald and Gynther (1963) and Gynther (1972) hypothesis that the greater the acculturation differences between the races, the greater the likelihood that Afro-Americans will have higher scale scores on certain scales of the MMPI, most likely **F, 8,** and **9** (Gynther & Green, 1980; Elion & Megargee, 1975). Therefore, while Afro- and Anglo-American differences on the MMPI may be dependent upon a variety of factors, what may be a major one is the degree to which a Black individual has been acculturated into the white society.

**Guidelines for Interpreting
Afro-American MMPI and MMPI-2 Profiles**

On the basis of the research I have reported in this section, I would suggest the following guidelines be used in interpreting an MMPI profile from an Afro-American.

1. When working with a nonpsychiatric acculturated population of Afro-Americans, I recommend that the MMPI be interpreted in the same way that you would interpret the test for a white client.

2. When working with a nonpsychiatric nonacculturated population of Afro-Americans, I recommend that you make allowances for the lack of acculturation by subtracting T-score points from elevated scores on **F, 4, 8,** and **9** scales. I recommend that you subtract 10 T-score points from the **8** scale score and 5 T-score points from the other three scales.

3. If the Afro-American client is from a psychiatric population, such as one that is incarcerated or under psychiatric care, treat the MMPI scores as being reflective of the individual's condition. If the Afro-American has higher scores than a white in a similar setting, most likely the MMPI scores are indicating more pathology.

## HISPANICS

In a major review of the research done regarding the use of the MMPI with Hispanics, Velasquez (1992) found 86 studies, most of which focused on comparisons with whites. These studies were done on Hispanics in drug/alcohol treatment, correctional, psychiatric, rehabilitation, and nonclinical or normal settings. The MMPI has been widely used in Hispanic populations to make diagnostic decisions, to describe pathology, and as an aid in treatment planning. I will separate the studies that have been done into those with normal populations and those with deviant populations.

**Normals**

Using surname and self-report to separate a Mexican-American sample from an Anglo-American sample, Montgomery, Arnold, and Orozco (1990) found that level of acculturation far outweighed age and social class as influences on elevations of the Wiggins Content Scales, Harris-Lingoes subscales, and Serkownek subscales. When level of acculturation and age were controlled, the significant differences were reduced to zero. These authors concluded that acculturation is an important moderator variable that must be considered when interpreting the MMPI for Hispanic-Americans.

Regional differences are another factor that can contribute to differential performance for ethnic groups. Mexican Americans vary along a continuum of acculturation that ranges from extremely Mexican-oriented to extremely Anglo-oriented. Montgomery and Orozco (1985) found that for a group of Mexican-American college students there were differences on 10 of 13 MMPI scales when compared to white students. When these authors controlled for acculturation using the Acculturation Rating Scale for Mexican-Americans (ARSMA), there were differences only on the **L** and **5** scales.

Whitworth (1988) tested the acculturation hypothesis by giving the MMPI to 150 Anglo-Americans and 300 Mexican-Americans. Half of the Mexican-Americans who spoke Spanish took a Spanish form, and the other half who spoke English took the standard form. The Spanish speaking group was significantly different from the other two groups at the .001 level on the following scales: **L, F, 1, 2, 4, 5, 6, 7, 8,** and **0.** The author concluded that if Mexican-Americans are fluent enough to be tested in English, MMPI differences should be relatively small and have little effect on the clinical interpretation of the MMPI.

McGill (1980) found no significant differences between Black and Anglo welfare recipients on the MMPI, but did find significant differences between Mexican-American and Anglo welfare recipients on the **L, 5,** and **9** scales and between Mexican-Americans and Blacks on the **L, K,** and **9** scales.

Scale **9** was lower for Mexican-Americans, and the other scales were higher.

## Deviant Populations

Velasquez and Callahan (1990a) found lower scores on MMPI scales **4, 5,** and **0** for Hispanic veterans diagnosed as alcoholics compared to a group of white veterans diagnosed as alcoholics, suggesting the Hispanic alcoholics may be better adjusted than Anglo alcoholics. Both groups had on the average **2-8/8-2** profile codetypes. These authors suggested that the Hispanic family attitude of support and caretaking behavior toward the subjects may account for some of the difference in scores.

Velazquez and Gimenez (1987) found the MMPI had limited utility for placing Mexican-American state hospital patients into DSM-III diagnostic groups. Hispanic-American patients with schizophrenia and affective disorders did not differ from each other on the MMPI. These results are consistent with findings for Anglo populations.

In a small but carefully matched sample of Native-Mexican and Caucasian-American male alcoholics, Venn (1988) found no significant differences except Mexican-Americans scored higher than Caucasians on scale **L**.

## Guidelines for Interpreting
## Hispanic MMPI and MMPI-2 Profiles

1.  In a nonpsychiatric setting, if a Hispanic test taker reports that he/she thinks in English and identifies as an American, interpret the profile the same way you would for an Anglo-American. The only scales on which you are likely to have unusual elevations are **L** and **5**.

2.  If Spanish is the primary language of the test taker and/or he/she was raised in some other country,

be cautious about MMPI interpretations, especially on scales **L, F, 1, 2, 4, 5, 6, 7, 8,** and **0**.

3. In a psychiatric setting, MMPI Hispanic-American profiles probably reflect pathology in the same way that they do in a white population.

4. In a drug or alcohol treatment setting, the MMPI profiles scale scores for Hispanic-Americans may be lower than those of an Anglo population.

## ETHNIC AND CULTURAL DIFFERENCES

I asked four questions at the end of the introduction to this chapter regarding ethnic and cultural differences on the MMPI and MMPI-2 that I now can answer.

### 1. Are there significant differences between Anglo-Americans and members of other groups such as Afro-Americans, Hispanics, and Native Americans on the MMPI and MMPI-2?

The answer is yes, under some circumstances. Minority group membership becomes important as an influence on answers to MMPI items if the individual identifies primarily with an ethnic group that has attitudes and a world view that are different from that of the white culture.

### 2. If differences do exist, are they due to test bias, socioeconomic class factors, or to measuring some real differences in behavior between minorities and Anglo-Americans?

Test bias may take a number of forms. In the case of the MMPI, the bias is most likely related to the fact that for many Afro-Americans an alertness to others' intentions because of the possibility of prejudice may show up as an elevation on scale **6**, and an alienation from the majority culture may show up as an elevation on scale **8**. In neither case would the elevations suggest the same level of pathology as they would if a white client had similar elevations.

I believe that social class plays a role in how an individual responds to the MMPI items. The experiences of lower-class whites are different in a number of ways from experiences of lower-class Afro-Americans and Hispanics. For example, while lower-class males, in general, are more likely than middle-class males to be stopped for questioning by police, minorities are much more likely to receive special attention from law enforcement officers. This would tend to make minority lower-class individuals' attitudes toward authority figures different from that of white lower-class individuals.

With the passage of time, Blacks have probably assimilated some of the world view of the more dominant white culture, but this does not mean that the Black experience does not continue to influence how answers are given to the MMPI items. From this point of view, acculturation is important. The extent to which answers will differ between groups will depend upon the acculturation process the individual has been exposed to and assimilated.

Even a score within normal limits may not mean the same thing for a minority subject that it does for a majority member. Answers to items still have a degree of projective possibilities. For example, Macaranas-Sittler (1986) found that Afro-American, Hispanic-American, and Native American college students had an external locus of control-internal locus of responsibility (EC-IR) while Anglo students had an internal focus of control-internal locus of responsibility (IC-IR).

### 3. If differences exist, are new norms for that cultural group needed?

The differences that are found do not seem to exist for the minority group as a whole but apparently only for subgroups. Jones and Thorne (1987) pointed out that developing separate norms for different cultural groups could become a never ending process. There are likely to be many regional differences; that is, Afro-Americans reared in an isolated area of Georgia would need different norms than an Afro-American reared in Harlem. Subgroups, especially for Hispanics, could be from any of several countries, e.g., Mexico, Cuba, or Argentina, and could have been in the U.S. for varying lengths of time.

### 4. Without separate norms, how should a clinician approach interpreting MMPIs from minority groups?

The lack of separate norms for ethnic groups throws the problem of test interpretation back to the clinician who must know something about the cultures with which he/she is working and have a way of estimating the level of acculturation of the individual or groups under consideration.

What does all this mean to the test interpreter? Ask about the background of the test taker: What is the person's major identification? How acculturated is the person's subgroup into the attitudes and world view of the majority culture. How much prejudice has the individual experienced?

Jones and Thorne (1987) have suggested that the test taker become a collaborator in helping the clinician understand what test responses mean.

> Obtaining post assessment narratives is particularly useful when the usual, more or less etic instruments have been used. Narrative accounts help to reconceptualize the data by providing access to subjects' impressions about what they believed the instrument was attempting to assess, what the items or questions meant to them, and what meaning the test-taking situation held for them; in short, what motives, expectations, and understandings they brought to the assessment situation. (p. 493)

## CROSS-NATIONAL USE OF THE MMPI

In recent years, an influx of Mexicans, Cubans, and Vietnamese have immigrated to the U.S. Some of these individuals are being tested in mental health facilities and other social service agencies. In colleges and universities, there are also a large number of foreign students, especially from such countries as Iran, India, Nigeria, and China. Most clinicians who have occasion to use the MMPI with foreign nationals will use it with individuals who are living in the U.S. Few of us will have the opportunity to test someone in a foreign country such as Brazil or Japan, but an understanding of how individuals in those countries differ from American norms can be instructive.

The need to interpret MMPIs of individuals from a variety of foreign countries raises two questions: (1) Does thinking in a foreign language affect the measurement of personality, especially with the MMPI? and (2) If it does, how should we modify the interpretation of MMPI profiles for foreign nationals?

In the *Psychological Abstracts* for 1990-1992 there were abstracts of articles on the MMPI from researchers in the following English speaking countries: Australia, Canada, England, New Zealand, and South Africa. The largest number of published papers were from Canada (50). Most of these articles appeared in journals published in the U.S. These articles show that the MMPI appears to have the same validity in those cultures as it does in this country. Despite this validity, it is interesting to note that very little is being done with the MMPI in England (3 articles).

Many European countries have translated the MMPI into their language and have done research using it as an assessment instrument. In Butcher and Pancheri's book (1976) on cross-national MMPI research, the authors have discussed methods that need to be used to insure a valid translation from one language to another. One method is to translate from English into the foreign language then have someone else translate from that language back into English to be sure that the item meaning has been retained. It is also necessary to rewrite some items because they would be meaningless in another culture, for example, the item on who was the greater man, Washington or Lincoln.

During the period 1990-1992, Belgium, Finland, France, Germany, Italy, Netherlands, Norway, Poland, Spain, Sweden,

Switzerland, USSR, and Yugoslavia all published at least some studies using the MMPI. The main foreign users of the MMPI for personality research during those years were the USSR (now Russia) with 33 studies and Italy with 26. These studies indicate that the MMPI appears to be a valid measure of personality when used with these European populations.

Much of what we know regarding national differences on the MMPI is based on work by Butcher and Pancheri (1976) and Butcher and Clark (1979). Butcher and Pancheri (1976) studied differences between normal American subjects and normal individuals from Israel, Pakistan, Mexico, Costa Rica, Italy, Switzerland, and Japan using translations of the MMPI that were developed using specific criteria for evaluating their adequacy. Butcher and Pancheri initially felt that it was doubtful that the structure and content of personality would be the same in all countries. However, after translating the MMPI into a number of languages, they found an impressively similar factor structure for the MMPI not only for Western European groups but for other national groups as well. As one would expect when comparing samples of subjects of such diverse origin, some differences existed in factor loading for some scales, but for most purposes it seems that whatever personality structure underlies the MMPI for Americans seems to apply to other cultures as well.

Butcher and Pancheri (1976) concluded that, "It is evident from the factor-analytic study that the factor structure of the MMPI is maintained across different cultural samples, not only when dealing with normal populations, but also when pathological subjects from different countries take the MMPI in their native languages" (p. 134).

Butcher and Pancheri (1976) also presented the results of item analyses, and a study of extreme item-endorsement to demonstrate that the MMPI item pool has a high degree of generality for normal populations speaking other languages. That is, normal subjects from different countries taking the test in different language translations respond to MMPI item content in an essentially similar manner to the United States population. This does not mean, however, that their MMPI profiles look exactly like those of the U.S. population. A study of profiles of normal individuals from different national groups (Butcher & Pancheri, 1976) showed that the mean profiles of the Swiss and Italians are most like U.S. samples, Mexican and Costa Rican samples are somewhat different, and the Pakistani and Japanese mean profiles are so different that if these MMPIs were used to screen for pathology, many of them would be falsely labeled pathological.

While Butcher and Pancheri were impressed with the ability of the MMPI to discriminate among different diagnostic samples across cultures, they did feel that sufficient differences did exist between Western and non-Western subjects in endorsement patterns for scales that measure psychopathology to caution against blind acceptance of MMPI scale scores to diagnose psychopathology. They suggested the need for additional research to verify the generality of these clinical scales.

The primary development of the translation of the MMPI into other languages has been done by Butcher and his associates. Translations now in use in other non-European countries include Brazil, Chile, China, India, Israel, Japan, Mexico, and Pakistan. Cheung and Song (1989) reviewed 26 studies of the clinical application of the Chinese version of the MMPI. They found that the clinical scales were able to differentiate between normals and psychiatric patients, with profiles for the different diagnostic groups being similar to those found in the U.S. The average T-scores for scales **F, 2,** and **8** are high for Chinese normals and were further elevated in the patient groups. These authors concluded that the Chinese MMPI was a useful diagnostic instrument.

## SUMMATION OF CULTURAL EFFECTS

In summation, a review of the above studies indicates the following:

1.  For an individual from a different culture who is part of a normal population, a reasonable expectation is

that the clinical scale scores are elevated in direct proportion to how dissimilar that culture is to the American culture. More elevated profiles and, therefore, more false positives (calling people pathological when they are not) can be expected when making judgments about such national groups as Iranians and Japanese because these cultures are quite dissimilar from the American culture. Fewer false positives will be found when judging elevations in such national groups as the Germans or French because these cultures are quite similar to the U.S. culture.

2. Some scale elevations for people from a normal population will not indicate the same symptoms cross-culturally. For example, Butcher and Pancheri found symptom exaggeration on the MMPI for Italians. They felt this might be a manifestation of the general characteristic of Italians to dramatize problems. A good way to become acquainted with some of these cultural symptom differences would be to read the book by Butcher and Pancheri (1976).

3. When a clinician is working with a psychiatric or other deviant population, the MMPI should be a moderately good indicator of degree and kind of psychopathology. While caution is necessary, apparently rather good concordance exists for the symptoms of psychiatric problems from one national group to another.

CHAPTER **VIII**

# THE MMPI AND MMPI-2 IN MEDICAL SETTINGS

Wayne Anderson

In this book we have been stressing that an individual's response to MMPI items reflects a variety of factors. When interpreting a profile, the clinician needs to take into consideration the nature of the clientele and the situation in which the MMPI was taken. This precaution becomes especially important when the MMPI is used in a medical setting because illness and/or pain often produce symptoms that contribute to elevations on some scales. The clinician must be aware that these patients' responses may be a consequence of the illness and/or pain and may not reflect preexisting psychopathological personality characteristics.

The assumption that patients with pain of no known etiology will present with higher levels of emotional disturbance as measured by the MMPI than patients who have an identifiable organic pathology is only partially supported by the research evidence. Therefore, in a medical setting, if some scales are given a standard interpretation such as we present in the chapter on the clinical scales (Chapter IV), this can lead to misleading conclusions about the nature of the patient's dynamics and prognosis. I, therefore, believe that clinicians should avoid standard interpretive rules when assessing a patient in a medical setting. Although high scores on scales **1, 2,** and **3** of the MMPI are often an indication of an ongoing functional disorder or what we used to call a neurosis, it will become clear that for persons with physical problems, other factors may be operating to push these scales into the level where one makes clinical interpretations.

In this chapter I will first present information about pain as it influences profile elevations and then discuss the two most common sources of pain—back pain and headaches. Following that, I will summarize the findings on closed head injuries and some other medical conditions for which the MMPI has been used, including the possible relationship between depression as measured by the MMPI-2 scale and cancer. I then will close with a summary of my conclusions about how to use the MMPI and MMPI-2 in medical settings.

## A TWO-FACTOR THEORY OF PAIN

A recent review of the research literature on pain by Fernandez and Turk (1992) helps explain the problem clinicians have in differentiating functional from organic medical conditions with the use of the MMPI. The Fernandez and Turk review supports the position that pain can be separated into sensory and affective components. **Sensory pain** can be experienced as external, such as pressure and temperature, or internal, such as aches or burning. The **affective component of pain** is the level of arousal of unpleasant emotions such as anger, fear, and sadness. These emotions are qualitatively different from the sensory component but add to the overall discomfort felt by the patient.

When describing the sensory aspects of pain, patients will use words like sharp or throbbing, and when describing the emotional aspects, they will use words like nagging and terrifying. While these two components of pain may not be universal, these distinctions do appear in both Romance and Germanic languages. How much of the variance in pain reported by a patient is accounted for by the affective component depends upon the source of the pain and the personality of the patient. For example, Leavitt, Garron, Whisler, and

Sheinkop (1978) in a study of patients with back pain attributed 38% of the variance to emotional discomfort, while Reading (1979) in a study of patients with dysmenorrhoea attributed 10% of the variance to an emotional distress component.

Fernandez and Turk (1992) cautioned that while research clearly points to the existence of these two aspects of pain, it is unlikely that individuals will be able to make conscious discriminations in the relative contribution of these two components to their personal sense of pain. The authors concluded that while pain has these two different dimensions, it is difficult to measure them. Part of the problem is their lack of independence. As the sensation of physical discomfort increases, there is a corresponding increase in the negative emotional reaction of the patient, such as fear or anger, that in turn can accentuate the sensation of physical pain that again increases the patient's emotional discomfort.

In line with Fernandez and Turk's findings, Wade, Price, Hamer, and Schwartz (1990), using regression analyses of a number of instruments including the MMPI, found that anger and frustration are critical concomitants of the pain experience. They examined the relative contribution of frustration, fear, anger, and anxiety to the unpleasantness and depression that 143 pain patients experienced. They found that these emotions are all part of the emotional unpleasantness associated with pain and make the pain less tolerable.

The sex of a patient may be a factor in the effect of pain on the individual. Haley, Turner, and Romano (1985) studied 63 patients who were heterogenous for site of pain and found that women's ratings of pain level were correlated with degree of depression, but for men the pain ratings were correlated with amount of physical activity—the more pain, the fewer activities in which the men engaged.

A follow-up of 54 former patients of a multidisciplinary clinic for evaluation of chronic pain was done by Brennan, Barrett, and Garretson (1986). When the amount of initial pain and physical disability was taken into account, the psychological test scores (MMPI included) at the initial evaluation did not predict future chronic pain. While later in this chapter I will cite studies that show that some kinds of prediction with the MMPI are possible, the clinician needs to keep in mind that, at least in part, the elevated scores on psychological tests may be a reflection of the sensory components of the pain, that is, the actual physical effects of the trauma. For one individual, elevated scale scores on the MMPI may reflect the patient's emotional response to pain, and in another individual, the elevations may reflect physical sensations connected with tissue damage and/or the limitations the pain places on the patient's activity level. The clinician's problem becomes one of judging the relative contribution of the emotional (affective) component towards elevating the patient's MMPI scale scores.

## MMPI PAIN PROFILES

An early error in research using the MMPI for pain patients was to group together patients with specific sources of pain, such as headache or lower back pain, and to develop a mean group profile. It turned out that a profile derived this way reflected the dynamics of only a minority of the actual patient profiles that had been used to create it. A more useful method of research has been to cluster profiles into groups based on profile similarity, study the characteristics of those clients with these profiles, and then define rules by which an individual profile can be matched into an appropriate group.

Costello, Hulsey, Schoenfeld, and Ramamurthy (1987) did a meta-clustering of 57 profile types from 10 studies and found that they were able to reduce these profiles to four, which they labeled *P-A-I-N*. These four profile types were common to both men and women and represented patient groups with a variety of painful medical conditions, and a mixture of etiologies and levels of chronicity.

The authors defined **Type P** as an MMPI profile with elevations greater than 70 on scales **1**, **2**, **3**, **4**, **7**, and **8**. While scores on scales **L** and **K** were not allowed to exceed

65, scores on scales **6, 9,** and **0** were often also elevated above 70 (Costello et al. 1987). The Type P pain group was markedly disturbed, with people in it who made many claims of ill health, emotional instability, and constant pain. They were most likely to have had a specific incident at the onset of the pain and to have the most interference in their ordinary functioning as a result of the pain. While they frequently sought medical attention, patients in this profile type showed the least overall improvement as a result of treatment.

Profile **Type A** had elevations greater than T-score 70 on scales **1** and **3,** with the **2** scale less than 69 and 9 or more T-score points below scales **1** and **3**. This is the "conversion V" that is so frequently reported in the literature on medical patients. The authors found the least number of empirical correlates for this group, which seemed to be between **Types P** and **N** on the variables studied.

**Type I** had scores greater than 70 on **1, 2,** and **3** with no other elevated scales. This group had undergone the most surgeries, the most hospitalizations, and the longest periods of disability. They also had made the least physical improvement in treatment. While they were the most physically impaired, they did appreciate the help that was given to them. They also tried to adapt to the limitations on their daily activities imposed by their pain and seemed to make progress in coping emotionally with their pain.

**Type N** had no scale elevations over 65. This group was the best educated with the highest monthly income of all four groups. These individuals were moderate in how they described their pain and the impact that pain had on their daily functioning. Their pain was very responsive to treatment and was of short duration.

In a later study, Costello, Schoenfeld, Ramamurthy, and Hobbs-Hardee (1989) found support for the rules that they had developed in their earlier research (Costello et al., 1987) to divide patients' MMPI profiles into the four chronic pain profile types. They also found that pain Types P and N were extremes on a Factor 1, Profile Elevation, and Types A and I were extremes on Factor 2, Optimism-Pessimism.

Curtiss, Kinder, Kalichman, and Spana (1989) also supported the existence of four subgroups of pain patients based on personality functioning. The four subgroups had differences in the experience and expression of anxiety and anger, suggesting that differential treatment of chronic pain patients based on their MMPI profiles and gender is called for.

These four pain profile types are frequently reported in other studies; for example, Henrichs (1987) found them in chronic pain patients with varying types of pain and with varying duration. These profiles types are not always found, however. Robinson, Swimmer, and Rallof (1989) used 125 adult chronic pain patients' MMPI profiles to test the P-A-I-N classification system and found that 69% of the profiles in their sample were not classified into one of these four pain profiles.

## PREEXISTENT TENDENCY FOR SOMATIZATION OR RESPONSE TO PAIN

When the MMPI was first used to try to diagnose chronic pain, it was expected that the test would allow professionals in medical settings to separate patients with chronic pain due to organic causes from patients with pain due to functional or "psychogenic" bases in order to plan appropriate treatment. Very early in the use of the MMPI, McKinley and Hathaway (1943) made the point that when a functional (neurotic) basis for symptoms is suspected, but the patient presents a normal MMPI profile, the need for further medical evaluation is indicated.

But does the opposite hold true? Does a high score on the MMPI mean that a functional process underlies the patient's medical condition? The conversion V—that is, scales **1** and **3** clinically elevated and scale **2** at least 10 T-score points lower—was long felt to indicate a psychogenic or somataform disorder. In recent years, it has become clear that the situation is not as simple as we first thought and that some of the interpretations and conclusions that we drew from these elevated scales are questionable. The conversion V, for example, occurs in profiles of patients who have a definite organic basis for their chronic pain (Franz, Paul, Bautz, Choroba, & Hildebrandt, 1986). Osborne's (1979) review of research on medical patients showed that when the MMPI is given as part of a medical evaluation, a common occurrence is to have elevations on the conversion V.

A different approach to answering the question as to what extent elevations on the conversion V are due to preexisting personality traits and to what extent they are the result of the pain and discomfort the patient is suffering was made by Wade, Dougherty, Hart, and Cook (1992). They clustered the MMPIs of 59 chronic pain patients and came up with four clusters very similar to those found by Costello et al. (1989). Wade et al. (1992) started with the hypothesis that the five major dimensions of personality as measured by the NEO-PI (Costa & McCrae, 1985), namely Neuroticism, Extraversion, Openness to Experience, Agreeableness, and Conscientiousness, are stable over time. The authors hoped that by using the NEO-PI they would be able to find out what the patients' personalities had been before the chronic pain condition developed.

The only relationship Wade et al. found between the four MMPI clusters and the NEO-PI was between Neuroticism and the MMPI profile they called Emotionally Overwhelmed. With its elevations of over 70 T-score on scales **1, 2, 3, 4, 6, 7,** and **8,** this profile is very similar to the highly disturbed Type P cluster of Costello et al. (1989). The Emotionally Overwhelmed group had intense anxiety, depression, hostility, and vulnerability as measured by the NEO-PI. Persons with this profile appeared to have a predisposition toward a large affective component in their illness/pain; that is, their pain and suffering seemed to be largely due to their preexisting personality characteristics.

Wade et al. indicated that the other three group profiles, which they found to be similar to Costello et al.'s P-A-I-N clusters (1989), did not seem to have an underlying neurotic character style since these profiles did not correlate with the NEO-PI. Wade et al. concluded that an MMPI elevation on scale **2** for pain patients was more likely to be a reflection of the individuals' emotional/behavioral adjustments to chronic pain, whereas elevations on scales **1** and **3** more likely reflected patients' endorsement of somatic items associated with their illness and therefore were not the result of preexisting psychopathology.

Kinder, Curtiss, and Kalichman's (1986) research on anxiety and anger in chronic pain also supports the hypothesis that underlying traits may have preexisted and influenced a patient's reaction to pain. These researchers had 77 chronic pain patients take the *State-Trait Personality Inventory* and the *Anger Expression Scale*. Trait Anxiety was a predictor of elevations on MMPI scales **1, 2** and **3** for both males and females, indicating that these scales do seem to reflect long-term, stable personality traits. These authors believed that these elevations are not solely a response to a chronic medical condition.

An interesting additional finding of Kinder et al. (1986) was that the person's awareness of Trait Anger was negatively related to elevations on scales **1, 2,** and **3** on the MMPI in males. That is, given two male patients with equal Trait Anxiety, the one who can admit to experiencing his anger will have lower scores on **1, 2,** and **3** MMPI scales. This indicates that a relationship may exist between the denial of anger and the functional component of the pain response. These authors suggested that working with these males to recognize their angry feelings may be a helpful treatment approach.

This finding, that the inability to express anger may be related to pain, is supported by a study of 90 chronic headache and low back pain patients who were compared to a group of healthy people by Franz, Paul, Bautz, Choroba, and Hildebrandt (1986). These authors factor analyzed items that differentiated pain patients from normal subjects and found three factors. The third factor they labeled Frankness—the ability to express feelings of anger and aggressiveness in social situations. Pain patients had much less of this ability than the healthy control group.

## SIGNS OF MENTAL ILLNESS AND PAIN

I have been stressing how the consequences of a chronic illness can elevate a patient's T-scores on MMPI scales **1**, **2**, and **3**, and while I have mentioned that some profiles have other elevations, I have not elaborated on this fact. The **8** scale is elevated in Type P of the P-A-I-N clusters found by Costello, Hulsey, Schoenfeld, and Ramamurthy (1987). Does this mean that the P Type of pain patient has schizophrenic characteristics? Moore, McFall, Kivlahan, and Capestany (1988) used the Harris and Lingoes subscales (Harris & Lingoes, 1955) for the schizophrenia scale to find the differences in responses for a group of schizophrenics, a group of non-psychotics, and a group of chronic pain patients who had elevated scores on the **8** scale.

Their results indicate that the endorsement of unusual sensory experiences and items that indicate life is a strain are the major contributors to the elevation of scale **8** in pain patients. The diagnosed schizophrenic patients had more bizarre thought processes, social isolation, defective inhibition and fewer somatic complaints. Pain patients were higher on items that asked about muscles twitching, sense of balance, and numbness in the skin. For pain patients with elevated scale **8** scores, then, an examination of items or subsets of items helps clarify the diagnosis.

In discussing the problem of pathological elevations of scale **8** in pain patients, Henrichs (1987) cited studies that showed medications and seizure disorders can cause some of the symptoms reported on scale **8**. Demerol can cause dysphoria, disorientation, agitation, and transient hallucinations, and codeine can cause delirium.

Some special scales, Schizophrenia-Organicity (**S-O** scale), Psychiatric-Organic (**P-O** scale), and Pseudo-Neurological (**P-N** scale) may be useful in the differential diagnosis of patients with brain damage from patients with schizophrenia and schizophrenics who are also brain-damaged. For further information on these scales, see Puente, Rodenbough, and Horton (1989) and Watson (1984).

## Predicting Treatment Outcome with the MMPI

Given that elevations on the MMPIs of some patients are the result of emotional behavioral responses to chronic pain, can they still be used as predictors of treatment outcome? Akerlind, Hornquist, and Bjurulf (1992), after reviewing 21 prognostic studies based on individual MMPI scales, found that two elevated scale scores were significant predictors of negative outcome in 15 of the studies. An elevated scale **3** was a negative predictor in 11 of the studies, and elevated scale **7** was a negative predictor in 6 of the studies. These authors felt that elevations on these scales were indicators of poor prognosis.

In their own study of 80 long-term back pain patients, Akerlind et al. (1992) found that poor long-term prognosis was related to the number of scales over 70 on the MMPI plus an elevation on scales **1** or **3**. This is consistent with studies that I examined in the previous section entitled "Preexistent Tendency for Somatization or Response to Pain." Akerlind et al. (1992) relate this finding to Caldwell and Chase's (1977) pain-fear hypothesis that states that this type of patient has a pessimistic and defeatist attitude toward the future because of a fear that the pain is going to remain and increase. This fear of pain leads to a restriction of activity to avoid pain-provoking situations and the development of a chronic sick role. Akerlind et al. (1992) concluded that the reason for the MMPI not predicting better is because some patients with elevated scales do learn to cope with pain and do gain confidence.

Support for this conclusion is found in a number of studies. Kleinke (1991) found that the MMPI-2 scores in a group of 120 chronic-pain patients were positively correlated with self-blame/escape and negatively correlated with social support. Strategies (methods) that patients used in coping with their depression contributed significant variance over demographics and level of depression in predicting rehabilitation outcome. Kleinke (1991) concluded that a cognitive-behavioral mediation model is helpful for understanding the relation between depression and chronic pain. Like Akerlind et al. (1992), Kleinke believed that by increasing patients' confidence in their ability to cope and manage their pain, they will become better rehabilitation risks.

## LOW BACK PAIN: SOME CONTRADICTORY FINDINGS

I found more studies on the MMPI regarding back pain than any other medical conditions, probably because it is such a common problem. Low back pain is frequently expected to have a heavy functional component. Because diagnosis and the resultant treatment are often based on the patient's subjective report about the pain, medical professionals have been eager to find a tool to help them make a differential diagnosis between actual low back pain and malingering.

Part of the problem appears to be that some chronic pain programs have a fair amount of success in treating low back pain while others do not. As a result, the findings on the adequacy of the MMPI as a predictor vary widely.

Some studies have found improvement as a result of treatment. Seven hundred two patients treated for low back pain in a multidisciplinary treatment program who showed considerable disability on the MMPI at admission had significant improvement at discharge (McArthur, Cohen, Gottlieb, & Naliboff, 1987). This is not a consistent finding, however. In a study by McCreary, Naliboff, and Cohen (1989), back pain clinic patients with elevated MMPI profiles had more dysfunction upon examination and showed poorer response to treatment than back pain patients with more normal profiles.

Naliboff, McCreary, McArthur, and Cohen (1988) cluster analyzed the MMPI profiles of 634 chronic low back pain patients and identified 4 subgroups each for males and females: (1) severely disturbed, (2) hypochondriacal, (3) unelevated, and (4) reactive depression and somatization with denial of affect. None of the subgroups differed on intake measures or treatment outcome. All groups improved following a behaviorally oriented inpatient pain treatment program and later showed significant decreases in MMPI scale elevations.

Kleinke and Spangler (1988) assessed the treatment outcome of 72 chronic back pain patients. High scores on the MMPI **3** scale were correlated with high self-ratings of pain, but patients with high scores on scales **3** and **2** had the most improvement on self-rated pain and mood. These authors found no relationship between demographics and improvement outcome measures.

Using 305 male and 330 female chronic pain patients, Guck, Meilman, Skultety, and Poloni (1988) identified three male and four female MMPI subgroups similar to those found in other studies. Long-term follow-up found few treatment differences in the men's groups and none for the four women's groups.

Ornduff, Brennan, and Barrett (1988) compared 42 chronic back pain patients with 80 nonpain subjects on MMPI scale **2** and the **3** scale subscales, *Bodily Concern* and *Psychological Denial*. High **2** scale elevations among pain patients were partially accounted for by the endorsement of a disproportionate number of Bodily Concern items. Pain patients' scores on the Bodily Concern subscale were significantly related to more indices of pain duration and severity than were scores on the Psychological Denial subscale.

Uomoto, Turner, and Herron (1988) looked at outcome of lumbar laminectomy for 69 males and 69 females with chronic back pain and found that the MMPI had only moderate ability to predict successful outcome. They suggested caution in using the MMPI to make surgery outcome predictions.

Given these varied resources, it would seem premature to 2ecommend the use of the MMPI for predicting treatment outcome with patients with low back pain. It may be, however, that the problem is not in the MMPI but in the variation in success rates of the different treatment programs.

## HEADACHE PAIN

### Types of Headache

Kinder, Curtiss, and Kalichman (1991, 1992) have reviewed studies clustering MMPI profiles of patients with chronic headaches. These studies were remarkably consistent in finding four profile types. While the general shape of these four profiles was similar to those found for back pain patients, chronic headache sufferers had only two profiles that had marked elevations. A much smaller percentage of headache patients had elevated profiles than did patients with low back pain. In fact, Mathew (1992) found in his study that most patients with cluster headaches showed normal profiles on the MMPI. In the Kinder et al. studies (1991, 1992), only 35 out of 177 female and 18 out of 52 male patients had markedly elevated profiles. Males and females had slightly different profile types with the females having more profiles with scales **1** and **3** elevated and scale **2** lower (the conversion V), and males having higher **2** scales than the **1** and **3** scales.

In a review of the MMPI and its use with headache patients, Williams, Thompson, Haber, and Raczynski (1986) concluded that there are differences in MMPI indications of psychopathology among headache types, with post-traumatic and conversion headache patients having the highest elevations on MMPI scales, muscle contraction and combined headache groups next, and migraine and cluster types having the least distressed profiles. In general, male profiles showed more disturbance than females with scale **2** typically higher than scales **1** and **3**. In female patients scales **1** and **3** were higher than **2**.

Levor, Cohen, Naliboff, McArthur, and Heuser (1986) studied 33 patients who had severe migraine headaches. They suggested a model of the migraine sufferer as a person whose social functioning, emotional serenity, and physical energy are diminished over the three days preceding an attack. They concluded that the triggers for migraine in these patients are the routine stressors that would be unremarkable in a non-headache group. They developed a formula based on MMPI scales **1, 3, 9,** and **F** that in combination with daily hassles accounted for 43% of the variance in frequency of headaches. These MMPI scales were all sub-clinical, however. The fact that scale **9** correlated .59 frequency of headaches is an unusual and interesting finding.

Patients with tension-type primary headaches reported a higher level of daily hassles (microstress) than patients with migraine headaches. Tension-type headache sufferers also had higher MMPI scores on scales **1, 3,** and **7** but not on scale **2** than migraine patients (De-Benedittis & Lorenzetti, 1992). These authors suggested that headache patients see minor life events as more threatening because of the pain and see more stress around them than non-headache sufferers. These patients may be trapped in a circle of headache and stress that perpetuate each other.

Robinson, Geisser, Dieter, and Swerdlow (1991) found no relationship between five MMPI cluster groups of 485 headache sufferers and five diagnostic categories of headache sufferers that differed on measures of pain severity, sex, and age. These authors proposed that when MMPI profile types are developed from cluster analysis then these profiles will be an indication of the patient's response to pain and are likely to be the result of psychological status, pain coping style, and social support rather than headache-related personality style.

Kurlman, Hursey, and Mathew (1992), using the MMPI-2 to study three types of headache sufferers, found no relationship between MMPI-2 cluster type and diagnosis; however, they conclude that the MMPI-2 does offer additional information not available through medical diagnosis alone.

In summation, patients with migraine and cluster headaches tend to have MMPI profiles that fall within the normal range.

On the other hand, tension and post-traumatic stress patients are more likely to have elevations on the MMPI clinical scales. This suggests that the latter groups may have personality characteristics that cause them to react more strongly to hassles that they encounter.

### Headache Treatment

Can the MMPI predict those patients who profit from treatment? Can the MMPI predict who will remain in treatment? Tsushima, Stoddard, Tsushima, and Daly (1991) found that non-trauma headache patients with elevated MMPI scales **4, 6,** and **9** are more likely to drop out of treatment than patients with post-traumatic headache who also have elevations on these scales. These authors concluded that different characteristics underlie the drop-out behavior for different pain conditions.

A biofeedback treatment program significantly reduced the pain total index (PTI) and depression as measured by the MMPI in 20 tension headache patients (Grazzi, Frediani, Zappacosta, & Boiardi, 1988).

Werder, Sargent, and Coynes (1981) studied 51 patients diagnosed with migraine, muscle contraction, and combined headaches who were in a self-regulation training treatment program using biofeedback, progressive relaxation, autogenic phrases, and guided imagery. Those who were unsuccessful had higher scores on scales **1** and **3** with lower scores on scale **2** of the MMPI. The successful group had peak scores on scales **2** and **0**. These authors suggested that the elevation on scale **2** indicates more internally felt discomfort and thus higher motivation, and that scale **0** may indicate patients who are more able to use self-regulation treatment techniques.

## HEAD INJURY

Closed head injured patients are another medical group with which the MMPI has been frequently used. In one study,

Gass (1991) was concerned that, although the MMPI is widely used with brain-damaged patients, the test had items on the clinical scales that reflected actual physical and cognitive symptoms of brain lesions. Endorsement of these symptoms on the MMPI, therefore, could be totally unrelated to psychopathology or personality characteristics. Gass studied the MMPI-2 item endorsements of 75 closed-head-trauma patients. He found two factors: Factor 1 was Neurologic Complaints ("I find it hard to keep my mind on a task or job."), and Factor 2 was Psychiatric Complaints ("It is safer to trust nobody."). The 14 items on Factor 1 could lead to T-score increments on MMPI-2 scales **1** (13 points), **2** (12 points), **3** (10 points), **7** (12 points), and **8** (20 points). Gass made several recommendations for interpreting the MMPI-2 of head injured patients: check the Harris & Lingoes subscales for cognitive and somatic complaints; look for elevations on the MMPI-2 content scales **DEP, BIZ, SOD** and **FAM**; and score the test twice, once with and once without the Factor 1 items.

Ditty and Lynch (1987) compared a recovered group of closed head injury patients who were working, going to school, or in a sheltered workshop with a group of non-recovered closed head injured patients and found that MMPI scale **4** was significantly lower in the recovered group. The higher score on the **4** scale for the non-recovered patients was reflected in their significantly higher scores on the Adaptive Behavior Scale areas of Violent and Destructive, Antisocial, Rebelliousness, and Untrustworthiness. In line with the Gass study just cited, (Gass, 1991), both groups had **8** scale scores over 70, but there was no difference on this scale between groups.

## OTHER MEDICAL CONDITIONS

### Cancer

MMPI differences have been found between individuals who have cancer and those who do not, although it is not clear in most studies whether these MMPI differences reflect pre-illness personality characteristics that are connected in some way with the development of cancer or whether the MMPI scale elevations are the consequences of the illness.

Identical twins, one with hematologic malignancy and the other as a bone marrow donor, took the MMPI. The female patients scored higher on scales **1, 2, 3,** and **6** than their twins (Friedrich, Smith, Harrison, Colwell, Davis, & Fefer, 1987). There were no corresponding differences for men. Female patients were different from their nonpatient twin in their tendencies to repress their feelings, show less anger, and be more externally directed. Friedrich et al. (1987) recognized that the differences that they had found might be due to the emotional turmoil and physical distress of the illness but left open the possibility that people who develop a malignancy might be psychologically different from those who do not.

Additional support for the possibility of pre-illness personality differences in personality between those who develop cancer and those who do not is found in a study by Persky, Kempthorne-Rawson, and Shekelle (1987). The depression score of the MMPI was correlated with incidence of cancer in the first 10 years of a 20-year follow-up of 1,522 men. Repression was not associated with cancer risk. This study agrees with other findings that depression might promote the development and spread of malignant neoplasms.

Women who had a mastectomy for breast cancer had higher scores than those receiving chemotherapy on scales **1, 6, 7, 8,** and **9** of the MMPI. Compared with a group of healthy nurses, the mastectomy group had higher scores on scales **1, 2, 3, 5** and **8** (Kirkcaldy & Kobylinska, 1987).

Getting tests on a patient after a condition such as cancer has developed makes it difficult to sort out what is causing the test elevations. Cancer itself is likely to cause reactions that show up as elevated scale scores on the MMPI. On the other hand, the Persky et al. study (1987), cited above, was on a large sample tested before the cancer developed and is evidence that depression may be related in some way to its onset.

## Multiple Sclerosis

Two studies on multiple sclerosis (MS) patients' responses to the MMPI provide us with very similar results as to the effect of the illness on the elevation of particular scale scores. Mueller and Girace (1988) believed that the self-report of patients with multiple sclerosis reflects the physical consequences of the illness and not personality characteristics. They removed 22 items related to symptoms of multiple sclerosis, such as dizziness, fatigue, visual problems, incontinence, motor problems, paralysis, and tremor and gave the new MMPI to 26 MS patients and a control group. Profiles on the rescored MMPIs were significantly lower, and the MS group was significantly lower than the control group on scales **1** (14 points), **3** (9 points), and **8** (9 points). Scale **2** however, was basically unchanged. It still was in the moderately elevated range. The mean MS profile changed from an **8-1-3** code to a **2-4-9** code, which the authors point out is much more in line with dynamics involved in having MS. If a clinician decides to use the MMPI with the critical items deleted, the authors recommended adding some portion of the missing items based on the number of items that are answered on the revised form. For example, on scale **1** there are 33 items. The correction deletes 10 of them; thus, if the patient answers 15 items after the correction, the clinician would add 5 points (1/3 of 15) to correct for the missing items.

Meyerink, Reitan, and Selz (1988) found similar scales lower when they removed 30 items symptomatic of MS for 83 patients' MMPIs. They provided a table showing the elevation of MS profiles due to items that reflect their physical condition: scale **1** (15 T-score points), scale **2** (3 to 4 T-score points), scale **3** (3 to 6 T-score points), and scale **8** (5 to 7 T-score points). While they found less elevation on scales **3** and **8** and more on scale **2** than Mueller and Girace (1988) did, their results still point to the need for caution in interpreting some of these scale elevations on the profiles of MS patients. I would suggest taking 15 T-score points off scale **1** and taking 5 to 9 T-score points off scales **3** and **8** to get a more accurate picture of the psychological function of MS patients being evaluated.


**Stroke**


Gass and Lawhorn (1991) developed a scale composed of 21 items that have content related to speech problems, weakness, fatigue, hypesthesia, tremor, and visual disturbance as a correction for the MMPI profiles for 98 stroke patients. Pre-correction profiles had elevations on scales **1, 2, 3,** and **8**. Following correction, a significant drop occurred in all four scales with the greatest drop being on scales **1** and **3**. The depressive codetypes increased from 29% to 43% after the correction was used.


## CONCLUSIONS AND OBSERVATIONS

The following are observations and conclusions that summarize the findings of the many research studies that have been reviewed.

1. Elevations on MMPI scales **1, 2, 3,** and **8** may be a consequence of the patient's illness or pain and not an indication of neurosis or psychosis. It is usual for medical patients to have elevations on MMPI scales **1, 2,** and **3**.

2. Unusual sensory experiences caused by pain or illness can be major contributors to the elevation of scale **8**.

3. Medications for pain, such as demerol and codeine, can cause disorientation, which shows up as an elevated scale **8**.

4. If a patient in pain has no objective source for the pain and presents with a normal MMPI profile, further medical evaluation is indicated.

5. Persons who repress their anger are likely to report more pain and have higher scores on the neurotic triad than those patients who express it more openly.

6. The more chronic and intense the pain is, the more likely the patient is to have MMPI scale elevations over T-score of 70.

7. The more scales elevated over a T-score of 70 (65 on MMPI-2), the less improvement can be expected as a result of treatment.

8. Patients who have many scale elevations on their MMPI profile are likely to have a preexisting neurotic condition as measured by the NEO-PI or high Trait Anxiety as measured by the State-Trait Personality Inventory.

9. High scale **2** appears to be connected with both incidence of and mortality from cancer.

10. For certain conditions, such as multiple sclerosis and stroke, using correction scales made up of items that relate to symptoms caused by the condition gives a more accurate picture of patients' psychological condition.

11. For different medical conditions, there seem to be different MMPI predictors of treatment and prognosis. For example, headache patients with high scales **2** and **0** on the MMPI are better treatment risks than patients with scales **1** and **3** higher than scale **2**. For closed head injuries, patients with a low **4** scale are better treatment risks than patients with a high **4** scale.

# APPENDIX
## VALIDITY, CLINICAL, AND RESEARCH SCALES
### Intercorrelations for Two Normal Populations*

| | Validity | | | Clinical Scales | | | | | | | | | |
|---|---|---|---|---|---|---|---|---|---|---|---|---|---|
| | L | F | K | 1 | 2 | 3 | 4 | 5 | 6 | 7 | 8 | 9 | 0 |
| **L** | | −.10 | .38 | −.01 | .05 | .07 | −.20 | .11 | −.05 | −.29 | −.27 | −.22 | −.07 |
| L | | −.06 | .26 | .14 | .07 | .19 | −.03 | −.05 | .04 | .00 | .06 | −.17 | −.02 |
| **F** | −.10 | | −.25 | .36 | .31 | .06 | .40 | −.05 | .28 | .34 | .54 | .25 | .27 |
| F | −.06 | | −.44 | .24 | .45 | .11 | .34 | .08 | .29 | .43 | .60 | .23 | .36 |
| **K** | .38 | −.25 | | −.21 | −.15 | .13 | −.15 | .02 | −.00 | −.62 | −.54 | −.30 | −.45 |
| K | .26 | −.44 | | .14 | −.25 | .27 | .20 | .12 | −.02 | −.04 | −.02 | −.13 | −.51 |
| **1** | −.01 | .36 | .−21 | | .51 | .29 | .24 | .19 | .21 | .44 | .43 | .13 | .25 |
| 1 | .14 | .24 | .14 | | .45 | .66 | .33 | .14 | .24 | .47 | .47 | .06 | .12 |
| **2** | .05 | .31 | −.15 | .51 | | .28 | .39 | .23 | .33 | .62 | .52 | −.03 | .52 |
| 2 | .07 | .45 | −.25 | .45 | | .35 | .30 | .06 | .32 | .64 | .48 | −.14 | .57 |
| **3** | .07 | .06 | .13 | .29 | .28 | | .16 | .13 | .17 | .12 | .13 | .03 | −.00 |
| 3 | .19 | .11 | .27 | .66 | .35 | | .44 | .15 | .37 | .42 | .39 | .06 | −.08 |
| **4** | −.20 | .40 | −.15 | .24 | .39 | .16 | | −.05 | .43 | .47 | .56 | .42 | .13 |
| 4 | −.03 | .34 | .20 | .33 | .30 | .44 | | .17 | .31 | .44 | .53 | .33 | −.08 |
| **5** | .11 | −.05 | .02 | .19 | .23 | .13 | −.05 | | .07 | .16 | .08 | −.06 | .12 |
| 5 | −.05 | .08 | .12 | .14 | .06 | .15 | .17 | | .03 | .18 | .19 | .19 | −.18 |
| **6** | −.05 | .28 | −.00 | .21 | .33 | .17 | .43 | .07 | | .39 | .44 | .20 | .13 |
| 6 | .04 | .29 | −.02 | .24 | .32 | .37 | .31 | .03 | | .44 | .45 | .10 | .11 |
| **7** | −.29 | .34 | −.62 | .44 | .62 | .12 | .47 | .16 | .39 | | .83 | .32 | .61 |
| 7 | .00 | .43 | −.04 | .47 | .64 | .42 | .44 | .18 | .44 | | .72 | .16 | .36 |
| **8** | −.27 | .54 | −.54 | .43 | .52 | .13 | .56 | .08 | .44 | .83 | | .44 | .48 |
| 8 | −.06 | .60 | −.02 | .47 | .48 | .39 | .53 | .19 | .45 | .72 | | .33 | .21 |
| **9** | −.22 | .25 | −.30 | .13 | −.03 | .03 | .42 | −.06 | .20 | .32 | .44 | | −.14 |
| 9 | −.17 | .23 | −.13 | .06 | −.14 | .06 | .33 | .19 | .10 | .16 | .33 | | −.31 |
| **0** | −.07 | .27 | −.45 | .25 | .52 | −.00 | .13 | .12 | .13 | .61 | .48 | −.14 | |
| 0 | −.02 | .36 | −.51 | .12 | .57 | −.08 | −.08 | −.18 | .11 | .36 | .21 | −.31 | |
| **A** | −.30 | .39 | −.71 | .37 | .52 | .05 | .42 | .14 | .31 | .90 | .79 | .32 | .61 |
| A | −.15 | .58 | −.71 | .19 | .61 | .06 | .14 | .02 | .29 | .59 | .48 | .11 | .64 |
| **R** | .32 | −.00 | .40 | .13 | .39 | .18 | −.06 | .18 | .10 | −.07 | −.11 | −.42 | .30 |
| R | .30 | −.05 | .34 | .27 | .32 | .26 | .03 | .07 | .09 | .17 | .06 | −.41 | .29 |
| **Es** | −.10 | −.09 | .14 | −.25 | −.24 | −.09 | −.02 | −.39 | −.07 | −.25 | −.20 | .03 | −.19 |
| Es | −.07 | −.42 | .45 | −.37 | −.51 | −.24 | −.03 | −.01 | −.29 | −.49 | −.39 | .03 | −.51 |
| **Lb** | .19 | .06 | .36 | .21 | .28 | .26 | .20 | .10 | .20 | −.01 | .00 | .05 | .14 |
| Lb | .17 | −.01 | .29 | .32 | .18 | .39 | 17 | −.03 | .14 | .14 | .09 | −.04 | −.09 |
| **Ca** | −.25 | .39 | −.61 | .47 | .63 | .13 | .42 | .14 | .30 | .86 | .74 | .23 | .66 |
| Ca | −.13 | .53 | −.65 | .32 | .62 | .13 | .18 | .05 | .24 | .57 | .44 | .12 | .63 |
| **Dy** | −.06 | .16 | −.21 | .17 | .22 | .04 | .13 | .21 | .13 | .32 | .27 | .07 | .25 |
| Dy | −.16 | .49 | −.66 | .17 | .54 | .00 | .08 | .06 | .28 | .56 | .40 | .08 | .63 |
| **Do** | −.03 | −.10 | .15 | −.10 | −.13 | −.02 | −.10 | −.04 | −.06 | −.18 | −.19 | .01 | −.19 |
| Do | −.09 | −.38 | .44 | −.17 | −.46 | .00 | .00 | .12 | −.15 | −.44 | −.29 | .07 | −.57 |
| **Re** | .39 | −.25 | .52 | −.06 | −.01 | .11 | −.29 | .19 | −.07 | −.37 | −.38 | −.31 | −.12 |
| Re | .29 | −.41 | .51 | .07 | −.11 | .18 | −.14 | .05 | −.07 | −.12 | −.20 | −.32 | −.15 |
| **Pr** | −.16 | .34 | −.67 | .24 | .26 | −.07 | .27 | −.02 | −.00 | .59 | .59 | .31 | .47 |
| Pr | −.13 | .53 | −.69 | .09 | .35 | −.13 | .02 | −.00 | −.00 | .26 | .30 | .19 | .46 |
| **St** | −.05 | −.12 | .38 | −.16 | −.23 | .06 | −.00 | −.26 | .14 | −.38 | −.31 | .17 | −.53 |
| St | −.02 | −.23 | .41 | −.14 | −.33 | .03 | .08 | .14 | −.11 | −.29 | −.19 | .18 | −.61 |
| **Cn** | −.54 | .24 | −.42 | −.14 | .20 | .01 | .38 | .08 | .21 | .45 | .43 | .44 | .13 |
| Cn | −.40 | .36 | −.46 | −.01 | .25 | −.06 | .20 | .11 | .11 | .20 | .23 | .32 | .14 |

*Bold figures—847 graduate students from Ball State U. and non-student volunteers from the community. No known clinical patients included.

Light figures—50,000 medical outpatients at the Mayo Clinic. No psychiatric patients included (Swenson, Pearson, & Osborne, 1973).

# APPENDIX
## VALIDITY, CLINICAL, AND RESEARCH SCALES
### Intercorrelations for Two Normal Populations*

New Scales

| | A | R | Es | Lb | Ca | Dy | Do | Re | Pr | St | Cn |
|---|---|---|---|---|---|---|---|---|---|---|---|
| **L** | −.30 | .32 | −.10 | .19 | −.25 | −.06 | −.03 | .39 | −.16 | −.05 | −.54 |
| L | −.15 | .30 | −.07 | .17 | −.13 | −.16 | −.09 | .29 | −.13 | −.02 | −.40 |
| **F** | .39 | .00 | −.09 | .06 | .39 | .16 | −.10 | −.25 | .34 | −.12 | .24 |
| F | .58 | −.05 | −.42 | −.01 | .53 | .49 | −.38 | −.41 | .53 | −.23 | .36 |
| **K** | −.71 | .40 | .14 | .36 | −.61 | −.21 | .15 | .52 | −.67 | .38 | −.42 |
| K | −.71 | .34 | .45 | .29 | −.65 | −.66 | .44 | .51 | −.69 | .41 | −.46 |
| **1** | .37 | .13 | −.25 | .21 | .47 | .17 | −.10 | −.06 | .24 | −.16 | −.14 |
| 1 | .19 | .27 | −.37 | .32 | .32 | .17 | −.17 | .07 | .09 | −.14 | −.01 |
| **2** | .52 | .39 | −.24 | .28 | .63 | .22 | −.13 | −.01 | .26 | −.23 | .20 |
| 2 | .61 | .32 | −.51 | .18 | .62 | .54 | −.46 | −.11 | .35 | −.33 | .25 |
| **3** | .05 | .18 | −.09 | .26 | .13 | .04 | −.02 | .11 | −.07 | .06 | .01 |
| 3 | .06 | .26 | −.24 | .39 | .13 | .00 | −.00 | .18 | −.13 | .03 | −.06 |
| **4** | .42 | −.06 | −.02 | .20 | .42 | .13 | −.10 | −.29 | .27 | .00 | .38 |
| 4 | .14 | .03 | −.03 | .17 | .18 | .08 | −.00 | −.14 | .02 | .08 | .20 |
| **5** | .14 | .18 | −.39 | .10 | .14 | .21 | −.04 | .19 | −.02 | −.26 | .08 |
| 5 | .02 | .07 | −.01 | −.03 | .05 | .06 | .12 | .05 | .00 | .14 | .11 |
| **6** | .31 | .10 | −.07 | .20 | .30 | .13 | −.06 | −.07 | −.00 | .14 | .21 |
| 6 | .29 | .09 | −.29 | .14 | .24 | .28 | −.15 | −.07 | −.00 | −.11 | .11 |
| **7** | .90 | −.07 | −.25 | −.01 | .86 | .32 | −.18 | −.37 | .59 | −.38 | .45 |
| 7 | .59 | .17 | −.49 | .14 | .57 | .56 | −.44 | −.12 | .26 | −.29 | .20 |
| **8** | .79 | −.11 | −.20 | .00 | .74 | .27 | −.19 | −.38 | .59 | −.31 | .43 |
| 8 | .48 | .06 | −.39 | .09 | .44 | .40 | −.29 | −.20 | .30 | −.19 | .23 |
| **9** | .32 | −.42 | .03 | .05 | .23 | .07 | .01 | −.31 | .31 | .17 | .44 |
| 9 | .11 | −.41 | .03 | −.04 | .12 | .08 | .07 | −.32 | .19 | .18 | .32 |
| **0** | .61 | .30 | −.19 | −.14 | .66 | .25 | −.19 | −.12 | .47 | −.53 | .13 |
| 0 | .64 | .29 | −.51 | −.09 | .63 | .63 | −.57 | −.15 | .46 | −.61 | .14 |
| **A** | | −.16 | −.32 | −.12 | .85 | .31 | −.19 | −.39 | .64 | −.38 | .49 |
| A | | −.10 | −.68 | −.13 | .84 | .88 | −.60 | −.41 | .66 | −.49 | .45 |
| **R** | −.16 | | −.09 | .33 | .00 | .00 | −.07 | .37 | −.18 | −.15 | −.33 |
| R | −.10 | | −.12 | .31 | −.03 | −.08 | −.09 | .36 | −.16 | −.21 | −.37 |
| **Es** | −.32 | −.09 | | .00 | −.23 | −.57 | .56 | .00 | −.15 | .20 | .09 |
| Es | −.68 | −.12 | | .03 | −.61 | −.64 | .60 | .25 | −.53 | .54 | −.02 |
| **Lb** | −.12 | .33 | .00 | | −.05 | −.04 | .07 | .22 | −.17 | .29 | .08 |
| Lb | −.13 | .31 | .03 | | −.10 | −.20 | .10 | .12 | −.15 | .14 | −.04 |
| **Ca** | .85 | .00 | −.23 | −.05 | | .30 | −.19 | −.33 | .58 | −.40 | .41 |
| Ca | .84 | −.03 | −.61 | −.10 | | .80 | −.57 | −.38 | .61 | −.51 | .44 |
| **Dy** | .31 | .00 | −.57 | −.04 | .30 | | −.55 | −.09 | .20 | −.16 | .11 |
| Dy | .88 | −.08 | −.64 | −.20 | .80 | | −.63 | −.39 | .61 | −.53 | .35 |
| **Do** | −.19 | −.07 | .56 | .07 | −.19 | −.55 | | .08 | −.18 | .21 | −.14 |
| Do | −.60 | −.09 | .60 | .10 | −.57 | −.63 | | .33 | −.54 | .61 | −.02 |
| **Re** | −.39 | .37 | .00 | .22 | −.33 | −.09 | .08 | | −.49 | .20 | −.43 |
| Re | −.41 | .36 | .25 | .12 | −.38 | −.39 | .33 | | −.54 | .17 | −.47 |
| **Pr** | .64 | −.18 | −.15 | −.17 | .58 | .20 | −.18 | −.49 | | −.30 | .27 |
| Pr | .66 | −.16 | −.53 | −.15 | .61 | .61 | −.54 | −.54 | | −.48 | .30 |
| **St** | −.38 | −.15 | .20 | .29 | −.40 | −.16 | .21 | .20 | −.30 | | .20 |
| St | −.49 | −.21 | .54 | .14 | −.51 | −.53 | .61 | .17 | −.48 | | .06 |
| **Cn** | .49 | −.33 | .09 | .08 | .41 | .11 | −.14 | −.43 | .27 | .20 | |
| Cn | .45 | −.37 | −.02 | −.04 | .44 | .35 | −.02 | −.47 | .30 | .06 | |

*Bold figures—847 graduate students from Ball State U. and non-student volunteers from the community. No known clinical patients included.

Light figures—50,000 medical outpatients at the Mayo Clinic. No psychiatric patients included (Swenson, Pearson & Osborne, 1973).

*MMPI & MMPI-2*

# REFERENCES

Adams, J. (1971). Defensiveness on the MMPI as a function of the warmth of test introduction. *Journal of Consulting and Clinical Psychology, 36,* 444.

Akerlind, I., Hornquist, J.O., & Bjurulf, P. (1992). Psychological factors in the long-term prognosis of chronic low back pain patients. *Journal of Clinical Psychology, 48,* 596-605.

Alfano, A.M., Nerviano, V.J., Thurstin, A.H. (1987). An MMPI-based clinical typology for inpatient alcoholic males: Derivation and interpretations. *Journal of Clinical Psychology, 43,* 431-437.

Alfano, D.E., Neilson, P.M., Paniak, C.E., & Finlayson, M.A. (1992). The MMPI and closed head injury. *Clinical Neuropsychologist, 6,* 134-142.

Allen, J.P., Faden, V.B., Miller, A., & Rawlings, R.R. (1991). Personality correlates of chemically dependent patients scoring high versus low on the MacAndrew scale. *Psychological Assessment, 3,* 273-276.

Altman, H., Gynther, M., Warbin, R., & Sletten, I. (1972). A new empirical automated MMPI interpretive program: The **6-8/8-6** code type. *Journal of Clinical Psychology, 28,* 495-498.

Altman, H., Warbin, R., Sletten, I., & Gynther, M. (1973). Replicated empirical correlates of the MMPI **8-9/9-8** code type. *Journal of Personality Assessment, 37,* 369-371.

Anderson, T., & Leitner, L.M. (1991). The relationship between the Defense Mechanisms Inventory and reported symptomatology in college females. *Personality and Individual Differences, 12,* 967-969.

Anderson, T., & Meshot, C.M. (1992). The relationship of the Eating Disorders Inventory with the SCL-90 and MMPI in college women. *Personality and Individual Differences, 13*, 249-253.

Anderson, W. (1956). The MMPI: Low **Pa** scores. *Journal of Counseling Psychology, 3*, 226-228.

Anderson, W., & Bauer, B. (1985). Clients with MMPI high **D-Pd**: Therapy implications. *Journal of Clinical Psychology, 41*, 181-188.

Anderson, W., & Duckworth, J. (1969). New MMPI scales and the college student. *University of Missouri Testing and Counseling and Service Report, 23*(7).

Anderson, W., & Holcomb, W.R. (1983). Accused murderers: Five MMPI personality types. *Journal of Clinical Psychology, 39*, 761-768.

Anderson, W.P., & Kunce, J.T. (1984). Diagnostic implications of markedly elevated MMPI **Sc** scale scores for nonhospitalized clients. *Journal of Clinical Psychology, 40*, 925-930.

Anderson, W. Kunce, J., & Rich, R. (1979). Sex offenders: Three personality types. *Journal of Clinical Psychology, 35*, 671-676.

Appledorf, M., & Hunley, P. (1975). Application of MMPI alcoholism scales to older alcoholics and problem drinkers. *Journal of Studies on Alcohol, 36*, 645-653.

Archer, R.P. (1992). MMPI-A: *Assessing adolescent psychopathology.* Hillsdale, NJ: Lawrence Erlbaum.

Archer, R.P., & Klinefelter, D. (1992). Relationships between MMPI codetypes and **MAC** scale elevations in adolescent psychiatric samples. *Journal of Personality Assessment, 58*, 149-159.

Arnold, P. (1970). *Marriage counselee MMPI profile characteristics with objective signs that discriminate them from married couples in general.* Unpublished doctoral dissertation, University of Minnesota.

Balogh, D.W., Merritt, R.D., Lennington, L., Fine, M., & Wood, J. (1993). Variants of the MMPI **2-7-8** code type: Schizotypal correlates of high point **2**, **7**, or **8**. *Journal of Personality Assessment, 61*, 474-488.

Barefoot, J.C., Beckham, J.C., Peterson, B.L., & Haney, T.L. (1992). Measures of neuroticism and disease status in coronary angiography patients. *Journal of Consulting and Clinical Psychology, 60*, 127-132.

Barger, B., & Hall, E. (1964). Personality patterns and achievement in college. *Educational and Psychological Measurement, 24*, 339-346.

Barley, W.D., Sabo, T.W., & Greene, R.L. (1986). Minnesota Multiphasic Personality Inventory normal **K+** and other unelevated profiles. *Journal of Consulting and Clinical Psychology, 54*, 502-506.

Barron, F. (1953). An ego-strength scale which predicts response to psychotherapy. *Journal of Consulting Psychology, 17*, 327-333.

Barron, F. (1956). Ego strength and the management of aggression. In G.S. Welsh & W.G. Dahlstrom (Eds.), *Basic readings on the MMPI in psychology and medicine*. Minneapolis: University of Minnesota Press.

Barron, F. (1969). *Creative persons and creative process*. New York: Holt, Rinehart, and Wilson.

Bartol, C.R. (1991). Predictive validation of the MMPI for small-town police officers who fail. *Professional Psychology Research and Practice, 22*, 127-132.

Beck, N.C., McRae, C., Henrichs, T. F., Sneider, L., Horwitz, B., Rennier, G., Thomas, S., & Hedlund, J. (1989). Replicated item level factor structure of the MMPI: Racial and sexual differences. *Journal of Clinical Psychology, 45*, 553-560.

Ben-Porath, Y.S., Butcher, J.N., & Graham, J.R. (1991). Contribution of the MMPI-2 content scales to the differential diagnosis of schizophrenia and major depression. *Psychological Assessment: A Journal of Consulting and Clinical Psychology, 3,* 634-640.

Ben-Porath, Y.S., Hostetler, K., Butcher, J.N., & Graham, J.R. (1989). New subscales for the MMPI-2 Social Introversion (**Si**) scale. *Psychological Assessment, 1,* 169-174.

Bertelson, A.D., Marks, P.A., & May, G.D. (1982). MMPI and race: A controlled study. *Journal of Consulting and Clinical Psychology, 50,* 316-318.

Biaggio, M.K., & Godwin, W.H. (1987). Relation of depression to anger and hostility constructs. *Psychological Reports, 61,* 87-90.

Birtchnell, J., & Kennard, J. (1983). What does the MMPI Dependency scale really measure? *Journal of Clinical Psychology, 39,* 532-542.

Block, J., & Bailey, D. (1955, May). *Q-sort item analyses of a number of MMPI scales.* Officer Education Research Laboratory, Technical Memorandum, OERL-TM-55-7.

Bolla-Wilson, K., & Bleecker, M.L. (1989). Absence of depression in elderly adults. *Journal of Gerontology, 44,* 53-55.

Borden, J.W., Clum, G.A., & Broyles, S.E. (1989). MMPI correlates of panic disorder and panic attacks. *Journal of Anxiety Disorders, 3,* 107-115.

Bornstein, R.A., Rosenberger, P., Harkness-Kling, K., & Suga, L. (1989). Content bias of the MacAndrew's Alcoholism scale in seizure disorder patients. *Journal of Clinical Psychology, 45,* 339-341.

Bowler, R.M., Mergler, D., Rauch, S.S., & Bowler, R.P. (1992). Stability of psychological impairment: Two year follow-up of former microelectronics workers' affective and personality disturbance. *Women and Health, 18,* 27-48.

Bowler, R.M., Rauch, S.S., Becker, C.H., & Hawes, A. (1989). Three patterns of MMPI profiles following neurotoxin exposure. *American Journal of Forensic Psychology, 7,* 15-31.

Brennan, A.F., Barrett, C.L., & Garretson, H.D. (1986). The prediction of chronic pain outcome by psychological variables. *International Journal of Psychiatry in Medicine, 16,* 373-387.

Brown, R., Munjack, D., & McDowell, D. (1989). Agoraphobia with and without current panic attacks. *Psychological Reports, 64,* 503-506.

Burke, H.R. (1983). Markers for the MacAndrew and the Cavior Heroin Addiction MMPI scales. *Journal of Studies on Alcohol, 44,* 558-563.

Burke, H.R., & Marcus, R. (1977). MacAndrew MMPI alcoholism scale: Alcoholism and drug addictiveness. *Journal of Psychology, 96,* 141-148.

Butcher, J. (1965). Manifest aggression: MMPI correlates in normal boys. *Journal of Consulting Psychology, 29,* 446-454.

Butcher, J.N. (1990). *MMPI-2 in psychological treatment.* New York: Oxford University Press.

Butcher, J.N. (1993). Symptom underreporting: A new approach to an old problem. *MMPI-2 & MMPI-A News & Profiles: A Newsletter of the MMPI-2 Workshops and Symposia, 4,* 5.

Butcher, J.N., Braswell, L., & Raney, D. (1983). A cross-cultural comparison of American Indian, Black, and White inpatients on the MMPI and presenting symptoms. *Journal of Consulting and Clinical Psychology, 51,* 587-594.

Butcher, J.N., & Clark, L.A. (1979). Recent trends in cross-cultural MMPI research and application. In James N. Butcher (Ed.), *New developments in the use of the MMPI.* Minneapolis: University of Minnesota Press.

Butcher, J.N., Dahlstrom, W.G., Graham, J.R., Tellegen, A., & Kaemmer, B. (1989). *MMPI-2 (Minnesota Multiphasic Personality Inventory-2): Manual of administration and scoring.* Minneapolis: University of Minnesota Press.

Butcher, J.N., Graham, J.R., Williams, C.L., & Ben-Porath, Y.S. (1990). *Development and use of the MMPI-2 content scales.* Minneapolis: University of Minnesota Press.

Butcher, J.N., & Han, K. (1993). *Development of an MMPI-2 scale to assess the presentation of self in a superlative manner: The **S** scale.* Paper given at the 28th Annual Symposium of Recent Developments in the Use of the MMPI/MMPI-2/MMPI-A, St. Petersburg, FL.

Butcher, J.N., & Pancheri, P. (1976). *A handbook of cross-national MMPI research.* Minneapolis: University of Minnesota Press.

Butcher, J.N., & Pope, K.S. (1992). The research base, psychometric properties, and clinical uses of the MMPI-2 and MMPI-A. *Canadian Psychology, 33,* 61-78.

Butcher, J.N., & Williams, C.L. (1992). *Essentials of MMPI-2 and MMPI-A interpretation.* Minneapolis: University of Minnesota Press.

Caldwell, A. (1972). *Families of MMPI pattern types.* Paper presented at the Seventh Annual Symposium on the MMPI, Mexico City, Mexico.

Caldwell, A. (1974). *Characteristics of MMPI pattern types.* Paper presented at the Ninth Annual Symposium on the MMPI, Los Angeles.

Caldwell, A. (1977). *Families of MMPI code types.* Paper presented at the Twelfth Annual Symposium on the MMPI, Tampa, FL.

Caldwell, A. (1985). *MMPI clinical interpretation.* Paper presented at the Advanced Psychological Studies Institute, Los Angeles.

Caldwell, A.B. (1988). *MMPI supplemental scale manual.* Los Angeles: Caldwell Report.

Caldwell, A.B. (1991). MMPI-2 content scales: What you say is what you get. *Contemporary Psychology, 36*, 550-561.

Caldwell, A.B. (1992). *Comparing the MMPI & MMPI-2.* Symposium conducted at the meeting of the American Psychological Association, Washington, DC.

Caldwell, A.B. (1994). *MMPI-2 interpretation.* A workshop presented at the national meeting of the Society for Personality Assessment, Chicago.

Caldwell, A.B., & Chase, C. (1977). Diagnosis and treatment of personality factors in chronic low back pain. *Clinical Orthopaedic and Related Research, 129*, 141-149.

Canter, A., Day, C.W., Imboden, J.B., & Cluff, L.E. (1962). The influence of age and health status on the MMPI scores of a normal population. *Journal of Clinical Psychology, 18*, 71-73.

Carkhuff, R.R., Barnette, L., & McCall, J.N. (1965). *The counselor's handbook: Scale and profile interpretation of the MMPI.* Urbana, IL: R.W. Parkinson and Associates.

Carson, R. (1969). Interpretative manual to the MMPI. In J. Butcher (Ed.), *MMPI: Research developments and clinical applications* (pp. 279-296). New York: McGraw-hill.

Carson, R. (1972). *MMPI profile interpretation.* Paper read at the Seventh Annual Symposium on the MMPI, Mexico City, Mexico.

Carson, R. (1985). *The MMPI and DSM-III diagnosis.* Paper presented at the Advanced Psychological Studies Institute. Los Angeles, CA.

Cernovsky, Z. (1984). **Es** scale level and correlates of MMPI elevation: Alcohol abuse vs. MMPI scores in treated alcoholics. *Journal of Clinical Psychology, 40*, 1502-1509.

Cernovsky, Z.Z. (1985a). MacAndrew Alcoholism scale and repression: Detection of false negatives. *Psychological Reports, 57*, 191-194.

Cernovsky, Z.Z. (1985b). Relationship of the masculinity-femininity scale of the MMPI to intellectual functioning. *Psychological Reports, 57,* 435-438.

Chance, J.E. (1957). Some correlates of affective tone of early memories. *Journal of Consulting Psychology, 21,* 203-205.

Cheung, F.M., & Song, W.Z. (1989). A review of the clinical applications of the Chinese MMPI. *Psychological Assessment, 1,* 230-237.

Chojnacki, J.T., & Walsh, W.B. (1992). The consistency of scores and configural patterns between the MMPI and MMPI-2. *Journal of Personality Assessment, 59,* 276-289.

Clopton, J.R., Weiner, R.H., & Davis, H.G. (1980). Use of the MMPI in identification of alcoholic psychiatric patients. *Journal of Consulting and Clinical Psychology, 48,* 416-417.

Cofer, C.N., Chance, J., & Judson, A.J. (1949). A study of malingering on the MMPI. *Journal of Psychology, 27,* 491-499.

Cole, D.W. (1991). *The MMPI-2 and Megargee's classification system.* Paper presented at the annual convention of the American Psychological Association, San Francisco.

Colligan, R.C., & Offord, K.P. (1987). The MacAndrew Alcoholism scale applied to a contemporary normative sample. *Journal of Clinical Psychology, 43,* 291-293.

Colligan, R.C., & Offord K.P. (1988). Changes in MMPI factor scores: Norms for the Welsh **A** and **R** dimensions from a contemporary normal sample. *Journal of Clinical Psychology, 44,* 142-148.

Colligan, R.C., Osborne, D., Swenson, W.M., & Offord, K.P. (1984). The MMPI: Development of contemporary norms. *Journal of Clinical Psychology, 40,* 100-107.

Colligan, R.C., Osborne, D., Swenson, W.M., & Offord, K.P. (1989). *The MMPI: A contemporary normative study of adults* (2nd ed.). Odessa, FL: Psychological Assessment Resources.

Conley, J. (1981). An MMPI typology of male alcoholics: Admission, discharge, and outcome comparisons. *Journal of Personality Assessment, 45,* 33-39.

Coons, P.M., Bowman, E.S., & Milstein, V. (1988). Multiple personality disorder: A clinical investigation of 50 cases. *Journal of Nervous and Mental Disease, 176,* 519-527.

Costa, P.T., & McCrae, R.R. (1985). *The NEO Personality Inventory Manual.* Odessa, FL: Psychological Assessment Resources.

Costello, R. (1977). Construction and cross-validation of an MMPI Black-White Scale. *Journal of Personality Assessment, 41,* 514-519.

Costello, R.M., Hulsley, T.L., Schoenfeld, L.S., & Ramamurthy, S. (1987). P-A-I-N: A four-cluster MMPI typology for chronic pain. *Pain, 30,* 199-209.

Costello, R.M., Schoenfeld, L.S., Ramamurthy, S., & Hobbs-Hardee, B. (1989). *Journal of Psychosomatic Research, 33,* 315-421.

Costello, R., & Tiffany, D. (1972). Methodological issues and racial (Black-white) comparisons on the MMPI. *Journal of Consulting and Clinical Psychology, 38,* 161-168.

Cottle, W.C. (1953). *The MMPI: A review.* Lawrence, KS: University of Kansas Press.

Craig, R. (1984a). A comparison of MMPI profiles of heroin addicts based on multiple methods of classification. *Journal of Personality Assessment, 48,* 115-129.

Craig, R. (1984b). MMPI substance abuse scales on drug addicts with and without concurrent alcoholism. *Journal of Personality Assessment, 48,* 495-499.

Craig, R.J., & Olson, R.E. (1990). MMPI characteristics of drug abusers with and without histories of suicide attempts. *Journal of Personality Assessment, 55,* 717-728.

Crumpton, E., Cantor, J.M., & Batiste, C. (1960). A factor analytic study of Barron's ego-strength scale. *Journal of Clinical Psychology, 16*, 283-291.

Cuadra, C.A. (1953). *A psychometric investigation of control factors in psychological adjustment*. Unpublished doctoral dissertation, University of California.

Curtiss, G., Kinder, B.N., Kalichman, S., & Spana, R. (1989). Affective differences among subgroups of chronic pain patients. *Anxiety Research, 1*, 65-73.

Dahlstrom, L.E. (1986). MMPI findings on other American minority groups. In W.G. Dahlstrom, D. Lachar, & L.E. Dahlstrom (Eds.), *MMPI patterns of American minorities* (pp. 50-86). Minneapolis: University of Minnesota Press.

Dahlstrom, W.G. (1992). Comparability of two-point high-point code patterns from original MMPI norms to MMPI-2 norms for the restandardization sample. *Journal of Personality Assessment, 59*, 153-164.

Dahlstrom, W.G., Lachar, D., & Dahlstrom, L.E. (Eds.). (1986). *MMPI patterns of American minorities*. Minneapolis: University of Minnesota Press.

Dahlstrom, W.G., & Welsh, G.S. (1960). *An MMPI handbook: A guide to use in clinical practice and research*. Minneapolis: University of Minnesota Press.

Dahlstrom, W.G., Welsh, G., & Dahlstrom, L. (1972). *An MMPI handbook: Volume I, clinical interpretation*. Minneapolis: University of Minnesota Press.

Dana, R.H., & Whatley, P.R. (1991). When does a difference make a difference? MMPI scores and African-Americans. *Journal of Clinical Psychology, 47*, 400-406.

Daniels, E.E., & Hunter, W.A. (1949). MMPI personality patterns for various occupations. *Journal of Applied Psychology, 33*, 559-565.

Davis, K. (1971). *The actuarial development of a female 4-3 MMPI profile.* Unpublished doctoral dissertation, St. Louis University.

Davis, K., & Sines, J. (1971). An antisocial behavioral pattern associated with a specific MMPI profile. *Journal of Consulting and Clinical Psychology, 36,* 229-234.

De-Benedittis, G., & Lorenzetti, A. (1992). Minor stressful life events (daily hassles) in chronic primary headache: Relationship with MMPI personality patterns. *Headache, 32,* 330-334.

De Groot, G.W., & Adamson, J.D. (1973). Responses of psychiatric inpatients to the MacAndrew alcoholism scale. *Quarterly Journal of Studies on Alcohol, 34,* 1133-1139.

Denier, C.A., Thevos, A.K., Latham, P.K., & Randall, C.L. (1991). Psychosocial and psychopathology differences in hospitalized male and female cocaine abusers: A retrospective chart review. *Addictive Behaviors, 16,* 489-496.

DiFrancesca, K.R., & Meloy, J.R. (1989). A comparative clinical investigation of the "How" and "Charlie" MMPI subtypes. *Journal of Personality Assessment, 53,* 396-403.

Ditty, J.A., & Lynch, K.P. (1987). Prediction of recovery for closed-head-injured adults: An evaluation of the MMPI, the Adaptive Behavior Scale, and a "Quality of Life" rating scale. *Journal of Clinical Psychology, 43,* 699-707.

Doob, L. (1960). *Becoming more civilized: A psychological exploration.* New Haven, CT: Yale University Press.

Drake, L.E. (1962). MMPI patterns predictive of achievement. *Journal of Counseling Psychology, 9,* 164-167.

Drake, L.E., & Oetting, E.R. (1959). *An MMPI codebook for counselors.* Minneapolis: University of Minnesota Press.

Duckworth, J. (1983). *The **MAC** scale: A report on three studies.* Paper presented to the Eighteenth Annual Symposium on the MMPI, Tampa, FL.

Duckworth, J.C. (1975). *MMPI interpretation manual for counselors and clinicians* (2nd ed.). Muncie, IN: Accelerated Development.

Duckworth, J.C., & Anderson, W.P. (1986). *MMPI interpretation manual for counselors and clinicians* (3rd ed.). Muncie, IN: Accelerated Development.

Edwards, D.W., Morrison, T.L., & Weissman, H.N. (1993). The MMPI and MMPI-2 in an outpatient sample: Comparisons of code types, validity scales, and clinical scales. *Journal of Personality Assessment, 61*, 1-18.

Elion, V.H., & Megargee, E.I. (1975). Validity of the MMPI **Pd** scale among Black males. *Journal of Consulting and Clinical Psychology, 43*, 166-172.

Elliott, T.R., Anderson, W.P., & Adams, N.A. (1987). MMPI indicators of long-tern therapy in a college counseling center. *Psychological Reports, 60*, 79-84.

English, H.B., & English, A.C. (1959). *A comprehensive dictionary of psychological and psychoanalytical terms.* New York: Longmans, Green and Co.

English, R.W. (1971). Correlates of stigma towards physically disabled persons. *Rehabilitation Research and Practice Review, 2*, 1-17.

Erickson, W.D., Luxenberg, M.G., Walbek, N.H., & Seely, R.K. (1987). Frequency of MMPI two-point code types among sex offenders. *Journal of Consulting and Clinical Psychology, 55*, 566-570.

Evans R.G. (1984). The test-retest index and high **F** MMPI profiles. *Journal of Clinical Psychology, 40*, 516-518.

Evans, R.G., & Dinning, W.D. (1983). Response consistency among high **F** scale scorers on the MMPI. *Journal of Clinical Psychology, 39*, 246-248.

Fernandez, E., & Turk, D.C. (1992). Sensory and affective components of pain: Separation and synthesis. *Psychological Bulletin, 112,* 205-217.

Finn, S.E., & Tonsager, M.E. (1992). Therapeutic effects of providing MMPI-2 test feedback to college students awaiting therapy. *Psychological Assessment, 4,* 278-287.

Finney, J.C., Smith, D.F., Skeeters, D.E., & Auvenshire, C.D. (1971). MMPI alcoholism scale: Factor structure and content analysis. *Quarterly Journal of Studies on Alcohol, 32,* 1055-1060.

Fowler, R.D., & Athey, E.B. (1971). A cross-validation of Gilberstadt and Duker's **1-2-3-4** profile type. *Journal of Clinical Psychology, 27,* 238-240.

Fowler, R.D., & Coyle, F.A. (1969). Collegiate normative data on MMPI content scales. *Journal of Clinical Psychology, 25,* 62-63.

Fowler, R.D., Teal, S., & Coyle, F.A. (1967). The measurement of alcoholic response to treatment by Barron's ego strength scale. *Journal of Psychology, 67,* 65-68.

Franz, C., Paul, R., Bautz, M., Choroba, B., & Hildebrandt, J. (1986). Psychosomatic aspects of chronic pain: A new way of description based on MMPI item analysis. *Pain, 26,* 33-43.

Friedman, A.F., Webb, J.T., & Lewak, R. (1989). *Psychological assessment with the MMPI.* Hillsdale, NJ: Lawrence Erlbaum Associates.

Friedrich, W., & Loftsgard, S. (1978). A comparison of the MacAndrew alcoholism scale and the Michigan Alcohol Screening Test in a sample of problem drinkers. *Journal of Studies on Alcohol, 39,* 1940-1944.

Friedrich, W.N., Smith, C.K., Harrison, S.D., Colwell, K.A., Davis, A.K., & Fefer, A. (1987). MMPI study of identical twins: Cancer patients and bone marrow donors. *Psychological Reports, 61,* 127-130.

Galluci, N.T., Kay, D.C., & Thornby, J.I. (1989). The sensitivity of 11 substance abuse scales from the MMPI to change in clinical status. *Psychology of Addictive Behaviors, 3*, 29-33.

Gass, C.S. (1991). MMPI-2 interpretation and closed head injury: A correction factor. *Psychological Assessment, 3*, 27-31.

Gass, C.S. (1992). MMPI-2 interpretation of patients with cerebrovascular disease: A correction factor. *Archives of Clinical Neuropsychology, 7*, 17-27.

Gass, C.S., & Lawhorn, L. (1991). Psychological adjustment following stroke: An MMPI study. *Psychological Assessment, 3*, 628-633.

Gentry, M.M., & Meyer, C.T. (1990). *A validation study of the MMPI-2 sex role scales: An analysis of the **GM**, **GF**, and **Mf** scales.* Paper presented at the meeting of the American Psychological Association, Boston.

Getter, H., & Sunderland, D.M. (1962). The Barron ego strength scale and psychotherapy outcome. *Journal of Consulting Psychology, 26*, 195.

Gilberstadt, H. & Duker, J. (1965). *A handbook for clinical and actuarial MMPI interpretation.* Philadelphia: W.B. Saunders.

Gilliland, A.R., & Colgin, R. (1951). Norms, reliability, and forms of the MMPI. *Journal of Consulting Psychology, 15*, 435-438.

Glosz, J.T., & Grant, I. (1981). Prognostic validity of the MMPI. *Journal of Clinical Psychology, 37*, 147-151.

Goldwater, L., & Duffy, J.F. (1990). Use of the MMPI to uncover histories of childhood abuse in adult female psychiatric patients. *Journal of Clinical Psychology, 46*, 392-398.

Good, P., & Brantner, J. (1961). *The physician's guide to the MMPI.* Minneapolis: University of Minnesota Press.

Good, P., & Brantner, J. (1974). *A practical guide to the MMPI.* Minneapolis: University of Minnesota Press.

Goodstein, L.D. (1954). Regional differences in MMPI responses among male college students. *Journal of Consulting Psychology, 18*, 437-441.

Gottesman, I.I., & Prescott, C.A. (1989). Abuses of the MacAndrew alcoholism scale: A critical review. *Clinical Psychology Review, 9*, 223-242.

Gough, H.G. (1948). A new dimension of status: II. Relationship of the **St** scale to other variables. *American Sociological Review, 13*, 534-537.

Gough, H.G. (1949). A short social status inventory. *Journal of Educational Psychology, 40*, 52-56.

Gough, H.G. (1951). Studies of social intolerance: III. Relationship of the **Pr** scale to other variables. *Journal of Social Psychology, 33*, 257-262.

Gough, H.G. (1952). A personality scale for social responsibility. *Journal of Abnormal and Social Psychology, 47*, 73-80.

Gough, H.G. (1954). Some common misconceptions about neuroticism. *Journal of Consulting Psychology, 18*, 408-413.

Gough, H.G., McClosky, H., & Meehl, P.E. (1951). A personality scale for dominance. *Journal of Abnormal and Social Psychology, 46*, 360-366.

Graham, J. (1977). *The MMPI: A practical guide.* New York: Oxford University Press.

Graham, J.R. (1978). Review of MMPI special scales. In P. McReynolds (Ed.), *Advances in psychological assessment* (Vol. IV, pp. 11-55). San Francisco: Jossey-Bass.

Graham, J.R. (1987). *The MMPI: A practical guide* (2nd ed.). New York: Oxford Press.

Graham, J.R. (1990). Congruence between MMPI and MMPI-2 codetypes. *MMPI-2 News and Profiles, 1*(12), 1-2.

Graham, J.R. (1991). Comments on Duckworth's review of the Minnesota Multiphasic Personality Inventory-2. *Journal of Counseling and Development, 69,* 570-571.

Graham, J.R., & Mayo, M.A. (1985, March). *A comparison of MMPI strategies for identifying black and white male alcoholics.* Paper presented at the 20th Annual Symposium on Recent Developments in the Use of the MMPI, Honolulu.

Graham, J.R., & McCord, G. (1982, March). *Correlates of "normal range" MMPI scores for nonclinical subjects.* Paper presented at the 17th Annual Symposium on Recent Developments in the Use of the MMPI, Tampa, FL.

Graham, J., Schroeder, H., & Lilly, R. (1971). Factor analysis of items on the Social Introversion and Masculinity-femininity scales of the MMPI. *Journal of Clinical Psychology, 27,* 367-370.

Graham, J.R., & Strenger, V.E. (1988). MMPI characteristics of alcoholics: A review. *Journal of Consulting and Clinical Psychology, 56,* 197-205.

Gravitz, M. (1970). Validity implications of normal adult MMPI **L** scale endorsement. *Journal of Clinical Psychology, 26,* 497-499.

Grazzi, L., Frediani, F., Zappacosta, B., & Boiardi, A. (1988). Psychological assessment in tension headache before and after biofeedback treatment. *Headache, 28,* 337-338.

Greene, R.L. (1978). An empirically derived MMPI carelessness scale. *Journal of Clinical Psychology, 34,* 407-410.

Greene, R. (1980). *The MMPI: An interpretive manual.* New York: Grune & Stratton.

Greene, R.L. (1987). Ethnicity and MMPI performance: A review. *Journal of Consulting and Clinical Psychology, 55,* 497-512.

Greene, R.L. (1991). *The MMPI-2/MMPI: An interpretive manual.* Boston: Allyn and Bacon.

Greene, R.L., & Garvin, R.D. (1988). Substance abuse/dependence. In R.L. Greene (Ed.), *The MMPI: Use in specific populations* (pp. 159-197). San Antonio: Grune & Stratton.

Greene, R.L., Arredondo, R., & Davis, H.G. (1990). *The comparability between the MacAndrew Alcoholism Scale-Revised (MMPI-2) and the MacAndrew Alcoholism Scale (MMPI)*. Paper presented at the annual meeting of the American Psychological Association, Boston.

Greene, R.L., Week, N.C., Butcher, J.N., Arredondo, R., & Davis, H.G. (1992). A cross-validation of MMPI-2 substance abuse scales. *Journal of Personality Assessment, 58*, 405-410.

Grier, W.H., & Cobbs, P.M. (1968). *Black rage*. New York: Basic Books.

Grow, R., McVaugh, W., & Eno, T.D. (1980). Faking and the MMPI. *Journal of Clinical Psychology, 36*, 910-917.

Guck, T.P., Meilman, P.W., Skultety, F.M., & Poloni, L.D. (1988). Pain-patient Minnesota Multiphasic Personality Inventory (MMPI) subgroups: Evaluation of long-term treatment outcome. *Journal of Behavioral Medicine, 11*, 159-169.

Gulas, I. (1973). MMPI 2-pt. codes for a "normal" college male population: A replication study. *Journal of Psychology, 84*, 319-322.

Guthrie, G.M. (1949). *A study of the personality characteristics associated with the disorders encountered by an internist*. Unpublished doctoral dissertation, University of Minnesota.

Guthrie, G.M. (1952). Common characteristics associated with frequent MMPI profile types. *Journal of Clinical Psychology, 8*, 141-145.

Gynther, M. (1961). The clinical utility of "invalid" MMPI **F** scores. *Journal of Consulting Psychology, 25*, 540-542.

Gynther, M.D. (1972). White norms and black MMPI's: A prescription for discrimination? *Psychological Bulletin, 78,* 386-402.

Gynther, M.D. (1989). MMPI comparisons of Blacks and Whites: A review and commentary. *Journal of Clinical Psychology, 45,* 878-883.

Gynther, M., Altman, H., & Sletten, I. (1973). Replicated correlates of MMPI two-point code types: The Missouri actuarial system. *Journal of Clinical Psychology, 29,* 263-289.

Gynther, M., Altman, H., & Warbin, R. (1972). A new empirical automated MMPI interpretative program: The **2-4/4-2** code type. *Journal of Clinical Psychology, 28,* 598-601.

Gynther, M., Altman, H., & Warbin, R. (1973a). Behavioral correlates for the Minnesota Multiphasic Personality Inventory **4-9/9-4**. code types: A case of the emperor's new clothes? *Journal of Consulting Psychology, 40,* 259-263.

Gynther, M., Altman, H., & Warbin, R. (1973b). A new actuarial-empirical automated MMPI interpretive program: The **4-3/3-4** code type. *Journal of Clinical Psychology, 29,* 229-231.

Gynther, M., Altman, H., & Warbin, R. (1973c). A new empirical automated MMPI interpretive program: The **2-7/7-2** code type. *Journal of Clinical Psychology, 29,* 58-59.

Gynther, M., Altman, H., & Warbin, R. (1973d). A new empirical automated MMPI interpretive program: The **6-9/9-6** code type. *Journal of Clinical Psychology, 29,* 60-61.

Gynther, M., Altman, H., Warbin, R., & Sletten, I. (1972). A new actuarial system for MMPI interpretation: Rationale and methodology. *Journal of Clinical Psychology, 28,* 173-179.

Gynther, M., Altman, H., Warbin, R., & Sletten, I. (1973). A new empirical automated MMPI interpretative program: The **1-2/2-1** code type. *Journal of Clinical Psychology, 29,* 54-57.

Gynther, M., Burkhart, B.R., & Hovanitz, C. (1979). Do face-valid items have more predictive validity than subtle items? The case of the **Pd** scale. *Journal of Consulting and Clinical Psychology, 47*, 295-300.

Gynther, M.D., Fowler, R.D., & Erdberg, P. (1971). False positives galore: The application of standard MMPI criteria to a rural, isolated, Negro sample. *Journal of Clinical Psychology, 27*, 234-237.

Gynther, M.D., & Green, S.B. (1980). Accuracy may make a difference, but does a difference make for accuracy? A response to Pritchard and Rosenblatt. *Journal of Consulting and Clinical Psychology, 48*, 268-272.

Gynther, M., & Shimkunas, A. (1965). Age, intelligence, and MMPI **F** scores. *Journal of Consulting Psychology, 29*, 383-388.

Haley, W.E., Turner, J.A., & Romano, J.M. (1985). Depression in chronic pain patients: Relation to pain activity and sex differences. *Pain, 23*, 337-343.

Hall, G.C.N. (1989). WAIS-R and MMPI profiles of men who have sexually assaulted children: Evidence of limited utility. *Journal of Personality Assessment, 53*, 404-412.

Hall, G.C.N., Graham, J., & Shepherd, J.B. (1991). Three methods of developing MMPI taxonomies of sexual offenders. *Journal of Personality Assessment, 56*, 2-13.

Hall, G.C.N., Maiuro, R.D., Vitaliano, P.P., & Proctor, W.C. (1986). The utility of the MMPI with men who have sexually assaulted children. *Journal of Consulting and Clinical Psychology, 54*, 493-496.

Hall, G.C.N., Shepherd, J.B., & Mudrak, P. (1992). MMPI taxonomies of child sexual and nonsexual offenders: A cross-validation and extension. *Journal of Personality Assessment, 58*, 127-137.

Hanvik, L.J. (1951). MMPI profiles in patients with low-back pain. *Journal of Consulting Psychology, 15*, 350-353.

Harmon, M. (1980). The Barron Ego Strength scale: A study of personality correlates among normals. *Journal of Clinical Psychology, 36,* 433-436.

Harris, R.E., & Lingoes, J.C. (1955). *Subscales for the MMPI: An aid to profile interpretation.* Unpublished manuscript, University of California.

Hathaway, S.R., & Monachesi, E.D. (1958). *MMPI studies of ninth-grade students in Minnesota schools.* Unpublished materials.

Henrichs, T.F. (1987). MMPI profiles of chronic pain patients: Some methodological considerations that concern clusters and descriptors. *Journal of Clinical Psychology, 43,* 650-660.

Heppner, P., & Anderson, W. (1985). The relationship between problem solving, self-appraisal, and psychological adjustment. *Cognitive Therapy & Research, 9,* 415-427.

Hibbs, B.J., Kobas, J.C., & Gonzalez, J. (1979). Effects of ethnicity, sex, and age on MMPI profiles. *Psychological Reports, 45,* 591-597.

Hjemboe, S., & Butcher, J.N. (1991). Couples in marital distress: A study of personality factors as measured by the MMPI-2. *Journal of Personality Assessment, 57,* 216-237.

Hoffman, H., Loper, R., & Kammeier, M. (1974). Identifying future alcoholics with MMPI alcoholism scales. *Quarterly Journal of Studies on Alcohol, 35,* 490-498.

Hokanson, J.E., & Calden, G. (1960). Negro-white differences on the MMPI. *Journal of Clinical Psychology, 16,* 32-33.

Holcomb, W.R., Adams, N.A., & Ponder, H.M. (1984). Are separate Black and White norms needed?: An IQ-controlled comparison of accused murderers. *Journal of Clinical Psychology, 40,* 189-193.

Holland, T. (1979). Ethnic group differences in MMPI profile pattern and factorial structure among adult offenders. *Journal of Personality Assessment, 43*, 72-77.

Hovanitz, C., & Gynther, M.D. (1980). The prediction of impulsive behavior: Comparative validities of obvious vs. subtle MMPI hypomania **(Ma)** items. *Journal of Clinical Psychology, 36*, 422-427.

Hovanitz, C. Gynther, M.G., & Marks, P. (1983). The prediction of paranoid behavior: Comparative validities of obvious vs. subtle MMPI paranoid **(Pa)** items. *Journal of Clinical Psychology, 39*, 407-411.

Hovey, H., & Lewis, E. (1967). Semi-automatic interpretation of the MMPI. *Journal of Clinical Psychology, 23*, 123-124.

Huber, N., & Danahy, S. (1975). Use of the MMPI in predicting completion and evaluating changes in a long-term alcoholism treatment program. *Journal of Studies on Alcohol, 36*, 1230-1237.

Huesmann, L.R., Lefkowitz, M.M., & Eron, L.D. (1978). Sum of MMPI scales **F**, **4**, and **9** as a measure of aggression. *Journal of Consulting and Clinical Psychology, 46*, 1071-1078.

Hutton, H.E., Miner, M.H., Blades, J.R., & Langfeldt, V.C. (1992). Psychiatric inpatient MMPI profiles: An exploration for potential racial bias. *Journal of Counseling Psychology, 37*, 213-215.

Hutton, H.E., Miner, M.H., & Langfeldt, V.C. (1993). The utility of the Megargee-Bohn typology in a forensic psychiatric hospital. *Journal of Personality Assessment, 60*, 572-587.

Hyer, L., Fallon, J.H., Harrison, W.R., & Boudewyns, P.A. (1987). MMPI overreporting by Vietnam combat veterans. *Journal of Clinical Psychology, 43*, 79-83.

Hyer, L., Woods, M., Harrison, W.R., Boudewyns, P., & O'Leary, W.C. (1989). MMPI **F-K** index among hospitalized Vietnam veterans. *Journal of Clinical Psychology, 45*, 250-254.

Jensen, A.R. (1957). Authoritarian attitudes and personality maladjustment. *Journal of Abnormal and Social Psychology, 54,* 303-311.

Johnson, M.E., & Brems, C. (1990). Psychiatric inpatient MMPI profiles: An exploration for potential racial bias. *Journal of Counseling Psychology, 37,* 213-215.

Jones, E.E. (1978). Black-White personality differences: Another look. *Journal of Personality Assessment, 42,* 244-252.

Jones, E.E., & Thorne, A. (1987). Rediscovery of the subject: Intercultural approaches to clinical assessment. *Journal of Consulting and Clinical Psychology, 55,* 488-495.

Kalichman, S.C. (1988). Empirically derived MMPI profile subgroups of incarcerated homicide offenders. *Journal of Clinical Psychology, 44,* 733-738.

Keane, T.M., Malloy, P.F., & Fairbank, J.A. (1984). Empirical development of an MMPI subscale for the assessment of combat-related posttraumatic stress disorder. *Journal of Consulting and Clinical Psychology, 52,* 888-891.

Keiller, S.W., & Graham, J.R. (1993). The meaning of low scores on MMPI-2 clinical scales of normal subjects. *Journal of Personality Assessment, 61,* 211-223.

Keller, L.S., & Butcher, J.N. (1991). *Assessment of chronic pain patients with the MMPI-2.* Minneapolis: University of Minnesota Press.

Kelley, C.K., & King, G.D. (1979a). Behavioral correlates of infrequent two-point MMPI code types at a university mental health center. *Journal of Clinical Psychology, 35,* 576-585.

Kelley, C.K., & King, G.D. (1979b). Behavioral correlates of the **2-7-8** MMPI profile type in students at a university mental health center. *Journal of Consulting and Clinical Psychology, 47,* 679-685.

Kelley, C.K., & King, G.D. (1980). Two and three point classification of MMPI profiles in which scales **2,7**, and **8** are the highest elevations. *Journal of Personality Assessment, 44*, 25-33.

Kennedy, W.A. (1962). MMPI profiles of gifted adolescents. *Journal of clinical Psychology 18*, 148-149.

Kennedy, B.P., & McPeake, J.D. (1987). MacAndrew Alcoholism scale and repression: Detection of false negatives, a failure to replicate. *Psychological Reports, 60*, 839-842.

Kinder, B.N., Curtiss, G., & Kalichman, S. (1986). Anxiety and anger as predictors of MMPI elevations in chronic pain patients. *Journal of Personality Assessment, 50*, 651-661.

Kinder, B.N., Curtiss, G., & Kalichman, S. (1991). Cluster analyses of headache-patient MMPI scores: A cross-validation. *Psychological Assessment: A Journal of Consulting and Clinical Psychology, 3*, 226-231.

Kinder, B.N., Curtiss, G., & Kalichman, S. (1992). Affective differences among empirically derived subgroups of headache patients. *Journal of Personality Assessment, 58*, 516-524.

King, G.D., & Kelley, C.K. (1977a). Behavioral correlates for **spike 4**, **spike 9**, and **4-9/9-4** MMPI profiles in students at a university mental health clinic. *Journal of Clinical Psychology, 33*, 718-724.

King, G.D., & Kelley, C.K. (1977b). MMPI behavioral correlates of **spike 5** and two-point code types with scale **5** as one elevation. *Journal of Clinical Psychology, 33*, 180-185.

Kirkcaldy, B.D., & Kobylinska, E. (1987). Psychological characteristics of breast cancer patients. *Psychotherapy and Psychosomatics, 48*, 32-43.

Klein, S., & Cross, H. (1984). Correlates of the MMPI **Lb** scale in a college population. *Journal of Clinical Psychology, 40*, 185-188.

Kleinke, C.L. (1991). How chronic pain patients cope with depression: Relation to treatment outcome in a multidisciplinary pain clinic. *Rehabilitation Psychology, 36*, 207-218.

Kleinke, C.L., & Spangler, A.S. (1988). Predicting treatment outcome of chronic back pain patients in a multidisciplinary pain clinic: Methodological issues and treatment implications. *Pain, 33*, 41-48.

Kleinmuntz, B. (1960). An extension of the construct validity of the ego-strength scale. *Journal of Consulting Psychology, 24*, 463-464.

Kleinmuntz, B. (1961). The college maladjustment scale (**MT**): Norms and predictive validity. *Educational and Psychological Measurement, 20*, 381-386.

Kolotkin, R.L., Revis, E.S., Kirkley, B.G., & Janick, L. (1987). Binge eating in obesity: Associated MMPI characteristics. *Journal of Consulting and Clinical Psychology, 55*, 872-876.

Koss, M.P., & Butcher, J.N. (1973). A comparison of psychiatric patients' self-report with other sources of clinical information. *Journal of Research in Personality, 7*, 225-236.

Kranitz, L. (1972). Alcoholics, heroin addicts, and nonaddicts: Comparisons on the MacAndrew alcoholism scale of the MMPI. *Quarterly Journal of Studies on Alcohol, 33*, 807-809.

Kunce, J., & Anderson, W. (1976). Normalizing the MMPI. *Journal of Clinical Psychology, 32*, 776-780.

Kunce, J., & Anderson, W. (1984). Perspectives on uses of the MMPI in nonpsychiatric settings. In P. McReynolds & G.J. Chelune (Eds.), *Advances in psychological assessment.* San Francisco: Jossey-Bass.

Kunce, J., & Callis, R. (1969). Vocational interest and personality. *Vocational Guidance Quarterly, 18*, 34-40.

Kurlman, R.G., Hursey, K.G., & Mathew, N.T. (1992). Assessment of chronic refractory headache: The role of the MMPI-2. *Headache, 32*, 432-435.

Kurlychek, R., & Jordan, L. (1980). MMPI profiles and code types of responsible and nonresponsible criminal defendants. *Journal of Clinical Psychology, 36*, 590-593.

Lachar, D. (1974). *The MMPI: Clinical Assessment and Automated Interpretation*. Los Angeles, CA: Western Psychological Services.

Lachar, D., Berman, W., Grisell, J.L., & Schoof, K. (1976). The MacAndrew alcoholism scale as a general measure of substance misuse. *Journal of Studies on Alcohol, 37*, 1609-1615.

Lachar, D., & Wroebel, T.A. (1979). Validation of clinicians' hunches: Construction of a new MMPI critical item set. *Journal of Consulting and Clinical Psychology, 47*, 277-284.

Leavitt, F., Garron, D.C., Whisler, W.W., & Sheinkop, M.B. (1978). Affective and sensory dimensions of low back pain. *Pain, 4*, 273-281.

Lees-Haley, P.R. (1991). MMPI-2 **F** and **F-K** scores of personal injury malingerers in vocational neuropsychological and emotional distress claims. *American Journal of Forensic Psychology, 9*, 5-14.

Levitt, E.E. (1989). *The clinical application of MMPI special scales*. New York: Lawrence Erlbaum.

Levitt, E.E. (1990). A structural analysis of the impact of MMPI-2 on MMPI. *Journal of Personality Assessment, 55*, 562-577.

Levor, R.M., Cohen, M.J., Naliboff, B.D., McArthur, D., & Henser, R.D. (1986). Psychosocial precursors and correlates of migraine headache. *Journal of Consulting and Clinical Psychology, 54*, 347-353.

Lewak, R. (1993). *Low scores on scale 6: A case history*. Paper presented at the annual convention of the Society of Personality Assessment, San Diego, California.

Lewak, R.W., Marks, P.A., & Nelson, G.E. (1990). *Therapist Guide to the MMPI & MMPI-2*. Muncie, IN: Accelerated Development.

Lewandowski, D., & Graham, J.R. (1972). Empirical correlates of frequently occurring two-point MMPI code types: A replicated study. *Journal of Consulting and Clinical Psychology, 39,* 467-472.

Light, K.C., Herbst, M.C., Bragdon, E.E., & Hinderliter, A.L. (1991). Depression and Type A behavior pattern in patients with coronary artery disease: Relationships to painful versus silent myocardial ischemia and b-endorphin responses during exercise. *Psychosomatic Medicine, 53,* 669-683.

Lilienfeld, S.O. (1991). Assessment of psychopathy with the MMPI and MMPI-2. *MMPI-2 News and Profiles: A Newsletter of the MMPI-2 Workshops and Symposia, 2,* 2.

Long, C.J. (1981). The relationship between surgical outcome and MMPI profiles in chronic pain patients. *Journal of Clinical Psychology, 37,* 744-749.

Loper, R. (1976). *MMPI in a counseling service setting.* Paper presented at the Eleventh Annual Symposium on the MMPI, Minneapolis, MN.

Lough, O, & Green, M. (1950). A comparison of the Minnesota Multiphasic Personality Inventory and the Washburne S-A Inventory as measures of personality of college women. *Journal of Social Psychology, 32,* 23-30.

MacAndrew, C. (1965). The differentiation of male alcoholic outpatients from nonalcoholic psychiatric outpatients by means of the MMPI. *Quarterly Journal of Studies on Alcohol, 26,* 238-246.

MacAndrew, C. (1979a). **Mac** scale scores of three samples of men under conditions of conventional versus independent scale administration. *Journal of Studies on Alcohol, 40,* 138-141.

MacAndrew, C. (1979b). On the possibility of the psychometric detection of persons who are prone to the abuse of alcohol and other substances. *Addictive Behavior, 4,* 11-20.

MacAndrew, C. (1981). What the **Mac** scale tells us about men alcoholics: An interpretive review. *Journal of Studies on Alcohol, 42*, 604-625.

Macaranas-Sittler, N. (1986). *Psychological frames of reference: Cross-cultural dimension.* Poster presented at the annual meeting of the Southwestern Psychological Association meeting. Fort Worth, TX.

MacKinnon, D.W. (1962). The nature and nurture of creative talent. *American Psychologist, 17*, 484-495.

Maffeo, P.A., Ford, T.W., & Lavin, P.F. (1990). Gender differences in depression in an employment setting. *Journal of Personality Assessment, 55*, 249-262.

Marks, P., Seeman, W., & Haller, D. (1974). *The actuarial use of the MMPI with adolescents and adults.* Baltimore, MD: The Williams and Wilkins.

Mathew, N.T. (1992). Cluster headache. *Neurology, 42*, 22-31.

McArthur, D.L., Cohen, M.J., Gottleib, H.J., & Naliboff, B.D. (1987). Treating chronic low back pain: 1. Admissions to initial follow-up. *Pain, 29, 1-22.*

McCreary, C., Naliboff, B., & Cohen, M. (1989). A comparison of clinically and empirically derived MMPI groupings in low back pain patients. *Journal of Clinical Psychology, 45*, 560-570.

McDonald, R.L., & Gynther, M.D. (1963). MMPI differences associated with sex, race and class in two adolescent samples. *Journal of Consulting Psychology, 27,* 112-116.

McGill, J.C. (1980). MMPI score differences among Anglo, Black, and Mexican-American welfare recipients. *Journal of Clinical Psychology, 36,* 147-151.

McGrath, R.E., & O'Malley, W.B. (1986). The assessment of denial and physical complaints: The validity of the **Hy** and associated MMPI signs. *Journal of Clinical Psychology, 42,* 754-760.

McKinley, J.C., & Hathaway, S.R. (1943). The identification and measurement of the psychoneuroses in medical practice: The Minnesota Multiphasic Personality Inventory. *Journal of the American Medical Association, 122,* 161-167.

Meehl, P. (1951). *Research results for counselors.* St. Paul, MN: State Department of Education.

Megargee, E.I. (1993). Using MMPI-2 with criminal offenders: A progress report. *MMPI-2 & MMPI-A News & Profiles: A Newsletter of the MMPI-2 Workshops & Symposia, 4,* 2-3.

Megargee, E., & Bohn, M. (1979). *Classifying criminal offenders.* Beverly Hills, CA: Sage Publications.

Megargee, E.I., & Carbonell, J.L. (1991). Personality factors associated with frequent sick call utilization in a federal correctional institution. *Journal of Prison and Jail Health, 10,* 19-42.

Megargee, E.I., & Mendelsohn, G.A. (1962). A cross-validation of twelve MMPI indices of hostility and control. *Journal of Abnormal and Social Psychology, 65,* 431-438.

Mello, N., & Guthrie, G. (1958). MMPI profiles and behavior in counseling. *Journal of Counseling Psychology, 5,* 125-129.

Meyerink, L.H., Reitan, R.M., & Selz, M. (1988). The validity of the MMPI with multiple sclerosis patients. *Journal of Clinical Psychology, 44,* 764-769.

Mitler, C., Wertz, C., & Counts, S. (1961). Racial differences on the MMPI. *Journal of Clinical Psychology, 17,* 159-161.

Montgomery, G.T., Arnold, B.R., & Orozco, S. (1990). MMPI supplemental scale performance of Mexican Americans and level of acculturation. *Journal of Personality Assessment, 54,* 328-342.

Montgomery, G.T., & Orozco, S. (1985). Mexic al Americans' performance on the MMPI as a function of level of acculturation. *Journal of Clinical Psychology, 41,* 203-212.

Moore, J.E., McFall, M.E., Kivlahan, D.R., & Capestany, F. (1989). Risk of misinterpretation of MMPI Schizophrenia Scale elevations in chronic pain patients. *Pain, 32,* 207-213.

Morgan, H.H. (1952). A psychometric comparison of achieving and non-achieving college students of high ability. *Journal of Consulting Psychology, 16,* 292-298.

Mueller, S.R., & Girace, M. (1988). Use and misuse of the MMPI: A reconsideration. *Psychological Reports, 63,* 483-491.

Munley, M.J., & Gilbert, T.E. (1965). The **Pd** scale of the MMPI for college students. *Journal of Clinical Psychology, 21,* 48-51.

Munley, P.H. (1991). A comparison of MMPI-2 and MMPI T-scores for men and women. *Journal of Clinical Psychology, 47,* 87-91.

Munley, P.H., & Zarantonello, M.M. (1989). A comparison of MMPI profile types across standard and contemporary norms. *Journal of Clinical Psychology, 45,* 229-239.

Nacev, V. (1980). Dependency and ego-strength as indicators of patient's attendance in psychotherapy. *Journal of Clinical Psychology, 36,* 691-695.

Naliboff, B.D., McCreary, C., McArthur, D.L., & Cohen, M.J. (1988). MMPI changes following behavioral treatment of chronic low back pain. *Pain, 35,* 271-277.

Navran, L. (1954). A rationally derived MMPI scale to measure dependence. *Journal of Consulting Psychology, 18,* 192.

Nelson, L.D. (1987). Measuring depression in a clinical population using the MMPI. *Journal of Consulting and Clinical Psychology, 55,* 788-790.

Nelson, L.D., & Cicchetti, D. (1991). Validity of the MMPI Depression scale for outpatients. *Psychological Assessment, 3,* 55-59.

Nelson, L.D., & Marks, P.A. (1985). Empirical correlates of infrequently occurring MMPI code types. *Journal of Clinical Psychology, 41,* 477-482.

Nichols, D.S. (1987). *Interpreting the Wiggins MMPI content scales. Clinical notes on the MMPI, No. 10.* Minneapolis: National Computer Systems.

Norman, R.D., & Redlo, M. (1952). MMPI personality patterns for various college age groups. *Journal of Applied Psychology, 36,* 404-409.

Nyman, A.J., & LeMay, M.L. (1967). Differentiation of types of college misconduct offenses with MMPI subscales. *Journal of Clinical Psychology, 23,* 99-100.

Ollendick, D., Otto, B., & Heider, S. (1983). Marital MMPI characteristics: A test of Arnold's signs. *Journal of Clinical Psychology, 39,* 240-246.

Ornduff, S.R., Brennan, A.F., & Barrett, C.L. (1988). The Minnesota Multiphasic Personality Inventory (MMPI) Hysteria **(Hy)** Scale: Scoring bodily concern and psychological denial subscales in chronic back pain patients. *Journal of Behavioral Medicine, 11,* 131-146.

Osborne, D. (1979). Use of the MMPI with medical patients. In J.N. Butcher (Ed.), *New developments in the use of the MMPI* (pp. 141-163). Minneapolis: University of Minnesota Press.

Osborne, R.T., Sander, W.B., & Young, F.M. (1956). MMPI patterns of college disciplinary cases. *Journal of Counseling Psychology, 3,* 52-56.

Otto, R.K., Lang, A.R., Megargee, E.I., & Rosenblatt, A.I. (1988). Ability of alcoholics to escape detection by the MMPI. *Journal of Consulting and Clinical Psychology, 56,* 452-457.

Page, R., & Bozler, S. (1982). A cross-cultural MMPI comparison of alcoholics. *Psychological Reports, 50,* 639-646.

Palmer, S.A., Lambert, M.J., & Richards, R.L. (1991). The MMPI and premenstrual syndrome: Profile fluctuations between best and worst times during the menstrual cycle. *Journal of Clinical Psychology, 47,* 215-221.

Panton, J.H. (1979). MMPI profile configurations associated with incestuous and nonincestuous child molesting. *Psychological Reports, 45,* 335-338.

Paolo, A.M., Ryan, J.J., & Smith, A.J. (1991). Reading difficulty of MMPI-2 subscales. *Journal of Clinical Psychology, 47,* 529-532.

Parmer, J.C. (1991). Bulimia and object relations: MMPI and Rorschach variables. *Journal of Personality Assessment, 56,* 266-276.

Parsons, O.A., Yourshaw, S., & Borstelmann, L. (1968). Self-ideal-self-discrepancies on the MMPI: Consistencies over time and geographic region. *Journal of Counseling Psychology, 15,* 160-166.

Patalano, F. (1980). MMPI two point code type frequencies of drug abusers in a therapeutic community. *Psychological Reports, 46,* 1091-1027.

Penk, W.E., Robinowitz, R., Black, J., Dolan, M., Bell, W., Dorsett, D., Ames, M., & Noriega, L. (1989). Ethnicity: Post-traumatic stress disorder (PTSD) differences among Black, White, and Hispanic veterans who differ in degrees of exposure to combat in Vietnam. *Journal of Clinical Psychology, 45,* 729-736.

Persky, V.W., Kempthorne-Rawson, J., & Shekelle, R.B. (1987). Personality and risk of cancer: 20 year follow-up of the Western Electric study. *Psychosomatic Medicine, 49,* 435-449.

Persons, R., & Marks, P. (1971). The violent **4-3** MMPI personality type. *Journal of Consulting and Clinical Psychology, 36,* 189-196.

Peterson, C.D. & Dahlstrom, W.G. (1992). The derivation of gender-role scales **GM** and **GF** for MMPI-2 and their relationship to scale **5 (Mf)**. (1992). *Journal of Personality Assessment, 59,* 486-499.

Pothast, M.D. (1956). *A personality study of two types of murderers.* Unpublished doctoral dissertation, Michigan State University.

Priest, W. (1993). *The MMPI-2 Depression Scale and the measurement of depression in the elderly.* Unpublished doctoral dissertation, Ball State University, Muncie, IN.

Pritchard, D., & Rosenblatt, A. (1980). Racial bias in the MMPI: A methodological review. *Journal of Consulting and Clinical Psychology, 48,* 263-267.

Puente, A.E., Rodenbough, J., & Horton, A.M., Jr. (1989). Relative efficacy of the **Sc-O**, **P-O**, **P-N**, and **Sc** MMPI scales in differentiating brain-damaged, brain-damaged schizophrenic, schizophrenic, and somatoform disorders in an outpatient setting. *Journal of Clinical Psychology, 45,* 99-105.

Reading, A.E. (1979). The internal structure of the McGill Pain Questionnaire in dysmenorrhoea patients. *Pain, 7,* 353-358.

Rhodes, R.J. (1969). The MacAndrew alcoholism scale: A replication. *Journal of Clinical Psychology, 25,* 189-191.

Richey, K. (1991). *Women incest survivors: An MMPI cluster analysis.* Unpublished doctoral dissertation, Ball State University, Muncie, IN.

Riley, W.T., & McCranie, E.W. (1990). The Depressive Experiences Questionnaire: Validity and psychological correlates in a clinical sample. *Journal of Personality Assessment, 54,* 523-533.

Robinson, M.E., Geisser, M.E., Dieter, J.N., & Swerdlow, B. (1991). The relationship between MMPI cluster membership and diagnostic category in headache patients. *Headache, 31,* 111-115.

Robinson, M.D., Swimmer, G.I., & Rallof, D. (1989). The P-A-I-N MMPI classification system: A critical review. *Pain, 37,* 211-214.
*MMPI & MMPI-2*

Robyak, J.E., Prange, M., & Sands, M. (1988). Drinking practices among Black and White alcoholics and alcoholics of different personality types. *Journal of Personality Assessment, 52,* 487-498.

Roman, D.D., & Gerbing, D.W. (1989). The mentally disordered criminal offender: A description based on demographic, clinical, and MMPI data. *Journal of Clinical Psychology, 45,* 983-990.

Rose, A. (1947). A study of homesickness in college freshmen. *Journal of Social Psychology, 26,* 185-202.

Rosen, E. (1956). Self-appraisal and perceived desirability of MMPI personality traits. *Journal of Counseling Psychology, 5,* 44-51.

Rosen, H., & Rosen, R.A. (1957). Personality variables and role in a union business agent group. *Journal of Applied Psychology, 41,* 131-136.

Schenkenberg, T., Gottfredson, D., & Christensen, P. (1984). Age differences in MMPI scale scores from 1,189 psychiatric patients. *Journal of Clinical Psychology, 40,* 1420-1426.

Schill, T., Wang, S., & Thomsen, D. (1986). MMPI **F**, **4**, and **9** as a measure of aggression in a college sample. *Psychological Reports, 59,* 949-950.

Schlenger, W.E., & Kulka, R.A. (1987). *Performance of the Keane-Fairbank MMPI scale and other self-report measures in identifying post-traumatic stress disorder.* Paper presented at the annual meeting of the American psychological Association, New York.

Schotte, C., Maes, M., Cluydts, R., & de-Doncker, D. (1991). MMPI characteristics of the DSM-III-R avoidant personality disorder. *Psychological Reports, 69,* 75-81.

Schroeder, D.J., & Piercy, D.C. (1979). A comparison of MMPI two-point codes in four alcoholism treatment facilities. *Journal of Clinical Psychology, 35,* 656-663.

Schwartz, M.F., & Graham, J.R. (1979). Construct validity of the MacAndrew Alcoholism scale. *Journal of Consulting and Clinical Psychology, 47*, 1090-1095.

Schwartz, M., & Krupp, N. (1971). The MMPI "conversion V" among 50,000 medical patients: A study of incidence, criteria and profile elevation. *Journal of Clinical Psychology, 27*, 89-95.

Schwartz, M., Osborne, D., & Krupp, N. (1972). Moderation effects of age and sex in the association of medical diagrams and **1-3/3-1** MMPI profiles. *Journal of Clinical Psychology, 28*, 502-505.

Shondrick, D.D., Ben-Porath, Y.S., & Stafford, K.P. (1992). Forensic application of the MMPI-2. *MMPI-2 News & Profiles: A Newsletter of the MMPI-2 Workshops & Symposia, 3*, 6-7.

Smith, C.P., & Graham, J.R. (1981). Behavioral correlates for the MMPI standard **F** scale and for a modified **F** scale for Black and white psychiatric patients. *Journal of Consulting and Clinical Psychology, 49*, 455-459.

Snyder, C.M., & Graham, J.R. (1984). The utility of subtle and obvious subscales based on scale-specific ratings. *Journal of Clinical Psychology, 40*, 981-985.

Snyder, D.K., & Regts, J.M. (1990). Personality correlates of marital satisfaction: A comparison of psychiatric, maritally distressed and nonclinic samples. *Journal of Sex and Marital Therapy, 16*, 34-43.

Srole, L., Langner, T.S., Michael, S.T., Opler, M.K., & Rennie, T.A.C. (1962). *Mental health in the metropolis: The Midtown Manhattan Study.* New York: The Blakiston Division, McGraw-Hill.

Steenman, H.F., Hermann, B.P., Wyler, A.R., & Richey, E.T. (1988). The MacAndrew Alcoholism scale in epilepsy: A high false positive error rate. *Journal of Clinical Psychology, 44*, 457-460.

Strassberg, D.S. (1991). Interpretive dilemmas creased by the Minnesota Multiphasic Personality Inventory 2 (MMPI-2). *Journal of Psychopathology and Behavioral Assessment, 13,* 53-59.

Strassberg, D.S. (1992). Erratum to Strassberg (1991). *Journal of Psychopathology and Behavioral Assessment, 14,* 93-94.

Streit, K., Greene, R.L., Cogan, R., & Davis, H.G. (1993). Clinical correlates of MMPI depression scales. *Journal of Personality Assessment, 60,* 390-396.

Sutker, P.B., Archer, R.P., Brantley, P.J., & Kilpatrick, D. (1979). Alcoholics and opiate addicts: Comparison of personality characteristics. *Journal of Studies on Alcohol, 40,* 635-644.

Sutker, P.B., Brantley, P.J., & Allain, A. (1980). MMPI response patterns and alcohol consumption in DUI offenders. *Journal of Consulting and Clinical Psychology, 48,* 350-355.

Svanum, S., & Ehrmann, L.C. (1992). Alcoholic subtypes and the MacAndrew Alcoholism scale. *Journal of Personality Assessment, 58,* 411-422.

Svanum, S., Levitt, E., & McAdoo, W. (1982). Differentiating male and female alcoholics from psychiatric outpatients: The MacAndrew and Rosenberg alcoholism scales. *Journal of Personality Assessment, 46,* 81-84.

Swenson, W. (1961). Structured personality testing in the aged: An MMPI study of the geriatric population. *Journal of Clinical Psychology, 17,* 302-304.

Swenson, W., Pearson, J., & Osborne, O. (1973). *An MMPI source book.* Minneapolis: University of Minnesota Press.

Tamkin, A.S., & Klett, C.J. (1957). Barron's ego strength scale: A replication of an evaluation of its construct validity. *Journal of Consulting Psychology, 21,* 412.

Tanner, B.A. (1990a). Composite descriptions associated with rare MMPI two-point code types: Codes that involve scale **5**. *Journal of Clinical Psychology, 46*, 425-431.

Tanner, B.A. (1990b). Composite descriptions associated with rare MMPI two-point code types in an adult urban psychiatric setting: Codes that involve scale **0**. *Journal of Clinical Psychology, 46*, 791-795.

Trimboli, F., & Kilgore, R. (1983). A psychodynamic approach to MMPI interpretation. *Journal of Personality Assessment, 47*, 614-626.

Trunnell, E.P., Turner, C.W., & Keye, W.R. (1988). A comparison of the psychological and hormonal factors in women with and without premenstrual syndrome. *Journal of Abnormal Psychology, 97*, 429-436.

Tsushima, W.T., Stoddard, V.M., Tsushima, V.G., & Daly, J. (1991). Characteristics of treatment drop-outs among two samples of chronic headache patients. *Journal of Clinical Psychology, 47*, 199-205.

Uecker, A., Boutilier, L., & Richardson, E. (1980). "Indianism" and MMPI scores of men alcoholics. *Journal of Studies on Alcohol, 41*, 357-362.

Uomoto, J.M., Turner, J.A., & Herron, L.D. (1988). Use of the MMPI and MCMI in predicting outcome of lumbar laminectomy. *Journal of Clinical Psychology, 44*, 191-197.

Velasquez, R.J. (1992). Hispanic-American MMPI research (1990-1992): A comprehensive bibliography. *Psychological Reports, 70*, 743-754.

Velasquez, R.J., & Callahan, W.J. (1990a). MMPI comparisons of Hispanic- and White-American veterans seeking treatment for alcoholism. *Psychological Reports, 67*, 95-98.

Velasquez, R.J., & Callahan, W.J. (1990b). MMPIs of Hispanic, Black, and White DSM-III schizophrenics. *Psychological Reports, 66*, 819-822.

Velasquez, R.J., Callahan, W.J., & Carrillo, R. (1989). MMPI profiles of Hispanic-American inpatient and outpatient sex offenders. *Psychological Reports, 65,* 1055-1058.

Velasquez, R.J., & Gimenez, L. (1987). MMPI differences among three diagnostic groups of Mexican-American state hospital patients. *Psychological Reports, 60,* 1071-1074.

Venn, J. (1988). Low scores on MMPI scales **2** and **0** as indicators of character pathology in men. *Psychological Reports, 62,* 651-657.

Vincent, K.R. (1990). The fragile nature of MMPI code types. *Journal of Clinical Psychology, 46,* 800-802.

Volentine, S.Z. (1981). The assessment of masculinity and femininity: Scale **5** of the MMPI compared with the BSRI and the PAQ. *Journal of Clinical Psychology, 37,* 367-374.

Wade, J.B., Dougherty, L.M., Hart, R.P., & Cook, D. (1992). Patterns of normal personality structure among chronic pain patients. *Pain, 48,* 37-43.

Wade, J.B., Price, D.D., Hamer, R.M., & Schwartz, S.M. (1990). An emotional component analysis of chronic pain. *Pain, 40,* 303-310.

Walfish, S., Massey, R., & Krone, A. (1990). MMPI profiles of cocaine-addicted individuals in residential treatment: Implications for practical treatment planning. *Journal of Substance Abuse Treatment, 7,* 151-154.

Walfish, S., Stenmark, D.E., Shealy, S.E., & Krone, A.M. (1991). MMPI profiles of impaired nurses. *International Journal of the Addictions, 26,* 189-194.

Walfish, S., Stenmark, D.E., Shealy, S.E., & Krone, A.M. (1992). MMPI profiles of women in codependency treatment. *Journal of Personality Assessment, 58,* 211-214.

Walker, D.E., Blankenship, V., Ditty, J.A., & Lynch, K.P. (1987). Prediction of recovery for closed-head-injured adults: An evaluation of the MMPI, the Adaptive Behavior Scale, and a "Quality of Life" Rating Scale. *Journal of Clinical Psychology, 43,* 699-909.

Walsh, S.S., Penk, W.E., Bitman, D.B., Keane, T.M., Wickis, J., & LoCastro, J. (1990, August). *MMPI/MMPI-2 comparisons among substance abusers.* Paper presented at the annual meeting of the American Psychological Association, Boston.

Walters, G.D., Greene, R.L., Jeffrey, T.B., Kruzich, D.J., & Haskin, J.J. (1983). Racial variations on the MacAndrew Alcoholism scale of the MMPI. *Journal of Consulting and Clinical Psychology, 51,* 947-948.

Walters, G.D., & Solomon, G.S. (1982). Methodological note on deriving behavioral correlates for MMPI profile patterns: Case of the female **4-5-6** configuration. *Psychological Reports, 50,* 1071-1076.

Ward, L.C. (1991). A comparison of T-scores from the MMPI and the MMPI-2. *Psychological Assessment, 3,* 688-690.

Watson, C.G. (1984). The schizophrenia-organicity **(Sc-O)** and psychiatric-organic **(P-O)** scales: A review. *Journal of Clinical Psychology, 40,* 1008-1023.

Webb, J., McNamara, K., & Rogers, A. (1981). *Configural interpretation of the MMPI and CPI.* Columbus, OH: Ohio Publishing.

Weed, N.D., Butcher, J.N., Ben-Porath, Y.S., & McKenna, T. (1992). New measures for assessing alcohol and drug abuse with the MMPI-2: The **APS** and **AAS**. *Journal of Personality Assessment, 58,* 389-404.

Weiner, D.N. (1948). Subtle and obvious keys for the MMPI. *Journal of Consulting Psychology, 12,* 164-170.

Welsh, G.S. (1956). Factor dimensions **A** and **R**. In G.S. Welsh and W.G. Dahlstrom (Eds.), *Basic readings on the MMPI in psychology and medicine* (pp. 264-281). Minneapolis: University of Minnesota Press.

Welsh, G.S. (1965). MMPI profile and factor scales **A** and **R**. *Journal of Clinical Psychology, 21,* 43-47.

Werder, D.S., Sargent, J.D., & Coynes, L. (1981). MMPI profiles of headache patients using self-regulation to control headache activity. *Headache, 21,* 164-169.

Wetter, M.W., Baer, R.A., Berry, D.T.R., Robison, L.H., & Sumpter, J. (1993). *Psychological Assessment, 5,* 317-323.

White, W.G., (1974). *A psychometric approach for adjusting selected MMPI scale scores obtained by Blacks.* Unpublished doctoral dissertation, University of Missouri-Columbia.

Whitworth, R.H. (1988). Anglo- and Mexican-American performance on the MMPI administered in Spanish or English. *Journal of Clinical Psychology, 44,* 891-897.

Wiggins, J.S. (1966). Substantive dimensions of self-report in the MMPI item pool. *Psychological Monographs, 80* (22, Whole No. 630.)

Wiggins, J.S., & Rumrill, C. (1959). Social desirability in the MMPI and Welsh's factor scales **A** and **R**. *Journal of Consulting Psychology, 23,* 100-106.

Williams, D.E., Thompson, J.K., Haber, J.D., & Raczynski, J.M. (1986). MMPI and headache: A special focus on differential diagnosis, prediction of treatment outcome, and patient-treatment matching. *Pain, 24,* 143-158.

Wilson, R.L. (1980). *Comparative validities of subtle vs. obvious MMPI Hysteria items: Predicting the elusive neurosis.* Master's thesis, Auburn University.

Wiltse, L., & Rocchio, P. (1975). Preoperative psychological tests as predictors of success of chemonucleolysis in the treatment of the low-back syndrome. *The Journal of Bone and Joint Surgery, 57*, 478-483.

Young, R., Gould, E., Gluck, I.D., & Hargraves, W. (1980). Personality inventory correlates of outcome in a follow up study of psychiatric hospitalization. *Psychological Reports, 46*, 903-906.

# SUBJECT INDEX

## A

summation 459-60
CYN scale 388

# D

D, Depression, scale 2 107-38
Depression scale 107-38
Do scale (Dominance scale) 340-5
    codetypes 343
    general information 341-2
    high scores 342
    low scores 342
    MMPI & MMPI-2 T-scores for
      men, *Table* 293-4
    MMPI & MMPI-2 T-scores for
      women, *Table* 295-6
    summary/interpretation of Do
      scale 343
    summary/interpretation of Dy
      and Do combination 344-5
Dy scale (Dependency scale) 335-9
    codetypes 338
    general information 336-7
    high scores 338
    items in MMPI but not MMPI-2,
      *Table* 298
    low scores 338
    means & standard deviations for
      times, *Table* 299
    MMPI & MMPI-2 T scores for
      men, *Table* 300-1
    MMPI & MMPI-2 T scores for
      women, *Table* 203-3
    summary/interpretation for Dy
      scale 339
    summary/interpretation of Dy
      and Do combination 344-5

# E

Es scale (Ego-Strength scale) 322-9
    codetypes 328
    general information 324-6
    high scores 326-7
    low scores 327-8
    MMPI-MMPI-2 T-scores for men,
      *Table* 293-4
    MMPI-MMPI-2 T-scores for
      women, *Table* 295-6
    summary/interpretations 329

Ethnic differences on MMPI-2
    439-60
        questions and answers 454-6

# F

F (Infrequency or Feeling Bad) scale
    49-63
        general information 50-1
        high scores 51-2
        low scores 58-9
        summary/interpretations 60-1
F minus K (dissimulation) index
    81-2
        general information 81-2
False response set, *Figures* 46, 47
FB validity scale 75-7
Feeling bad (F) scale 49-63
FEM scale 388
Frequency of highpoint pairs,
    *Tables* 86,87

# G

GF supplementary scale 385
GM supplementary scale 384-5

# H

Harris and Lingoes subscales
    for scale 3 157
    for scale 4 195
    for scale 6 227
    for scale 8 265
    for scale 9 280
HEA scale 388
Head injury 475-6
Headache pain 473-5
    treatment 475
    types of 473-5
Hispanics 451-4
    deviant populations 453
    interpretation guidelines 453-4
    normals 452-3
Hs, Hypochondriasis, scale 1
    85-106
Hy, Hysteria, scale 3 139-62
Hypochondriasis (Hs) scale 85-106
Hysteria (Hy) scale 139-62

# S

# NAME INDEX

## A

Adams, J. 67,483
Adams, N.A. 136, 284, 449,494, 502
Adamson, J.D. 374, 493
Akerlind, I. 470-1,483
Alfano, A.M. 96, 117, 130, 237, 250,483
Alfano, D.E. 99, 111, 483
Allain, A. 121,517
Allen, J.P. 381,483
Altman, H. 56, 94, 98, 101, 118, 120, 126, 132, 179, 186, 191, 223, 225, 238, 262, 483, 500
Ames, M. 447-8, 513
Anderson, T. 115, 128,483-4
Anderson, W.P. 8, 11, 16, 18-9, 23, 25, 89, 91, 108, 112, 114, 122, 136, 140, 143, 164, 168, 170, 176, 178, 184, 187, 199, 203, 214, 217, 220, 230, 233, 245, 248, 250, 252, 258, 259, 267, 272, 283-5, 310, 313, 325-8, 332, 337-8, 341-2, 350, 354-5, 364, 370, 436, 484, 494, 502, 506
Appledorf, M. 378, 484
Archer, R.P. 4, 94, 99, 103, 121, 136, 151, 375, 484, 517
Arnold, B.R. 452, 510
Arnold, P. 169, 183, 216, 284, 325,484
Arredondo, R. 381, 386-7, 499
Athey, E.B. 96, 495
Auvenshire, C.D. 375, 377, 495

## B

Baer, R.A. 55, 521
Bailey, D. 310, 318, 486
Balogh, D.W. 130, 237, 256, 485
Barefoot, J.C. 99, 485
Barger, B. 193, 204, 485
Barley, W.D. 72, 485
Barnette, L. 190, 204, 217, 489

Barrett, C.L. 463, 472, 487, 512
Barron, F. 25, 245, 323-4, 485
Bartol, C.R. 168, 271, 485
Batiste, C. 323-4, 492
Bauer, B. 122, 178,484
Bautz, M. 467-8, 495
Beck, N.C. 445, 485
Becker, C.H. 90, 145, 232, 248, 487
Beckham, J.C. 99, 485
Bell, W. 447-8, 513
Ben-Porath, Y.S. 5, 9, 54, 114, 250, 284, 386-7, 389, 406, 411, 486, 488, 516, 520
Berman, W. 374-5, 377, 507
Berry, D.T.R. 55, 521
Bertelson, A.D. 449, 486
Biaggio, M.K. 115, 486
Birtchnell, J. 336, 338, 341, 486
Bitman, D.B. 121, 213, 520
Bjurulf, P. 470-1, 483
Black, J. 447-8, 513
Blades, J.R. 179, 447, 503
Blankenship, V. 169, 520
Bleecker, M.L. 110, 486
Block, J. 310, 318, 486
Bohn, M. 7, 121, 168, 175-6, 179, 187, 191-2, 251, 258-9, 262, 510
Boiardi, A. 475, 498
Bolla-Wilson, K. 110, 486
Borden, J.W. 90, 486
Bornstein, R.A. 380, 486
Borstelmann, L. 310, 513
Boudewyns, P.A. 54, 82, 503
Boutilier, L. 378, 518
Bowler, R.M. 90, 145, 232, 248, 486-7
Bowler, R.P. 90, 145, 232, 248, 486
Bowman, E.S. 114, 491
Bozler, S. 377, 512
Bragdon, E.E. 111, 508
Brantley, P.J. 121, 375, 517
Brantner, J. 52, 125, 167, 208, 249, 273, 283, 286, 496
Braswell, L. 448, 487

Brems, C. 449, 504
Brennan, A.F. 463, 472, 487, 512
Brown, R. 128, 487
Broyles, S.E. 90, 486
Burke, H.R. 374-5, 487
Burkhart, B.R. 168, 501
Butcher, J.N. 3-5, 9, 37, 41, 53, 68,
    77, 91, 97, 109, 111, 114, 142-3,
    168-9, 171, 189, 201, 217, 232,
    235, 247, 250, 252, 271, 284,
    310, 317, 325, 341, 377, 386-9,
    406, 411, 436, 448, 457-60,
    486-8, 499, 502, 504, 506, 520

## C

Calden, G. 168, 502
Caldwell, A. 27, 41, 44, 59, 67, 89,
    94-6, 100-1, 104, 109, 119-20,
    122, 124-5, 127-29, 131-4, 142,
    150, 167, 177, 179, 182, 184,
    186-7, 189, 202-3, 206, 216,
    223-4, 232, 246, 257, 259-61,
    270, 276, 286, 375-6, 470, 488-9
Callahan, W.J. 223, 255-6, 448,
    453, 518-9
Callis, R. 22, 108, 231, 506
Canter, A. 174, 489
Cantor, J.M. 323-4, 492
Capestany, F. 248, 469, 511
Carbonell, J.L. 450, 510
Carkhuff, R.R. 190, 204, 217, 489
Carrillo, R. 256, 519
Carson, R. 54, 71, 73, 125, 128,
    146, 165, 180-2, 184, 188, 201,
    204-6, 208, 216, 218-9, 261, 272,
    274, 285-6, 489
Cernovsky, Z.Z. 203, 328, 379,
    489-90
Chance, J.E. 315, 379, 490
Chase, C. 470, 489
Cheung, F.M. 459, 490
Chojnacki, J.T. 419, 490
Choroba, B. 467-8, 495
Christensen, P. 51, 90, 143, 168,
    216, 232, 247, 270, 515
Cicchetti, D. 110, 511
Clark, L.A. 458, 487
Clopton, J.R. 381, 490
Cluff, L.E. 174, 489

Clum, G.A. 90, 486
Cluydts, R. 124, 515
Cobbs, P.M. 445, 499
Cofer, C.N. 379, 490
Cogan, R. 114, 517
Cohen, M.J. 471-3, 507, 509, 511
Cole, D.W. 7, 490
Colgin, R. 24, 496
Colligan, R.C. 41, 68, 90, 110, 143,
    168, 201-2, 216, 270-1, 284, 306,
    309, 317, 378, 490
Colwell, K.A. 477, 495
Conley, J. 117, 122, 192, 260, 491
Cook, D. 467, 519
Coons, P.M. 114, 491
Costa, P.T. 467, 491
Costello, R.M. 223, 247, 444, 464-5,
    467-9, 491
Cottle, W.C. 287, 491
Counts, S. 168, 510
Coyle, F.A. 277, 324, 495
Coynes, L. 475, 521
Craig, R.J. 103, 134, 173, 178, 190,
    379, 491
Cross, H. 333, 505
Crumpton, E. 323-4, 492
Cuadra, C.A. 370, 492
Curtiss, G. 466, 468, 473, 492, 505

## D

Dahlstrom, L.E. 45, 51, 53, 67, 71,
    73, 88, 96, 118, 143, 149, 154,
    166-8, 171, 182, 184-5, 231,
    233-4, 276, 326, 388, 442, 492
Dahlstrom, W.G. 3, 9, 18, 26, 41,
    45, 51, 53, 67-8, 71, 73, 85-8, 91,
    96, 107, 109, 118, 139, 143, 149,
    154, 163, 166-8, 171, 182, 184-5,
    197, 213, 217, 222, 229, 231-4,
    243, 247, 267, 271, 276, 281,
    284, 310, 317, 323, 325-6, 341,
    350, 377, 385, 388-9, 418, 441-2,
    488, 492, 513
Daly, J. 475, 518
Dana, R.H. 446, 492
Danahy, S. 376, 503
Daniels, E.E. 22, 164, 492
Davis, A.K. 477, 495

Davis, H.G. 114, 381, 386-7, 490, 499, 517
Davis, K. 179, 493
Day, C.W. 174, 489
De Groot, G.W. 374, 493
De-Benedittis, G. 474, 493
de-Doncker, D. 124, 515
Denier, C.A. 122, 493
Dieter, J.N. 474, 514
DiFrancesca, K.R. 251, 258, 493
Dinning, W.D. 57, 494
Ditty, J.A. 169, 476, 493, 520
Dolan, M. 447-8, 513
Doob, L. 445, 493
Dorsett, D. 447-8, 513
Dougherty, L.M. 467, 519
Drake, L.E. 95, 126, 135, 181, 183, 188, 190, 193, 209-10, 219, 222, 224-5, 240, 253, 263, 274, 278, 286, 288-9, 493
Duckworth, J.C. 8, 313, 326-7, 330, 332, 337-8, 342, 354-5, 364, 375, 377-8, 380, 436, 484, 493-4
Duffy, J.F. 182, 496
Duker, J. 95-7, 100-1, 126-7, 129, 175, 179, 190, 238. 254-5, 257, 262, 275, 496

**E**

Edwards, D.W. 417-8, 494
Ehrmann, L.C. 382, 517
Elion, V.H. 447, 450, 494
Elliott, T.R. 136, 284, 494
English, A.C. 439, 494
English, H.B. 439, 494
English, R.W. 354, 494
Eno, T.D. 82, 499
Erdberg, P. 247, 445, 501
Erickson, W.D. 177, 180, 185, 187, 494
Eron, L.D. 174, 271, 503
Evans, R.G. 57, 494

**F**

Faden, V.B. 381, 483
Fairbank, J.A. 82, 385, 504
Fallon, J.H. 54, 503

Fefer, A. 477, 495
Fernandez, E. 462-3, 495
Fine, M. 130, 237, 256, 485
Finlayson, M.A. 99, 111, 483
Finn, S.E. 434, 495
Finney, J.C. 375, 377, 495
Ford, T.W. 110, 509
Fowler, R.D. 96, 247, 277, 324, 445, 495, 501
Franz, C. 467-8, 495
Frediani, F. 475, 498
Friedman, A.F. 96, 495
Friedrich, W.N. 378, 477, 495

**G**

Galluci, N.T. 376, 496
Garretson, H.D. 463, 487
Garron, D.C. 463, 507
Garvin, R.D. 374, 499
Gass, C.S. 90, 99, 111, 117, 145, 247-8, 476, 479, 496
Geisser, M.E. 474, 514
Gentry, M.M. 385, 496
Gerbing, D.W. 173, 251, 515
Getter, H. 324, 326, 496
Gilberstadt, H. 95-7, 100-1, 126-7, 129, 175, 179, 190, 238, 254-5, 257, 262, 275, 496
Gilbert, T.E. 170, 511
Gilliland, A.R. 24, 496
Gimenez, L. 453, 519
Girace, M. 478, 511
Glosz, J.T. 250, 496
Gluck, I.D. 324 , 522
Godwin, W.H. 115, 486
Goldwater, L. 182, 496
Gonzalez, J. 41, 51, 68, 91, 143, 168, 216, 271, 502
Good, P. 52, 125, 167, 208, 249, 273, 283, 286, 496
Goodstein, L.D. 24, 497
Gottesman, I.I. 374, 497
Gottfredson, D. 51, 90, 143, 168, 216, 232, 247, 270, 515
Gottleib, H.J. 471, 509
Gough, H.G. 55, 341, 350, 354-6, 363-4, 497
Gould, E. 324, 522
Graham, J.R. 3, 5, 9, 41, 68, 91, 93, 98, 109, 114-5, 117-20,

# I

Imboden, J.B. 174, 489

# J

anick, L. 234, 506
Jeffrey, T.B. 374, 378, 520
Jensen, A.R. 355-6, 504
Johnson, M.E. 449, 504
Jones, E.E. 444, 455-6, 504
Jordan, L. 259, 507
Judson, A.J. 379, 490

# K

Kaemmer, B. 3, 9, 41, 68, 91, 109,
   143, 168, 217, 232, 247, 271,
   284, 310, 317, 325, 341, 377,
   388-9, 488
Kalichman, S.C. 176-7, 191, 466,
   468, 473, 492, 504-5
Kammeier, M. 379, 502
Kay, D.C. 376, 496
Keane, T.M. 82, 121, 213, 385, 504,
   520
Keiller, S.W. 93, 115, 146, 174, 219,
   274, 504
Keller, L.S. 97, 111, 142, 235, 252,
   504
Kelley, C.K. 116, 121, 123-4, 126,
   130, 133-4, 136, 151, 154, 176,
   181, 185, 190, 209, 222, 239-40,
   273, 287, 504-5
Kempthorne-Rawson, J. 112, 477,
   513
Kennard, J. 336, 338, 341, 486
Kennedy, B.P. 380, 382, 505
Kennedy, W.A. 24, 505
Keye, W.R. 112, 518
Kilgore, R. 44, 71, 92, 102, 109,
   113, 125, 142-4, 154, 171, 182,
   184, 203-6, 216, 218, 225, 232,
   257, 270, 273-4, 276, 283, 285,
   518
Kilpatrick, D. 375, 517
Kinder, B.N. 466, 468, 473, 492, 505
King, G.D. 116, 121, 123-4, 126,
   130, 133-4, 136, 151, 154, 176,

181, 185, 190, 209, 222, 239-40,
   273, 287, 504-5
Kirkcaldy, B.D. 477, 505
Kirkley, B.G. 234, 506
Kivlahan, D.R. 248, 469, 511
Klein, S. 333, 505
Kleinke, C.L. 111, 145, 471-2, 505-6
Kleinmuntz, B. 25, 384, 506
Klett, C.J. 325-6, 517
Klinefelter, D. 103, 484
Kobas, J.C. 41, 51, 68, 91, 143,
   168, 216, 271, 502
Kobylinska, E. 477, 505
Kolotkin, R.L. 234, 506
Koss, M.P. 9, 506
Kranitz, L. 375, 506
Krone, A.M. 173, 273, 519
Krupp, N. 98-9, 516
Kruzich, D.J. 374, 378, 520
Kulka, R.A. 385, 515
Kunce, J.T. 11, 16, 18-9, 22-3, 25,
   89, 91, 108, 112, 114, 140, 143,
   164, 170, 176, 199, 203, 214,
   217, 230-1, 233, 245, 248, 250,
   252, 258, 267, 272, 283, 285,
   327, 370, 484, 506
Kurlman, R.G. 474, 506
Kurlychek, R. 259, 507

# L

Lachar, D. 9, 95, 104, 116, 119,
   124, 129, 131, 134, 144, 150-1,
   166, 183-4, 188, 221, 224, 240,
   246, 256, 260, 263, 269, 374-5,
   377, 492, 507
Lambert, M.J. 133, 513
Lang, A.R. 379, 512
Langfeldt, V.C. 176, 179, 192, 251,
   258, 447, 503
Langner, T.S. 441, 516
Latham, P.K. 122, 493
Lavin, P.F. 110, 509
Lawhorn, L. 117, 479, 496
Leavitt, F. 463, 507
Lees-Haley, P.R. 52, 82, 507
Lefkowitz, M.M. 174, 271, 503
Leitner, L.M. 115, 483
LeMay, M.L. 190, 512
Lennington, L. 130, 237, 256, 485

Levitt, E.E. 8, 375, 388, 507, 517
Levor, R.M. 473, 507
Lewak, R.W. 96, 219, 434, 495, 507
Lewandowski, D. 98, 119, 186, 190, 223, 508
Lewis, E. 22-3, 108, 135, 164, 185-6, 190, 199, 203, 214, 218, 224, 234, 238, 250, 253, 262-3, 268, 273, 503
Light, K.C. 111, 508
Lilienfeld, S.O. 169, 508
Lilly, R. 286, 498
Lingoes, J.C. 7, 12, 109, 142, 166, 215, 246, 269, 410-1, 469, 502
LoCastro, J. 121, 213, 520
Loftsgard, S. 378, 495
Long, C.J. 92, 95, 99-100, 508
Loper, R. 217, 379, 502, 508
Lorenzetti, A. 474, 493
Lough, O. 247, 508
Luxenberg, M.G. 177, 180, 185, 187, 494
Lynch, K.P. 169, 476, 493, 520

# M

MacAndrew, C. 374, 376, 378-381, 386, 508-9
Macaranas-Sittler, N. 455, 509
MacKinnon, D.W. 21, 245, 509
Maes, M. 124, 515
Maffeo, P.A. 110, 509
Maiuro, R.D. 172, 252, 501
Malloy, P.F. 82, 385, 504
Marcus, R. 374-5, 487
Marks, P. 66, 72, 94, 98, 101-3, 118-9, 121, 123, 125-7, 129, 132, 135, 148, 150-4, 170, 179, 181-3, 185-6, 188, 191, 193, 209-10, 216, 221, 223-4, 238-40, 255-7, 260, 262, 277-8, 434, 449, 486, 503, 507, 509, 512-3
Massey, R. 173, 273, 519
Mathew, N.T. 473-4, 506, 509
May, G.D. 449, 486
Mayo, M.A. 374, 498
McAdoo, W. 375, 517
McArthur, D.L. 471-3, 507, 509, 511
McCall, J.N. 190, 204, 217, 489
McClosky, H. 341, 497

McCord, G. 16, 18-9, 498
McCrae, R.R. 467, 491
McCranie, E.W. 109, 514
McCreary, C. 471-2, 509, 511
McDonald, R.L. 450, 509
McDowell, D. 128, 487
McFall, M.E. 248, 469, 511
McGill, J.C. 452, 509
McGrath, R.E. 142, 509
McKenna, T. 386-7, 520
McKinley, J.C. 466, 510
McNamara, K. 135, 520
McPeake, J.D. 380, 382, 505
McRae, C. 445, 485
McVaugh, W. 82, 499
Meehl, P.E. 166, 174, 341, 497, 510
Megargee, E.I. 7, 121, 163, 168, 175-6, 179, 187, 191-2, 251, 258-9, 262, 379, 384, 447, 450, 494, 510, 512
Meilman, P.W. 472, 499
Mello, N. 173, 174, 253, 510
Meloy, J.R. 251, 258, 493
Mendelsohn, G.A. 384, 510
Mergler, D. 90, 145, 232, 248, 486
Merritt, R.D. 130, 237, 256, 485
Meshot, C.M. 128, 484
Meyer, C.T. 385, 496
Meyerink, L.H. 478, 510
Michael, S.T. 441, 516
Miller, A. 381, 483
Milstein, V. 114, 491
Miner, M.H. 176, 179, 192, 251, 258, 447, 503
Mitler, C. 168, 510
Monachesi, E.D. 188, 502
Montgomery, G.T. 452, 510
Moore, J.E. 248, 469, 511
Morgan, H.H. 220, 342, 351, 511
Morrison, T.L. 417-8, 494
Mudrak, 172, 252, 501
Mueller, S.R. 478, 511
Munjack, D. 128, 487
Munley, M.J. 170, 511
Munley, P.H. 107, 418-9, 511

# N

Nacev, V. 337, 511
Naliboff, B.D. 471-3, 507, 509, 511

Navran, L. 336, 511
Neilson, P.M. 99, 111, 483
Nelson, G.E. 434, 507
Nelson, L.D. 110, 152, 511-2
Nerviano, V.J. 96, 117, 130, 237, 250, 483
Nichols, D.S. 388, 512
Noriega, L. 447-8, 513
Norman, R.D. 24, 108, 512
Nyman, A.J. 190, 512

## O

O'Leary, W.C. 82, 503
O'Malley, W.B. 142, 509
Oetting, E.R. 95, 126, 135, 181, 183, 188, 190, 193, 209-10, 219, 222, 224-5, 240, 253, 263, 274, 278, 286, 288-9, 493
Offord, K.P. 41, 68, 90, 110, 143, 168, 201-2, 216, 270-1, 284, 306, 309, 317, 378, 490
Ollendick, D. 169, 183, 216, 284, 512
Olson, R.E. 103, 134, 491
Opler, M.K. 441, 516
Ornduff, S.R. 472, 512
Orozco, S. 452, 510
Osborne, D. 41, 68, 90, 99, 110, 143, 168, 201-2, 216, 270-1, 284, 467, 490, 512, 516
Osborne, O. 305-6, 309, 332, 347-8, 517
Osborne, R.T. 222, 512
Otto, B. 169, 183, 216, 284, 512
Otto, R.K. 379, 512

## P

Page, R. 377, 512
Palmer, S.A. 133, 513
Pancheri, P. 436, 457-60, 488
Paniak, C.E. 99, 111, 483
Panton, J.H. 177, 284, 513
Paolo, A.M. 271, 513
Parmer, J.C. 188, 513
Parsons, O.A. 310, 513
Patalano, F. 187, 513
Paul, R. 467-8, 495

Pearson, J. 305-6, 309, 332, 347-8, 517
Penk, W.E. 121, 213, 447-8, 513, 520
Persky, V.W. 112, 477, 513
Persons, R. 179, 513
Peterson, B.L. 99, 485
Peterson, C.D. 385, 513
Piercy, D.C. 121, 178, 515
Poloni, L.D. 472, 499
Ponder, H.M. 449, 502
Pope, K.S. 201, 488
Pothast, M.D. 187, 514
Prange, M. 450, 515
Prescott, C.A. 374, 497
Price, D.D. 463, 519
Priest, W. 110, 514
Pritchard, D. 442, 446, 514
Proctor, W.C. 172, 252, 501
Puente, A.E. 470, 514

## R

Raczynski, J.M. 473, 521
Rallof, D. 466, 514
Ramamurthy, S. 464-5, 467-9, 491
Randall, C.L. 122, 493
Raney, D. 448, 487
Rauch, S.S. 90, 145, 232, 248, 486-7
Rawlings, R.R. 381, 483
Reading, A.E. 463, 514
Redlo, M. 24, 108, 512
Regts, J.M. 169, 516
Reitan, R.M. 478, 510
Rennie, T.A.C. 441, 516
Rennier, G. 445, 485
Revis, E.S. 234, 506
Rhodes, R.J. 374, 514
Rich, R. 114, 176, 258, 484
Richards, R.L. 133, 513
Richardson, E. 378, 518
Richey, E.T. 380, 516
Richey, K. 187, 252, 514
Riley, W.T. 109, 514
Robinowitz, R. 447-8, 513
Robinson, M.D. 466, 514
Robinson, M.E. 474, 514
Robison, L.H. 55, 521
Robyak, J.E. 450, 515

Thomsen, D. 174, 271, 515
Thornby, J.I. 376, 496
Thorne, A. 455-6, 504
Thurstin, A.H. 96, 117, 130, 237, 250, 483
Tiffany, D. 223, 247, 491
Tonsager, M.E. 434, 495
Trimboli, F. 44, 71, 92, 102, 109, 113, 125, 142-4, 154, 171, 182, 184, 203-6, 216, 218, 225, 232, 257, 270, 273-4, 276, 283, 285, 518
Trunnell, E.P. 112, 518
Tsushima, V.G. 475, 518
Tsushima, W.T. 475, 518
Turk, D.C. 462-3, 495
Turner, C.W. 112, 518
Turner, J.A. 463, 472, 501, 518

# U

Uecker, A. 378, 518
Uomoto, J.M. 472, 518

# V

Velasquez, R.J. 223, 255-6, 448, 451, 453, 518-9
Venn, J. 115, 287, 453, 519
Vincent, K.R. 26, 519
Vitaliano, P.P. 172, 252, 501
Volentine, S.Z. 202, 519

# W

Wade, J.B. 463, 467, 519
Walbek, N.H. 177, 180, 185, 187, 494
Walfish, S. 173, 273, 519
Walker, D.E. 169, 520
Walsh, S.S. 121, 213, 520
Walsh, W.B. 419, 490
Walters, G.D. 182, 374, 378, 520
Wang, S. 174, 271, 515
Warbin, R. 56, 94, 120, 126, 132, 179, 191, 223, 224, 262, 483, 500

Ward, L.C. 281, 520
Watson, C.G. 470, 520
Webb, J.T. 96, 135, 495, 520
Weed, N.D. 386-7, 520
Week, N.C. 386-7, 499
Weiner, D.N. 7, 110, 143, 168, 216, 270, 520
Weiner, R.H. 381, 490
Weissman, H.N. 417-8, 494
Welsh, G.S. 45, 51, 53, 67, 71, 73, 88, 96, 118, 143, 149, 154, 166-8, 171, 182, 184-5, 231, 233-4, 276, 309, 311, 313, 316, 326, 388, 492, 521
Werder, D.S. 475, 521
Wertz, C. 168, 510
Wetter, M.W. 55, 521
Whatley, P.R. 446, 492
Whisler, W.W. 463, 507
White, W.G. 450, 521
Whitworth, R.H. 452, 521
Wickis, J. 121, 213, 520
Wiggins, J.S. 8, 28, 114, 310, 317, 388, 521
Williams, C.L. 4, 5, 9, 37, 53, 387, 389, 488
Williams, D.E. 473, 521
Wilson, R.L. 143, 521
Wiltse, L. 99, 522
Wood, J. 130, 237, 256, 485
Woods, M. 82, 503
Wroebel, T.A. 9, 507
Wyler, A.R. 380, 516

# Y

Young, F.M. 222, 512
Young, R. 324, 522
Yourshaw, S. 310, 513

# Z

Zappacosta, B. 475, 498
Zarantonello, M.M. 107, 511

# CODETYPE INDEX

## Listed by Clinical Scale

## Listed by Supplementary Scale

## JANE C.
## DUCKWORTH

Jane Duckworth has a Ph.D. in psychology from the University of Missouri at Columbia and presently is a professor emerita in the Department of Counseling Psychology and Guidance Services at Ball State University. She has worked with the MMPI in two college counseling centers and a psychiatric clinic and has done MMPI research with the following groups: divorced people, married couples, college students, and sex offenders. A current research interest is the interface between the MMPI and the Rorshcach in personality assessment. She has taught the MMPI course in the graduate Counseling Psychology program at Ball State University and conducts workshops on the MMPI in various parts of the United States and foreign countries. She is a diplomat in counseling psychology.

# WAYNE ANDERSON

Wayne Anderson has a Ph.D. in psychology from the University of Missouri-Columbia. For 30 years he had a dual appointment as a Professor of Psychology in the Psychology Department and Counseling Psychologist in the Counseling Center. Previously he was with the VA as a psychologist for seven years. After coming to Missouri in 1963, he developed the graduate course on the MMPI. Prentice-Hall recently published his book *Stress Management for Law Enforcement Officers* based on his work with local and state police. He presently is working on a book on child sexual abuse. Dr. Anderson has published over 80 articles and book chapters on various aspects of psychology (17 on the MMPI).

## FEEDBACK

To:
Jane Duckworth, Ph.D.
2004 Euclid
Muncie, Indiana 47304

The parts of *MMPI & MMPI-2: Interpretation Manual for Counselors and Clinicians*, 1995 edition, that I have found most helpful are (please note pages and reasons if appropriate):

I would find the book more useful if you would elaborate on the following (please note pages and reasons if appropriate):

Other Comments:

Name: —————————————————————————————

Organization: ————————————————————————

Street: ——————————————————————————————

City: ———————————————————————————————

State/Zip: ————————————————————————————

---

## SUGGESTIONS

---

To:
Jane Duckworth, Ph.D.
2004 Euclid
Muncie, Indiana 47304

A resource not listed in your *MMPI & MMPI-2: Interpretation Manual for Counselors and Clinicians,* 1995 edition, that I have found useful is the following:

I am enclosing a copy of an article I found useful. The article was taken from the following source:

Other Comments:

Name: _____

Organization: _____

Street: _____

City: _____

State/Zip: _____

## DATE DUE

| | | |
|---|---|---|
| DEC 1 4 1996 | | |
| MAY 0 5 1998 | | |
| NOV 0 7 1999 | | |
| MAY 3 7 2001 | | |
| | | |
| JUN 2 1 2005 | | |
| | | |
| | | |
| | | |
| | | |
| | | |
| | | |
| | | |
| | | |
| | | |
| | | |
| | | Printed in USA |

HIGHSMITH #45230